B2 First Trainer

Six practice tests with answers and Teacher's Notes

with digital pack

Shaftesbury Road, Cambridge CB2 8EA, United Kingdom

One Liberty Plaza, 20th Floor, New York, NY 10006, USA

477 Williamstown Road, Port Melbourne, VIC 3207, Australia

314–321, 3rd Floor, Plot 3, Splendor Forum, Jasola District Centre, New Delhi – 110025, India

103 Penang Road, #05–06/07, Visioncrest Commercial, Singapore 238467

Cambridge University Press & Assessment is a department of the University of Cambridge.

We share the University's mission to contribute to society through the pursuit of education, learning and research at the highest international levels of excellence.

www.cambridge.org
Information on this title: www.cambridge.org/9781009813686

© Cambridge University Press & Assessment 2025

The copyright in the material in this book is owned by or licensed to Cambridge University Press & Assessment, or reproduced with permission from other third-party copyright owners.

The contents of this book may be copied solely:

(i) under the terms of a valid licence from a collective licensing scheme operated by a reproduction rights organisation such as the Copyright Licensing Agency (UK), the Copyright Clearance Center (USA), the Copyright Agency Limited (Australia) and/or similar agencies in other territories;

(ii) where reproduction is permitted for personal reference or specific educational and teaching purposes under applicable copyright laws, including the UK's Copyright, Designs and Patents Act, 1988;

(iii) with the express prior written consent of Cambridge University Press & Assessment.

The answer sheets at the back of this book are designed to be copied and distributed in class.

First published 2025

20 19 18 17 16 15 14 13 12 11 10 9 8 7 6 5 4 3 2 1

Printed in Poland by Opolgraf

A catalogue record for this publication is available from the British Library

ISBN   978-1-009-81368-6   Student's Book with answers with digital pack
ISBN   978-1-009-81369-3   Student's Book without answers with digital pack

Cambridge University Press & Assessment has no responsibility for the persistence or accuracy of URLs for external or third-party internet websites referred to in this publication and does not guarantee that any content on such websites is, or will remain, accurate or appropriate.

Contents

Introduction 4

Training and Exam practice

Test 1	Reading and Use of English	10
	Writing	35
	Listening	46
	Speaking	55
Test 2	Reading and Use of English	65
	Writing	85
	Listening	94
	Speaking	102

Practice tests

Test 3	Reading and Use of English	109
	Writing	119
	Listening	121
	Speaking	125
Test 4	Reading and Use of English	127
	Writing	137
	Listening	139
	Speaking	143
Test 5	Reading and Use of English	145
	Writing	155
	Listening	157
	Speaking	161
Test 6	Reading and Use of English	163
	Writing	173
	Listening	175
	Speaking	179

Audioscripts 181

Teacher's notes & keys Tests 1 and 2 204

Practice test keys Tests 3–6 237

Sample answer sheets 243

Acknowledgements 247

Speaking visuals C1

Introduction

Who is *B2 First Trainer 3* for?

This book is suitable for anyone who is preparing to take the *B2 First* exam. You can use *B2 First Trainer 3* in class with your teacher or on your own at home.

What is *B2 First Trainer 3*?

B2 First Trainer 3 contains six practice tests for *B2 First*, each covering the Reading and Use of English, Writing, Listening and Speaking papers. Guided Tests 1 and 2 consist of both training and practice for the exam, while Tests 3–6 are entirely practice. All six tests are at exam level and are of *B2 First* standard.

Test 1 contains information about each part of each paper, plus step-by-step guidance to take you through each kind of *B2 First* task, with examples and tips clearly linked to the questions. It also presents and practises grammar, vocabulary and functional language directly relevant to particular task types. This is supported by work on correcting common grammar mistakes made by *B2 First* candidates in the exam, as shown by the **Cambridge Learner Corpus**. The **Keys** tell you the correct answers.

Test 2 also contains training for the exam, in addition to revision from Test 1. Here too there is language input, as well as some step-by-step guidance to task types with further examples, advice and tips. In Writing, there is a full focus on the task types not covered in Test 1.

Tests 3–6 contain a wide range of topics, text types and exam items, enabling you to practise the skills you have developed and the language you have learnt in Tests 1 and 2.

How to use *B2 First Trainer 3*

Test 1 Training

- For each part of each paper, you should begin by studying **Task information**, which tells you the facts you need to know, such as what the task type tests and the kinds of questions it uses.
- Throughout Test 1, you will see information marked **Tip!** These tips give you practical advice on how to tackle each task type.
- **Remember!** boxes also give you quick reminders about grammar or vocabulary points that are useful for the exam.
- In all papers, training exercises help you develop the skills you need by working through example items of a particular task type.
- **Useful language** sections present and practise grammatical structures, vocabulary or functional expressions that are often tested by particular task types.
- Many exercises involve focusing on and correcting common language mistakes made by actual *B2 First* candidates, as shown by the **Cambridge Learner Corpus** (www.cambridge.org/corpus).

- In **Listening**, you are prompted to use the downloadable audio, e.g. 🎧1. If you are working on your own, you will need to be able to access the downloadable audio files.
- In **Writing**, Test 1 covers Part 1 (essay), as well as the article, letter and report tasks in Part 2. You study some **examples** to help you perfect your skills. The **Keys** contain answers to the exercises, plus **sample answers** and **examiner commentaries**. You finish each part by writing your own text, using what you have learnt in **Useful language**.
- In **Speaking**, you are prompted to use one of the downloadable audio files, e.g. 🎧18, and complete tasks while you listen to examples of each part of the paper. You can practise speaking on your own or with a partner, using what you have learnt in **Useful language**.
- You then work through an exam-style task. With the Exam practice tasks, **Advice** boxes suggest ways of dealing with particular exam items.
- Answers to all items are in the **Keys**.

Test 2 Training

- Test 2 contains many of the same features as Test 1, including exercises that focus on exam instructions, texts and tasks, **Tip!** information, **Remember!** boxes, **Advice** for many exam items, **Useful language** and **Keys**.
- There is further work based on mistakes frequently made by B2 First candidates, as shown by the **Cambridge Learner Corpus**.
- Test 2 **Writing** covers Part 1 (essay) plus the email and review tasks in Part 2, along with **sample answers** for the tasks.
- You should try to do the exam tasks under exam conditions where possible.

Tests 3–6 Exam practice

- In Tests 3, 4, 5 and 6, you can apply the skills and language you have learnt in guided Tests 1 and 2.
- You can do these tests and the four papers within them in any order, but you should always try to keep to the time recommended for each paper. For the Listening paper, you must **listen to each recording twice only**.
- It will be easier to keep to the exam instructions if you can find somewhere quiet to work and ensure there are no interruptions.
- For the Speaking paper, it is better if you can work with a partner, but if not, you can follow the instructions and do all four parts on your own.
- You can check your answers for yourself in the **Keys**, and also study the Listening audioscripts after you have completed the tasks.
- Sample answers with examiner commentaries are given in the **Keys** for the **Writing tasks**.
- Sample answers for the **Speaking tasks** are included in the audioscripts.

Other features of *B2 First Trainer 3*

- Full-colour **visual materials** for the Speaking paper of all six tests in the Speaking visuals section (pages C1–C22).
- The **teacher's notes** give teachers ideas on how to make the most of *B2 First Trainer 3* in a class setting.
- **Photocopiable sample answer sheets** for the Reading and Use of English, Listening, and Writing are at the back of the book. Before you take the exam, you should study these so that you know how to mark or write your answers correctly, if you are taking the paper-based test.
- The **downloadable audio files** contain recordings for the Listening papers of the six *B2 First* tests plus recordings from different parts of the Speaking paper in Tests 1 and 2 to serve as examples, and sample answers to Parts 1–4 of the Speaking paper in Tests 3–6.

The *B2 First* examination

Level of the *B2 First* examination

B2 First is at Level B2 on the Common European Framework (CEFR). When you reach this level, these are some of the things you should be able to do:

- You can scan written texts for the information you need, and understand detailed instructions or advice.
- You can understand or give a talk on a familiar subject, and keep a conversation going on quite a wide range of subjects.
- You can make notes while someone is talking, and write an essay that presents different opinions.

Grading

- The overall *B2 First* grade that you receive is based on the total score you achieve in all four papers.
- The Writing, Listening and Speaking papers each carry 20% of the possible marks. The Reading and Use of English paper carries 40% of the possible marks, with this being divided into 20% for Reading and 20% for Use of English.
- There is no minimum score for each paper, so you don't have to 'pass' all four in order to pass the exam.
- Candidates who achieve **Grade A** (Cambridge English Scale scores of 180–190) are given the First Certificate in English stating that they demonstrated ability at Level C1. Those who achieve **Grade B** or **Grade C** (Cambridge English Scale scores of 160–179) receive the First Certificate in English at Level B2. If a candidate's performance is below Level B2, but is within Level B1 (Cambridge English Scale scores of 140–159), they will be given a certificate stating that they demonstrated ability at Level B1.
- Whatever your grade, you will receive a Statement of Results. This includes a graphical profile of how well you did in each paper and shows your relative performance in each one.

Content of the *B2 First* examination

The *B2 First* examination has four papers, each consisting of a number of parts. For details on each part, see the page reference under the *Task information* heading in these tables.

Reading and Use of English 1 hour 15 minutes

Parts 1 and 3 mainly test your vocabulary; Part 2 mainly tests your grammar. Part 4 often tests both. There is one mark for each correct answer in Parts 1, 2 and 3. Answers to Part 4 can be awarded one or two marks. If you are taking the paper-based test, you can write on the question paper, but you must remember to transfer your answers to the separate answer sheet before the end of the test.

The total length of texts in Parts 5–7 is about 1,850 words. They are taken from newspaper and magazine articles, fiction, reports, advertisements, correspondence, messages and informational material such as brochures, guides or manuals. There are two marks for each correct answer in Parts 5 and 6; there is one mark for each correct answer in Part 7.

Part	Task type	No. of questions	Format	Task information
1	Multiple-choice cloze	8	You choose from words A, B, C or D to fill in each gap in a text.	page 10
2	Open cloze	8	You think of the correct word to fill in each gap in a text.	page 15
3	Word formation	8	You think of the correct form of a prompt word to fill in each gap in a text.	page 19
4	Key word transformations	6	You have to complete a sentence using a given key word so that it means the same as another sentence.	page 22
5	Multiple choice	6	You read a text followed by questions with four options: A, B, C or D.	page 25
6	Gapped text	6	You read a text with some missing paragraphs, then fill in the gaps by choosing paragraphs from a jumbled list.	page 29
7	Multiple matching	10	You read a text divided into sections (or several short texts) and match the relevant sections to statements.	page 32

Writing 1 hour 20 minutes

You have to do Part 1 (question 1) plus any **one** of the Part 2 tasks. In Part 2, you can choose one of questions 2–4. The possible marks for Part 1 and Part 2 are the same. In all tasks, you are told who you are writing to and why.

Part	Task type	No. of words	Format	Task information
1	Question 1: essay	140–190	You give your opinion on a topic using the two ideas given, plus an idea of your own.	page 35
2	Questions 2–4 possible tasks: article, email, letter, report or review	140–190	You write one text, from a choice of three text types, based on a situation.	pages 39, 42, 44, 88, 91

Listening about 40 minutes

You will both hear and see the instructions for each task, and you will hear each of the four parts twice. You will hear pauses announced, and you can use this time to look at the task and the questions. At the end of the test, if you are taking the paper-based test, you will have five minutes to copy your answers onto the answer sheet. If you are taking the digital test, you will have two minutes to check your answers.

If one person is speaking, you may hear information, news, instructions, a commentary, a documentary, a lecture, a message, a public announcement, a report, a speech, a talk or an advertisement. If two people are talking, you might hear a conversation, a discussion, an interview, part of a radio play, etc.

Part	Task type	No. of questions	Format	Task information
1	Multiple choice	8	You listen to unrelated monologues or conversations between interacting speakers, and you choose from answers A, B or C.	page 46
2	Sentence completion	10	You listen to a monologue lasting about three to four minutes, and you complete the sentences with the missing information.	page 49
3	Multiple matching	5	You listen to five themed monologues of about 30 seconds each, and you choose five correct options from a list of eight possible answers.	page 51
4	Multiple choice	7	You listen to a conversation between two or more speakers, lasting about three to four minutes, and you choose from answers A, B or C.	page 53

Speaking 14 minutes per pair of candidates

You will probably do the Speaking test with one other candidate, though sometimes it is necessary to form groups of three. There will be two examiners, but one of them does not take part in the conversation. The examiner will indicate who you should talk to in each part of the test.

Part	Task type	Minutes	Format	Task information
1	Interview	2	The examiner asks you some questions and you give information about yourself.	page 55
2	Long turn	1 minute per candidate	You talk on your own (for about a minute) about two photographs the examiner gives you. Then the examiner asks the other candidate to comment on the same photographs (for about 30 seconds). The examiner then gives the other candidate a different set of two photographs and the process is repeated.	page 57
3	Collaborative task	3 minutes (a 2-minute discussion followed by a 1-minute decision-making task)	You have a conversation with the other candidate. The examiner gives you some material and a task to complete together.	page 60
4	Discussion	4	You have a discussion with the other candidate, guided by questions from the examiner, about the topics in Part 3.	page 63

Further information

The information about *B2 First* contained in *B2 First Trainer 3* is designed to be an overview of the exam. For a full description of the *B2 First* examination, including information about task types, testing focus and preparation for the exam, please see the *B2 First* Handbook, which can be obtained from
https://www.cambridgeenglish.org/exams-and-tests/first/preparation

Cambridge University Press & Assessment
The Triangle Building
Shaftesbury Road
Cambridge
CB2 8EA

Test 1 Training — Reading and Use of English Part 1

Task information

- In Part 1, you read a text with gaps and choose the correct word from four options (A, B, C or D) to fill each gap.
- There is one example plus eight gaps.
- Part 1 mainly tests vocabulary.
- Part 1 tests what the words in the options mean, but it also tests which words go together (collocations).
- This part also tests how words are used in sentences. For example, you might need to know if a word is followed by a preposition, or if it is followed by the infinitive or *-ing* form of a verb.
- Part 1 may also test words which connect ideas in the text (linking words).

Useful language Verb–noun collocations

1 Complete the sentences with words from the box.

> account   action   adjustments   advantage   appearance
> breakthrough   chances   charge   connection   emphasis
> pressure   revenge   questions   use

Tip! When you learn a new word, find out how the word is used in a sentence. Learn that as well as what the word means.

1 Someone needs to take .... of the situation or there will be chaos.
2 I think the machine will work if you make the necessary ....
3 Don't take any .... on the mountain – be as careful as you can.
4 Try not to put too much .... on Gary – he's having a hard time at the moment.
5 The actor made her first .... in public yesterday, after a three-month break.
6 It is important to take .... of everyone's needs when designing a course.
7 Can you make .... of this equipment or should I have it moved out of the music room?
8 The teacher always puts the .... on the students' successes, rather than their mistakes.
9 It wasn't reasonable to make any kind of .... between the two events.
10 We took .... of all the facilities the hotel provided while we were staying there.
11 The problem is getting worse and worse – someone needs to take .... soon!
12 The scientists were delighted to finally make a significant .... after years of hard work.
13 In the film, the hero took .... on his enemies in an amusing way.
14 You can put your .... to the speaker after the talk.

2 Complete the phrases with *make, put* or *take*. Use Exercise 1 to help you.

1 .... advantage of
2 .... use of
3 .... the emphasis on
4 .... a connection
5 .... revenge
6 .... an adjustment
7 .... pressure on someone
8 .... a breakthrough
9 .... charge
10 .... a question to someone
11 .... account of
12 .... an appearance
13 .... a chance
14 .... action

Useful language Adverb collocations

3 Match the adverbs (1–6) with the adjectives (a–f).

1 brightly	a disappointed
2 closely	b populated
3 conveniently	c connected
4 bitterly	d forbidden
5 densely	e coloured
6 strictly	f located

4 Complete the sentences with collocations from Exercise 3.

1 My favourite café is very .... – it's right next to our college!
2 This is a .... part of the city, so it's always quite noisy.
3 He always wears .... clothes which reflect his cheerful nature.
4 They felt .... when they failed to win an award for their film.
5 I think the two ideas are very ....
6 Smoking is .... on all public transport here.

Tip! The options in Part 1 often have similar meanings, but only one option fits in each sentence.

5 Choose the correct word (**A**, **B**, **C** or **D**) to complete the sentences.

1 They enjoyed the show ....
   A significantly   B powerfully   C tremendously   D strongly

2 .... speaking, that isn't quite correct.
   A Strictly   B Accurately   C Precisely   D Exactly

3 The book was .... successful, but never became a bestseller.
   A rather   B roughly   C slightly   D reasonably

4 What .... are you trying to say?
   A correctly   B strictly   C exactly   D accurately

5 The film was .... fantastic!
   A completely   B absolutely   C thoroughly   D fully

6 Many people here are .... concerned about the threat to local wildlife.
   A completely   B totally   C entirely   D deeply

7 Is this information .... available?
   A largely   B deeply   C widely   D highly

8 I'd .... recommend reading this article!
   A strongly   B completely   C powerfully   D extremely

Reading and Use of English Part 1

Useful language Verbs + prepositions

6 Choose the correct options in *italics* to complete the sentences.

1 We will *respond / answer* to your queries as soon as possible.
2 She has *specialised / focused* in the history of science throughout her career.
3 Everyone here is *allowed / entitled* to some time off in the evenings.
4 They eventually *succeeded / managed* in contacting me.
5 My best friend doesn't *agree / approve* of eating meat.
6 The teacher *discouraged / advised* us from spending more than two hours on our homework.
7 I will *provide / give* you with as much information as I can.
8 They were wrongly *blamed / accused* of breaking the window.

| Tip! | Always read the text before and after the gap very carefully. The option you choose needs to work grammatically with the rest of the sentence. |

 Cambridge English: *B2 First* candidates often make mistakes with using verb + preposition combinations in the correct way. Example: *I want you to come ~~in~~ **to** my town.*

Useful language Adjectives + prepositions

7 For questions **1–8**, read the text below and decide which answer (**A, B, C** or **D**) best fits each gap.

My basketball team

I play in a wheelchair basketball team and I love it! We train once a week after school and play in matches twice a month. I've always been quite good at sport, but I'm delighted to have discovered one that I'm **(1)** .... about.

All the team members have become close friends over time, which makes us very **(2)** .... of one another. We also have a brilliant coach who's never too **(3)** .... of our performance, even on a bad day because she knows how **(4)** .... we are to do well! She's very **(5)** .... at her job, so we've all learnt a great deal from her, including how to handle the challenges **(6)** .... to basketball.

At matches, our friends and families always come along to support us, and I'm sure that's been partly **(7)** .... for our winning so many matches. But we players need to take the credit, too. I've become much more **(8)** .... in myself since I joined the team, so I can say things like that without blushing these days!

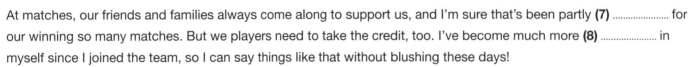

1	**A** stubborn	**B** addicted	**C** eager	**D** passionate
2	**A** loyal	**B** understanding	**C** sympathetic	**D** helpful
3	**A** critical	**B** negative	**C** annoyed	**D** pessimistic
4	**A** devoted	**B** fond	**C** keen	**D** emotional
5	**A** qualified	**B** trained	**C** skilled	**D** respected
6	**A** precise	**B** specific	**C** accurate	**D** exact
7	**A** involved	**B** reliable	**C** concerned	**D** responsible
8	**A** sure	**B** confident	**C** certain	**D** convinced

Useful language Verbs with similar meanings

8 For sentences 1–8, decide which answer (**A**, **B**, **C** or **D**) best fits each gap.

> **Remember!**
> Think about the meaning of the verb, but also about its 'grammar'. What can come after the verb? For example, is it followed by a noun/-ing form or an infinitive with to?

1 Everyone in the class .... of the way in which the teacher dealt with the problem.
   A agreed   **B** appreciated   **C** admired   **D** approved
2 We all want to .... our goals in life if we possibly can!
   A succeed   **B** obtain   **C** gain   **D** achieve
3 Everyone .... interesting ideas to the discussion.
   A contributed   **B** donated   **C** offered   **D** presented
4 He was only .... to have lost his phone!
   A imagining   **B** playing   **C** acting   **D** pretending
5 We need to find out how many students .... our proposal for the college garden.
   A support   **B** boost   **C** confirm   **D** assist
6 As the sun .... into the sky, the air became warmer.
   A raised   **B** lifted   **C** rose   **D** advanced
7 This catering business was .... over 100 years ago!
   A settled   **B** established   **C** set   **D** installed
8 Let's .... what this room would be like if we painted and decorated it!
   A invent   **B** dream   **C** imagine   **D** believe

Useful language Fixed phrases and idioms

Cambridge English: *B2 First* candidates often make mistakes in using idioms.
Example: ~~In the other hand~~ **On the other hand**, your website is not very attractive.

9 Complete the sentences with words from the box. There are four extra words that you do not need to use.

| fact | far | feelings | heart | mind | much | pain | question | sight | sign | sudden |

1 I love my little cousins with all my .... !
2 There was no .... of Dan's ball anywhere in the park.
3 That's a terrible thing to say – the idea never crossed my .... !
4 As .... as I know, tomorrow's band practice is going ahead as usual.
5 There's no internet here – it's a real .... !
6 The bird disappeared all of a .... before I managed to photograph it.
7 As a matter of ...., you're the first person to ever ask me that!

10 Choose the correct options in *italics* to complete the sentences.
1 It's difficult to learn the lyrics of several songs by *heart / memory / brain*.
2 Don't ask me about that; it's nothing to *have / think / do* with you.
3 I was under the *idea / impression / imagination* that she wanted to join the team.
4 I'm sorry I'm late – I completely lost *sense / track / idea* of time!
5 When I saw the palace, it *took / kept / threw* my breath away!
6 We will contact you in *next / further / due* course.
7 We have a bit of extra time in this city, so let's *take / get / make* the most of it!

Test 1 Exam practice — Reading and Use of English Part 1

For questions **1–8**, read the text below and decide which answer (**A, B, C** or **D**) best fits each gap. There is an example at the beginning (**0**).

Mark your answers **on the separate answer sheet**.

Tip! You need to understand the text as a whole in order to do the task. That's why you should always read the text quickly before you answer the questions.

Example:

0   A absolutely   B strictly   C deeply   D entirely

0 [A] [B] [C▬] [D]

Changing the world – one meal at a time

Many people all over the world are **(0)** .... concerned about the environment. As a result, they are gradually **(1)** .... more environmentally friendly lifestyles. One of the ways in which they are **(2)** .... action is by changing the way they eat. Around a billion tonnes of food are thrown away each year and food waste often **(3)** .... methane, a harmful greenhouse gas.

No individual is personally **(4)** .... for changing the whole world, but many people are altering their diets in order to **(5)** .... in a small way. Many try to eat what's **(6)** .... available locally rather than a lot of imported food, or eat less meat and more plants, especially beans and greens.

It isn't necessary to become completely vegetarian or vegan all of a **(7)** .... Simply having a meat-free day once a week can **(8)** .... a difference. Planning meals in advance and using up leftover food also helps to reduce unnecessary waste.

Advice
The example, and questions 1, 2, 3, 6 and 8 all test collocations. Question 7 tests a fixed phrase.

1	A using	B adopting	C welcoming	D accepting
2	A doing	B taking	C having	D setting
3	A generates	B breeds	C results	D leads
4	A blamed	B obliged	C responsible	D guilty
5	A donate	B support	C contribute	D add
6	A highly	B extremely	C strongly	D widely
7	A sudden	B rush	C flash	D moment
8	A give	B put	C bring	D make

Test 1 Training — Reading and Use of English Part 2

Task information

- In Part 2, you read a text with gaps and write one word in each gap.
- There is one example plus eight gaps.
- Part 2 mainly tests grammar: the missing words are usually auxiliary verbs, articles, pronouns or prepositions.
- Part 2 can also test linking words, phrasal verbs and fixed phrases.

Useful language Articles, quantifiers and determiners

1 Choose the correct options in *italics* to complete the text.

Tip! Sometimes, more than one answer is possible. You must write only one word for each gap.

Brave baby penguins!

(1) *Few / Some* baby emperor penguins have been filmed jumping into the sea from **(2)** *a / such* high cliff. **(3)** *The / This* extraordinary thing is that **(4)** *any / these* baby penguins have never actually swum before. They look as if they are trying to fly as they fall. Once they reach **(5)** *some / the* water, they are able to swim immediately. I would not be brave **(6)** *enough / so* to do that, but of course I am not **(7)** *a / the* baby penguin!

2 Choose the correct options in *italics* to complete the sentences. Sometimes both options are correct.

1. They called, but there was *no / not* answer.
2. *Every / Each* seat was taken when we got on the bus.
3. Has there been *many / much* interest in the new chess club?
4. *Any / None* of the people could solve the puzzle – it was too hard for all of them.
5. *Little / Few* is known about the history of this ruined castle.
6. We had *lots / plenty* of time to get to the station.
7. There weren't *many / any* clouds in the sky that day.
8. That's *one / some* of the tallest buildings in the world!
9. Luckily, I had brought a *little / some* money with me.
10. My sister and I are *all / both* good swimmers.

Useful language Prepositions

Cambridge English: *B2 First* candidates often use incorrect prepositions.
Example: *By the way, I have a question to **for** you.*

3 Complete the sentences with *at*, *in*, *of*, *on* or *with*.
1 Along .... her knowledge of her subject, she has great communication skills.
2 Only a handful .... people noticed the famous actor in the crowd.
3 Everyone seemed to be .... a good mood that day.
4 Please contact us .... your earliest convenience.
5 Their hard work will be worth it .... the long run.
6 The constant noise was beginning to get .... his nerves.
7 I am writing .... respect to your complaint about the delay to your flight.
8 Most people at the concert were .... their twenties.

4 Complete each sentence with a preposition.
1 They often confuse him .... his brother because they look so similar.
2 Each number corresponds .... a different colour.
3 All the children recovered .... the illness in a few days.
4 The classrooms are all equipped .... the latest technology.
5 The birds are adapting .... living in a warmer climate.
6 The presenter commented .... the team's poor performance.
7 They reacted .... the announcement with surprise.
8 Suddenly, a deer emerged .... the forest.

Useful language Relative pronouns

5 Choose the correct options in *italics* to complete the sentences. Sometimes more than one option is possible.

1 This is the painting *that / what / which* was stolen and then returned to the museum.
2 My cousin's car, *who / which / that* is very old, often breaks down.
3 The man *whom / whose / which* wallet they found was very grateful.
4 My aunt Lucie, *that / who / whom* lives in Paris, has invited me to stay.
5 The village I come from, *that / what / which* is very small, is famous for its cheese.
6 The friend to *which / whom / whose* I sent the parcel never received it.
7 The place *that / where / which* they swam was very quiet.
8 Try to find out *what / that / which* your sister would like for her birthday.

6 Rewrite the sentences, correcting the mistakes. Sometimes more than one answer is possible.

1 This is the house that I used to live.

....

2 Is that the person whose helped you when you fell off your bike?

....

3 I wonder whom backpack this is.

....

4 The only part of the film what confused me was the ending.

....

5 Paolo's friend Linda, which studies maths, managed to fix his laptop.

....

6 I'm having dinner with Tao, who parents are fantastic cooks.

....

> **Tip!** Contractions count as two words, so a contraction such as *that*'s or *they*'ve will never be an answer in Part 2.

Reading and Use of English Part 2

Test 1 Exam practice — Reading and Use of English Part 2

For questions **9–16**, read the text below and think of the word which best fits each gap. Use only one word in each gap. There is an example at the beginning **(0)**.

Write your answers **IN CAPITAL LETTERS on the separate answer sheet**.

Example: | 0 | A | B | O | U | T |

Gaming can bring people together

Some people are concerned **(0)** .... the impact of computer and video games. It is of course true that some players become addicted to them and once that has happened, it may be hard to know **(9)** .... to do about it.

There are also many positive aspects of gaming, however. **(10)** .... many gamers will tell you, it has become a means for many to communicate regularly **(11)** .... those they care most about. This is true for people of all ages, not just those in **(12)** .... teens or twenties.

Nowadays, almost **(13)** .... has a family member or friend living so far away that it is impossible to spend time with them **(14)** .... person. Gaming is a great way of bringing people together, **(15)** .... anyone needing to leave their own home.

Gaming provides a chance to catch up on news, exchange gossip and simply relax. Moreover, it costs relatively **(16)** .... compared to travelling great distances to meet up.

Tip! You must spell your answers correctly.

Advice
9 This is an indirect question, so a question word is needed here.
11 Which preposition is needed here?
13 What is the pronoun that means 'all people'?
15 This means that nobody needs to leave their own home.
16 Gaming doesn't cost much compared to making a long journey.

Test 1 Training — Reading and Use of English Part 3

Task information

- In Part 3, you read a text with gaps and make a word to fill each gap, using a word given in capital letters at the end of the line.
- There is one example plus eight gaps.
- Part 3 mainly tests vocabulary.
- Part 3 also tests grammar and spelling.
- In Part 3, you need to decide what kind of word goes in each gap (e.g. a noun, an adjective, an adverb or a verb).
- You need to know how to add prefixes and suffixes to change the words in capital letters, and how to make changes inside those words if necessary.

Useful language Suffixes

1 What kind of word (noun, adjective, adverb or verb) do you need to complete each sentence?

1. The college café is a good place to .... **SOCIAL**
2. That actor is great, she speaks very .... **NATURAL**
3. Those two tennis players win a lot of matches together – they form a great .... **PARTNER**
4. The artist used a combination of colours that was very .... **EFFECT**
5. They were .... accused of a crime they didn't commit. **WRONG**
6. People go there to think because it is such a quiet and .... place. **PEACE**
7. They were asked to make the first .... as soon as possible. **PAY**

> **Remember!**
> A prefix comes at the beginning of a word (e.g. *im*possible) and a suffix comes at the end of a word (e.g. happi*ness*).

2 Now complete the sentences in Exercise 1 by adding a suffix to the word in capitals.

> **Remember!**
> When you add a suffix, you may have to make some spelling changes.

3 Use the correct form of words 1–8 below the text to complete the gaps.

Bright futures

The careers **(1)** .... we received at our school was very helpful. The teacher who provided it was very kind and everyone admired her **(2)** .... Not all students **(3)** .... took the advice she gave, but the fact that she was so positive and **(4)** .... often changed their attitude towards their future goals and persuaded them to aim higher.

As a result, the number of applications for university places increased **(5)** .... while I was there. Thanks to the videos we were shown and the visits that were arranged to different university departments, the whole idea of what being a university student involved became less **(6)** .... to us all.

The school principal always gave her **(7)** .... for these visits, even when they were during the school day, which was great. So, when we eventually had to make a decision and **(8)** .... on the application forms exactly why we wanted to study a particular subject, it wasn't too difficult for anyone.

1. guide
2. patient
3. necessary
4. encourage
5. steady
6. mystery
7. approve
8. specific

Useful language Spelling

Cambridge English: *B2 First* candidates often misspell words that they know. Frequently misspelt words are *which*, *because*, *beautiful*, *different* and *interesting*.

4 Complete the gaps in these words with one or two letters.

1 happ..........ly
2 independ..........nt
3 suspic..........us
4 succe..........ful
5 beautifu..........y
6 fascinat..........ng
7 negati..........ly
8 appear..........nce

Tip! Some words have different spellings in American and British English, e.g. *flavour* (British English) and *flavor* (American English). Both spellings will be marked as correct in the exam.

Useful language Plural nouns

5 Decide whether a plural or singular form of **player** is needed to complete each sentence. Sometimes both are possible.

1 The .... celebrated after winning the match.
2 The .... in that team are some of the best in the world.
3 She is one of the best .... in the world.
4 The .... will have to rest for a week now.
5 Is that .... going to be selected for the team?
6 The .... enjoy having a good meal after a game.

Useful language Different tenses and verb forms

6 Complete each sentence with a form of the word **wide**.

1 The entrance to the theatre was .... last year.
2 They are thinking of .... the pavement here.
3 I'd like to .... my knowledge of chemistry.
4 Did they .... the discussion at the end to include everyone in the room?
5 My little cousin .... her eyes enormously whenever I mention cake!

Useful language Making extra changes to words

7 Complete the sentences with the correct form of the words in capitals.

1 The book turned out to be very different from what the novelist had .... intended. **ORIGIN**
2 The thing I love most about my cousin is her ....! **GENEROUS**
3 The scientists made some interesting .... **OBSERVE**
4 The students here are all very .... and want to do well. **AMBITION**
5 She's good at making plans quickly and carrying them out – she's very .... **DECIDE**
6 When we first arrived in the town, the people were quite ...., but after we'd lived there for a few months, they were much more welcoming. **FRIEND**

Tip! You often need to do more to change the word in capitals than simply add a suffix or a prefix. For example, you may need to add both a prefix and a suffix.

20 | Test 1 Training

Reading and Use of English Part 3

Test 1 Exam practice — Reading and Use of English Part 3

For questions **17–24**, read the text below. Use the word given in capitals at the end of some of the lines to form a word that fits in the gap **in the same line**. There is an example at the beginning **(0)**.

Write your answers **IN CAPITAL LETTERS on the separate answer sheet**.

Tip! You will always need to change the word in capitals in some way. You should read the text carefully, because sometimes you need a negative form.

Example: **0** F A S C I N A T I N G

New deep-sea species

Everyone knows the world's oceans are full of (0) .... creatures. Nevertheless, it's always exciting to think that there are still plenty of (17) .... to be made. Recently, a group of (18) .... set off on a deep-sea expedition aiming to explore underwater mountain ranges off the coast of Chile. They wanted to increase their (19) .... of the diverse sea life there.

FASCINATE

DISCOVER
SCIENCE

KNOW

What they found was totally (20) ....! In less than a month, the expedition recorded 100 deep-sea animals that they had never seen before, (21) .... species of corals and sponges. (22) .... , they recorded new types of octopus and jellyfish, as well as many other fantastic creatures that are of interest to researchers.

BELIEVE

INCLUDE
ADDITION

The remote area explored was (23) .... the size of Italy. The team had started with high (24) .... because they knew that this place was likely to contain some previously unknown species. However, the number they found was far greater than they had ever imagined it would be.

ROUGH
EXPECT

Advice

17 Make sure you spell this plural noun correctly!

20 People **couldn't** believe it because it was so amazing.

22 The word that completes the gap here means the same thing as *In addition*, but only one word can be used to complete the gap.

24 A noun is needed after the adjective *high*. Notice that there is no article before *high* in the text, so the noun in the gap can't be singular.

Test 1 Training — Reading and Use of English Part 4

Task information

- In Part 4, you have to rewrite sentences.
- There are six sentences.
- Each sentence is followed by a word in CAPITALS and the beginning and end of a second sentence.
- You have to fill the gap in the second sentence using between two and five words, including the word in capitals, so that the second sentence has the same meaning as the first sentence.
- The word in capitals must not be changed at all.
- Part 4 mainly tests grammar.
- Part 4 also tests vocabulary, fixed phrases and idioms.
- You get two marks for each correct answer: one mark for the first part of the answer and one for the second part.

Useful language Reported speech

1 Rewrite the sentences using the reporting verbs in the box. Don't write more than five words in the gap, including the reporting verb. Don't change the form of the verb.

| accused | advised | demanded | invited | offered | refused |

Tip! Only change the words that you need to. You don't get extra marks for using synonyms (e.g. *new / different*) and you may make a mistake.

Remember! When you report a conversation, present simple verbs become past simple verbs, verbs in the past simple become verbs in the past perfect, and so on.

1 'Would you like to come to our party?' Alex and Chris said to Toni.
   Alex and Chris .... party.

2 'I think you should take up a new sport,' Tariq said to Louis.
   Tariq .... a new sport.

3 'You can't make me play football with you in the rain!' Frankie said to his brother.
   Frankie .... with his brother in the rain.

4 'You broke my phone!' Susan said to Tomas.
   Susan .... her phone.

5 'Would you like me to bring some fruit for the picnic?' Peder asked.
   Peder .... some fruit for the picnic.

6 'I must know what is happening!' Gabriella said.
   Gabriella .... happening.

2 Rewrite the questions using reported speech.

1 'Where is the supermarket?' asked Mario.
   Mario asked ....

2 'Who left the flowers?' asked my sister.
   My sister asked ....

3 'Are your cousins coming?' Gerry asked me.
   Gerry asked me ....

4 'What does the teacher think?' Mo asked.
   Mo asked ....

Useful language Comparatives and superlatives

3 Complete the sentences using words from the box. Use some words more than once.

as   fewer   least   little   more   most   much

1 They're really nice people – the .... time I spend with them, the .... I like them.
2 That's the .... surprising news I've ever heard! Everyone was expecting that to happen!
3 The film wasn't .... interesting .... I'd hoped it would be.
4 She wanted to spend as .... time as possible inside the museum so she could get outside into the sunshine.
5 Yellow is a .... cheerful colour than grey, I think!
6 Could you give me .... green beans than you gave Julia, please? I don't like them very much.
7 I loved it – it's one of the .... amazing books I've ever read!
8 There are .... people in this city than there were 50 years ago, so the streets are always crowded.

Useful language Three-part phrasal verbs

4 Complete each phrasal verb (**1–6**) with one word. Then match them with the definitions (**a–f**).

1 look ...... to   a use / do / eat something less
2 stand up ......   b feel excited about something that's going to happen
3 come up ......   c have nothing left of something
4 run ...... of   d support someone / an idea
5 cut down ......   e accept something / someone without complaining
6 put ...... with   f think of a new idea / plan

5 Complete the sentences with the correct form of phrasal verbs from Exercise 4.

1 I'm not going to .... all the mess in this flat from now on! Let's tidy it up!
2 I think we've .... sugar – I can't find any in the kitchen.
3 The children are .... the summer holidays.
4 I'm hoping someone will .... a solution soon!
5 We're trying to .... salt because consuming a lot of it isn't very healthy.
6 David .... Chiara when some of her colleagues criticised her decision to work from home.

Test 1 Exam practice — Reading and Use of English Part 4

For questions **25–30**, complete the second sentence so that it has a similar meaning to the first sentence, using the word given. **Do not change the word given**. You must use between **two** and **five** words, including the word given. There is an example at the beginning **(0)**.

 Tip! Contractions (e.g. *they're*, *won't*) count as two words in your answer.

Example:

0   It's over five days since Sam's last message.

   TOUCH

   Sam hasn't ……………………………………………………………… least five days.

This gap can be filled by the words 'been in touch for at', so you write:

Example: | 0 | BEEN IN TOUCH FOR AT |

Write **only** the missing words **IN CAPITAL LETTERS on the separate answer sheet**.

---

25 'Thanks for your great idea for entertaining the kids,' Nola said to Jain.

   COMING

   Nola ……………………………………………………… with a great idea for entertaining the kids.

26 Spend as much time as you can on this painting, because that's what will improve it.

   BETTER

   The more time you spend on this painting, ……………………………………………………… be.

27 'Do you like windsurfing?' my aunt asked my brother.

   KEEN

   My aunt asked my brother ……………………………………………………… windsurfing.

28 I'm considering eating less cheese and drinking less milk.

   DOWN

   I'm thinking ……………………………………………………… cheese and milk.

29 'I won't accept your bad behaviour any longer!' the teacher said to the children.

   REFUSED

   The teacher ……………………………………………………… with the children's bad behaviour any longer.

30 I was pleased to find the job easier than expected.

   DEMANDING

   I was pleased that the job wasn't ……………………………………………………… thought it would be.

Advice

25 What reporting verb should be used here? What phrasal verb means 'have / suggest an idea'?

27 Be careful about word order!

30 What comparative structure often follows a negative verb? What tense should you use to talk about something that happened or was true **before** another time in the past?

Test 1 Training — Reading and Use of English Part 5

Task information

- In Part 5, you read a long text and answer multiple-choice questions about it.
- There are six questions. Each question has four options (A, B, C and D).
- In Part 5, there are usually questions about the opinions, feelings or attitudes of the writer or someone in the text. There may also be questions about what point the writer is making in a paragraph. Some questions could be about the writer's purpose: why the writer says something or why the writer includes some information. There can also be questions asking about what a word or phrase in the text refers to and in some questions, you have to work out what a word or phrase means by using the surrounding text.

Useful language Opinion and attitude

1 Match the sentences about learning to play chess (**1–5**) with the opinions (**a–e**).

1 It would be great if anyone who wanted to learn to play chess had the opportunity to do so, but unfortunately, that is not the case.
2 People who learn to play chess tend to become better at solving problems and better thinkers in general.
3 There are players who say that learning to play chess is extremely challenging, but they're wrong.
4 I don't know why more people aren't learning to play chess.
5 I can't think of anything less entertaining than learning to play chess, to be honest.

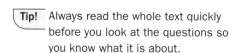

Always read the whole text quickly before you look at the questions so you know what it is about.

a It is a boring thing to do.
b It should be more accessible.
c It is not actually very difficult.
d It is surprising that it isn't more popular.
e It is a good way of developing the mind.

2 Read the extract quickly. What is happening?

> Dan and Lucy watched through the first-floor window as the new neighbours gave instructions to the men struggling to carry all their furniture into the house.
>
> 'I'd love a piano,' said Lucy.
>
> 'Have you seen the sofa?' Dan asked. 'And the armchairs? Far too old-fashioned, don't you think?'
>
> 'Don't be silly,' Lucy replied. 'Who cares about that kind of thing, anyway?'
>
> She'd noticed the sports equipment in some of the boxes, including a couple of badminton rackets, and thought they might have more than just music in common. There was something about the way they smiled and laughed, too. She imagined herself knocking on their door with the cake she'd just baked. Or maybe they could come round for dinner …
>
> 'At least they don't have a car,' Dan said. 'It isn't easy to manage without one around here. I like the look of those bikes. They must be pretty fit – and care about the environment.'
>
> Lucy wasn't so sure. Maybe they had a car, but it was being repaired. Or maybe they couldn't afford one. She'd offer them a lift to the supermarket later, she decided.

3 Choose the correct options in *italics* about Dan and Lucy's attitudes towards their new neighbours. Underline the parts of the extract which give you the answers.

1 Dan *admires / looks down on* their taste in furniture.
2 Lucy *welcomes / does not welcome* the idea of making friends with them.
3 *Dan / Lucy* respects the new neighbours for not having a car.

Useful language Feelings

4 Read the paragraph below quickly. What is the group learning to do?

> Tip! The incorrect options usually contain ideas that appear in the text, but they are not the answer to the question.

When I'd joined the art group, I hadn't expected everyone to be so encouraging and helpful. Having thought they might find me annoying if I kept asking questions, I'd said almost nothing for the first few lessons. I'm not brilliant at drawing and had been a bit worried that signing up for the intermediate class might have been too ambitious. However, I soon realised that no one else was that great either, which cheered me up. I'd initially found a seat at the back, in the corner furthest away from the teacher. That made it harder for me to see the carefully chosen objects she brought in for us to draw every week, but when she noticed I was having trouble, she insisted that I should sit closer to the front.

5 Choose the correct option (**A**, **B**, **C** or **D**) to answer the question below. Underline the part of the paragraph in Exercise 4 which gives you the answer.

How does the writer feel about the art group he joined?
- **A** eager to do well in it
- **B** irritated by some people in it
- **C** puzzled by the teacher's choices
- **D** relieved to be as good as the others

6 Why are the other options wrong?

Useful language Referencing

> Tip! Even if there isn't a question about referencing in Part 5, understanding references will help you to follow the text you're reading and this will help you to answer some of the questions!

7 Read the two extracts and answer the questions. How did you find the correct answer?

In town centres being modernised in most parts of the country, there are usually one or two old buildings of great interest to historians. Preserving **those** should be a priority.

1 What does *those* refer to?
- **A** town centres
- **B** most parts of the country
- **C** one or two old buildings
- **D** historians

Several species were recorded by scientists on the expedition, including tree frogs and lizards. **The former** were of particular interest because they had never been seen in that area before.

2 What does *the former* refer to?
- **A** several species
- **B** tree frogs
- **C** scientists
- **D** lizards

Test 1 Exam practice — Reading and Use of English Part 5

You are going to read an article about a journey on a cruise ship in Norway. For questions **31–36**, choose the answer (**A**, **B**, **C** or **D**) which you think fits best according to the text.

Mark your answers **on the separate answer sheet**.

Tip! The questions follow the order in which the information appears in the text.

My Norway cruise adventure

Last year, I went on a cruise in Norway. In many ways, the ship I was on looked like any modern cruise ship. There were major differences, however. When I went to meet the captain, he showed me the flatscreen displays used to control the ship. 'You see, if we increase speed …' He nodded at the first officer, who tapped a screen. 'We use up the power in the batteries and use more liquid natural gas.' Another nod and the ship slowed down a little. 'At this speed, we're at our most economical.' The chief engineer asked me to remember the first hybrid electric / petrol-engine cars. 'We're at that stage with ships,' he said. Liquified natural gas has been criticised for its methane gas emissions, but on this ship, other pollutants were reduced and the batteries allowed four hours of low-emission sailing in environmentally sensitive areas. The ship's twin 43-ton batteries were each in a tennis-court-sized container.

We were on our way to the most northerly part of Europe, far beyond most places inside the Arctic Circle where any humans live permanently. We were hoping to see stars and the Northern Lights (beautifully coloured moving lights that can sometimes be seen in the sky in that area). There was an astronomer on board, ready to answer our questions

line 24 if the latter appeared. As this was a winter cruise, the weather played a major part: storms had already made it impossible for us to board at Bergen, our intended point of departure. We'd had to meet the ship in Trondheim instead, then leave rapidly as another storm came rushing in. I was, in fact, enjoying the unexpected. Instead of a hike up a mountain near Ålesund, I found myself visiting the aviation museum in Bodø – not something I'd normally choose, but I was soon lost in Norwegian history and also had time for a coastal walk, spotting three sea eagles before hurrying back to the departing ship.

Later, at dinner, we were told there was a good chance of seeing the aurora borealis. Dinner, by the way, was never one of those giant buffets found on many cruises. The cruise company takes the issue of food waste seriously and table service significantly reduces it. The dishes themselves were absolutely delicious and delivered by the friendliest crew I've ever come across. After dinner, the ship's lights were turned down and for the next few hours, we watched silently as the aurora display grew, faded, then reappeared.

Over the next few days, we moved around the top Arctic edge of Europe, heading east into colder air. At dawn one morning, I could hardly last a minute outside holding a camera with my bare hands. The sea looked hard and dark, with white lines across it, and the island bays were silent with ice, unwelcoming. At Honningsvåg, on the island of Magerøya, we stopped and most people boarded coaches for a tour to Nordkapp, Europe's most northerly point. Several others chose a snowshoe walk. That left a tiny, rather nervous-looking group, including me, who had chosen to swim in the Barents Sea.

A short bus ride delivered us to Skarsvåg, the most northerly fishing village in the world and the scene of my remarkable, crazy, final experience of the trip. We were taken to a sauna and, after a few minutes in the 80°C heat, I went outside and descended some steps into the sea. The air temperature was −15 °C. I surprised myself by actually swimming a few metres. Then my toes and fingers started begging me to get out. Once I had, however, I was gripped by a strong desire to go back in. I really can't explain why I did, apart from the fact that it was so magical to swim surrounded by the Arctic winter in all its terrible beauty. Later, in a café, I ate waffles with cloudberry jam, washed down with hot coffee. I bought some locally knitted socks and at last, my feet warmed up.

31 What does the writer emphasise in the first paragraph?
  A how out-of-date the cruise ship had already become
  B the lack of luxurious facilities for the cruise passengers
  C attempts to lower the amount of pollution caused by the cruise
  D how well the cruise ship captain got on with the rest of the crew

32 What does 'the latter' refer to in line 24?
  A stars
  B the Northern Lights
  C the astronomer on board
  D passengers' questions

33 In the second paragraph, the writer describes being
  A willing to accept changes to the planned schedule.
  B relieved that a challenging activity had been cancelled.
  C concerned about potentially dangerous sailing conditions.
  D disappointed to miss so much of the natural surroundings.

34 What is the writer's opinion of the catering on board?
  A The staff were what made it so exceptional.
  B It made up for the lack of other entertainment.
  C It was a particularly positive aspect of the cruise.
  D The food was so good, it was a pity there wasn't more of it.

35 In the fourth paragraph, it is suggested that the colder weather affected
  A the passengers' enjoyment of some activities.
  B the choice of locations where the ship could stop.
  C people's decisions whether or not to leave the ship.
  D the writer's feelings about the surrounding landscape.

36 What does the writer say about swimming in the sea?
  A It had long-term impacts.
  B It was incredibly dangerous.
  C It proved to be irresponsible.
  D It inspired unexpected reactions.

Advice

31 What is talked about a lot in the first paragraph?

33 Options A–D all start with adjectives describing feelings. Look for information in the third paragraph that shows how the writer was feeling.

35 When you're asked a question about what is suggested in a particular part of the text, think about what the writer means by choosing particular words or phrases.

Test 1 Training — Reading and Use of English Part 6

Task information

- In Part 6, you read a long text with gaps and choose the correct sentence to fill each gap.
- There are six gaps and seven sentences to choose from, so there is one option that you do not need to use.
- Part 6 tests how a text is structured. You need to know how referencing words and linking words and phrases are used to connect ideas in a text.

Useful language Referencing

1 Complete the sentences using referencing words from the box. Sometimes more than one answer is possible.

Tip! Look for pronouns and other words in the text and the options which refer to people, things and ideas. Underline these referencing words and what they refer to.

| afterwards | elsewhere | others | so | that | them | then | there | these | this |

1 Italy is a beautiful country. That's why so many people enjoy having holidays ....
2 Researchers have published some interesting findings. Many people are reading .... with interest.
3 Professional chefs often create complex dishes. Many people cooking at home avoid doing ....
4 The team had no matches scheduled for March, so they decided to take a break ....
5 Some scientists say more research is needed. .... disagree.
6 Tourists often visit the main sights first. They usually have a meal ....

Useful language Linking words and phrases

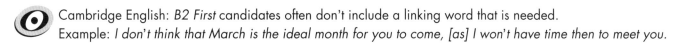

Cambridge English: *B2 First* candidates often don't include a linking word that is needed.
Example: *I don't think that March is the ideal month for you to come, [as] I won't have time then to meet you.*

2 Match the sentences (**1–4**) with the sentences (**a–d**) that follow them.

1 Sending astronauts into space is very expensive.
2 Conditions in space are very different from those on the Earth.
3 It could be argued that too much research has been devoted to space and space travel.
4 Scientists are always hoping to discover water on other planets.

a As a result, every space mission is extremely complex.
b That's because astronauts might be able to use it if they landed there.
c That's why relatively few countries have been able to do so.
d On the other hand, some of it has been found to be useful on Earth, too.

3 Complete the sentences using linking words and phrases from the box.

| for instance | furthermore | in contrast | in spite of this | nor |

1 Winter there is dark and cold. ...., summer brings long bright days and hot weather.
2 These devices are easy to use. ...., they cost very little.
3 The director rarely gives interviews. .... does her actor husband.
4 Websites often collect data on users. They may, ..., store information about their locations.
5 The explorers were tired and hungry. ...., they carried on.

Test 1 Exam practice — Reading and Use of English Part 6

You are going to read an article about sports. Six sentences have been removed from the article. Choose from the sentences **A–G** the one which best fits each gap (**37–42**). There is one extra sentence which you do not need to use.

Tip! Read the article quickly to see what it is about before you look at the options.

Mark your answers **on the separate answer sheet.**

Why have leisure sports become so competitive?

When I cycle west out of the town where I live, I have two choices. One is a steep hill that climbs and climbs for around 20 minutes, but it feels like much longer. I have to be in first gear, standing up and pedalling like mad, and when I get to the top, I stop to let my lungs return to some kind of normality. The alternative is a gently sloping, curving road, on which I can use gears that make me look relaxed (and strong) as I climb, and I can stay seated. **37** Time passes smoothly and fitness improves without too much thought or effort being given to it. Most of the time, I choose that route. **38** It's a fitness test, as well as a demonstration of faith in the 'no pain, no gain' principle, and it means the brain can switch off so that the body can do all the work.

It might also be a sign that I am getting drawn into the world of obsessed sporting fanatics. **39** I wonder how close I am to becoming the type of person who plans holidays around burning carbohydrates, who tracks and compares speeds as if something really, really important depended on it. The statistics-hungry sports enthusiast is a product of our time, a symptom of a need to turn what once passed for relaxing hobbies into strict regimes that make our work routines seem positively leisurely.

There are all sorts of social and cultural pressures on the way people spend their free time. **40** In that way, they can demonstrate they have the right kit, clothing and so on, which marks them out as someone with money and supposedly good taste. It could also be to do with feeling part of something bigger, part of a community.

Technology is changing the way people experience sports. Wearable gadgets, from internet-connected watches to head cameras, put amateurs, superficially at least, on a level with professionals. **41** And social media is full of people informing others of the route they used to climb a certain hill and sharing images from their extreme-sports weekend. The ability to share physical activity achievements like this fuels the desire to be seen to be engaged in exercise.

Not so long ago, many people laboured in physical jobs and spent their free time socialising, gardening, catching up on sleep and perhaps doing some fishing. If they cycled, it was usually to get to work and back home. If they ran, it was to catch the bus. Sport was a spectator experience; you paid to let other, more gifted people sweat it out. Now, our day jobs might not be so physically hard, but they are mentally tough. People in offices tend to have little freedom and are constantly monitored and evaluated. The worry that we will lose out if we do not work late or answer emails at midnight is incredibly harmful. **42** After all, this is the only time where we can have some control over what we do.

A	They allow us to keep an eye on our well-being and health while on the move.	**E**	Sometimes, however, it's impossible to resist the challenge of the steeper climb.
B	Despite this, sport is an arena in which we can all pretend to be the same.	**F**	So, a cyclist might cycle fast up a hill both to be physically active and to show off.
C	These include the road-racers, hill-runners and rock-climbers who are always trying to achieve 'personal bests'.	**G**	If cycling with a friend, it's even possible to chat a bit.
D	We push ourselves so hard in our leisure lives as a reaction to this.		

Advice

38 Look for an option that introduces a contrast to the idea in the previous sentence.

39 Look for examples of dedicated sports enthusiasts.

41 Look for an explanation of how wearable gadgets can help people who are doing sport.

Test 1 Training — Reading and Use of English Part 7

Task information

- In Part 7, you read several short texts or a long text divided into sections.
- There are ten questions.
- The questions don't follow the order in which the information appears in the text(s).
- You have to choose the section or short text (usually A, B, C or D – occasionally E as well) which answers each question.

Useful language Functional verbs

1 Match the verbs in the box with the sentences.

> accept   confess   deny   disapprove   question   recommend   stress

1. (I think they've behaved very badly.) ....
2. (I was the one who ate your chocolate bar.) ....
3. (I think you'd enjoy that book.) ....
4. (I don't think your plan will work.) ....
5. (I think that was absolutely the best day I've ever had!) ....
6. (OK, you're right, that's what we should do.) ....
7. (No, I didn't forget to book the tickets.) ....

2 Read the extracts from Part 7 texts. Then choose the correct options in *italics* to complete the sentences.

1. 'This was definitely the worst decision we could possibly have made.'
   The person is *explaining / emphasising / questioning* how bad an idea was.

2. 'I think it's reasonable to think that people should try to use their cars less often in order to improve air quality, so I'm not sure why the other people at the meeting disagreed with me.'
   The person is *defending / recommending / doubting* their own point of view.

3. 'I know it's often claimed that teenagers are addicted to their phones, but that isn't actually the case.'
   The person is *suggesting / regretting / challenging* an idea that many people have.

4. 'I think that anyone who goes out and does something to protect the environment deserves our admiration.'
   The person *criticises / challenges / respects* people who take action for the environment.

5. 'It's lazy and selfish to drop litter in the countryside, in my opinion.'
   The person is *explaining / criticising / denying* some behaviour.

6. 'The council say they're going to build a new sports centre. I think that's a great idea.'
   The person *approves of / justifies / explains* a proposal.

7. 'I know I'm right about that.'
   The person is *claiming / hoping / wishing* to be correct.

8. 'There are fewer and fewer birds in our local area. I think that planting more trees would improve the situation.'
   The person is *challenging / accepting / proposing* a solution.

Test 1 Exam practice — Reading and Use of English Part 7

You are going to read an article about four teenagers who went to escape rooms – places where groups of people can solve a series of puzzles together for fun. For questions **43–52**, choose from the people (**A–D**). The people may be chosen more than once.

Mark your answers **on the separate answer sheet.**

Which person

recognises the value of someone's experience?	43
regrets worrying about the time limit?	44
recalls insisting on a new approach?	45
suspects that someone cheated?	46
wishes they had asked for help?	47
justifies their decision to ignore some advice?	48
assumes they will do better another time?	49
admits boasting about their skills?	50
objects to a comment someone made?	51
explains why they backed someone up?	52

Tip! There is only one correct answer to each question, but there may be something in another text or section which distracts you (makes you want to choose the wrong answer).

Solving puzzles in an escape room

Four teenagers describe going to an escape room for the first time.

A Jay

Three friends and I booked an 'escape room' for an hour last weekend. None of us had ever tried it before. An escape room is an indoor space that players are locked into – although of course they can be let out any time if necessary – until they have solved a series of puzzles or until their time is up. The theme of this escape room was detective fiction and we had to solve a burglary case. We managed the first few puzzles all right, but then they became more challenging. The others wanted to carry on doing everything together, but I was concerned it was taking too long and eventually persuaded everyone to work separately, then compare answers. It did speed us up, but not enough – our session was over before we'd solved the crime. Anyway, I'm sure we'd succeed if we ever tried again, having learned from our mistakes.

B Cole

The theme of our escape room was science fiction. We weren't allowed to have our phones with us, but I'm pretty sure one of my friends brought theirs in with them and used it a couple of times. Some people wanted to ask the organiser for clues halfway through, which you can do, but my best friend didn't want to. I agreed with her and said so – it would have felt like giving up and I knew we'd succeed on our own if we really tried. It was great fun and everyone was delighted when we solved the final puzzle. Going to an escape room is a really enjoyable way to spend a rainy weekend afternoon. I think the fact that one person in our group had tried a few escape rooms before helped enormously, to be honest. But that doesn't mean it would have been impossible otherwise.

C Mara

I'd heard a lot about escape rooms before going to one for the first time with three of my friends. I must say I'd been keen to let them know how great I thought I'd be at it because I've always been pretty good at problem solving. They were nice enough not to remind me of that when I turned out not to be so brilliant in the end! The main thing I discovered was that it's a team effort and completing the puzzles within the time given often depends on understanding that. The escape room we went to was a treasure hunt and each of us turned out to be better at solving some types of clue than others. I spent ages trying to find a hidden animal in a 3D computer image. If I'd got one of my friends to do it with me, I wouldn't have wasted so much time.

D Leon

The theme of my first escape room was life in a medieval castle. One of my friends announced that it would be too easy because they'd seen so many historical films set in that period. That was a bit silly and rather arrogant, in my opinion. The main thing I'd do differently if I tried another escape room would be to forget about how fast or slow our progress was. I think I spoiled it for myself a little by focusing too much on whether or not we'd complete all the tasks before the end of the session. I did enjoy the various challenges, though. There was one I got very absorbed in – my friend tried to tell me how to do it, but I preferred to carry on in my own way – it was a kind thought, but I knew I was just about to solve it.

Test 1 Training — Writing Part 1 (essay)

Task information

- The essay task in Part 1 tests your ability to present opinions in an essay.
- The task consists of notes and information which you use to write between 140 and 190 words.
- You must write about the information and the notes given and think of a new idea of your own.
- You will need about 40 minutes for this task, including time to plan and check your work.

Planning the essay

Tip! Plan your essay before you start writing.

1a Read the Part 1 essay task below.

You **must** answer this question. Write your answer in **140–190** words in an appropriate style.

In your English class you have been talking about online classroom learning. Now, your English teacher has asked you to write an essay.

Write your essay using **all** the notes and giving reasons for your point of view.

What are the advantages and disadvantages of online classroom learning?

Notes

Write about:

1. location
2. connections with other students
3. .... (your own idea)

---

b What does *online classroom learning* mean?

....

c What do you have to write about in the essay?

....

d Look at note 1. Think about where you learn when you attend an online class. What are the advantages of this? Are there any disadvantages?

....

e Look at note 2. Think about making connections with other students. Are there advantages to learning online with other students? Are there disadvantages?

....

2 Which of these sentences from a candidate's answer to the question in Exercise 1a refer to note 1 and which refer to note 2?

   a You can't get to know people on a more personal level as easily. ....

   b It is more flexible because you can study anywhere at any time. ....

   c You may not have a suitable dedicated space to work. ....

   d There's no opportunity for chatting during breaks. ....

   e You might be interrupted while you're trying to study. ....

   f You get to talk to people from all over the world. ....

3a Which of these points would be suitable for note 3 in Exercise 1a?

- remote learning
- conversation
- social opportunities
- variety of tasks
- qualifications

> **Tip!** Your own idea (for note 3) should not overlap with either of the other points, and it should not simply be a conclusion for notes 1 and 2.

b What are the advantages and disadvantages of the points you chose in Exercise 3a?

c Think of your own idea for note 3.

Organising your essay

4a Which of the following would be the best structure for the essay in Exercise 1a? Why?

A

Introduction

Paragraph 1: advantages and disadvantages of note 1

Paragraph 2: advantages and disadvantages of note 2

Paragraph 3: advantages and disadvantages of note 3

Conclusion

C

Introduction

Main body: advantages and disadvantages of notes 1, 2 and 3

Conclusion

B

Introduction

Paragraph 1: advantages of notes 1, 2 and 3

Paragraph 2: disadvantages of notes 1, 2 and 3

Conclusion

b Read the sentences below. Using structure B from Exercise 4a, decide which paragraph you would put the sentences into.

1. Additionally, you can feel a sense of shared goals, despite not being face to face.
2. On the other hand, your studies can be disrupted by other people around you, or by background noise.
3. There are advantages and disadvantages to learning a language in an online classroom.
4. However, there can be difficulties with technology, such as people breaking up, or being on mute and not realising it.
5. Similarly, there is some fantastic software that allows learners to use interactive tools and watch videos or listen to recordings simultaneously.
6. To sum up, there are both advantages and disadvantages to learning a language in an online classroom, and personal preferences should be taken into consideration when choosing a course.
7. The advantages of studying remotely include being able to choose a suitable and comfortable place to work. What is more, you can even study when you're on the move, for example, on a train.

c There is no disadvantage for note 2 in the sentences in Exercise 4b. Write a suitable sentence for this note.

Using more formal language

5a Read the sentences which refer to using online platforms for classes. Match the informal words and phrases in bold in the sentences (**1–7**) with the more formal alternatives (**a–g**).

1 Participants may **accidentally** leave themselves on mute.
2 The audio can be muted **if that's helpful**.
3 Breakout rooms can **let people** share ideas with each other.
4 A participant may be asked to share their screen which **lets other people** see useful information.
5 One **problem** with using technology is that people's voices can break up due to a poor internet connection.
6 Participants may **use** the chat function.
7 Putting your hand up can **let people know you want** to contribute to the discussion.

a allows other participants to
b unintentionally
c enable participants to
d signal your intention
e difficulty
f when necessary
g make use of

> **Remember!**
> Remember: Avoid using language that is very informal in essays, such as informal fixed phrases and idioms (e.g. *It gets on my nerves!*).

b Read the sentences below. Decide which sentences use formal (F) and which use informal (I) language.

1 Some students can't be bothered to speak up and they let others do all the hard stuff. ....
2 There has been a considerable improvement in learning software during the last decade. ....
3 On balance, classroom learning is preferable to virtual lessons for a variety of reasons. ....
4 I don't really care whether I do my classes online or actually go somewhere to study. ....
5 It is more challenging to gain individual attention when the teacher is not in the same place. ....
6 They can just switch their camera off and mess about, which is a complete waste of time. ....

Writing Part 1

Linking words

6a Look at the sentences in Exercise 4b again. Underline the linking words and phrases. Are they used to add information or to compare and contrast ideas?

> **Remember!**
> Using linking words will make your essay more coherent and help you express ideas more clearly.

b Complete the table with the linking words and phrases from the box.

besides   equally   even so   even though   furthermore   in addition   in contrast   likewise   moreover   nevertheless   nonetheless   not only … but also   on the contrary   whereas

Adding information	Comparing and contrasting
Example: besides	*Example:* even so

Test 1 Exam practice — Writing Part 1 (essay)

You **must** answer this question. Write your answer in **140–190 words** in an appropriate style **on the separate answer sheet.**

In your English class you have been talking about online learning. Now, your English teacher has asked you to write an essay.

Write your essay using **all** the notes and giving reasons for your point of view.

> **Would a real partner or an AI partner be better for language practice?**
>
> **Notes**
>
> Write about:
>
> 1. personalised learning
> 2. interactive materials
> 3. ……………………………… (your own idea)

Advice

Use this checklist when you have finished the task.

- [ ] Have you included ideas for all three notes?
- [ ] Is your essay organised into paragraphs?
- [ ] Have you written 140–190 words?

Test 1 Training — Writing Part 2 (article)

In Part 2, you have three questions to choose from (Questions 2, 3 and 4), but you only answer one of them. Questions 2–4 will be three of the following: an article, an email, a letter, a report or a review.

Task information

- The article task in Part 2 tests your ability to write an interesting text for a magazine, newsletter or website.
- In the actual exam, you just choose one of the three tasks in Part 2. Read all the Part 2 questions and choose which one you will answer.
- In the exam, the Part 1 task and the Part 2 task both have the same number of marks. You need to give yourself the same amount of time for each answer.
- You may need to write descriptions, give examples, make comments or give your opinions.
- Think about who you are writing for and whether you should use formal or informal language.
- A short title will help to engage your readers.
- You should write between 140 and 190 words.

Engaging the reader

1a Match the titles (1–5) with the topics (a–e).

1. New from old: the best upcycling tips
2. The fun of hunting for 'treasure'
3. What your playlist says about you
4. Images with an impact
5. Thrill-seekers: what makes us tick?

a. arts and crafts
b. collecting things
c. extreme sports
d. music
e. photography

Tip! Read the instructions carefully to make sure you know who the reader of the article is. This will help you choose appropriate language.

b Do you think the titles in Exercise 1a are interesting? Why? / Why not?

2a The sentences below are the first lines of articles. Which ones make you want to read the rest of the article? Why?

1. Have you ever thought about spending your birthday underwater?
2. Many people do hobbies or sports in the evening and at the weekend.
3. Ever fancied diving off a cliff into the cool blue ocean?
4. Celebrations are good.

Tip! Articles often start with a rhetorical question (a question that doesn't need an answer). For example, *Have you ever felt you wanted to try an unusual sport?* might introduce an article on sports. Rhetorical questions can also be used within an article to involve the reader and make the style feel more direct.

b Rewrite the sentences as rhetorical questions.

1. You're wondering whether you're too old to take up competitive sport.
   Are you ....?
2. I don't know whether you've ever fancied learning to play an instrument.
   Have you ever ....?
3. I think you'd like to get some tips about strengthening your relationships.
   Would you like to ....?
4. You have some free time and want an interesting new project to do.
   Do you ....?

Tip! When you include a rhetorical question in your article, you often answer it in the following sentence. For example, *Are you looking for an interesting new hobby? If so, read on for our tips on the best ways to spend your free time.* Or *Are hobbies just for children? No, they aren't!*

Useful language Using dramatic adjectives

3a Look at the adjectives below. Write a different adjective that is more dramatic.

Example: surprising – *amazing*

1 annoying ....
2 bad ....
3 cold ....
4 difficult ....
5 funny ....
6 good ....
7 old ....
8 scary ....
9 tasty ....
10 tired ....

Tip! You should try to use some dramatic adjectives in your article, as these often make articles more interesting and exciting to read.

b Choose the more dramatic options in *italics* to complete the sentences.

1 We had a great time at the fairground. The rides were absolutely *thrilling / exciting*!
2 I was totally *interested in / fascinated by* the lecture about dinosaurs at the museum.
3 I felt completely *overwhelmed by / emotional about* the setting of the castle.
4 The story she told about how the painting ended up in the gallery was totally *interesting / unbelievable*.
5 The stones in the necklace are absolutely *priceless / expensive*.

Remember! Adding an adverb before an adjective can make the adjective even more dramatic. Keep a list of adverbs and adjectives that often go together, for example, *highly* intelligent, *absolutely* convinced, *deeply* concerned.

c Read the sentences in Exercise 3b again. Which adverbs are used in front of the dramatic adjectives?

 Cambridge English: *B2 First* candidates often use an adjective that is incorrect in the context.
Example: *It'll be a* ~~big~~ **great** *pleasure for us if you are willing to give a talk to our club.*

Giving opinions

4a Complete the phrases for giving opinions using words from the box.

| agree | concerned | conclusion | convinced |
| personally | see | seem | tend |

1 As I .... it, …
2 I've come to the .... that …
3 As far as (she / the average person) is ...., …
4 I .... to think that …
5 I'm (absolutely) .... / confident / certain that …
6 It would .... to me that …
7 .... speaking, …
8 Not everyone would .... (with me), but …

Tip! You can give your own opinions about the topic in an article. Make sure you choose suitable language for the reader of your article when giving an opinion.

b Decide which phrases can be used to introduce opinions.

1 To my mind, …
2 If you ask me, …
3 Imagine what you could …
4 I don't know about you, but I …
5 Whether you believe it or not, …
6 Listen to this! …

> **Tip!** It is important to both express your opinions and give reasons for them.

c Complete the sentences using phrases from Exercise 4b. There may be more than one correct answer.

1 .... achieve if you really put your mind to getting the best grades possible.
2 .... , employers are more likely to recruit those with skills beyond your academic qualifications.
3 .... , I'd say you should do as well at school as you possibly can, to give you the best chance in life.
4 .... You can do anything if you want it enough!
5 .... think that ambition is important, but being overly ambitious can lead to disappointment.
6 .... , it's important to have goals so that you gain a sense of fulfilment when you achieve them.

Test 1 Exam practice — Writing Part 2 (article)

Write your answer in **140–190 words** in an appropriate style **on the separate answer sheet**.

You see this announcement on an English-language website.

> *Articles wanted*
>
> **How should a visitor spend a day in your area?**
>
> How do you enjoy spending time in the place where you live? If a visitor came to your area for a day, what should they do and see?
>
> The best articles will be published on our website.

Write your **article**.

Advice

Use this checklist when you have finished the task.

- [ ] Have you included all the points / answered all the questions?
- [ ] Have you given reasons for your opinions, with examples?
- [ ] Have you used suitable language and dramatic adjectives?
- [ ] Have you written 140–190 words?

Test 1 Training — Writing Part 2 (letter)

Task information

- The letter task in Part 2 tests your ability to write, e.g. a formal job application or a letter to a magazine editor. You must write in an appropriate style.
- The instructions include a description of a situation. In response to this situation, you need write a letter of between 140 and 190 words.
- You should allow about 40 minutes for this task, including time at the end to check your work.
- You have to organise your letter into paragraphs, with a suitable beginning and ending.
- You should write full sentences with correct grammar and punctuation and use a good range of language with accurate spelling.

Tip! It is important to structure your letter well in the exam. It should begin with an opening formula (*Dear* …), state the reason for the letter, address any points in the task and end with an appropriate closing formula (*Yours* …).

Structuring a letter

1a Read the notice. What does the town council want someone to do?

> Dear residents,
>
> Next summer, we are planning to hold our first community festival, which will include talks and activities for local people and visitors to the town. We are looking for an Events Manager to lead the organisation of the event in the town.
>
> If you are interested, please send me your letter of application and explain why you would be suitable for the role.
>
> Anna Swan (Head of Events Committee at the Town Council)

b Look at the phrases (1–7). Where could they be included in a letter of application for the role in Exercise 1a? Decide if they should go in the opening (O), main body (B) or closing (C) section.

1. I have experience of planning events, including sports matches and last year's science festival at a nearby college. ....
2. Yours sincerely, ...
3. I am particularly interested in community events and have attended several similar festivals. ....
4. I am highly motivated, good at solving problems and I enjoy working under pressure to meet deadlines. ....
5. Dear Ms Swan, ...
6. I would like to apply for the role of Events Manager for the community festival. ....
7. I would be very pleased if you would consider me for the role and look forward to hearing from you. ....

2a Decide which of the phrases from the box are suitable ways to start a formal letter.

Tip! Think about who will read your letter. You should use formal language in a letter of application.

> Dear Mr Jackson,   Hello!   Hey! How's it going?   Hi there,   To whom it may concern   Dear Sir or Madam,

b Decide which of the phrases from the box are suitable to use at the end of a formal letter.

> Love from …   Yours faithfully,   Write back soon!   Yours sincerely,   See you later!

Vocabulary

> **Tip!** Try to include a range of vocabulary that is relevant to the topic you are writing about.

3a Match the words and phrases (**1–10**) with their definitions (**a–j**).

1 contribute to society
2 a sense of community
3 relevant qualifications
4 improve your career prospects
5 develop your CV
6 charity
7 skills and experience
8 give something back
9 internship
10 discover your strengths and weaknesses

a an organisation that helps people who need it
b find out what you're good at and what you're less good at
c participate in activities that help people around you
d an official record that shows you have the necessary skills
e a period of work experience in a company
f do something positive for those around you in return for what you have received
g do useful things that can be added to a written document of your experiences
h abilities to do something well and knowledge from doing things
i a feeling that those around you matter
j make opportunities for progress at work

b Which of the words and phrases in Exercise 3a could be connected to volunteering? Which could be connected to work or gaining work experience? Are there any phrases that connect to all three topics?

Test 1 Exam practice — Writing Part 2 (letter)

Write your answer in **140–190 words** in an appropriate style **on the separate answer sheet**.

You see this notice on an English-language website:

Volunteers wanted!

We are currently creating new wildlife areas on our farms and we are looking for volunteers who love the countryside to help us.

Write to Angela Tome, Volunteer Leader, explaining why you would like to volunteer, why you think wildlife protection is important, and what relevant experience you have.

Write your **letter**.

Advice
Use this checklist when you have finished the task.

☐ Have you explained why you would like to volunteer?
☐ Have you explained why you think wildlife protection is important?
☐ Have you included examples of useful ideas and experience?
☐ Have you used formal language?
☐ Have you started and finished your letter in an appropriate way?
☐ Have you written 140–190 words?

Test 1 Training — Writing Part 2 (report)

Task information

- The report task expects you to give some factual information and make recommendations or suggestions.
- The instructions include a description of a situation. You have to write a report of between 140 and 190 words.
- Allow about 40 minutes for this task, including time at the end to check your work.
- The report may be for a teacher, a school director or classmates, etc. You therefore have to write in an appropriate style.
- Organise your text into a report format, using headings if needed.
- Write full sentences and try to use correct grammar and punctuation with a good range of language and accurate spelling.

Structuring a report

> **Tip!** You must include one section per point in your report. Using appropriate headings can help you organise your report.

1a Read the report. What went well at the event? What did not go well?

Introduction

I **was** recently **chosen** to take part in a national swimming competition. The aim of this report is to provide feedback to the organisers about how the event **might be improved** in future.

Arrival at the venue

There were many competitors at the event and limited parking. This meant long queues at the drop-off point, which led to some competitors being late for races.

Facilities for competitors

Firstly, the changing facilities were spacious and clean. Secondly, although snacks were available, these ran out during through the event. What is more, there was no quiet area.

Organisation of races

The races **were organised** well, with events **being called** in advance for swimmers to warm up. However, one race **was overlooked**, so some swimmers did not get to compete.

Recommendations

I would strongly recommend giving each competitor a specific drop-off time in order to prevent queues. I suggest that a more plentiful supply of snacks should be available. I would advise arranging a quiet area where swimmers can get 'in the zone'. Finally, the running order of the races **should be double-checked**, so that none **are overlooked**.

b Look at the structure of the report in Exercise 1a. Decide which of the following statements are true.

1. The reason for the report is stated clearly at the beginning.
2. Each point is explained in its own section.
3. Positive and negative points are addressed in different sections from each other.
4. Each section has a relevant heading which describes the information that will follow.
5. The language in the report is informal.
6. Some suggestions for improvements are included.

Grammar

2a Look at the words in **bold** in the report in Exercise 1a. Are they active or passive? Why?

> **Remember!**
> We often use the passive voice (e.g. *The doors to the concert* **were opened** *at 7.30*) in reports. This is more formal than the active (e.g. *The duty manager* **opened** *the doors to the concert at 7.30*).

b Rewrite the sentences using the passive voice. There may be more than one change to make in each sentence.

1 They didn't put seat numbers on the tickets, so no one knew where to sit.

....

2 They let too many people into the festival and didn't provide enough facilities for them all.

....

3 The organisers didn't send the participants the address for the event.

....

4 Nobody had cleaned or tidied the kitchens, so we couldn't go ahead with our cooking event.

....

5 They cancelled the game at the last minute, but didn't inform anyone.

....

Test 1 Exam practice — Writing Part 2 (report)

Write your answer in **140–190 words** in an appropriate style **on the separate answer sheet**.

Your English teacher has asked you to write a report for the college magazine about how the college encourages students to be environmentally friendly.

In your report, you should:

- describe how students help to care for the environment at the college
- explain why such activities are important
- recommend other ways the college could help the environment.

Write your **report**.

Advice

Use this checklist when you have finished the task.

- ☐ Have you addressed all the points?
- ☐ Have you given reasons for your opinions, with examples?
- ☐ Have you used formal language, including the passive voice?
- ☐ Have you used appropriate headings?
- ☐ Have you written 140–190 words?

Test 1 Training — Listening Part 1

Task information

- In Part 1, you will hear eight short, unrelated recordings, which are either dialogues or monologues.
- The recording for each question will be about 30 seconds long.
- There is a sentence to tell you about the context of the recording: who will be speaking and the topic.
- There will be eight questions or stems and three options for the answer. You will hear each recording twice.
- The questions will test whether you can understand topic, gist, detail, function, purpose, speaker's attitude, feelings or opinions and agreement between speakers.

> **Tip!** You will hear and read a sentence that tells you about the context. Use this to help you prepare for what you will hear. For example, think about how many speakers you will hear and what the situation will be.

Focus of the question

1 Match the context sentences (**1–6**) with the descriptions (**a–f**).

1. You hear a man talking about some scientific research. What is he doing?
2. You hear two friends talking about bungee jumping. What does the man think of it?
3. You hear a woman talking about giving a presentation. She says that she felt …
4. You hear a woman talking about playing in a football match. What mistake did she make?
5. You hear two friends talking about a film. They agree that …
6. You hear a man talking on a sports podcast. What type of information is he giving?

a. The question focuses on someone's opinion.
b. The question focuses on someone's feelings.
c. The question focuses on what someone is trying to do when speaking (e.g. persuading, warning, encouraging).
d. The question focuses on the overall general meaning (the gist) of what is said.
e. The question focuses on what the speakers agree on.
f. The question focuses on a specific detail of what is said.

2 Look at the question from a Part 1 task. Decide which statement (**a–f**) best matches the question *What is she doing?*.

> You hear a woman talking about the creation of new supersonic airliners. What is she doing?
>
> **A** questioning the motives of potential passengers
> **B** explaining the reasons for ongoing research
> **C** criticising the aims of a current project

a. The question focuses on the topic the woman talks about.
b. The question focuses on the gist or overall general meaning of what she talks about.
c. The question focuses on a specific detail of what she talks about.
d. The question focuses on what her purpose is when she talks.
e. The question focuses on what the woman's attitude is.
f. The question focuses on what the woman feels about something.

3 🎧 1 Now listen to the recording and choose the correct answer.

4 Read the audioscript and underline the words that show the correct answer.

> It seems that experts in the aviation industry are wasting time and resources with their investigations into supersonic flight. My suspicion is it's just about showing off their engineering capabilities. Flights on aircraft like this will surely only be possible for the super-rich, rather than the rest of us. When the supersonic airliner Concorde was conceived back in the mid-1900s, there really was a genuine need to speed up the flow of information and ideas across continents, as in those days, we still relied on printed material or personal interaction a fair bit. Those kinds of reasons for developing aircraft no longer apply in the era of digital online communication.

Vocabulary focus

5 Match the adjectives (**1–8**) with the adjectives with similar meanings (**a–h**).

1	unwise	a	sweet
2	thrilled	b	immediate
3	fascinating	c	foolish
4	second-hand	d	used
5	sore	e	painful
6	dedicated	f	excited
7	cute	g	absorbing
8	instant	h	committed

> **Tip!** Try to develop a wide vocabulary of different adjectives that describe things and people. This will help you to match the meaning of what you hear on the recording with the meaning of questions and options in the listening test.

6 Match the adjectives (**1–8**) with the adjectives with a roughly opposite meaning (**a–h**).

1	stunning	a	awful
2	courageous	b	innocent
3	guilty	c	unattractive
4	refreshing	d	unclear
5	urgent	e	encouraging
6	depressing	f	unimaginative
7	brilliant	g	unimportant
8	obvious	h	cowardly

Test 1 Exam practice — Listening Part 1

🎧 2) You will hear people talking in eight different situations. For questions **1–8**, choose the best answer (**A**, **B** or **C**).

1   You hear two friends talking about bungee jumping.
    What is the man's attitude to the people who do it?
    A   He disapproves of the risks they take.
    B   He is curious about their motivation.
    C   He admires their sense of adventure.

2   You hear two friends talking about trainers.
    What do they disagree about?
    A   how comfortable trainers are to wear
    B   how much value for money trainers offer
    C   how good trainers look on people

3   You hear a woman talking about when she studied at a music school.
    What does she say about it?
    A   It was difficult to enjoy free time.
    B   Students were extremely competitive.
    C   She realised the importance of practice.

4   You hear two friends talking about an animated movie they saw.
    Why does the woman mention the cat called KJ?
    A   to show how well made she thought the movie was
    B   to support a view she has about the movie's plot
    C   to suggest the movie had too many characters

5   You hear part of a talk about photography.
    What is the main reason the woman thinks most people take photos?
    A   to share their experiences with others
    B   to record key moments in their lives
    C   to express their appreciation of beauty

6   You hear a man talking about a documentary.
    What was the documentary about?
    A   the preservation of wildlife
    B   the dangers that wildlife faces
    C   the behaviour of wildlife

7   You hear a man telling a friend about a long bike ride he did alone.
    How did he feel about it?
    A   satisfied with how fast he cycled
    B   pleased to be free to choose his own route
    C   proud of the amount of effort he made

8   You hear two friends talking about a podcast on food and nutrition.
    What annoys the man about the podcast presenters?
    A   their belief in the importance of vegetarianism
    B   their tendency to repeat the same arguments
    C   their assumption that it is easy to eat healthily

Tip! Use the time you have before the recording is played to prepare yourself well. Read the context sentences and questions carefully.

Tip! Check you know whether there are one or two speakers and which speaker is the focus of the question.

Tip! Don't worry too much about options A, B and C the first time you listen. Instead, try to get an understanding of what the speaker(s) is/are saying in relation to each question.

Tip! Use the second time you listen to check you are confident in your choice of option (A, B or C). If you aren't sure, choose the one that is closest to what you understood.

Advice

1 Does the man say that the people who bungee jump take a lot of risks? Does he say anything that sounds as if he is interested in why they bungee jump? Does he say anything that shows a positive view of their sense of adventure?

2 When does the woman seem to have a more negative reaction to what the man says? What words does she use to show that she has a different view from him?

Test 1 Training — Listening Part 2

Task information

- In Part 2, you listen to one person talking about a topic and fill in missing information in a set of notes (ten sentences in total).
- You must write down the exact word or phrase that you hear to fill the gap.
- You may be asked to spell a name or write a number.
- The questions follow the order of the information in the recording.
- You should write down only the words and phrases you hear – no more than three words for each answer. You will not be asked to make any changes to the words you hear.
- The recording will be between three and four minutes long.

> **Tip!** You will have time to read the ten sentences before you listen. For each gap, decide what kind of word(s) you need to listen for (e.g. a noun, adjective or verb). Many answers are likely to be nouns, so think about whether you are listening for an object, a place or a person.

1 Read the introduction to this Part 2 task. What will the man talk about?

You will hear a man called Kevin Pendit giving a talk about organising a festival of short films made by film students around the world.

2 Look at the examples of Part 2 questions below. Read the sentences and think about what words could go in the gaps.

Kevin says that **(1)** .... was the most important stage in planning the film festival.
Kevin felt extremely lucky to get sponsorship from a **(2)** .... company to help fund the film festival.
Kevin was told that it was extremely important to have a **(3)** .... in mind for the film festival.
Kevin succeeded in getting a **(4)** .... to head the team of judges for the film festival.

> **Tip!** As you listen, pay attention to changes of topic; a change usually indicates that you should be focusing on the information in the next sentence.

3 🎧 3 Now listen and complete the sentences with words you hear. Then listen again.

4 Read the audioscript and check your answers.

Hi. I'm Kevin Pendit, here to tell you all about the film festival I organised last year. I'm still a film student and it was my first time doing something like this. I wanted to show short films made by other film students in different parts of the world. When undertaking a project like this, planning is essential. I had lots of ideas about how to go about generating publicity, and I knew that I wanted the film festival to be an example of the creativity and diversity there is out there among young filmmakers. But research is key. I did a lot of this beforehand, so I'd know exactly what I was doing. The next thing was funding, of course, and I was incredibly lucky. I'd actually negotiated a sponsorship deal with a travel company, but they pulled out early on. Thankfully, a technology company then came forward and agreed to provide financial backing, a lot more generously, in return for having their name in all publicity material.
Of course, there are loads of important factors to consider besides funding. I listened to advice from others and learned that a theme is vital. After considering various ideas, I decided to go with 'community', as I think it's something we're losing in the modern world. I wanted to raise awareness in my target audience, which was primarily younger people.
There were prizes for the best films in different categories, which meant I needed a panel of judges. I knew an arts journalist on a local paper who was happy to join, plus a friend of mine who's a big film expert. I asked one well-known film director to be in charge of the team, but he was too busy, so I turned to my college tutor, who happily took on that role.

5 Look at the audioscript again. Underline words the speaker uses that show you which sentence of the task you should be focused on.

Test 1 Exam practice — Listening Part 2

🎧 4 You will hear a woman called Natalya Erikson giving a talk about her work as a curator, who organises exhibitions at a museum of contemporary art. For questions **9–18**, complete the sentences with a word or short phrase.

Tip! Quickly go through the incomplete sentences, including the words before and after the gaps. This will help you get an idea of what the recording is about.

Working as a curator in an art museum

Natalya says that her mother's work as an art **(9)** .... influenced her choice of career.

Natalya says that her previous experience of **(10)** .... gave her relevant skills for her current work.

Natalya likes to use the phrase **(11)** '..' to describe the main kind of work that she does.

The museum where Natalya works is well known for its collection of work from artists in **(12)** ....

Natalya is particularly proud of the work she did on a recent exhibition of students' **(13)** .... for an art college.

Natalya admits that she finds **(14)** .... of artworks less inspiring than other aspects of her job.

Natalya says that her talent for **(15)** .... is very helpful when organising big exhibitions.

Natalya is currently preparing for a talk she will give about **(16)** .... soon.

Natalya is hoping to purchase a picture painted on a **(17)** .... surface for the museum's collection.

Natalya advises those interested in becoming a curator to focus their initial plans on working in **(18)** ....

Tip! You will hear the information on the recording in the same order as you see it in the sentences.

Advice

9 Natalya mentions these jobs: art dealer, art teacher and artist. Which job did her mother have?

10 What did Natalya gain experience of on a student magazine?

12 Which part of the world does the museum's most celebrated collection come from?

16 Natalya mentions these subjects for talks: exhibition design, a spotlight on a particular artist and photography. Which one is the subject of her next talk?

Test 1 Training — Listening Part 3

Task information

- In Part 3, you hear five short monologues.
- You have to choose from a list of eight options which one best matches what you hear. There are three options that you won't need to use.
- Each monologue will be about 30 seconds long.
- The options on the page, A–H, don't follow the order of the information in the recording.
- Part 3 tests your understanding of gist, detail, attitude, opinion, feeling and purpose.

1 Look at the example of a Part 3 task. You will also hear these instructions.

You will hear five short extracts in which people are talking about training to become a chef. For questions **19–23**, choose from the list (**A–H**) how each speaker says they felt during their training.

> **Tip!** All five speakers will talk about a similar topic. You will be able to hear and read what this is before you listen. Use the time before listening to read the instructions and the options to make sure you have a clear idea of what you need to listen for.

2 Look at the list of options for this task before listening to the first speaker.

- **A** pleased to be recognised for doing better than others
- **B** annoyed about being given less pleasant tasks
- **C** upset about making unnecessary mistakes
- **D** nervous about taking on extra responsibility
- **E** confused by some complicated instructions
- **F** determined to avoid conflict with others
- **G** grateful to receive plenty of support
- **H** disappointed by a low level of challenge

> **Tip!** In the task, the correct option is a brief summary of what a speaker has said. The speaker normally uses more or different words to express the same idea as the correct option.

3 🎧 5 Listen to the first speaker and choose the option from Exercise 2 that best matches what she says. Then listen again.

4 Read the audioscript and <u>underline</u> information that shows the correct answer.

> All my previous cooking experience failed to prepare me for the intensity of chef training, producing dishes on a large scale, with so much information to take in: safety instructions, food hygiene, preventing cross-contamination between things like nuts and other foods. To be honest, I'd thought I'd be a more skilled cook than other students and then I put bicarbonate of soda instead of the flavour enhancer MSG into an Asian stir fry. If only I'd bothered to check the label! On top of that, I did it on more than one occasion. I was totally gutted – I mean, so irritated with myself! It made me feel a bit less self-important, anyway!

5 🎧 6 Listen to the second speaker and choose the correct option from Exercise 2. Listen again to check your answer.

6 Read the audioscript and <u>underline</u> information that shows the correct answer. Then identify anything that might have made you consider other options.

> **Tip!** Listen carefully so that you can rule out incorrect options and choose the correct one, which most accurately matches what the speaker has said.

> I'd heard that my chef training course would be a lot of hard work. And it was. I think I'd have enjoyed it more if there'd been less theoretical stuff – you know, nutrition, kitchen hygiene, menu planning, cost control and so on. But the thing I really appreciated was how positive everyone was about each other's work. The kitchen culture was very much stepping in to lend each other a hand. That meant that you didn't even mind doing less exciting chores like peeling potatoes or scrubbing kitchen surfaces. I really got into the cooking side of the course and I was so proud of my pastry skills by the end.

7 Read extracts from what other speakers might say. Complete the sentences with the correct form of the verbs in brackets.

1 I wish there .... (be) fewer boring tasks to do. It always seemed to be me who was asked to do them.
2 I felt very anxious and if I .... (give) a choice, I .... (turn down) the opportunity to play the role of head chef.
3 Everything seemed quite easy. I .... (like) it if the course .... (demand) a bit more from students.
4 It was a shame that I had a couple of arguments with other students. I wish I .... (keep) my temper and, afterwards, I made sure it never happened again.
5 The recipe was very complex and I got the stages in the wrong order. If someone else .... (not stop) me, I .... (do) it all wrong.

8 🎧 7 Listen and check your answers. Then match each sentence with one of the options (A–H) in Exercise 2.

Tip! The five speakers will have different voices. Some voices will be male and some will be female. You may also hear a variety of accents.

Test 1 Exam practice — Listening Part 3

🎧 8 You will hear five short extracts in which people are talking about a long-distance train journey they went on. For questions **19–23**, choose what regret (**A–H**) each speaker expresses about the trip. Use the letters only once. There are three extra letters which you do not need to use.

Tip! Quickly read the instructions and options A–H. Study the options and underline any key words.

A having a disagreement with another passenger
B not having enough ways of avoiding boredom
C opting for higher price tickets
D not reading some important information properly
E choosing a route that involved delays
F missing out on views of scenery
G deciding to travel alone
H not being able to communicate with other passengers

Speaker 1 — 19
Speaker 2 — 20
Speaker 3 — 21
Speaker 4 — 22
Speaker 5 — 23

Advice
Speaker 1: What does she say about the mountains at sunrise?
Speaker 2: What does he say about his way of getting from southwest England to Aberdeen?
Speaker 3: What does she say was a pity?
Speaker 4: What does he say he should have done?
Speaker 5: What made her journey seem very long?

Tip! The speakers may mention things that could relate to several options, but only one option will be the correct match. The other option(s) will not match correctly.

Test 1 Training — Listening Part 4

Task information

- In Part 4, you will hear an interview or an exchange between two or more speakers. There are seven multiple-choice questions and each one has three options.
- You will be tested on your understanding of gist and detail and also on the speakers' attitudes, feelings and opinions.
- The questions follow the order of the recording as you are listening.
- The instructions will give you information about who the speakers are and what they will be talking about.
- The recording will be 3–4 minutes long.

1 Work with a partner. Discuss these questions.
1 What sports do you enjoy?
2 How important is the human mind for doing well at sports?
3 Do you know anything about the work of sports psychologists?

> **Tip!** The questions that the interviewer will ask are very similar to the written questions. Listen carefully to how the person being interviewed answers. Then choose the option that most closely matches what you heard.

2 🎧 9 Read the introduction and the two questions. Then listen and choose the correct option for each question.

You will hear part of an interview with a man called Jim Gallagher, who works as a sports psychologist helping athletes to improve their performance through psychological techniques.

1 When asked what first led him to study sports psychology, Jim explains that he
   A felt a strong desire to help others.
   B was motivated by a particular experience.
   C had been interested in the subject for a long time.

2 What has Jim found particularly useful when working with sports people?
   A He is naturally patient.
   B He has an optimistic attitude.
   C He understands their viewpoint.

> **Tip!** The person who is interviewed in Part 4 will use different words to express themselves from the words used in the multiple-choice options. Part 4 tests your ability to understand the meaning of what is said and match this to a similar idea in one of the options.

3 Read the audioscript and check your answers.

> **Interviewer:** What first made you study sports psychology, Jim?
> **Jim:** It's common for people to become sports psychologists to figure themselves out. I've been learning about techniques on my own for ages, but I'll never forget the turnaround in myself when I won a major ski-racing event. The difference was clear. I'd been aware how much your head gets in the way of winning at things long before making a career of it and getting an academic qualification. I've since seen many transformations, assisting sportspeople who lacked sufficient confidence to come out on top. It's very rewarding.
> **Interviewer:** What's been useful in your work as a sports psychologist?
> **Jim:** Well, some athletes have doubts about the mental side, instead focusing on the physical aspects of what they do. Having been in the same position previously, I get that, and they get that I do. It means they're more willing to take on board what I'm putting across. I try to teach them to come back from losing, to look on the bright side and go forward. Developing psychological skills can take a frustrating amount of time. It's hard to play the waiting game, but worth it in the long run.

4 Complete the sentences using the most suitable words from the box.

| a career | a path | barriers | fulfilment | inspiration |

1 It was a desire to pass on my skills that drew me to .... as a coach.
2 Financial support enabled her to overcome .... and become a champion.
3 Young athletes often take .... from their sporting heroes.
4 Gymnasts have to follow .... of great discipline to master their routines.
5 Seeking .... in life through football, Marcia puts all her energy into daily training.

5 Match the idiomatic phrases (**1–6**) with the explanations (**a–f**).

1 take things in your stride
2 play the waiting game
3 get in the way of
4 look on the bright side
5 come out on top
6 take something on board

a have an optimistic outlook on a situation despite difficulties
b have success after a struggle
c be patient when something takes a long time
d handle difficulties calmly
e accept and understand information or advice
f block progress

Test 1 Exam practice — Listening Part 4

🎧 **10** You will hear an interview with a man called Abe Halliday, who is talking about his work as a music producer, directing musicians, both creatively and technically, in the recording studio. For questions **24–30**, choose the best answer (**A**, **B** or **C**).

24 What does Abe say about becoming a music producer?
 A He looked at it as a way of learning more about music.
 B He faced more problems than he had expected to.
 C He followed a similar path to someone he admired.

25 What does Abe enjoy most about his job?
 A working with talented people
 B applying his technical skills
 C having the freedom to be creative

26 What does Abe say about the negative sides of his work?
 A He finds dealing with financial matters dull.
 B He has difficulties keeping equipment in good condition.
 C He dislikes recording outside of normal working hours.

27 How did Abe get the best out of one musician he worked with?
 A He gave her plenty of praise.
 B He agreed to her demands.
 C He set clear rules for behaviour.

28 How did Abe feel about producing the music for a popular advertisement recently?
 A surprised at how the public reacted to it
 B relieved to have got it done quickly
 C embarrassed to be connected with it

29 How does Abe feel about recording soon with the band Furious Sleepers?
 A excited about trying some new ideas
 B nervous about the pressure he will be under
 C confident that they will be satisfied with his work

30 What does Abe think is the most important advice for people who want to become music producers?
 A Become an expert in using music-production technology.
 B Focus on training your ears with different types of music.
 C Build relationships with people in the music industry.

Advice

25 What is Abe's number one pleasure?

27 How did Abe talk to the musician? What kind of things did he say to her?

29 What does Abe say he is sure about?

30 What does Abe say is really essential?

Test 1 Training — Speaking Part 1

Task information

- Part 1 of the Speaking test usually lasts about two minutes.
- There are two examiners. One of the examiners asks you the questions. The other listens and assesses what you say.
- At the start of the test, the interlocutor tells you the names of both examiners, then asks you for your name. You give your marksheets to the interlocutor.
- Then the interlocutor asks you questions. You don't talk to the other candidate in this part of the test.
- The questions are about personal topics, such as your work / studies, your family, your free time and your likes and dislikes.

Focus Understanding the task

1a Look at the topics below. Which topics would you expect to answer questions about in Part 1?

environmental problems	new inventions
facilities in the local area	public transport in your country
future plans	the lives of famous people
friends	travel experiences
hobbies	your birthday
important news stories	

Tip! This part is all about you. You don't need to speak to your partner.

Tip! You can prepare for this part of the test by talking with friends about personal topics, but don't try to memorise responses. You need to make sure you answer the question you are asked.

b 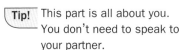 Listen to two candidates, Kemi and Yuki, answering questions in Part 1 of the test. Which topics from Exercise 1a do they talk about?

c 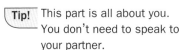 Listen again and write down the questions they were asked.

d Look at the topics in Exercise 1a which are not suitable for Part 1 questions. Change the topic focus and write a suitable Part 1 question.

Tip! Listen carefully to the question and note whether it is about the past, the present or the future. Make sure you use the correct tense to answer the question.

Useful language Expressing likes and dislikes

2a In Part 1 of the test, you may be asked to talk about things you like or don't like. Look at some comments from different candidates. Complete each comment with one word.

1. I'm really .... on cycling. It's something I try to do every weekend if I can.
2. I'm not particularly interested .... spending time on a beach. I would much .... visit a city or some historical sights.
3. I don't .... which university I go to, as long as I can study geography.
4. Unlike many people, I can't .... surprises, so I would hate it if someone organised a surprise party for me.
5. I enjoy .... the latest films at the cinema with them and we usually go for a burger afterwards.
6. Everyone knows I'm really .... fashion, so I often get clothes as presents.
7. I'm not a huge .... of art, but I'm looking forward to going to the galleries in Italy in the summer. They're supposed to be amazing.

b Look at the comments again. Which topics from Exercise 1a do the comments refer to?

c Here are some more Part 1 questions. They are all about likes and dislikes. Use expressions from Exercise 2a to write an answer for each question.

1. Is looking at art in museums something you like doing?
2. How do you feel about doing puzzles with numbers or words?
3. Do you enjoy playing computer games?
4. Tell us about a photo you like.
5. What is your favourite time of year?

> **Remember!**
> Adverbs are a good way of making your opinions stronger (e.g. *really, so, absolutely*) or weaker (e.g. *quite, a bit, slightly*).

d 🎧 12 Now listen to the recording and give your answer.

e 🎧 13 Listen to some candidates answering the questions. Do they have the same opinions as you?

Test 1 Exam practice   Speaking Part 1

1 Work with a partner. Take turns to ask and answer these questions. Ask questions in any order.

Part 1   2 minutes (3 minutes for groups of three)

Interlocutor	First we'd like to know something about you.
	Family and friends
	• How do you like to spend your time with friends?
	• Do you and your friends enjoy doing the same hobbies?
	• Where did you meet your best friend?
	• What would you like to do with your family this weekend?
	• Do you and your family often watch TV together?

2 🎧 14 Now listen to the recording and answer the questions you hear.

> **Advice**
> Try to use reasons and examples to give a longer answer. The examiner may ask *Why?* or *Why not?* to encourage you to extend your response.

Test 1 Training — Speaking Part 2

Task Information

- Part 2 of the Speaking test lasts about four minutes.
- The examiner gives you two photographs to talk about for about one minute. You compare the photographs and answer a question about them. The question is written above the photographs.
- You listen to your partner speaking, then you answer a shorter question connected to one or both of the photographs. You have about 30 seconds for your answer.
- No one will interrupt you when you are giving your 'long turn' response. You do not interact with your partner.
- If your answer to the 'follow-up' question is too short, the examiner may ask *Why?* or *Why not?* to encourage you to say more.

Focus Understanding the task

1 Read the ideas some students discussed about Part 2 of the Speaking test. Decide whether the comments are about things that you should or should not do in this part of the test.

- Ask your partner what they think about the photographs.
- Make guesses about what the photographs show.
- Choose your favourite photograph and talk about it.
- Describe everything you can see in the photographs.
- Talk about the similarities and differences between the photographs.
- Use linking words.
- Stop talking as soon as you have answered the question.
- Listen to what your partner says.
- Make suggestions to your partner.
- Answer the question above the photographs.
- Speak for a minute about your partner's photographs.

2 🎧15 Look at photos A and B on page C1 and read the questions. Listen to Mika talking about the photographs. Did she follow the correct advice from Exercise 1 above?

3a After Mika finishes speaking, her partner is asked a question about Mika's photographs. What do you think the question could be?

b 🎧16 Listen to Asif. What question does he answer? Does he follow the advice from Exercise 1?

Useful language Giving reasons

4a The comments below relate to photograph A on page C1. Match the sentence beginnings (**1–6**) with the endings (**a–f**).

1 It looks like an office due
2 I'd guess it's quite a relaxed workplace because of
3 It looks like the presentation has already started, given
4 She actually seems quite relaxed as
5 I don't know how big the audience is since
6 My guess is that she's about to explain her report owing

a the casual clothes the people are wearing.
b she's smiling at the other people.
c to the fact that there's data on the screen.
d to the style of furniture.
e that there's information showing on the screen.
f I can only see two people with the presenter.

Tip! Part 2 tests your ability to give an extended response and organise what you say appropriately. Using linking words and expressions to introduce reasons is one way of doing this.

b Now look at some comments for photo B on page C1. Complete them with one word in each gap.

1 .... that they're all smiling, I'd say they are feeling reasonably confident.
2 The man on the left must be the instructor .... the others are all looking at him and he looks like he's wearing some kind of uniform.
3 They are probably beginner .... there don't seem to be any steep slopes around them.
4 .... to the fact that they're all standing in line, I expect they are about to practise some basic moves on the skis.
5 Although there's snow everywhere, I imagine they're not particularly cold, ... to the sunshine.
6 They're probably feeling a bit nervous .... of their lack of experience.

5 🎧17 Look again at the photos on page C1. Listen to the recording and give your answer. Remember to follow the advice from the examiners.

Tip! Look at the whole picture – the location, the people, the weather – to find ideas to answer the question.

Tip! When you answer the follow-up question about your partner's photos, you can also give reasons. Remember you only have about 30 seconds for this response, though.

Tip! Speaking quickly is not the same as speaking fluently. Don't rush your response – take your time to think about how to organise and connect your ideas.

Test 1 Exam practice — Speaking Part 2

Look at the exam instructions below and the photos on C2 and C3. Then do this exam task in pairs.

Part 2 4 minutes (6 minutes for groups of three)

> **Interlocutor** In this part of the test, I'm going to give each of you two photographs. I'd like you to talk about your photographs on your own for about a minute, and also to answer a question about your partner's photographs.
>
> (*Candidate A*), it's your turn first. Here are your photographs on page C2 of the Speaking appendix. They show **people taking a break in different situations**. I'd like you to compare the photographs and say **why you think the people need to take a break**.
>
> All right?
>
> **Candidate A**
>
> ⏱ *1 minute* ....
>
> **Interlocutor:** Thank you.
>
> (*Candidate B*), do you enjoy painting pictures? (Why? / Why not?)
>
> **Candidate B**
>
> ⏱ *Approximately 30 seconds* ....
>
> **Interlocutor:** Thank you.
>
> Now (*Candidate B*), here are your photographs on page C3 of the Speaking appendix. They show **people making different types of changes**. I'd like you to compare the photographs and say **what the people might find difficult about making these changes**.
>
> All right?
>
> **Candidate B:**
>
> ⏱ *1 minute* ....
>
> **Interlocutor:** Thank you.
>
> (*Candidate A*), would you like to make any changes to your house? (Why? / Why not?)
>
> **Candidate A**
>
> ⏱ *Approximately 30 seconds* ....
>
> **Interlocutor** Thank you.

Advice
The examiner will ask you to stop talking after one minute, so you need to be sure you have compared both photographs and answered the question in that time.

Tip! You can talk about what you think happened before the photo was taken or what might happen later. In this way, you can demonstrate a wide range of language.

Test 1 Training — Speaking Part 3

Task information

- Part 3 of the Speaking test lasts about four minutes in total.
- The examiner gives you a task to discuss with your partner. There is one main discussion question with five written prompts which are connected to the question.
- You have 15 seconds to read the task, then two minutes to discuss the question and prompts.
- The examiner then asks you to try to reach a decision about something. You have about one minute for this stage.
- For Part 3, you need to listen and respond to your partner.
- In this part of the test, you need to discuss different options, make suggestions, express opinions and agree or disagree with your partner.

Focus Understanding the task

1a Look at the information below about the different stages of Part 3 of the Speaking test. Put the information into the correct order under *What you need to do* in the table. Some information can go in more than one place.

- Listen carefully.
- Read the question and the options.
- Take turns.
- Think about your opinion on the topic.
- Think of useful vocabulary.
- Talk to your partner.
- Talk about each of the prompts.
- Try to reach an agreement.
- Think about which option to start your discussion with.

What the examiner does	What you need to do	Advice
The examiner introduces the topic.		
The examiner gives you the task.		
The examiner reads out the discussion question.		
The examiner reads out the decision question.		

b Complete the advice using verbs from the box. Then add the advice to the table in Exercise **1a**.

| agree | disagree | give | link | reach | repeat | run | rush | start |

1 Don't .... through all the prompts.
2 It's OK if you don't .... with each other.
3 Don't try to .... an agreement yet.
4 Don't .... speaking until the examiner tells you to.
5 Don't worry if you .... out of time to discuss all the prompts.
6 You can ask the examiner to .... what they say if you need to.
7 You can agree to .... with your partner.
8 Ask your partner to .... their opinion.
9 Try to .... the prompts to the main question on the page.

Useful language Comparing prompts

2 Look at the Part 3 task on page C4. What is the topic of the discussion?

3 🎧 18 Listen to two candidates doing this task. What do they do well? What could they do better?

4 To organise your discussion and connect the prompts, you can use linking words and expressions. Complete the expressions in the table with one word in each gap.

Introduce new points	(1) .... move on to … (2) .... we look at …? How (3) .... this point? (4) .... on to the next point, …
Contrast points	(5) .... the other hand, … That point is a reason in favour. (6) ...., this next point is an argument against. (7) .... contrast, … That point is a reason in favour, (8) .... this point is an argument against.
Make positive connections between points	That's just (9) .... important as … What's (10) ...., this point also … In (11) ...., this point also … It's (12) .... important to … as it is to …

5 Look at how some other candidates connected the prompts from the Speaking Part 3 task in Exercise 2. Complete their comments, then check with Exercise 4.

1 I think getting the best price is a good reason to plan, ... being flexible is a reason not to plan too much.
2 Avoiding crowds and having time to relax are .... important things to consider.
3 I take your point about avoiding crowds. So, ... move on to the issue of being flexible.
4 OK, ... about saving money? Is that a reason to plan in advance?
5 Planning means you can book the activities you want to do. In ...., not having fixed plans gives you the flexibility to decide what to do when you get there.
6 Booking ahead saves money. .... is more, it makes it easier to book tickets for popular attractions.
7 So, ... we now look at whether planning in advance affects flexibility?
8 Careful planning means you can avoid crowds. .... addition, you may pay less for your tickets and accommodation.
9 A well-planned holiday means you can book attractions in advance. ...., this also means you can't change your plans when you get there.

6 Work with a partner to practise the task in Exercise 2. Remember to organise what you say by connecting the prompts.

> **Tip!** Comparing options is a good way of giving extended responses.

> **Tip!** You don't need to reach a decision in the first part of your discussion, so there is no need to rush through all the options.

> **Tip!** Keep the main question in mind during your discussion so that you keep focused on the task.

> **Remember!** Try to find different ways of talking about the prompts. For example, rather than saying *getting the best price*, you can say *pay less*.

Test 1 Exam practice — Speaking Part 3

Look at the exam instructions below and the question and ideas on page C5. Then do this exam task in pairs.

Part 3 — 4 minutes (5 minutes for groups of three)

Interlocutor: Now I'd like you to talk about something together for about two minutes.

Some people think that it's better to buy food from supermarkets, but other people prefer to use independent shops or markets.

Here are some things they think about and a question for you to discuss. First, you have some time to look at the task on page C5 of the Speaking appendix.

Now, talk to each other about **whether it's better to buy food from supermarkets instead of from independent shops and markets**.

Candidates: 2 minutes (3 minutes for groups of three)

Interlocutor: Thank you. Now you have about a minute to decide **what the best reason is for not buying food from a supermarket.**

Candidates: 1 minute (for pairs and groups of three)

Interlocutor: Thank you.

Advice

Listen carefully to the question the examiner asks. Sometimes you may have to talk about why something is not a good reason.

Test 1 Training — Speaking Part 4

Task information

- Part 4 of the test lasts about four minutes. This is the time for both candidates.
- In this part, the examiner asks general questions based on the same topic as Part 3.
- The examiner asks you different questions and may also ask you to respond to your partner's comments.
- The examiner may use gestures to encourage you to discuss a question with your partner.
- Part 4 tests your ability to talk about issues in more depth. You need to express your opinions and give reasons or examples to support your opinions.

Focus Understanding the task

1 Look at the task details below. Are they related to Part **1** or Part **4** of the Speaking test or both? Complete the table. Some details can go in both columns.

- You talk about general topics.
- You talk about personal topics.
- You talk on your own.
- You talk with your partner.
- The part lasts two minutes.
- The part lasts four minutes.
- The examiner may ask you *Why?* or *Why not?*
- The examiner may ask you if you agree with your partner.
- The questions may focus on how your opinion compares to other opinions.
- The questions are all about you.
- The questions are longer.
- The questions are shorter.

Part 1	Part 4

2 Match the Part **4** question beginnings (**1–5**) with the endings (**a–f**). Then <u>underline</u> the parts of the question that could be used to form questions for any topic.

1. Some people say that it's better to explore your own country
2. Should travelling by air
3. Is it always important to read reviews of places
4. Do you think it's true that
5. Some people believe that travelling helps them

a. before deciding where to go?
b. taking photos of places spoils the experience?
c. understand more about the world. Do you agree?
d. rather than travel abroad. What do you think?
e. for leisure be banned?

 Tip! Learning the common question structures used in Part 4 will help to prepare you for answering longer questions.

Useful language Thinking time and fillers

3 🎧 19 Listen to two candidates answering one of the questions from Exercise 2. What differences do you notice?

> **Tip!** It's OK to take a moment to think, but try to say something to fill the pause rather than staying silent.

4 Put the words in the correct order to make 'filler' expressions.

1 think. / me / let
....

2 answer. / difficult / that's / a / to / question
....

3 thought / not / that's / about / something / I've / before.
....

4 before. / about / thought / that / never / I've
....

5 honest, … / be / to
....

6 an / what / question! / interesting
....

7 saying / you / would / that / mind / again?
....

5 Which of the words from the box can you use to replace words in the expressions in Exercise 4?

| an issue   considered   fascinating   repeating   see   tricky |

6 Work in groups of three. Practise asking and answering the questions from Exercise 2.

Test 1 Exam practice   Speaking Part 4

Work in groups of three. Ask and answer these questions.

Part 4   4 minutes (6 minutes for groups of three)

Interlocutor
- Some people say that being able to buy all types of food all year round is a positive thing. Do you agree? (Why? / Why not?)
- Why do you think some people choose to grow their own fruit and vegetables?
- Do you think that cooking for yourself is always better than buying convenience foods? (Why? / Why not?)
- Is it better to go shopping regularly and only buy a few things each time or to buy larger quantities less often? (Why?)
- Some people say that online shopping is the best way to buy things. Do you agree? (Why? / Why not?)
- Some people think shopping is a fun thing to do. Other people think it is necessary, but boring. What do you think? (Why?)

Thank you. That is the end of the test.

What do you think?
Do you agree?
And you?

> **Advice** You do not need to speak to the assessor. They are not part of the discussion.

> **Tip!** Try not to interrupt your partner while they are preparing to speak.

Test 2 Training | Reading and Use of English Part 1

- How many questions are there in Part 1?
- How many options are there in each question?

Useful language Phrasal verbs

1 Choose one word from each box to make phrasal verbs which match the definitions (**1–5**).

count   date   go (×2)   run

for   from   into   on   through

> **Remember!**
> There are lots of different phrasal verbs and some of them have several different meanings. If you are keeping a vocabulary record, keep on adding the meanings as you learn them, with example sentences!

1 experience something difficult ....
2 meet by chance ....
3 have confidence that someone will do what they promised ....
4 try to achieve something ....
5 have existed since a certain time ....

2 Complete the sentences with the phrasal verbs from Exercise 1 in the correct form.
1 This statue .... the 17th century.
2 The ten-kilometre race is a real challenge, but I think you should .... it!
3 My brother .... a tough time when he was in his teens, but he's fine now.
4 I couldn't believe it when I .... Alex in the town centre!
5 I can always .... my sister to help me when I'm in trouble.

3 Choose the correct words in *italics* so that each phrasal verb matches its meaning.
1 die *in / out / over*: become rarer and rarer, then no longer exist
2 take *off / away / out*: suddenly become successful or popular
3 fall *off / over / out*: argue and stop being friends with someone
4 turn *up / down / in*: arrive or appear somewhere
5 show *away / out / off*: try to make people admire your abilities

4 Complete the sentences with the correct form of phrasal verbs from Exercise 3.
1 Most of the guests didn't .... until about nine o'clock.
2 Be careful what you say if you want to avoid .... with her.
3 My little brother is always .... how high he can jump!
4 The dinosaurs .... millions of years ago.
5 After their products were advertised online, the business finally ....

5 Match the phrasal verbs (**1–5**) with the definitions (**a–e**).
1 get across   a discourage from doing something
2 sum up   b briefly present the most important aspects
3 wear out   c successfully deal with a difficult situation
4 put off   d make someone very tired
5 sort out   e manage to make someone understand something

6 Complete the sentences with the correct form of phrasal verbs from Exercise 5.
1 It was a long presentation, but he .... everything .... very effectively at the end.
2 Don't let anyone .... you .... learning another language if that's what you really want to do!
3 You may have to explain your idea a few times in different ways if you want to .... your point ....
4 I had a problem with my bank, but luckily I was able to .... it .... in the end.
5 Looking after my three-year-old nieces has .... me .... !

7 Look at the sentences in Exercises 2, 4 and 6 again. Match the types of phrasal verbs with the rules (a–c).
1 the phrasal verbs in Exercises 1 and 2
2 the phrasal verbs in Exercises 3 and 4
3 the phrasal verbs in Exercises 5 and 6

a If the object is a noun, it can come after the phrasal verb or between the verb and the adverb / preposition.
b No object is possible.
c The object can only go after the phrasal verb.

Useful language Nouns with similar meanings

8 Choose the correct words in *italics* to complete the sentences. Sometimes both options are correct.
1 Our *opinions / views* on this issue are very similar.
2 She takes a very different *opinion / view* to his on the matter.
3 I wish I knew what her *attitude / opinion* is towards this proposal.
4 I like people with positive *attitudes / ideas*!
5 What's your favourite *way / means* of transport?
6 Cycling is probably the best *way / means* of getting there.
7 If you go rock climbing outdoors, you need to be aware of the *risks / dangers*.
8 If you go along that path, you're in *risk / danger* of falling!
9 Why don't we attempt to solve the problem using a different *process / method*?

Remember! Sometimes, words like *risk* or *threat* mean the same thing in a sentence, but in other sentences, only one of them can be used. This feature is often tested in Reading and Use of English Part 1.

Tip! Read as much as you can in English so you get used to the way in which words are used.

9 Look at the sentences in Exercise 8 which have an incorrect option. Rewrite them so that incorrect option becomes correct. The first of these sentences has been rewritten for you as an example.

Example: *2 She has a very different opinion to his on the matter.*

Cambridge English: *B2 First* candidates often use a noun that is not correct for the context.
Example: They claim that it is the best ~~way~~ **means** of transport.

Test 2 Exam practice — Reading and Use of English Part 1

For questions **1–8**, read the text below and decide which answer (**A**, **B**, **C** or **D**) best fits each gap. There is an example at the beginning (**0**).

Tip! Even if an option makes sense in a gap, it may be wrong because it doesn't collocate.

Mark your answers **on the separate answer sheet**.

Example:

0   **A**   run away   **B**   taken off   **C**   come up   **D**   gone over

0 | A | **B** | C | D

Indoor gardens

Houseplant sales have **(0)** .... recently as more and more people have been creating their own 'indoor gardens'. Having plants in a room is a relatively easy and inexpensive **(1)** .... of making it more attractive and welcoming, and many people enjoy **(2)** .... off the latest additions to their collection on social media.

If the idea of indoor gardening **(3)** .... to you, but you're not sure whether or not to **(4)** .... for it, all you need to do is look online. Plant influencers with over a million followers share videos and provide tips on how to get started and how to **(5)** .... the most of small spaces.

Some of the most popular houseplants include snake plants, spider plants and peace lilies. Swiss cheese plants, with leaves of up to a metre long, are also favourites. Many people end up absolutely **(6)** .... to their gardens and say they lose **(7)** .... of time while looking after them, something they appreciate in their **(8)** .... busy lives.

1	**A** technique	**B** step	**C** process	**D** means
2	**A** pointing	**B** setting	**C** showing	**D** giving
3	**A** draws	**B** attracts	**C** interests	**D** appeals
4	**A** go	**B** fall	**C** care	**D** head
5	**A** get	**B** make	**C** take	**D** have
6	**A** passionate	**B** devoted	**C** loyal	**D** emotional
7	**A** feeling	**B** sense	**C** track	**D** idea
8	**A** otherwise	**B** apart	**C** alternatively	**D** elsewhere

Advice
1 Remember the different meanings of these options. Which one makes sense here?

3 Only one of the options can be followed by the preposition *to*.

4, 5 and 7 test fixed phrases.

Test 2 Training — Reading and Use of English Part 2

- What should you always do before starting to fill in the gaps?
- How many words should you write in each gap?
- Can you write a contraction (e.g. *won't*) in the gap?

Useful language Auxiliary verbs

Tip! Passive forms are often tested in Part 2. If you have to complete a passive form with the auxiliary verb *be*, check carefully that you are using the right tense.

1 Complete each sentence with an auxiliary verb. Sometimes more than one answer is possible.

1. Hari didn't think he .... be able to repair his bike by Friday.
2. The children .... never seen snow, so they were very excited.
3. I think you .... to apologise to them.
4. They .... told to arrive at least half an hour early.
5. Do you really .... to make so much noise?
6. She ran as fast as she .... , but she still missed the bus.
7. My brother may .... been there with us, but I can't remember.
8. Look at this vase – it .... believed to be over 1,000 years old.

Useful language Linking words and phrases

2 Complete the sentences with the words from the box.

| apart | as | long | not | order | owing | view | whereas |

1. I think everyone enjoyed the picnic .... from me!
2. They didn't read any reviews before watching the film so .... to make up their own minds about it.
3. In .... of the weather today, I think we should stay indoors!
4. .... only is this shirt cheap, but it's also a lovely colour!
5. My father is quite short, ... my mother is quite tall.
6. .... to the long delay, all the train passengers were given a refund.
7. You can ride your bike on the road as .... as you wear a helmet.
8. We got up at five in the morning in .... to see the sun rise.

Tip! Read the whole sentence containing the gap carefully before you try to complete it. Don't just read one or two words on either side of the gap.

Useful language *so, such, too, enough, very*

Cambridge English: *B2 First* candidates often make mistakes when using *so* and *such*.
Example: We met ~~so~~ **such** nice people.

3 Choose the correct options in *italics* to complete the sentences about a group of hikers.

1. They hadn't realised that the village where they wanted to stay was *so / such / too* high up in the mountains.
2. They wondered whether it was *so / too / very* far for them to get there before dark.
3. Fortunately, they had brought *so / such / enough* food and water with them.
4. They knew they'd be *such / too / very* tired by the time they arrived, but they didn't mind.
5. On the way up the mountain, there were *so / such / enough* fantastic views that they kept on stopping to take photographs.

4 Correct the mistakes in the rest of the story.
1 They saw too many mountain goats on the rocks.
2 Eventually, it wasn't so light for them to see the path clearly.
3 Luckily, they reached the village before it was very dark for them to walk safely.
4 They were too relieved to have finally reached their destination.
5 It was so lovely place that they stayed there for a week!

Test 2 Exam practice — Reading and Use of English Part 2

For questions **9–16**, read the text below and think of the word which best fits each gap. Use only one word in each gap. There is an example at the beginning (**0**).

Tip! It's always worth writing a word in the gap. If you make a mistake, you won't get a mark, but you won't lose a mark, either.

Write your answers **IN CAPITAL LETTERS** on the separate answer sheet.

Example: 0 A N D

Solar batteries that can bend and stretch

Solar panels are seen more (**0**) ………………… more often on the roofs of buildings in many parts of the world. Solar batteries – known as cells – provide plenty of power as (**9**) ………………… as there is enough sun. Smaller solar cells are sometimes used in wearable technology such as smartwatches. For a long time, however, using them in smart clothing or other soft products has proved (**10**) ………………… difficult to be worth doing on (**11**) ………………… large scale.

However, this may soon change because solar cells have now (**12**) ………………… invented which can bend and stretch in different directions without breaking. The solar cells are (**13**) ………………… only easy to put into clothing, but also still (**14**) ………………… to work efficiently while being stretched and strained during use.

The new cells can be stretched to as much as 40% larger than their original size. So (**15**) ………………… is hoped that engineers and designers will soon come (**16**) ………………… with many interesting ways of using them.

Advice

9 What linking phrase means *if*?

12 Is this an active or a passive form of the verb *invent*? What is the tense here?

14 This means the solar cells can still work efficiently.

16 Which phrasal verb with *come* means 'to think of (an idea)'?

Test 2 Training — Reading and Use of English Part 3

- Can you use the word in capitals at the end of the line to create the answer for a gap on a different line?
- Do you always have to change the word in capitals?

Useful language Prefixes

1 Use the prefixes from the box to change the words below so they mean the opposite. You need to use one of the prefixes twice.

> **Tip!** Prefixes are often, but not always, used to form words with an opposite meaning.

dis-   il-   im-   in-   ir-   mis-   un-

1 ....moral
2 ....aware
3 ....experienced
4 ....organised
5 ....legal
6 ....lock
7 ....understand
8 ....regular

2 Complete the sentences with complete words from Exercise 1.

1 Our swimming instructor only started teaching last month, so he's very ....
2 I've lost my key, so I can't .... the front door.
3 I was initially .... of how difficult the situation was.
4 That artist uses a lot of .... shapes in her paintings.
5 I don't want anyone to .... the instructions, so I'll be as clear as I can.
6 Some people believe it is .... to eat meat.
7 The business was shut down by the police because what the owners did was ....
8 This office is a mess! Are your colleagues as .... as you are?

3 Complete the sentences with the prefixes from the box and a suitable form of the words in capitals. You will need to use one of the prefixes twice.

dis-   il-   im-   in-   inter-   ir-   mis-   re-   un-

1 The two families are finally .... their relationship after not speaking to one another for so long. **BUILD**
2 He always looks unhappy and .... with everyone and everything! **SATISFY**
3 The children love playing with the .... displays at the museum. **ACT**
4 She behaved very .... , so now she feels really guilty. **RESPONSIBLE**
5 Everyone at the party was dressed .... , in T-shirts and jeans. **FORMAL**
6 It is important not to give people .... information. **LEAD**
7 She felt annoyed she had been made to wait and tapped the table .... with her fingers. **PATIENT**
8 It isn't a good idea to buy food that has been imported .... **LEGAL**
9 Their kindness to me has been so great that it can never be .... **PAY**
10 The buses here never arrive on time – they're very .... **RELY**

Useful language Internal spelling changes

4 Create nouns from these words.

1 hot ....
2 anxious ....
3 high ....
4 think ....
5 prove ....
6 deep ....
7 long ....
8 visual ....
9 maintain ....

> **Tip!** Sometimes you have to change the spelling of the word in capitals quite a lot in order to form a new word.

5 Complete the sentences using words from Exercise 4.

1 The tree ended up growing to a great ....
2 You shouldn't accuse someone of a crime without any ....
3 We have given this matter a great deal of ....
4 This monkey's tail can be up to a metre in ....
5 My grandparents' .... is quite bad, so they both wear glasses.
6 Thinking about her driving test was causing her a lot of ....
7 The school minibus requires a lot of ....
8 The plants in the garden were drying up in the ....
9 I can't swim, so I always check the .... of the water before getting into a pool.

> **Tip!** In Part 3, you may sometimes have to form a compound word – a word formed from two words joined together. Words with a hyphen (e.g. *self-confident*) are never tested.

6 Complete the sentences with compound words formed from the words in capitals at the end of the sentences.

1 Some animals live in .... rivers and spend their whole lives in the dark. **GROUND**
2 My coat isn't .... , so I got very wet in the rain this morning. **WATER**
3 He struggled to complete his studies, but in the end it was .... **WORTH**
4 .... , recycling is another important issue. **FURTHER**
5 The view from the top of the hill was .... **BREATH**

Reading and Use of English Part 3

Test 2 Exam practice — Reading and Use of English Part 3

For questions **17–24**, read the text below. Use the word given in capitals at the end of some of the lines to form a word that fits in the gap **in the same line**. There is an example at the beginning (**0**).

Tip! You always have to change the word in capital letters. It never fits in the gap without a change.

Write your answers **IN CAPITAL LETTERS** on the separate answer sheet.

Example: | 0 | C | O | N | N | E | C | T | I | O | N | | | | | |

A fitness five-a-day?

Have you ever heard the term 'five-a-day' in (**0**) .... with exercise? Studies show that even small amounts of regular movement can be (**17**) .... to health. In fact, just three and a half minutes per day of (**18**) .... activity like stair-climbing will do you good. So, getting your fitness five-a-day doesn't mean big workouts of over an hour in (**19**) .... – it's micro-breaks of movement that can easily fit into your (**20**) ....

CONNECT

BENEFIT
ENERGY

LONG
LIFE

And (**21**) .... some expensive sports activities, this kind of 'exercise snacking' costs nothing. For example, you can start walking while on the phone or spend a few minutes a day dancing. You'll be able to change your (**22**) .... more easily if you can maintain your new habits, so make use of activities you already do on a (**23**) .... basis. Brushing your teeth is a mindless activity you do (**24**) .... every day, so why not use that time to get a mini workout in? And remember, doing something is always better than doing nothing!

LIKE

BEHAVE

DAY
AUTOMATIC

Advice

17 You'll need to replace the *t* at the end of benefit with a *c*, and add a few more letters.

19 You need to change the word in capitals a lot.

20 You need a compound noun here.

21 Are expensive sports activities similar to or different from ones that cost nothing?

Test 2 Training — Reading and Use of English Part 4

- In Part 4, can you change the word in capital letters?
- Does the word in capital letters count as one of the words in the answer?
- Do contractions (e.g. *I'm*, *They'd*) count as one or two words?

Useful language Active and passive forms

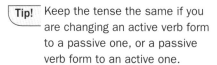
Tip! Keep the tense the same if you are changing an active verb form to a passive one, or a passive verb form to an active one.

1 Rewrite the sentences, changing the verb forms from passive to active or from active to passive.

1 I'm sure someone will find the stolen statue.
   I'm sure the stolen statue ....

2 They gave the extra food to homeless people.
   The extra food .... to homeless people.

3 They say that this tree is 200 years old.
   This .... 200 years old.

4 All the classes are taught by experienced swimming instructors.
   Experienced swimming instructors ....

5 Has anyone offered you a cup of coffee?
   .... a cup of coffee?

6 The painting is going to be sold tomorrow.
   They .... the painting tomorrow.

7 People believed that the last chef in that restaurant was one of the best in the world.
   The last chef in that restaurant .... one of the best in the world.

8 The editor is choosing the photographs for next week's magazine at the moment.
   The photographs for next week's magazine .... by the editor at the moment.

Useful language *-ing* or infinitive (with or without *to*)

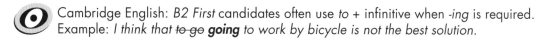
Cambridge English: B2 First candidates often use *to* + infinitive when *-ing* is required.
Example: *I think that* to go **going** *to work by bicycle is not the best solution.*

2 Complete the sentences with the correct form of the verb in brackets.

1 We hope .... (see) you again very soon.
2 Can you imagine .... (live) in that castle?
3 My parents let me .... (drive) their car once I'd passed my test.
4 Would you mind .... (talk) more quietly, please?
5 I'm not sure I can afford .... (go) to the concert.
6 Do many people choose .... (sit) at that table?
7 My little sister practised .... (throw) a ball into a bucket for an hour yesterday.
8 We fancied .... (try) a new flavour of ice cream.

3 Match the sentence beginnings (**1–6**) with the sentence endings (**a–f**).

1 My brother needs helping,
2 My brother needs to help us,
3 Working there meant starting at 7.30 every morning,
4 I meant to start work at 7.30 every morning,
5 They stopped eating
6 They stopped to eat

a but I didn't always keep to my good intentions.
b because they felt hungry.
c so please could somebody go to him?
d because they had had enough food.
e otherwise we'll never be ready before the guests arrive!
f which was tiring.

Useful language Conditional sentences and *wish / if only* to express ideas about the present and the future

4 Complete the sentences with the correct form of the verb in brackets. Use contractions where possible.

1 Mira wants a new bicycle. 'I wish I .... (can afford) one with lots of gears,' she says to her friend Lily.
2 Mira's college is 10 km away. 'If only I .... (not have to) cycle so far every day!' Mira says. 'I wish there .... (be) a bus!'
3 Lily thinks cycling is a good form of exercise. 'You .... (not be) so fit if you .... (go) to college by bus!' Lily says to Mira.
4 Lily thinks Mira should get a part-time job. 'Just imagine it: if you .... (get) a job, you .... (have) more money,' she says.
5 Mira thinks that's a very good idea. 'If I .... (look) for a weekend job, ... (you help) me?' she asks Lily. 'Of course!' Lily replies.

Useful language Conditional sentences and *wish / if only* to imagine how the past could have been different

5 Read the information about Selim. Then complete the sentences with the correct form of the verbs in brackets.

Selim has organised a barbecue on the beach with his friends. But, unfortunately, once they are all at the beach, it starts to rain.

1 Selim wishes he .... (check) the weather forecast earlier.
2 Selim thinks: 'If I .... (know) it .... (going to rain), I .... (postpone) the barbecue!'
3 Selim thinks: 'If only we .... (bring) some big umbrellas!'
4 Afterwards, Selim thinks: 'If I .... (plan) that better, we .... (not all have to go) home.

Useful language Past modal forms

6 Complete the sentences with the correct form of the verbs in brackets.

1 Most tourists go to the Natural History Museum to see the dinosaurs. Erica .... (must / see) them while she was there.
2 My brother borrowed my jacket and he lost it. I .... (should not / lend) it to him!
3 My parents said they were going to the café where my friend works, but he says they haven't arrived yet. They .... (may / change) their minds.
4 I sent them a message saying where to meet, but they're not here. They .... (can't / read) the message.

Test 2 Exam practice — Reading and Use of English Part 4

For questions **25–30**, complete the second sentence so that it has a similar meaning to the first sentence, using the word given. **Do not change the word given**. You must use between **two** and **five** words, including the word given. There is an example at the beginning (**0**).

Tip! Always write something in the gap. You get two marks for each completely correct answer and you'll usually get one mark if part of your answer is correct.

Example:

0   It's over five days since Sam's last message.

   TOUCH

   Sam hasn't ……………………………………………………… least five days.

This gap can be filled by the words 'been in touch for at', so you write:

Example: | **0** | BEEN IN TOUCH FOR AT |

Write **only** the missing words **IN CAPITAL LETTERS on the separate answer sheet**.

---

25   My parents gave all the children sweets at the end of the party.
   CHILD
   At the end of the party, ……………………………………………………… sweets by my parents.

26   'Please don't use my favourite mug any more,' Vanya said to her little sister.
   STOP
   Vanya asked her little sister ……………………………………………………… favourite mug.

27   'It's a pity this laptop is too expensive for me,' said Luke.
   AFFORD
   Luke wished he ……………………………………………………… get the laptop.

28   Although we were expecting Anna for dinner at seven, she arrived at eight o'clock.
   TURN
   Although we were expecting Anna for dinner at seven, she ……………………………………………………… until eight o'clock.

29   People think that this necklace is extremely valuable.
   THOUGHT
   This necklace ……………………………………………………… extremely valuable.

30   Stefan didn't listen to the teacher's instructions, which was a mistake.
   ATTENTION
   Stefan should ……………………………………………………… the teacher's instructions.

Advice

25 What form of the verb usually comes before *by* (someone)? The given word, *child*, is singular, but there were several children. How can you refer to individual children?

27 Luke is imagining a situation that is unfortunately not real at the moment. What modal verb is used with the verb *afford*?

30 What structure with *should* do you need to express a regret about the past? Which verb comes before the noun *attention* to form a phrase meaning *listen to*?

Test 2 Training — Reading and Use of English Part 5

- How many questions are there in Part 5?
- How many options are there to choose from in each question?
- Are the questions in the same order as the text?

Useful language Writer purpose

1 Quickly read the paragraph below. Where does the writer go running?

> I love running and it keeps me healthy, both mentally and physically. However, I know that runners are seen by many as a problem on city pavements, disliked for taking up too much space and sometimes even bumping into people. I accept that anyone wishing to exercise in public in this way needs to be aware of others, and I see it as my responsibility to ensure that I never make anyone feel uncomfortable. Personally, as someone who runs for an hour twice a day, I do my best to stay away from busy areas, especially when people are walking to and from work. When I do end up running through a crowded neighbourhood, I am always extremely careful to spend as little time as possible there.

2 Answer the question below. Underline the parts of the paragraph in Exercise **1** that give you the answer.

What is the writer doing in this paragraph?

- **A** criticising people who complain about runners
- **B** justifying spending so much time trying to get fit
- **C** explaining where the best places are for people to run
- **D** emphasising how hard she tries to avoid annoying people

3 Here are reasons why the other options in Exercise **2** are wrong. Match reasons **1–3** with the incorrect options (**A–D**).

1 The writer mentions that she runs for an hour twice a day, but she does not try to explain why this is a good thing to do. ....
2 The writer mentions where she runs, but does not say where others can go running. ....
3 The writer says that runners are not popular with everyone, but she doesn't say that this is an unreasonable attitude. ....

Useful language Working out the meaning of a word or phrase

4 Read the paragraph and answer the question below it.

> When Jim had first enquired about working part time in the café and met the manager, he'd made the mistake of taking what she said at face value. She was desperate to hire a new member of staff and now he realised that she had deliberately made it all sound far more flexible than it turned out to be. Before agreeing to start, he really should have asked some of the waiters what exactly the hours were and what the pay would be like. He hadn't liked the manager much anyway, but he needed the work.

line 2

Why does the writer say that Jim made a mistake by 'taking what she said at face value' in line 2?

- **A** He hadn't understood the manager.
- **B** He thought the manager seemed nice.
- **C** He didn't question what the manager said.
- **D** He accepted some money from the manager.

Tip! There are different types of question that ask you to work out the meaning of a word or phrase. Some questions directly ask you what the word or phrase means. Other questions are different, for example asking why the writer used a word or phrase. You should always be able to work out the meaning from the context.

Test 2 Exam practice — Reading and Use of English Part 5

You are going to read an article about a footballer from Nepal. For questions **31–36**, choose the answer (**A**, **B**, **C** or **D**) which you think fits best according to the text.

Mark your answers **on the separate answer sheet**.

Nepalese goal machine
Our reporter met football player Sabitra Bhandari

One winter's day in February 2024, Sabitra Bhandari set off to warm up as soon as the coach gave the sign. At the football stadium in Bordeaux, France, just two days after joining the Guingamp football team, Bhandari was about to make history. Samba, as she's called by everyone back home, became the first Nepalese player – male or female – to play in a top-level European match, coming onto the pitch in the 76th minute. When I met her afterwards, the 27-year-old told me she'd always dreamed of playing in Europe. She said she thought this was the time to prove herself and turn her dreams into reality by doing well at the level she'd grown up watching.

Despite everything she'd already done and her obvious talent, Bhandari told me she still regarded herself as having a lot to learn, especially technically. 'It was difficult,' she said, describing her experience playing against French team PSG shortly before our interview. 'I know I'm not the best [at] the technical and tactical aspects of play. It all comes down to coaching and I only started getting formally trained after I went to Kathmandu' (the capital of Nepal).

line 22 Bhandari's journey to France was nothing short of remarkable. It all started with a ball made from old socks in a hilly village 100 km northwest of Kathmandu. Playing with it on the rough ground of an empty field was one problem; hiding it from everyone else was another. 'I used to hide it below my bed,' she recalled. 'I even buried it several times for safety because whenever my mum or elder sister found it, they threw it away.' Determined to follow her dreams, she played volleyball – even switching schools and playing on a boys' team – and football. There were barefoot matches in the morning and in the lunch hour. It was a very busy schedule. 'I had to fetch fodder for the cattle before leaving for school,' she said. 'I used to do it quickly and play football before classes. I often got pulled aside after the morning assembly, as my clothes were dirty after playing.' Was it worth it? Bhandari told me she thought so, adding that those early struggles helped her develop the strong will that made her successful later in life.

One memory stood out, Bhandari said: forming a team with her female school friends to play in a local women's football tournament, which they won 2–0 in the final, both goals, of course, being scored by the barefoot Samba. She said she could still picture the second goal – a run that started from the muddy halfway line and with the fear of playing barefoot against opponents with boots. 'I knew I had to do it myself. So, I just kept on going, one defender at a time, and shot from outside the box.' It was this performance that caught the eye of Shukra Tamang, a local referee, who insisted that Bhandari should carry on playing football and go to the capital to look for opportunities.

She ended up scoring 53 goals in 46 matches for her national team and then went to India, where she scored almost two goals a game during the first season she spent there. In 2023, she did even better than that by managing close to three goals per 90 minutes for Gokulam Kerala in the Indian Women's League. And that was after coming back from a long absence because of a knee injury. Then she moved to France and the rest, as they say, is history. 'I've only wanted to score as many goals as I can ever since I can remember,' she told me. 'Having the ball at my feet, in front of goal, makes me comfortable rather than nervous.' That, she said, is when her confidence is higher than at any other time and she **thrives**.

31 What do we learn about Bhandari in the first paragraph?
- A She had not expected to play at a high level so soon.
- B She had always known she would become a star player.
- C She found it hard to believe how fortunate she had been.
- D She felt she was going to be able to achieve her ambitions.

32 What is implied in the second paragraph?
- A Bhandari's assessment of her own abilities is not very accurate.
- B Bhandari wished she had had more opportunities at a younger age.
- C Bhandari's playing style had recently been admired by another team.
- D Bhandari regretted not having paid more attention to her coaches' advice.

33 By using the phrase 'nothing short of remarkable' in line 22, the writer is
- A highlighting the challenges Bhandari faced.
- B responding to doubts about Bhandari's skill.
- C revealing how little is known about Bhandari.
- A correcting a mistake in the story Bhandari told.

34 What point does Bhandari make about her childhood in the third paragraph?
- A It was a time of great freedom.
- B It made people feel sorry for her.
- C It gave her a lot of determination.
- D It taught her the value of hard work.

35 Why is Bhandari's goal described in the fourth paragraph?
- A because she had never played so well
- B to explain why everyone admired her
- C because of the effect it had on her life
- D to justify how proud she was of herself

36 What does 'thrives' mean in the final line?
- A feels fantastic
- B risks making errors
- C starts to play better
- D becomes too relaxed

Tip! For each question, it's a good idea to underline the part(s) of the text that give you the answer.

Advice

32 A possible regret is suggested here. If something had happened earlier, she might be an even better player now.

33 Read what follows the first sentence of the third paragraph. This should help you choose the correct answer.

36 Is the tone positive or negative here? Is she potentially successful in this position or might she do something wrong at this point?

Test 2 Training — Reading and Use of English Part 6

- How many gaps are there in the Part 6 text?
- How many sentences are there to choose from to fill the gaps?

Tip! An option might appear to fit in a gap, but not actually make sense when you consider the rest of the paragraph or the whole passage.

Useful language Ensuring that the text makes sense

1 Choose the correct sentence (**a** or **b**) to follow each of sentences **1–5**.

1 Humans have bred horses for centuries.
  a They have used them not only for transport, but also for agriculture.
  b This explains why there are so many wild horses in the area.

2 The forest is enormous.
  a On the other hand, there aren't any trees.
  b None of the trees are very tall, though.

3 The dishes in their cookbooks are quick and easy to make.
  a As a result, they are popular with busy parents.
  b Most of them take far more time than expected.

4 The two artists had grown up in the same city.
  a However, this was the first time that they had actually met.
  b That's why neither of them spoke the same language.

5 Badminton is a game that can be played either indoors or outdoors.
  a So nobody can play it when it's windy.
  b So people can play it all year round.

Useful language More linking words

2 Replace the underlined linking word or phrase with a different linking word from the box with a similar meaning.

| alternatively   besides   consequently   finally   meanwhile   nevertheless   otherwise |

1 The mountain is difficult to climb. <u>However</u> .... , lots of people attempt it.
2 One way of reaching the ruins in the jungle from here is to walk, which takes three days. <u>Or</u> .... , you could go by helicopter.
3 Firstly, watching films at home is cheaper than going to the cinema. Secondly, there is no need to walk or take a bus. <u>Lastly</u> .... , there is a wider choice of films available online.
4 The scientists thought they might have taken the wrong approach to the research project. <u>Anyway</u> .... , they were running out of money.
5 The competition organisers knew they would have to repair the damage to the running track. <u>If not</u> .... , all the races would have to be cancelled.
6 The village was abandoned for 20 years. <u>During that time</u> .... , plants and trees grew everywhere.
7 The birds were fed every day by the visitors. <u>Therefore</u> .... , they stopped feeling afraid of humans.

Test 2 Exam practice — Reading and Use of English Part 6

You are going to read an article about an unusual mouse. Six sentences have been removed from the article. Choose from the sentences **A–G** the one which best fits each gap (**37–42**). There is one extra sentence which you do not need to use.

Mark your answers **on the separate answer sheet**.

A tidy mouse?

Mice like to keep themselves clean, but does this also apply to their homes? A video of a mouse in a man's garden shed in Wales showing the mouse repeating the same activities night after night has been seen as evidence that the mouse was tidying up its living area. However, experts say there could be other explanations for this strange behaviour.

The mouse, called 'Welsh Tidy Mouse' by the shed's owner, was recorded gathering small objects and placing them in a tray on the owner's work table – a behaviour that had been going on for months. **37** Then, a mouse was filmed collecting small metal items inside a box of bird food.

Assuming Welsh Tidy Mouse really was keeping its home nice and tidy, it wouldn't be the only animal to engage in 'cleaning' behaviour: bees and ants remove waste from their hives and tunnels; some fish clear other sea creatures from the areas where their eggs are; and some birds carry their babies' uneaten food away from their nests. **38** It could also be to get rid of smells that might attract other animals.

But whether Welsh Tidy Mouse was genuinely doing 'mousework', or some other activity, is a matter for debate. Although mice are careful to be clean, experts doubt that the mouse had actually looked around and thought the shed was messy and needed tidying up. **39** It is an unusual way of doing it, but female mice do build nests while they are pregnant.

40 They weren't things that are normally associated with being good for nests. Mice normally use materials that provide a bit of support and that will keep both themselves and their babies warm.

Alternatively, the mouse may simply have been curious. **41** Take pack rats, for example, a large type of rat found in North and Central America: they like to keep shiny things like bottle tops, keys and stolen jewellery in their nests. According to scientists, many of the mice that they have observed do seem to take pleasure in going out into the world around them, picking things up and dragging them back to a place that they seem to regard as good for storing things.

Whatever the reason for Welsh Tidy Mouse's behaviour, it appeared to find it enjoyable. **42** But it was still doing it night after night, even though it had probably learned that the shed owner always put everything back the following day. The fact that the mouse was doing something that had no obvious purpose may well mean that it found it satisfying in some way. As one scientist commented, humans have the chance to enjoy different aspects of life, so it's rather appealing to see a mouse acting in a way that doesn't actually seem to be of any practical use.

A	The behaviour isn't necessary for survival, after all.	**E**	It followed a similar incident a few years ago.
B	They could be trying to make use of the objects they collect.	**F**	Mice and other similar species often enjoy exploring new objects and interacting with them.
C	Instead, the mouse might be preparing a safe warm place for future babies.	**G**	Yet it is an odd case because of the type of objects that the mouse was gathering.
D	They may do this in order to reduce the risk of infection.		

Advice

37 *Then* in the sentence after the gap could introduce the next action or event in a sequence or refer back to a particular time. Which is it here?

39 The option that fills the gap contains a contrast to the idea in the sentence before the gap.

41 This paragraph is all about being curious, including the option that fills the gap.

Tip! The option you choose must not only follow on well from the sentence before the gap, it must also fit in with the sentence after the gap.

Test 2 Training   Reading and Use of English Part 7

- How many questions are there in Part 7?
- Do the questions follow the order of the information in the text(s)?

Tip! As in Part 5 of the Reading and Use of English paper, you must read the text carefully to work out what feeling, attitude or opinion is being expressed.

Useful language Feelings, opinions and attitudes

1 Read the extracts from Part 7 texts. Then complete the sentences with the words from the box.

| amused | bitter | encouraging | sophisticated | thoughtful | unhelpful | unrealistic | worrying |

1. It was very kind of my friends to visit my great-grandmother.
   The writer says his friends were ....

2. I was impressed by the sisters' knowledge of art and the smart way they dressed.
   The writer thinks the sisters were ....

3. I felt concerned when I saw all the pollution in the river.
   The writer says the state of the river was ....

4. Listening to what they were saying made me smile.
   The writer was .... by the conversation.

5. I don't think the plan will work – they want to do too much in too short a time.
   The writer thinks the plan is ....

6. My colleagues left me to find my own way to the hotel – they could have given me a lift!
   The writer says his colleagues were ....

7. I don't think I will ever forgive them.
   The writer feels ....

8. What they told me made me feel better.
   The writer says the news was ....

Useful language Paraphrase

Tip! Paraphrasing means using the same idea, but expressing it in different words. This is tested in Parts 4 and 5 of the Reading and Use of English paper, too.

2 Match the sentences (**1–6**) with the extracts from Part 7 texts (**a–f**).

1. There was general agreement about a proposal.
2. The spectators were delighted with a result.
3. A decision was controversial.
4. The timing of an event was inconvenient.
5. The ending was very moving.
6. A priceless object had been stolen.

a. Nearly everyone was in tears as they left the cinema.

b. There was a great deal of debate about whether the council had been right to go ahead with the road-widening project.

c. Everyone in the stadium clapped and cheered when the young athlete won a gold medal.

d. The vase was so precious that nobody could say what exactly it was worth. And now it was no longer in the glass case in the museum.

e. The director wanted staff to be involved in making a training video. Everyone thought it was a good idea.

f. We all had to get up extremely early to make it into the office for the presentation. Everyone complained about that.

Test 2 Exam practice — Reading and Use of English Part 7

You are going to read an article about a man who decided to explore his local area for a year. For questions **43–52**, choose from the sections (**A–D**). The sections may be chosen more than once.

In which section does the writer mention

a commitment he decided to make?	43
a place that is not in any way unique?	44
an effort to be more aware of his surroundings?	45
a relationship that no longer exists?	46
being responsible for doing some harm?	47
several benefits that he gained?	48
an aspect of his behaviour that made little sense?	49
how exactly to reach a particular location?	50
an initial concern about his project?	51
enjoying something over short periods?	52

Tip! If you see words from a question in a particular short text (or section of a longer text), that doesn't mean that you have found the answer to the question. Look for paraphrases instead.

Advice

43 What words do you often use when you make a commitment to do something?

46 Look for a sentence in the text that talks about a relationship that *did* exist.

48 Look for some adjectives that describe positive feelings.

49 Look for an adjective which means that something doesn't make sense.

52 The same word is used to talk about medicine!

Amazing discoveries on my doorstep
Explorer Alastair Humphreys finds adventure close to home

A There's a special place near where I live. To get there, you head down the road with all the rubbish along it, go under the motorway, then turn left by the second-hand car garage and the café with a spelling mistake in its name. When you reach the factory with the old metal pipes and enormous concrete chimney, push through the bushes opposite and you've arrived. Tall plants surround you, whispering in the wind. Birds call and race over pools where endangered water animals make their home. Wandering through this place is like being transported to a wilder, quieter, more hopeful world. This secret discovery, or one like it, lies on the edges of towns everywhere, part of the forgotten lands that we travellers ignore, preferring more exotic destinations. I spent a year searching for wildness close to home – and it was a fascinating journey.

B I'm lucky enough to have explored many parts of the world. While one or two of my adventures have been environmentally friendly, most of my travels have been less so, and have even been damaging to the wild places I love. I wondered if there was a different approach to exploration. I'd walked through distant countries and explored wild rivers, but not visited that local wood by the shopping centre or seen what was at the end of that ordinary-looking street in my town. That seemed ridiculous. It's a relatively modern idea that those hoping for adventure need to cross several time zones to satisfy their curiosity. Maybe what I hadn't yet discovered nearby could be just as fascinating as the most remote locations, if only I looked at it that way.

C Many societies, including mine, have lost their connection with the wild around them, and I wanted to try to put nearby nature back into my everyday life. I wanted to prove it's possible to get regular small doses of the delights of travelling without having to wait for a long holiday or the trip of a lifetime. So, I bought a map that covered where I live – 20 km by 20 km of a very ordinary corner of the world on the fringes of a big city – and promised myself I'd spend a year exploring it. Once a week, I visited a single area of just 1 km^2, and explored in detail every street, hill and building I found. I tried to be enthusiastically curious about everything I discovered, as I always am when I'm abroad.

D I worried at first that the plan might be too limited, that my boring neighbourhood couldn't compare with the mountains or coastlines I love. But I kept on with my mini-voyages, and the experience steadily became more meaningful. I had to deliberately slow myself down, sometimes forcing myself to sit on a fallen tree trunk, with no phone or music to distract me, and simply pay attention for a while. Taking a camera also helped me to slow down, pay attention and try to regard everywhere as equally potentially interesting. Travelling around my map for a year gave me much to think about and changed the way I think about travel. It made me calmer and healthier. It made me feel curious, grateful and more deeply aware of nature than ever before. The more you look, the more you see. The more you see, the more you learn and care. Your local area is a tiny part of the wider world. Care for it, love it and discover it. You might just find that it provides enough to explore for an entire lifetime.

Test 2 Training — Writing Part 1 (essay)

- Do you always have to write an essay in Part 1 of the Writing test for B2 First?
- How many notes are you given to write about?
- How many points of your own do you need to include?
- How many words do you have to write?

Tip! It is important to plan your essay. Decide what your arguments are going to be before you start writing.

Topic vocabulary

1a Read the exam task. <u>Underline</u> the general topic of the essay. What are the topics of the notes?

In your English class you have been talking about travel. Now, your English teacher has asked you to write an essay. Write your essay using **all** the notes and giving reasons for your point of view.

> 'It is better to go on holiday with family than with friends of the same age.' Do you agree?
>
> Notes
>
> Write about:
> 1. destination
> 2. cost
> 3. .... (your own idea)

b What would you include as your third point?

Tip! Make a list of useful vocabulary connected to the topic to include in your answer.

c Complete the definitions using words and phrases from the box.

| all-inclusive | budget | connection | itinerary | local speciality | peak season / off-season | self-catering | vacancy |

1 ....: accommodation, such as an apartment, that has cooking facilities so you can make your own meals
2 ....: the food a place is especially known for
3 ....: the amount you have to spend (n), or inexpensive (adj)
4 ....: a type of holiday where everything is included in the price, such as meals and drinks
5 ....: a train / bus / plane that leaves after another has recently arrived, to enable a journey to continue
6 ....: a room that is available at a hotel or guest house
7 ....: the busiest and least busy times of the year for travel, when prices are at their highest / lowest
8 ....: a list of places you plan to visit on a journey

d Complete the sentences with the correct form of the words and phrases from Exercise 1c.

1 If you elect to travel during the ...., be prepared to battle the crowds and spend a lot of money.
2 There were no .... at any of the campsites, so we camped in the wild instead.
3 I'm on a bit of a ...., so there'll be no luxuries on this trip.
4 Our .... is pretty extensive – we'll be moving on to a new place every day.
5 We missed our .... in Denver, so we had to stay the night in a hotel.
6 I always make an effort to at least try the ...., even if the dishes aren't to my taste.
7 .... is a good option for families because it can be cheaper and they can suit themselves at mealtimes.
8 I've never been on an .... holiday – I prefer having the option to eat out.

Giving opinions

2a What are the following phrases used for?

I personally feel that …
I partly / fully agree.
I completely disagree.
I firmly believe that …
I'm inclined to believe that …
I take the view that …

> **Tip!** In the essay, you should include suitable phrases to make your opinions clear. You may need to express strong or partial agreement/disagreement, for example, and use appropriate phrases to do this.

> **Tip!** Include reasons and/or examples for the opinions or points that you express.

b Which are the strongest expressions of opinion in Exercise 2a?

c Read a student's answer to the task in Exercise 1a. <u>Underline</u> any phrases that introduce the student's opinions.

> Some people believe it is preferable to go on holiday with family rather than friends of their own age. While there are advantages and disadvantages to both options, I would tend to agree with the statement in general.
>
> As far as destinations are concerned, I think it is likely that you will have travelled to the same places as a family, making it easier to reach a conclusion about where to go. However, friends are perhaps more likely to want to go on the same type of holiday, such as backpacking or sightseeing.
>
> When it comes to cost, I'm of the opinion that it is better to travel with family. This is because resources are shared, whereas with friends your own age, everyone is likely to be on a strict budget, which may limit the itinerary.
>
> To sum up, my view is that travelling with family can be a very positive experience, but there are some advantages to going on holiday with friends, too.

d Write a paragraph about the point you chose for Exercise 1b. Remember to include your opinions.

Grammar Introductions and conclusions

> **Tip!** It is important to include a clear introduction and conclusion in an essay. Use appropriate phrases to indicate the topic of your essay and when you are about to finish it.

3a Which of the sentences below are good ways to start an essay?
1 <u>To begin with</u>, I think that beach holidays are incredibly dull.
2 <u>This essay will talk about</u> the pros and cons of 'staycations'.
3 <u>Let me start by saying that</u> I completely disagree with the statement that travel makes you cleverer.
4 <u>I'd like to begin by</u> stating the obvious: travelling by car is more convenient than public transport.
5 <u>This essay will outline</u> the positive and negative aspects of international travel.
6 <u>First of all,</u> I'd like to point out that what makes a good holiday for one person might …

b Choose the correct options in *italics*.
1 To *conclude / sum* up, where you stay is as important as who you travel with.
2 In *conclusion / the summary*, I'd like to restate the point that flying is unethical and …
3 All things *considered / stated*, …
4 *Overall / Over all*, …
5 *Lastly / Last* but not least, …

Useful language Starting sentences with *It* or *There*

4 Rewrite the sentences, starting with *it* or *there*.

1. People often say that travel broadens the mind, but I'm not sure I agree.
   .... is often said ....
2. People have many different opinions about what makes ethical tourism.
   .... are many ....
3. Ordering food from a menu in another language can be challenging.
   .... can be ....
4. People have solutions to the challenges of travelling alone.
   .... are several possible solutions ....
5. Holidays can be expensive when you have to pay for tickets and entry fees.
   .... can be expensive to go ....
6. Choosing where to go on holiday is especially hard on a budget.
   .... is especially hard ....

Tip! Starting sentences with *It* or *There* can be a useful way to introduce common ideas and opinions where knowing who says them is unimportant.

Tip! Use a range of different grammatical structures in your writing to show the examiner what you know.

Test 2 Exam practice   Writing Part 1 (essay)

You **must** answer this question. Write your answer in **140–190** words in an appropriate style.

In your English class you have been talking about places to stay on holiday. Now, your English teacher has asked you to write an essay.

Write your essay using **all** the notes and giving reasons for your point of view.

Is it better to go camping or stay in a hotel when you are on holiday?

Notes

Write about:

1. comfort
2. the environment
3. .... (your own idea)

Advice

It is often easier to write about things you have experience of in the essay. However, it is also fine to invent information or offer opinions that you do not necessarily agree with if you prefer.

Test 2 Training — Writing Part 2 (email)

Task information

- The email task tests your ability to write to an English-speaking person, often a friend or colleague, in response to the situation described in the question.
- In your email of 140–190 words, you must include all the information asked for.
- You have about 40 minutes for this task, including time at the end to check your work.
- You must organise your email into paragraphs and give it a suitable beginning and ending.
- You must use an appropriate style and tone, depending on who your email is for.
- A good range of language, correct punctuation and spelling will get you higher marks.

Tip! It is important to structure your email so that it reads in a logical order. Remember to include a suitable opening and closing phrase.

Tip! The email you write in Part 2 is often to an English-speaking friend and for this, you should use informal language. Always check who has written the email to you and make sure that your reply uses suitable language for that person.

Opening and closing an email

1a Look at the phrases. Are they usually used at the start (S) or end (E) of an email?

1 Say hi to your brother! ....
2 Dear ... , ...
3 Great to hear from you. ....
4 Hi! ....
5 Hope to hear back from you soon. ....
6 Regards, ...
7 How are things? ....
8 Best wishes, ...
9 Take care, ...
10 Thanks in advance, ...

b Which of the phrases in Exercise 1a can be used in informal emails?

Formal and informal language

Tip! Read the whole email carefully before you start writing. Answer all the questions or address all the points that the email raises.

2a Read the email and the answer. Which one uses formal language? Which one uses informal language? How do you know?

You have received this email from your English-speaking friend, Bailey.

 **New message**

From: Bailey

Subject: Free-time courses

Hi**!**
I've been thinking about signing up for a course in my free time because I sometimes get bored at the weekends. The trouble is, **I've** no idea what kind of activity to do!

I know you've done some courses, **haven't you**? Which ones did you do? How did you find out about the courses? You know me **really** well, so what do you think I should do? Nothing boring, please!

Take care.

 SEND

Write your **email**.

New message

Dear Bailey,

It was particularly nice to hear from you. It has been a long time. I would be happy to offer you a few suggestions for courses. That is correct: I took a course on bicycle mechanics and I also took a course in computer programming. They were excellent and I enjoyed them very much.

I believe that you are a patient person and as such, you would be good at an activity that requires attention to detail. What would you think about registering for a course in jewellery making or woodworking? I believe you would do very well at those things.

It is possible to research courses online. There are two ways in which this can be done: either search for an interest you already have or do a general search for 'Courses near me'. I am sure you will find something that suits you.

I should go back to my studies now. Please let me know what you have decided to do.

Best regards,
Ellis

b Complete the language features (**1–4**) with the examples in bold from Exercise 2a.
1 informal punctuation, e.g. ....
2 contractions, e.g. *wouldn't, hadn't, I'd,* ....
3 question tags, e.g. *You don't like winter sports,* **do you?** ....
4 informal vocabulary, e.g. *loads, sign up, OK,* ....

c Rewrite the phrases from Ellis's email using informal language.
1 Dear Bailey, ...
2 It was particularly nice to hear from you. ....
3 That is correct: I took a course on bicycle mechanics. ....
4 They were very good. ....
5 I believe that you are a patient person. ....
6 What would you think about registering for a course? ....
7 Please let me know what you have decided to do. ....
8 Best regards, ...

Useful language Making suggestions and giving advice

Tip! In the email, you often have to give advice or make suggestions in response to a friend's email. Try to use a variety of phrases to give advice or make suggestions.

3a Read the phrases used to make suggestions and give advice. Complete them using the correct form of the words in brackets. Add any other words you need.
1 What about .... (take up / new sport)
2 If I were you, I'd .... (think about / what / interested in)
3 How about .... (sign up / completely different)
4 It might be a good idea .... (consider / strengths)
5 Why not .... (do / online search)
6 You might try .... (outdoors)
7 Why don't you .... (figure out / good at)

8 Maybe you should .... (get ideas / other people)
9 You could always .... (look out / ads around town)
10 It's worth .... (ask around / friends and family)

b Look at the completed sentences in Exercise 3a. Are the phrases followed by an infinitive, a *to* + infinitive or the *-ing* form of the verb?

Vocabulary

4a Match a word from A with a word from B to make interesting courses. You may need to use words more than once.

A   content   creative   music   portrait   pottery   script   web

B   composition   creation   design   making   painting   writing

b Choose the correct option in *italics* to complete the sentences.
1 A public-speaking course would help you *build / make* your confidence.
2 You'd make lots of new *networks / contacts*.
3 You might even *pick up / collect* transferable skills that could widen your career options.
4 Doing courses helps keep your mind *smart / sharp*.
5 Obviously, you'd make *piles / tons* of new friends and acquaintances.
6 Courses can give your mental and physical well-being a *boost / boast*.

Tip! It is a good idea to create a list of useful collocations (words that go together). Using correct collocations will improve the accuracy of your writing.

Test 2 Exam practice — Writing Part 2 (email)

You have received this email from your English-speaking friend, Dan.

Write your answer in **140–190 words** in an appropriate style **on the separate answer sheet**.

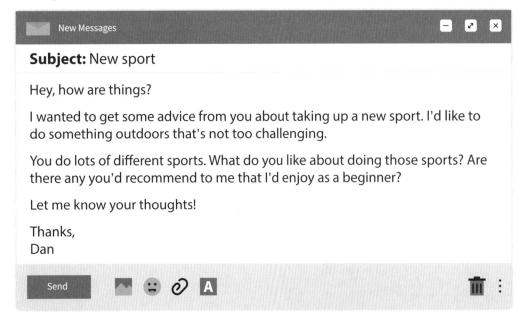

Subject: New sport

Hey, how are things?

I wanted to get some advice from you about taking up a new sport. I'd like to do something outdoors that's not too challenging.

You do lots of different sports. What do you like about doing those sports? Are there any you'd recommend to me that I'd enjoy as a beginner?

Let me know your thoughts!

Thanks,
Dan

Advice
Don't worry if you don't have much experience of the subject your friend would like advice about. It may help you to think about similar situations you have experienced or to use your imagination. Remember that you are being tested on your English ability, not your knowledge of a specific topic.

Write your **email**.

Test 2 Training — Writing Part 2 (review)

Task information

- The review task in Part 2 tests your ability to describe something you have experienced (e.g. a TV programme, a holiday or a product) and give your personal opinion of it, with a recommendation to the reader.
- You read a description of the topic, then write a review in 140–190 words. You should allow about 40 minutes for this task, including time at the end to check your work.
- The instructions also tell you where your review will be published (e.g. on a travel website). You therefore have to write in an appropriate style.
- You should write full sentences and try to use correct grammar, punctuation and spelling, and a good range of language.

Useful language Adjectives and adverbs

1a Which of the following might you write a review about?

> a campsite   a celebrity   a film   a game   a job   a meal   a website   an animal   an app

b Match the topics in Exercise 1a with the extracts from reviews (1–6).

1. It was relatively inexpensive to download, but not very user-friendly. I've used better ones!
   ....
2. The design was truly outstanding and navigation was really straightforward. I found what I needed quickly.
   ....
3. It was way too tough and the sauce a bit too rich for my liking, so I didn't leave a tip as I usually would.
   ....
4. The characters were incredibly true to life and the screenplay was especially impressive for a first-time scriptwriter.
   ....
5. It was pretty remote, but the amenities were extremely eco-friendly, like the rainwater swimming pool.
   ....
6. The graphics were exceptionally low quality and the soundtrack was very poor, but the story was truly groundbreaking. ....

c <u>Underline</u> the adjectives in the extracts in Exercise 1b and the adverbs that come before them. What is their function?

> Cambridge English: *B2 First* candidates often make errors when using adjectives ending in *-ed* and *-ing*.
> Example: *We were* ~~satisfying~~ **satisfied** *with the hotel.*

Features of a review

2a Read the review of an outdoor activity centre on page 92. What has the writer commented on?

Example: food

Alex
3 Oct

Review of Woodlands Outdoor Activity Centre

(1) .... The centre's in a beautiful setting and, in general, it was an enjoyable trip.

We met our instructors on the first morning. (2) .... We were also told what to do in an emergency.

I was looking forward to trying some new activities, especially kayaking and ziplining. Unfortunately, kayaking was cancelled because of poor weather and no alternative was suggested. (3) .... However, the ziplining went ahead and was brilliant.

I understand why they use the word 'cosy' in their adverts – the cabin was tiny! (4) ....

(5) .... The food was cooked to a high standard, but there wasn't a huge choice.

The spa looked stunning, but there was an additional payment for this. (6) ....

(7) .... However, be aware of the add-ons and arrange alternative entertainment in case activities are cancelled.

b Complete the gaps (**1–7**) in the review with the sentences a–g.
  a But the shower was hot and the beds were particularly comfortable.
  b We couldn't afford it, which was a shame.
  c I stayed at Woodlands Outdoor Adventure Centre in July.
  d I would definitely recommend Woodlands for a short stay.
  e This meant hanging around all morning with nothing to do.
  f We chose the meal plan, which was relatively inexpensive.
  g They were extremely friendly and knowledgeable.

c What did the reviewer like about the outdoor centre? What weren't they so keen on? Would they recommend the centre to other guests?

d Find and <u>underline</u> the descriptive language in the review in Exercise 2a.

e Which structure (A or B) does the review in Exercise 2a follow?

A
Overall recommendation (positive or negative)
Review of individual features: positive comments
Review of individual features: negative comments

B
General introduction: where / when / who, and positive / negative overall comment
Review of individual features in turn, with positive / negative comments
General recommendation

Tip! You can put the information in a review in different orders. For example, you can put all the positive comments together and all the negative comments together, or you can include the positives and negatives for each point in turn. However, you should make sure that the information follows a logical order.

f Which features would you include in a review of these places and things?

a café   a make-up or hair product   a mobile phone   a sports centre   a TV series

Expressing opinions and making comparisons

3a Complete the sentences with the words from the box. There may be more than one correct answer.

bonus   disappointing   downside   drawback   found   major   minuses   positive

1 The new shopping centre was really .... because it was a lot smaller than I expected.
2 Two .... aspects of the new cinema are the reclining chairs and superior-quality snacks on offer.
3 We .... that the room had not only not been cleaned, but it was really cold, too.
4 One .... of the holiday was the noisy group of people next door and the lack of soundproofing.
5 The storyline was interesting enough, but on the ...., the book got a bit boring in the middle.
6 Getting a free gift when I bought a membership to the club was a real ....
7 The concert was a .... flop – the headliner band didn't turn up and it rained non-stop.
8 One of the biggest .... of the 'eat in the dark' experience was not seeing the other diners.

b Choose the correct words in *italics* to complete the sentences.

1 In my opinion, the pizzas are *much more / not as* flavoursome at Denney's Diner than Olly's Café.
2 The website is the *most / least* trustworthy source of information ever. It's definitely all fake news.
3 I was not nearly as impressed by the wildlife park *as / than* I'd expected to be.
4 One thing to consider when buying a second-hand bicycle is how much value for money you get *in / by* comparison with a new bike.
5 The classes were far *less / more* entertaining than we'd hoped and we had a good laugh.
6 Adam thought the climbing route was slightly more *challenging / harder* than the ones he'd done before.

Test 2 Exam practice — Writing Part 2 (review)

Write your answer in **140–190 words** in an appropriate style **on the separate answer sheet**.

You see this announcement on an English-language website.

> *Reviews wanted*
>
> **Have you visited a shop recently that made an impression on you?**
>
> Write us a review of the shop, saying why you chose to visit it and what made the experience different from other shops you regularly go to. Tell us whether or not you would recommend this shop to other people.
>
> The best reviews will be published on our website.

Write your **review**.

Advice

You don't have to write about a real place, product or service in your review, but make sure it sounds realistic.

Test 2 Training — Listening Part 1

Choose the correct options.
- In Part 1, you will hear *six / eight* short recordings – these are usually *monologues / dialogues / both monologues and dialogues.*
- You will answer *gap-fill / multiple-choice* questions about the recordings.
- You will hear each text on the recording *once / twice.*

> **Tip!** In Listening Part 1, you will often be tested on your understanding of a speaker's feelings and attitudes. Make sure you have a good understanding of a range of both positive and negative adjectives to describe feelings and attitudes, e.g. *determined, dissatisfied, delighted, unfriendly.*

1 Look at this Part 1 task. What attitude or feeling do you need to listen for?

You hear a college student talking about a blog she writes about hill running.
What does she feel satisfied with?
- **A** the amount of college work she's doing
- **B** the rate of progress she's making
- **C** the popularity of the blog she writes

2 🎧20 Listen and choose the correct answer.

3 Look at the audioscript and check your answer.

> My last entry on my blog was about a 10 km run up in hills around 800 metres high. It was tough, I won't lie, and I could have pushed myself harder. Anyway, my posts are getting plenty of hits, which is awesome. I must be doing something right. But I may have taken on more than I can handle as I'm falling behind on my assignments. The blog about today's run might not be finished until tomorrow because I'm catching up on one. What with college deadlines, I guess I shouldn't have taken on all the training and blogging, but if I hadn't, I might have found excuses for not studying.

4 Read the audioscript in Exercise 3 again. <u>Underline</u> all the modal verbs and the verbs that follow them.

> **Remember!** Modal verbs can be used in many different ways in English to express possibility, give advice, make suggestions, give criticism, etc. They can also be used to talk about the past, the present and the future.

5 Now match each modal verb + verb that you underlined in Exercise **4** with the descriptions (**1–6**).
1. a possibility in the past that did not happen ....
2. a possibility in the past ....
3. a criticism of an action in the past ....
4. an assumption about the present ....
5. a possibility in the future (passive form) ....
6. a speculation about something in the past that is uncertain ....

> **Tip!** It is a good idea to study how modal verbs are used in English. This will help you, when listening, to understand a speaker's attitude and how they feel.

6 The adjectives below can all be used to describe a person's attitudes or feelings. Decide if each one indicates a more positive (P) or a more negative (N) attitude or feeling.

1. enthusiastic ....
2. critical ....
3. fascinated ....
4. reassured ....
5. flattered ....
6. puzzled ....
7. envious ....
8. appreciative ....
9. reluctant ....
10. resigned ....

7 🎧21 Listen to six speakers talking about three different topics. Choose the most appropriate adjective from Exercise **6** for each speaker. There are four adjectives that you will not need to use.

Test 2 Exam practice — Listening Part 1

🎧 22 You will hear people talking in eight different situations. For questions **1–8**, choose the best answer (**A, B** or **C**).

1. You hear a psychologist talking about attitudes to time.
   What point does he make?
   - A Enjoying the present moment might not always be possible.
   - B Thinking about the future may benefit you in the present.
   - C Expecting good things in the future can help them to happen.

2. You hear two friends talking about artificial intelligence.
   The woman is doubtful about how much AI could succeed in
   - A freeing people from boring and difficult tasks.
   - B taking over power and control of society.
   - C producing art and music that is original.

3. You hear a man talking about working in a shop.
   What is he doing?
   - A explaining why communication skills are important
   - B recommending it as an initial step on a career path
   - C identifying characteristics that make it challenging

4. You hear two friends talking about cooking without using ready-made ingredients.
   What do they agree about?
   - A It is too time-consuming to do all the time.
   - B It only suits certain types of people.
   - C It involves a lot of planning.

5. You hear a woman telling a friend about an app she likes for booking train tickets.
   Why does she recommend it?
   - A It makes the cheapest prices clear.
   - B It offers good customer support.
   - C It helps her save time.

6. You hear a man telling a friend about his efforts to develop greater self-discipline.
   How does he feel?
   - A determined to improve even more
   - B proud of his achievements so far
   - C pleased that it is easier than expected

7. You hear two friends talking about an exhibition they saw.
   What view does the woman express?
   - A She's reluctant to see more of the artist's work.
   - B She's critical of the techniques the artist uses.
   - C She's puzzled by the popularity of the artist.

8. You hear part of an interview with a novelist.
   What does she say about her childhood?
   - A Thinking about it helps inspire her to write.
   - B It is strange to consider how innocent she was.
   - C She regrets how much she has forgotten.

Test 2 Training — Listening Part 2

Choose the correct options.

- In Part 2, you will hear a text that lasts three or four minutes with *one speaker / two speakers*.
- You will complete *eight / ten* sentences with information from the recording.
- You will hear the recording *once / twice*.

> **Tip!** Always read the words before and after the gap in each sentence. This will help you to understand what kind of word is needed in the gap, in terms of both meaning and grammar.

1 You will hear a man called Frankie Banford talking about running his own coffee shop. Look at the sentences below and try to predict possible words that could go in the gaps.

Frankie uses the word '(1) ....' to describe his first two years running the coffee shop.

Frankie was surprised that some customers complained about the (2) .... in the coffee shop.

> **Tip!** Sometimes, a sentence in the task will be phrased like this:
> *Speaker X uses the word (1) .... to describe ...*
> You should always write exactly what the speaker says. Even if you know other synonyms for a word, write only the one(s) the speaker uses.

2 🎧 23 Listen and complete the sentences in Exercise 1 with the correct words.

Vocabulary focus Verbs and prepositions

> **Tip!** To help you learn which prepositions go with which verbs, it's a good idea to keep a record of verbs and prepositions that go together.

3 🎧 24 Complete the sentences using prepositions from the box. Then listen and check your answers.

| about | from | in | on | to | with |

1. Nobody's ever complained .... the quality of coffee here before!
2. Dealing .... customers takes up most of my energy when the shop's open.
3. The number of customers depends a lot .... what time of day it is.
4. I strongly believe .... the importance of serving coffee at the right temperature.
5. Customers sometimes ask how a latte differs .... a cappuccino.
6. I was worried about how customers might react .... a big price increase.

Vocabulary focus Adjectives and prepositions

4 🎧 25 Complete each sentence with a preposition. Pay attention to the adjective before each gap. Then listen and check your answers.

1. I never thought I'd be capable .... running a business single-handed for so long.
2. All our food's homemade and Sara is responsible .... preparing it.
3. She's incredibly good .... making delicious homemade pastries.
4. I'm very pleased .... the new décor since the coffee shop was redecorated.
5. The relaxed atmosphere in a small coffee shop is preferable .... that of a busy takeaway.
6. I remain very confident .... the future loyalty of my regular customers.

Test 2 Exam practice — Listening Part 2

🎧 26 You will hear a young woman called Marlene Niall talking about a course in fashion design she has just completed. For questions **9–18**, complete the sentences with a word or short phrase.

Fashion design course

Marlene uses the phrase '(9) ....' to describe how she viewed her own clothes designs before doing the course.

It was Marlene's (10) .... that impressed the tutors at the interview she attended before the course.

Marlene says that having experience of (11) .... made the course easier for her.

Marlene was proud of a children's clothing design project she created based on the theme of the (12) .... during her first year.

Marlene was excited by the (13) .... of the special fashion design software she was trained to use.

Marlene says that her favourite fabric to work with is (14) .... because of how it looks and feels.

Marlene found it particularly challenging to design and create a range of (15) .... for a fashion show in her final year.

Marlene was pleased to have chosen (16) .... for her long academic written assignment.

Marlene was pleasantly surprised to discover a talent for (17) .... when students worked on digital branding.

Marlene benefitted most from all the opportunities for (18) .... at a Fashion Marketing Agency during a work placement.

Advice

9 What adjective made from the verb *wear* does Marlene use? Did she previously see fashion design as something commercial or creative?

10 What did the tutors tell Marlene after her interview?

11 What had Marlene done a lot of before the course?

12 Marlene mentions several themes children might like. Which one did she opt for?

Test 2 Training — Listening Part 3

Choose the correct options.

- In Part 3 you will hear *five / six* short recordings of about 30 seconds each – these will be *monologues / dialogues*.
- You will match the correct option with each recording from a choice of *eight / ten* options.
- You will hear each recording *once / twice*.

> **Tip!** One of the options will express the same idea as something that one of the speakers says, but different words are used to express the idea. You should listen for paraphrases or ideas expressed across more than one sentence.

1 🎧 27 Listen to five short extracts, in which people are talking about taking part in a competition. Choose the option (**A–H**) that is closest in meaning to what each speaker says about the competition. There are three options that you do not need to use.

- **A** I learned some helpful techniques very quickly.
- **B** There was a lot of pressure for me to do well.
- **C** I had a great idea that was very useful.
- **D** All my time preparing was worthwhile.
- **E** Something put me off my performance.
- **F** I made some mistakes at an important moment.
- **G** People said I was much better than other competitors.
- **H** The number of people watching affected me.

Speaker 1 ....
Speaker 2 ....
Speaker 3 ....
Speaker 4 ....
Speaker 5 ....

> **Tip!** When you listen, you may hear the speaker talk about the other topics in options A–H, but they do not express the same idea as in the option. Only one of the answers will be correct.

2 🎧 28 Now listen to the full version of Speaker 3 from Exercise 1. Does anything she says make you consider any of the other options?

3 Read the audioscript and <u>underline</u> the three phrasal verbs the speaker uses. Try to explain what they mean.

> It was amazing how huge the audience was. Luckily, it didn't bother me as I was so focused on my performance and getting everything perfect and not making any silly errors. Apparently, someone's phone went off in the middle of my song, but I didn't even notice! There were ten singers in total and we all had to perform the same song. I couldn't believe the amount of praise I got. Apparently, I stood out from the rest. It was like a dream come true and I knew I'd got through to the next stage of the competition. My family were in the front row cheering. It was an overwhelming feeling.

> **Tip!** It is useful to be familiar with and understand the meaning of as many phrasal verbs at B2 level as you can. Being familiar with the meaning of phrasal verbs may help you to match what the speaker says with the option with a similar meaning.

4 Complete the sentences using phrasal verbs from the box. You may need to change the form of the verb.

come up with   get along   live up to   mess up   pay off   pick up   put in   stand out

1 In the final of the baking competition, the judges thought my cake .... from all the others.
2 My coach .... several brilliant ideas that enabled me to make the necessary improvements before the first day of the competition.
3 I had to .... an incredible amount of practice to get a place in the final of the chess competition.
4 All my hard work .... when I finally beat my biggest rival in one of the toughest matches of my life.
5 Despite all my training, I unexpectedly .... my routine during the gymnastics finals, which cost me first place.
6 I think I .... my full potential as an athlete today, achieving a faster speed than ever before.
7 It was great that all the other competitors and I .... with each other so well.
8 I learned many of my skills just from watching the greatest musicians playing – it's amazing what you can .... like that.

Test 2 Exam practice — Listening Part 3

🎧 29 You will hear five short extracts in which people are talking about surfing. For questions **19–23**, choose from the list (**A–H**) what each person says makes surfing special for them. Use the letters only once. There are three extra letters which you do not need to use.

A   I get a huge sense of achievement.

B   It encourages me to be a patient person.

C   I feel part of a community.

D   It teaches me to respect nature.

E   It teaches me to deal with fear.

F   I can forget difficult problems.

G   I can escape my daily routine.

H   It's a good way to keep fit.

Speaker 1 [ ] 19
Speaker 2 [ ] 20
Speaker 3 [ ] 21
Speaker 4 [ ] 22
Speaker 5 [ ] 23

Advice
19 What does Speaker 1 like to get away from when surfing?
20 What does Speaker 2 say is most rewarding about surfing?
21 What does Speaker 3 say makes surfing different from anything else?
22 What life skill has Speaker 4 gained from surfing?
23 What makes surfing a joy for Speaker 5?

Test 2 Training — Listening Part 4

Choose the correct options.
- In Part 4, you will hear *an interview / a monologue* lasting three or four minutes.
- You will answer *seven / eight* multiple-choice question with *three / four* options.
- You will hear the recording *once / twice*.

Tip! It is important to be able to follow what the speaker says across a number of sentences. People often use reference words, such as *it*, *they*, *this* and *that*, to avoid repetition. Practise noticing how speakers use reference words in listening texts. This will help you to understand what the speaker is referring to.

1. 🎧 30 Listen to the first part of an interview with an architect called Elena Lovejoy. Choose the best answer (A, B or C).

   Elena says that the main thing that made her want to be an architect was a long-held interest in
   - A how buildings affect people's feelings.
   - B what buildings tell us about history.
   - C why buildings are such different shapes.

2. Look at the audioscript and check your answer.

   > I've always been fascinated by buildings. <u>They</u> can cause emotions, such as a sense of wonder or excitement, or even fear. But <u>what</u> really developed my passion for them, and ultimately made me choose my career, was family trips, when my parents would point out significant or beautiful buildings, from old cottages and castles to the earliest skyscrapers. There's such a diversity of styles and <u>each</u> had a story. <u>It</u> made me curious about the past and the culture of times gone by and I think <u>that</u> inspired my desire to train as an architect.

3. Look at the underlined words in Exercise 2. Identify what they are referring to.

4. Complete the sentences with words from the box. In some cases, more than one answer is possible.

   | appealing | astonished | bizarre | eager | extraordinary | impressive |
   | modest | mysterious | remarkable | stunned | | |

   Tip! In Part 4 interviews, some questions will test your understanding of feelings, attitudes and opinions expressed by the speaker. Make sure you have a good knowledge of a range of words in English to describe feelings and attitudes.

   1. Modern architects are sometimes criticised for not creating buildings that are .... to the majority of people.
   2. Seeing the skyscraper for the first time, I was .... by its unusual design.
   3. Despite having won many awards for his work, he remains very .... about it all.
   4. Passers-by kept stopping to look up at the .... building. It was like nothing they'd ever seen before.
   5. As a young architect, she was .... to start immediately once she was given the chance to run her own project.
   6. What everyone found particularly .... about the new conference centre was how much space and light there was everywhere.

Test 2 Exam practice — Listening Part 4

🎧 31 You will hear an interview with a man called Dean Belinsky, who is talking about his interest in science and his career as a science journalist. For questions **24–30**, choose the best answer (**A**, **B** or **C**).

24 When talking about using a telescope for the first time as a child, Dean remembers feeling
   A   proud of his ability to identify some stars.
   B   frustrated that it took so long to set up.
   C   astonished at what he could see with it.

25 What does Dean say about a chemistry experiment he planned to do at home as a child?
   A   He was unaware how dangerous it was.
   B   He was sure that it was completely original.
   C   He was embarrassed about misunderstanding something.

26 When talking about becoming a communicator about science, Dean explains that
   A   he has noticed that the subject has increased in popularity.
   B   he feels uncertain about why he developed a desire to do this.
   C   he developed an ambition to do this while he was a university student.

27 What does Dean say about his decision to leave his job as a scientist to become a journalist?
   A   He was eager to test his abilities in a different field.
   B   He was convinced that he could communicate well.
   C   He was nervous about the loss of security.

28 What did the producer of the TV series *Sci World* find impressive about Dean?
   A   his enthusiasm for finding interesting stories
   B   his wide-ranging experience in science
   C   his ability to explain complex ideas

29 What does Dean say about the science topics he writes about for magazines and newspapers?
   A   Some fields are requested more than others.
   B   Certain news events influence his choices of focus.
   C   It is difficult to predict what will be most successful.

30 What helps Dean to communicate with the public about science?
   A   thinking about things in as unscientific way as he can
   B   trying to imagine things from the viewpoint of a curious child
   C   remembering his own understanding of things before he studies them

Advice!
25 What did Dean discover could be dangerous?
27 What does Dean say about his writing abilities?
29 What news event does Dean refer to?

Test 2 Training — Speaking Part 1

Choose the correct options.
- For Part 1 of the Speaking test, all the questions are about *general / personal* topics.
- You need to talk to *the examiner / your partner*.
- Your questions will be *the same as / different from* your partner's questions.
- The total time is *two / four* minutes.
- The questions will be connected to *one / more than one* topic.

> **Tip!** The examiner doesn't know you, so you can answer the questions in any way you like.

> **Tip!** There are two examiners in the room. You only talk to one of them. The other examiner may say 'hello' at the start of the test, but then they just listen and assess what you say.

Focus Understanding the task

1 What is the common theme of these questions? Complete the questions with one word in each gap.

1 .... did you spend your evening yesterday?
2 .... you enjoy taking photos with a phone?
3 .... was the last time you did some sport?
4 .... you rather watch a film in the cinema, on TV or on a computer?
5 .... us what you usually do when the weather is bad.

> **Remember!** The questions may be about your daily life, past experiences or future hopes and plans. Listen carefully so that you know which tense to use.

2 Complete the questions so that they have similar meaning to the questions in Exercise 1.

1 What .... yesterday evening?
2 Is .... something you often enjoy doing?
3 When did .... some sport?
4 Which do ....: watching a film in the cinema, on TV or on a computer?
5 How .... time when the weather is bad?

Exam skill Giving full answers

3 Look at these answers to the questions in Exercise 1. What do you notice about them?

1 I spent yesterday evening at a concert.
2 Yes, I do.
3 I did some sport yesterday.
4 I prefer watching films in the cinema.
5 When the weather is bad, I stay at home and watch TV.

4 🎧 32 Listen to two candidates answering the five questions from Exercise 1. Make notes on how they improve on the answers in Exercise 3.

	Information added	Alternative words used
1		
2		
3		
4		
5		

5 Work with a partner. Practise asking and answering the questions from Exercise 1. Try to give a full answer and avoid repeating words from the questions.

Test 2 Exam practice — Speaking Part 1

1 Work with a partner. Take turns to ask and answer these questions. Ask questions in any order.

Part 1 — 2 minutes (3 minutes for groups of three)

Interlocutor First, we'd like to know something about you.

Food and drink
- Do you prefer eating at home or going out to eat?
- What do you like to eat in the mornings?
- How good are you at cooking?
- Which do you prefer: food from your own country or food from other countries?
- Tell us about a meal you really enjoyed.

2 🎧 33 Now listen to the examiner on the recording and answer the questions you hear.

Advice

The examiner can choose questions from three different topics. You may not be asked questions on the same topic as your partner. If you have two or more questions, these may each be on a different topic.

Test 2 Training — Speaking Part 2

Choose the correct words.
- For Part 2 of the Speaking test, you and your partner have *the same / different* photographs to talk about.
- The examiner *will / will not* tell you what the photographs are about.
- The question *is / isn't* written down for you.
- You *ask / answer* a question about your partner's photographs.
- The total time is *two / four* minutes.

Focus Understanding the task

1 Some students practised Part 2 of the Speaking test and asked their teacher for feedback. Match the students' comments (**1–6**) about what they did with the teacher's feedback (**a–f**).

1 'I had lots to say about one of the photos.'
2 'I did everything I was asked to in 45 seconds.'
3 'I was still talking when you stopped me.'
4 'I found lots of ways to compare the two photos.'
5 'I know I made some grammar mistakes.'
6 'I couldn't remember the right words to describe some things in the photos.'

a 'Next time, give more details so you keep speaking for the full time.'
b 'That's OK, as long as you compared both photos and answered the question.'
c 'OK, but did you remember to talk about the other one as well?'
d 'OK, and did you also answer the question?'
e 'Next time, if you don't know the exact word, find a way to explain what you mean.'
f 'Don't worry. Accuracy is one part of the assessment, but it is not the only thing you are assessed on.'

2 Look at the students' comments about the follow-up question in Part 2. What advice could the teacher give?

- I didn't agree with what my partner said about the photos.
- I talked about both of the photos.
- I described what I could see in the photos.
- I was able to answer the question very quickly.

Tip! Start by making a quick comparison of the two photos before you discuss the question in depth. This way, you won't run out of time to talk about one of the pictures.

Useful language Common language errors

3a Read the sentences and phrases and correct any mistakes you find.
1. Both of the pictures shows people doing positive things for the environment.
2. … there is a group of people who seem to have just finished to clean the beach …
3. They look like happy and pleased with the result.
4. I think they have chose to do this because they can see the benefits immediately.
5. Do something like this in a group is a good idea.
6. … they can encourage each another …
7. … the results are not as easier to see …
8. They decided to go by bike or scooter rather of car.

3b 🎧 34 Look at the photos on page C6. Listen to a candidate answering a Part 2 question about the photos. He uses the language in Exercise 3a, but with no errors. Check your answers to Exercise 3a.

Tip! It is normal to make some mistakes when you are speaking. If you notice a mistake, you can correct it, but otherwise just carry on.

4 Work with a partner. Practise giving your own answer to the Part 2 question on page C6.

Test 2 Exam practice — Speaking Part 2

Look at the exam instructions below and the photos on pages C7 and C8. Then do this exam task in pairs.

Part 2   4 minutes (6 minutes for groups of three)

Interlocutor In this part of the test, I'm going to give each of you two photographs. I'd like you to talk about your photographs on your own for about a minute and also to answer a question about your partner's photographs.

(*Candidate A*), it's your turn first. Here are your photographs on page C7 of the Speaking appendix. They show **people feeling uncomfortable in different situations**. I'd like you to compare the photographs and say **why you think the people are finding it difficult to get comfortable**.

All right?

Candidate A

⏱ *1 minute* ....

Interlocutor: Thank you.

(*Candidate B*), do you enjoy going on long car journeys? (Why? / Why not?)

Candidate B

⏱ *Approximately 30 seconds* ....

Interlocutor Thank you.

Now (*Candidate B*), here are your photographs on page C8 of the Speaking appendix. They show **people spending time alone**. I'd like you to compare the photographs and say **why the people might want to spend time alone**.

All right?

Candidate B

⏱ *1 minute* ....

Interlocutor Thank you.

(*Candidate A*), do you enjoy spending time outdoors on your own? (Why? / Why not?)

Candidate A

⏱ *Approximately 30 seconds* ....

Interlocutor Thank you.

Advice

One way to keep talking for the full minute is to talk about what may have happened before and after the picture. For example, talk about what caused the situation or what the people might do next.

Test 2 Training — Speaking Part 3

Choose the correct words.

- For Part 3 of the Speaking test, you talk *on your own / with your partner*.
- You have *one question / two questions* to discuss.
- You *need / do not need* to discuss the prompts in a particular order.
- You need to try to reach a decision in the *first / second* stage of this part of the test.
- The total time is *three / four* minutes.

Useful language Making comparisons

1a Look at the question below. What situations do you think the question is referring to? Look at the sample Part 3 Speaking task on page C9. Which of the prompts did you predict?

> Is it important to get advice from other people in these situations?

b Use the words in the box to complete the comparative and superlative expressions. Decide whether the expressions describe a small difference, a big difference or no difference at all.

as   by   even   less   much   near   nearly   quite

	Big difference	Small difference	No difference
Getting advice about travel plans is (1) .... more important than getting advice about books.			
Making travel plans is not (2) .... as important as finding a new job.			
It's not (3) .... as important to get advice about buying gadgets as it is to get advice about health.			
Getting advice about health is (4) .... more important than getting advice about work.			
Getting advice about travelling is just (5) .... important as this.			
Health is (6) .... far the most important reason to get advice.			
Getting advice about travel is important, but slightly (7) .... important than getting advice about work.			
It's nowhere (8) .... as important to get advice about books.			

2 Look at the task on page C9 again. Choose three situations in which you think it is most important to get advice from other people. Then compare with your partner.

> **Remember!**
> When you are talking about big differences, putting stress on the words which describe the difference is a good way of emphasising your point.
> Example: *Health is <u>by</u> <u>far</u> the <u>most</u> <u>important</u> reason to get advice.*

> **Tip!** You do not have to agree with your partner. You could both present your choice and then 'agree to disagree'.

Test 2 Exam practice — Speaking Part 3

Look at the exam instructions below and the question and ideas on page C10. Then do this exam task in pairs.

Part 3 4 minutes (5 minutes for groups of three)

Interlocutor: Now I'd like you to talk about something together for about two minutes.

Some people think that it's always a good idea for towns to try to increase the number of tourists who visit, but other people disagree.

Here are some things they think about and a question for you to discuss. First, you have some time to look at the task on page C10 of the Speaking appendix.

Now, talk to each other about **whether it's always a good idea for towns to try to increase the number of tourists who visit.**

Candidates: 2 minutes (3 minutes for groups of three)

Interlocutor: Thank you. Now you have about a minute to decide **what the best reason is for trying to increase the number of tourists who visit a town.**

Candidates: 1 minute (for pairs and groups of three)

Interlocutor: Thank you.

> **Advice**
> The decision-making question may ask you to select one or more of the options. This question is not written down, so listen carefully to the examiner so that you know exactly what you have to do.

> **Tip!** Question tags (*don't you think?*, *is it?*, etc.) are a good way of inviting your partner to give their opinion.

Test 2 Training — Speaking Part 4

Choose the correct words.
- For Part 4 of the Speaking test, you *discuss / do not discuss* your decision in Part 3.
- The examiner asks you *some / all* of the questions on their list.
- You *may / may not* talk to your partner.
- The total time is *three / four* minutes for a pair of candidates.

Focus Understanding the task

1 Complete the assessment notes using the information below.

Grammar and Vocabulary	Discourse Management	Pronunciation	Interactive Communication

The range of structures used.
Using a range of linking words and cohesive devices.
Saying individual sounds clearly.
Responding to questions appropriately.
Giving extended responses.
Using word and sentence stress accurately.
The range of vocabulary used.

The amount of hesitation and repetition.
Using language which is accurate and appropriate.
Taking an active role in conversations.
Using intonation appropriately.
The amount of support needed in conversations.
The organisation of ideas.

2a 🎧 35 Listen to people answering four questions. Match the answers (1–4) with the questions (a–d).

____ a Is it better to get advice from family or from friends?
____ b Some people avoid giving advice. Why do you think this is?
____ c Some people search the internet for advice and recommendations. Is this a good idea?
____ d Do you think that reviews of books and films can be trusted?

b 🎧 35 Listen again and look at the Discourse Management assessment points from Exercise 1. What do the candidates do well? What could they improve?

3 Choose one of the questions from Exercise 2a to ask other students.

> **Tip!** After your partner has answered a question, the examiner may ask you if you agree. Make sure you listen carefully to the question and how your partner responds.

Useful language Acknowledging different opinions

4 Match the two halves of the phrases.

1 That makes   a valid point …
2 That's a   b true that …
3 I see what   c surprise me …
4 It's   d they think that …
5 That doesn't   e they mean …
6 I get why   f sense …

> **Remember!** Even if you disagree with an opinion you hear, you can acknowledge it and then use connecting words (e.g. *Nevertheless, However, but, yet*) to introduce a contrasting opinion.

5 🎧 35 Listen to the answers again and say whether you agree or disagree with them. Use language from Exercise 4 to acknowledge their point.

Test 2 Exam practice — Speaking Part 4

Work in groups of three. Ask and answer these questions.

Part 4   4 minutes (6 minutes for groups of three)

Interlocutor
- Is going shopping in a city centre a good way of using our free time? (Why? / Why not?)
- Do you think it's a good idea for all city centres to be closed to traffic? (Why? / Why not?)
- Do you think cities should preserve historical buildings or replace them with buildings which are more suitable for modern living? (Why?)
- Some people say that city centres as they are today will eventually disappear. Do you agree? (Why? / Why not?)
- Some popular cities have started charging tourists a tax to visit. Why do you think this is?
- Some people think the convenience of living in a town centre outweighs the problems. What do you think? (Why?)

Thank you. That is the end of the test.

What do you think?
Do you agree?
And you?

Advice
Think about a city you know. Use examples from your own experience to support your answers to the questions.

> **Tip!** Eye contact is really important when you are talking to someone. Remember to look at who you are talking to.

Test 3 — Reading and Use of English Part 1

For questions **1–8**, read the text below and decide which answer (**A**, **B**, **C** or **D**) best fits each gap. There is an example at the beginning (**0**).

Mark your answers **on the separate answer sheet**.

Example:

| 0 | **A** help | **B** make | **C** let | **D** assist |

| 0 | **A** ▬ | **B** ▭ | **C** ▭ | **D** ▭ |

Feeling grateful makes us happier

How can we **(0)** .... ourselves to feel happy? Studies have found that our attitude to life can **(1)** .... an important part. Taking a more optimistic **(2)** .... and learning to feel grateful for the good things in our lives can provide **(3)** .... against negative emotions. It can also increase our happiness **(4)** ....

Listing things at the end of every day that we feel grateful for can help us think more positively and feel better. This can be done in a **(5)** .... of ways, for example by **(6)** .... a daily gratitude diary, which can be written by hand or on your phone. Another quick and easy habit is simply writing down three things that **(7)** .... well every day and thinking about what was good about them. You can also tell someone what you are grateful for that day or send a thank-you message.

This might all sound rather simple, but it does seem that feeling grateful is **(8)** .... with increased social well-being.

1	**A** take	**B** give	**C** play	**D** hold
2	**A** belief	**B** approach	**C** thought	**D** strategy
3	**A** protection	**B** security	**C** defence	**D** safety
4	**A** levels	**B** degrees	**C** amounts	**D** extents
5	**A** volume	**B** collection	**C** set	**D** number
6	**A** keeping	**B** filling	**C** maintaining	**D** storing
7	**A** were	**B** did	**C** went	**D** looked
8	**A** combined	**B** associated	**C** attached	**D** considered

Test 3 — Reading and Use of English Part 2

For questions **9–16**, read the text below and think of the word which best fits each gap. Use only one word in each gap. There is an example at the beginning (**0**).

Write your answers **IN CAPITAL LETTERS** on the separate answer sheet.

Example: **0** E V E R Y

The French baguette

In 2022, the French baguette, a long, thin loaf of bread eaten by many French people **(0)** ...EVERY... day, was added to a list of culturally protected traditions by UNESCO, the United Nations Educational, Scientific and Cultural Organization. The list has traditions from over 130 countries on it. **(9)** .... from food, it also includes activities and events such **(10)** .... dances and festivals. UNESCO said that **(11)** .... including the bread on the list, it was protecting the traditional method **(12)** .... baking baguettes.

The origins of the stick-shaped bread are unknown. Some say the French emperor Napoleon Bonaparte invented the longer shape in **(13)** .... to make it easier for people to carry. Others say the bread was in **(14)** .... invented in the 1830s by an Austrian baker called August Zang. **(15)** .... is certain is that the bread has been at **(16)** .... centre of French life for more than a century and around 16 million baguettes a day are still produced in France.

Test 3 — Reading and Use of English Part 3

For questions **17–24**, read the text below. Use the word given in capitals at the end of some of the lines to form a word that fits in the gap **in the same line**. There is an example at the beginning (**0**).

Write your answers **IN CAPITAL LETTERS** on the separate answer sheet.

Example: `0` `L E A D I N G`

Sculptures made of sand

Have you ever been to a sand-sculpture festival? In Weymouth, on the south coast of England, visitors to SandWorld can see amazing work by some of the world's (**0**) .... sand sculptors – artists who make sculptures out of sand.   **LEAD**

The (**17**) .... sculptures can be seen in spring, summer and autumn. They're so (**18**) .... detailed, it's hard to believe they're just sand and water. Science-fiction adventures have provided the (**19**) .... for many of them and there are dinosaurs, too. New displays are added throughout the season and many visitors get the chance to observe the sculptors creating their (**20**) .... works of art.   **BREATH** / **BEAUTY** / **INSPIRE** / **IMPRESS**

Visitors can also create their own sand sculptures. There's plenty of advice available for anyone trying the activity out for the first time, so it's a fun and (**21**) .... day out for people of all ages. It's also easily (**22**) .... for people in wheelchairs. There's a charge for (**23**) .... to the attraction, with group tickets available. Alternatively, a season ticket will allow you an (**24**) .... number of visits throughout the summer.   **EDUCATE** / **ACCESS** / **ADMIT** / **LIMIT**

Test 3 — Reading and Use of English Part 4

For questions **25–30**, complete the second sentence so that it has a similar meaning to the first sentence, using the word given. **Do not change the word given**. You must use between **two** and **five** words, including the word given. Here is an example (**0**).

Example:

0 It's over five days since Sam's last message.

TOUCH

Sam hasn't ……………………………………… least five days.

The gap can be filled by the words 'been in touch for at', so you write:

Example: | **0** | BEEN IN TOUCH FOR AT

Write **only** the missing words **IN CAPITAL LETTERS** on the separate answer sheet.

---

25 I'm surprised that you're here!

EXPECT

I ……………………………………… be here!

26 Ben needed to try very hard to win the race.

GREAT

Ben had to ……………………………………… effort to win the race.

27 It is obvious that the coach is admired by all the players, without exception.

SINGLE

It is obvious that ……………………………………… up to the coach.

28 It's a pity I didn't buy as much food as we needed for everyone at the party!

ENOUGH

If only I ……………………………………… for everyone at the party!

29 Nobody understood Ferda's decision to leave her job.

DECIDED

Nobody understood ……………………………………… up her job.

30 I know that it isn't always easy to grow vegetables.

CAN

I know that ……………………………………… difficult.

Reading and Use of English Part 5

You are going to read an article about songwriting. For questions **31–36**, choose the answer (**A**, **B**, **C** or **D**) which you think fits best according to the text.

Mark your answers **on the separate answer sheet**.

A songwriting course in Wales
How our reporter wrote her first song

When I decided to try songwriting, I initially enrolled on a course online. The tutor calmed my nerves a little, telling me to ignore the voices in my head saying I was rubbish. I was also told to listen to the singers whose lyrics I most admired. I did this for hours on end, hoping that somehow, some of their incredible talent would flow into me. I watched videos of singer-songwriters in which they explained their desire to connect with their fans and to hear them say they felt the same way too, sometimes. There was clearly a shared and very human reason why so many different people wanted to write their songs. In the end, however, I realised that if I was ever going to actually write a song myself, I needed to go away somewhere for a few days and spend time with people who felt like I did. So, I signed up for a four-day songwriting course on the coast of Wales.

The setting was amazing and the course focused on the links between poetry and songwriting. Every morning, we sang together to exercise our lungs and ears. We went on rainy group walks and afterwards were encouraged to write freely, inspired by the wind and the sea, putting together unusual combinations of words to see if they meant something to us. In group sessions, we had fascinating discussions about what songs can do that poems can't. Music can, for example, make simple lyrics sound more meaningful, while poetry sits on the page, there for readers to analyse for as long as they want to. Or a single sound in a song may express an emotion that it might take an entire poem to convey. We analysed short sections of work by different singer-songwriters and talked about how songs are complex combinations of words, sounds, atmospheres and arrangements.

Then the time came for me to write my own song. I sat in my room with a tiny keyboard and a notebook covered in crossed out lyrics. The only rhythm in my ears was my heart beating rapidly. The only music in my mind was the rising panic of my inner critic screaming at me to stop. An idea finally started to emerge and I noted some words down on the page. We'd been advised to aim to express moods with our words and not worry about whether we were copying anyone. In fact, I noticed later how the tune I eventually came up with was heavily influenced by (and far worse than) one by an Irish band. But the most scary comment had been that whatever we did, our songs would all end up sounding like ourselves. We'd been encouraged to seek help from others on the course, so I discussed my idea with another participant, despite it making me feel uncomfortably exposed. We worked together to develop it into a story with a surprising ending, mixing ordinary lines with more unusual ones.

When I had to perform it for the group, I was terrified, but also strangely excited. As we'd built a shared sense of trust and loyalty, it felt all right that the song was not perfect. I was also very much aware that these courses aren't about writing hit singles, but the joy of trying out new things with new people. And my song wasn't a total disaster. Afterwards, I approached my tutors for a review. They were unsparing but kind. One said he'd have loved me to play around with first- and third-person points of view in the song, and maybe even speak the last verse. Another pointed out that some of it was quite hard to understand. However, they also said they loved the strength of feeling in it and reminded me that although not everyone would like my songs, I should never let that influence what I did next. That was my favourite piece of advice!

line 58

31 What problem did the writer have when she started learning about songwriting?

- **A** Her motivation for wanting to write songs differed from that of others.
- **B** One of her songwriting teachers put her off taking her interest further.
- **C** It was hard to progress without other songwriting students around her.
- **D** Hearing other people's songwriting efforts became boring after a while.

32 In the second paragraph, what does the writer suggest about the course in Wales?

- **A** She would have enjoyed it more if the weather had not been so awful.
- **B** She would have preferred to spend a little less time focusing on poetry.
- **C** She valued the in-depth understanding she gained of the subject matter.
- **D** She benefitted from spending time with students who were experts on music.

33 What does the writer say in the third paragraph about her idea for a song?

- **A** She was amazed it was so hard to come up with.
- **B** She was not initially keen to share it with anyone.
- **C** She was disappointed it was not particularly original.
- **D** She was unwilling to consider changing it in any way.

34 What point does the writer make about performing her song?

- **A** Her desire to impress overcame her anxiety.
- **B** It made her feel that she could do almost anything.
- **C** It turned out to be far easier than she had expected.
- **D** Her experiences on the course made her feel secure.

35 What does 'unsparing' mean in line 58?

- **A** very brief
- **B** totally honest
- **C** not at all negative
- **D** careful not to offend

36 In the text as a whole, what feeling does the writer emphasise?

- **A** her lack of confidence in her own abilities
- **B** her unwillingness to follow advice she was given
- **C** her eagerness to demonstrate what she can achieve
- **D** her relief at finding she could do as well as her coursemates

Test 3 — Reading and Use of English Part 6

You are going to read an article about making old furniture look beautiful. Six sentences have been removed from the article. Choose from the sentences **A–G** the one which best fits each gap (**37–42**). There is one extra sentence which you do not need to use.

Mark your answers **on the separate answer sheet**.

Upcycling furniture: be bold – that's the fun part
Some tips for finding second-hand items and giving new life to wooden furniture

If you're new to the idea of searching for second-hand – also known as pre-owned or pre-loved – furniture, it can be difficult to know where to start. Some people look online, but antique markets are also fun, especially if you go with a friend. Second-hand furniture often has a great deal of character and charm. It has soul and energy – and that's why so many people love it.

Dark brown furniture is the first thing to look for. Made from solid dark wood, it's often quite cheap. **37** Avoid anything with modern legs, though. Look for a solid, heavy frame and lovely curved wooden legs, or short, bun-shaped feet.

Avoid anything broken. Don't buy anything with a leg missing or drawers that don't slide in and out smoothly. **38** But never think that anything very cheap is too good to be true. That's where real happiness lies – in discovering reasonably priced pieces that you love.

When you've found a bargain that needs a bit of care, there's no point attempting to make it look brand new. It's surprising how far a good clean goes. Start with a vacuum cleaner with a special attachment to remove dust and dirt from all the interior and exterior surfaces. Then, using warm, soapy water and a soft cloth, clean the surfaces carefully. Wipe them with a soft, dry cloth afterwards. **39**

Avoid purchasing anything which smells bad – some smells are really hard to get rid of. **40** However, if your piece smells a little old and damp, you can spray white vinegar on the inside surfaces and leave it to dry. The vinegar will get rid of most smells. Give yourself space and time to work, wear sensible clothes and protect the surfaces surrounding your project with newspaper or an old sheet.

After that, you may want to paint your furniture. Many people think they're not artistic or they can't paint. **41** If you're a beginner, start with a small item of furniture. Look for something cheap and solid, such as a small pine table. By painting it, you'll transform it from something insignificant to something that really stands out in its environment. Try starting with blue – it goes with anything and everything. Or try a deep, gorgeous green. Then, if you find that you hate it, just paint over it. That's the beauty of paint.

Make sure the piece you want to paint is clean and dry, then simply start painting it all over in all directions. Don't worry about painting up and down in neat lines. You want the paint to spread out smoothly without brush marks. Once you've given it a first coat of paint, wait for the recommended amount of time (read the instructions on the paint tin!), then add a second coat and allow it to dry thoroughly. The best thing is that painting – and upcycling in general – is incredibly good for your mental health. **42** That takes your mind off everything else. But it isn't stressful; it's a lovely feeling. And at the end of it, you'll feel fantastic about the piece you've created.

A	Don't let feelings like that put you off.	**E**	Pine is also inexpensive, but can have more stains on it, which isn't so great.
B	Then it will look totally unique.		
		F	It requires you to concentrate on what you're doing.
C	If you do, it will annoy you forever.		
D	They can also transfer to any items you might want to store inside the piece.	**G**	Repeat if necessary and watch out for rough wood at the backs of drawers and the rear of furniture.

Test 3 — Reading and Use of English Part 7

You are going to read an article in which four people talk about meeting strangers by chance. For questions **43–52**, choose from the people (**A–D**). The people may be chosen more than once.

Which person says they

praised someone's talent?	43
misunderstood a question?	44
set up another meeting?	45
made up an excuse?	46
appreciated someone's humorous stories?	47
challenged a statement?	48
repaid someone's kindness?	49
calmed someone down?	50
overcame their dislike of someone?	51
discovered a shared interest?	52

That was a surprise!

Four people talk about unexpected meetings with strangers

A Gina

I was coming out of the cinema after watching a rather amusing comedy when a young woman behind me in the crowd of people leaving said it was a terrible film. I couldn't help turning round and disagreeing with her, immediately regretting it, as I'm actually rather shy. I'm still not sure why I responded. Perhaps it was simply that I'd enjoyed the film so much, I couldn't help defending it. Anyway, she just laughed and we carried on chatting, ending up having coffee together as she, like me, had been to see the film on her own. We instantly hit it off and it turned out that neither of us actually went to the cinema very often, but had been feeling a bit bored and wanted something to do. I suggested we should see each other again the following week and a year later, she's one of my closest friends.

B Rudi

One summer, I was spending a week cycling in the countryside when on one particularly hot day, I ran out of water. I came across a small village, but all the shops were closed and there was no drinking fountain in sight. Then a young man my age came out of a house and asked if I was OK. He gave me a glass of water and invited me in for some food. I noticed some beautiful pottery in his kitchen. He'd made it himself and was amazed when I told him that was something I did, too. His work was absolutely stunning, though, and he was very pleased when I said so. He insisted on giving me a small bowl as a present. When I got home, I sent him a small vase of mine to thank him. I hope we'll be able to meet again one day.

C Andy

I'd just left work and was walking home when this man came round a corner and walked straight into me. It would have been fine if he hadn't been carrying a coffee, and even that would have been fine if it hadn't gone all over my coat. Luckily, it was a thick coat, so I wasn't hurt. The thing was, he got really upset and quite angry with himself and I had to keep telling him it was OK and not to worry, until eventually he stopped apologising. He offered to buy me another coffee, but I was in a bad mood and just wanted to get away and go home. So I told him I was late for dinner with my aunt. I don't even have an aunt, but that's the first thing that came into my head, for some reason.

D Marian

I was in a café in an art gallery reading my book when someone asked if they could have the free chair next to me. I thought they wanted to take it to another table, so I was a bit surprised when they sat down at mine. In fact, while I'd been reading, the place had filled up and there weren't any free tables left. I was even more surprised when I looked at the woman's face and realised she was the presenter of a TV show I sometimes watch. I'd always found her style quite aggressive and irritating, so I can't say I was keen to start a conversation. But she was friendly and very different from the way she appeared on screen, so I soon found myself chatting away to her. She was very amusing about some of the famous people she'd worked with, too, which I enjoyed.

Test 3 — Writing Part 1

You **must** answer this question. Write your answer in **140–190** words in an appropriate style on the separate answer sheet.

1. In your English class you have been talking about the natural world. Now, your English teacher has asked you to write an essay.

   Write your essay using **all** the notes and giving reasons for your point of view.

   'People should be banned from nature reserves.'

   Do you agree?

   Notes

   Write about:

   1. damage
   2. litter
   3. .... (your own idea)

Test 3 — Writing Part 2

Write an answer to **one** of the questions **2–4** in this part. Write your answer in **140–190** words in an appropriate style on the separate answer sheet. Put the question number in the box at the top of the answer sheet.

2   You see this notice on an English-language website.

> **Would you like to work for a brand-new social media company?**
>
> We're looking for people to work in our marketing department who:
> - have experience of using a variety of social media
> - have strong English skills
> - are good at working as part of a team.
>
> Please write to the manager, George Harrow, explaining why you would be suitable.

Write your **letter of application**.

3   You see this announcement in an English-language magazine.

> **Reviews wanted**
>
> **The most interesting TV series ever**
>
> What is the most interesting TV series you've ever seen? What made it so interesting? What did you learn from it?
>
> Write us a review of the TV series. We will publish the best reviews next month.

Write your **review**.

4   You see this announcement on an English-language website.

> **Articles wanted**
>
> **The best present ever**
>
> What is the best present you have ever received? Why was it such a good present? Do you prefer giving or receiving presents?
>
> We will publish the best articles on our website.

Write your **article**.

Test 3 Listening Part 1

🎧 36 You will hear people talking in eight different situations. For questions **1–8**, choose the best answer (**A**, **B** or **C**).

1   You hear a podcaster talking about the issue of success in life.
    What is he doing?

    A   suggesting why some people try to become less competitive
    B   explaining what makes some people competitive
    C   advising on when being competitive is useful

2   You hear a man telling a woman about the yoga classes he attends.
    What does he emphasise about yoga?

    A   how varied the people it attracts are
    B   how many benefits it has given him
    C   how long it has been practised for

3   You hear two friends talking about football.
    They agree that in the best matches there are

    A   many surprises.
    B   very few mistakes.
    C   plenty of goals.

4   You hear a young man talking to a friend about learning to drive.
    He mentions driving near the town hall in order to show

    A   how hard it is to focus on lots of things at the same time.
    B   how important it is to know the rules of the road.
    C   how easy it is to make the wrong decision.

5   You hear a woman talking to a friend about a book she has just read.
    How did she feel about it?

    A   sympathetic to the main character
    B   surprised by the themes it dealt with
    C   disappointed by the quality of the writing

6   You hear two people talking about space exploration.
    What does the woman express approval of?

    A   searching for planets that could support life
    B   continuing to develop the necessary technology
    C   having more ordinary people travel into space

7   You hear a man talking about some psychology research.
    What finding was he unsurprised by?

    A   how wide people's social networks tend to be
    B   how important close social networks are for people
    C   how varied people are in maintaining their social networks

8   You hear two colleagues talking about their boss.
    They disagree about the importance of their boss

    A   working closely with employees.
    B   communicating honestly with employees.
    C   encouraging employees to be creative.

Test 3 — Listening Part 2

🎧 37 You will hear part of a travel podcast in which a man called Danny Blake is talking about a climb he did with friends and a guide up Mount Batur, a volcano in Bali, an island in Indonesia. For questions **9–18**, complete the sentences with a word, number or short phrase.

Climbing a volcano – Mount Batur, Bali, Indonesia

Danny was very relieved that his group were supplied with **(9)** .... by their guide Wayan at the start of the climb.

Wayan informed Danny's group that Mount Batur is approximately **(10)** .... metres at its highest point.

Danny was pleased that he was wearing **(11)** .... for the climb.

Danny says that he was amazed to feel **(12)** .... now and again after a short time hiking.

Several members of Danny's group requested **(13)** .... on the way up.

Danny says that the torches of other hikers resembled **(14)** .... shining in the darkness.

Danny uses the phrase **(15)** .... to describe his physical experience of the two-and-a-half-hour climb to the top.

Danny managed to prevent his **(16)** .... from being stolen by one of the monkeys they encountered.

Danny was pleased with his efforts to capture the **(17)** .... in a photograph.

Danny says that what impressed him about the black volcanic rocks of Mount Batur was how **(18)** .... they were.

Test 3 — Listening Part 3

🎧 38 You will hear five short extracts in which people are talking about learning to play a musical instrument. For questions **19–23**, choose from the list (**A–H**) what each person says about their experience. Use the letters only once. There are three extra letters which you do not need to use.

A   It's more enjoyable than I expected.

B   I find my rate of progress frustrating.

C   I've discovered the value of setting realistic goals.

D   My level of enthusiasm varies greatly.

E   I've become confident with my new skills quickly.

F   It's inspiring to hear other people's stories.

G   It's benefitted another aspect of my life.

H   I feel embarrassed about playing in front of others.

Speaker 1   **19**

Speaker 2   **20**

Speaker 3   **21**

Speaker 4   **22**

Speaker 5   **23**

Test 3 — Listening Part 4

🎧 39 You will hear an interview with a woman called Claire Kaledos, who is a personal trainer and helps people with personal health and fitness goals. For questions **24–30**, choose the best answer (**A**, **B** or **C**).

24 Claire discovered that gaining a professional qualification as a personal trainer is important

   A for avoiding legal problems.
   B as an initial goal on a long path.
   C when applying for positions at gyms.

25 What does Claire say surprised her after starting work?

   A the kinds of positive effects it had on her own life
   B the amount of responsibility she felt for people's lives
   C the level of competition there was for the work available

26 What image of herself did Claire emphasise in her social media profile as a personal trainer?

   A someone who educates and informs
   B someone who is energetic and motivating
   C someone who uses modern new ideas and methods

27 What did Claire find difficult about being self-employed?

   A getting time to relax
   B managing financial matters
   C finding suitable clients

28 What does Claire say about working with an actor called Jake Gardner?

   A He was delighted with the physical results.
   B He was happy to make changes to his lifestyle.
   C He was keen to introduce her to other celebrities.

29 What does Claire say is the main issue for many of her clients?

   A lack of confidence
   B giving up easily
   C busy schedules

30 During her time as a personal trainer, Claire says that she has become

   A more interested in communication skills.
   B more conscious of the value of self-care.
   C more understanding of her clients' feelings.

Test 3 — Speaking Parts 1 and 2

Part 1   40   2 minutes (3 minutes for groups of three)

Interlocutor First, we'd like to know something about you.

Life experiences
- How do you usually celebrate important events in your family? (Why do you do that?)
- How would you like to celebrate your next birthday? (Why?)
- Do you like taking lots of photos of important events? (Why? / Why not?)
- Have you ever entered any competitions? (What kind of competition was it?)
- Tell us about the type of job you would like to do in the future. (Why have you chosen that?)

Part 2   41   4 minutes (6 minutes for groups of three)

Interlocutor In this part of the test, I'm going to give each of you two photographs. I'd like you to talk about your photographs on your own for about a minute and also to answer a question about your partner's photographs.

(*Candidate A*), it's your turn first. Here are your photographs on page C11 of the Speaking appendix. They show **people who need to prepare well in different situations**. I'd like you to compare the photographs and say **what you think the people might find difficult about preparing for these situations**.

All right?

Candidate A
1 minute ....

Interlocutor Thank you.

(*Candidate B*), **do you enjoy classical music? (Why? / Why not?)**

Candidate B
Approximately 30 seconds ....

Interlocutor Thank you.

Now (*Candidate B*), here are your photographs on page C12 of the Speaking appendix. They show **people showing things in different situations**.

I'd like you to compare the photographs and say **why you think the people have decided to show these things**.

All right?

Candidate B
1 minute ....

Interlocutor Thank you.

(*Candidate A*), **Do you enjoy shopping with friends? (Why? / Why not?)**

Candidate A
Approximately 30 seconds ....

Interlocutor Thank you.

Test 3 Speaking Parts 3 and 4

Part 3 4 minutes (5 minutes for groups of three)

Interlocutor Now, I'd like you to talk about something together for about two minutes.

Here are some things many people think are helpful when someone moves to live somewhere new and a question for you to discuss. First, you have some time to look at the task on page C13 of the Speaking appendix.

Now, talk to each other about **whether you think these things are helpful when someone moves to live somewhere new.**

Candidates 2 minutes (3 minutes for groups of three)

Interlocutor Thank you. Now you have about a minute to decide **which two things are most helpful when someone moves to live somewhere new**.

Candidates 1 minute (for pairs and groups of three)

Interlocutor Thank you.

Part 4 4 minutes (6 minutes for groups of three)

Interlocutor
- What do you think someone new to the area where you live would enjoy about living there? (Why?)
- Do you think that it's a good idea to live in the same place your whole life? (Why? / Why not?)
- Why do you think people choose to live in a capital city?
- Which do you think is more important: what your home is like or where your home is? (Why?)
- Some young people like to stay at home when they study at college or university. Other young people think it's better to move away from home to study. What do you think? (Why?)
- Do you think that living in another country is easier now than it was in the past? (Why? / Why not?)

What do you think?
Do you agree?
And you?

Thank you. That is the end of the test.

Test 4 — Reading and Use of English Part 1

For questions **1–8**, read the text below and decide which answer (**A**, **B**, **C** or **D**) best fits each gap. There is an example at the beginning (**0**).

Mark your answers **on the separate answer sheet**.

Example:

| 0 | **A** responsible | **B** faithful | **C** reliable | **D** loyal |

Eco-shoes

There are few (0) .... statistics about the number of shoes manufactured every year for the world's eight billion humans. We do know, however, that modern shoes are (1) .... the hardest items to produce in an ecologically friendly way. That's because most shoes are (2) .... of a mixture of artificial cloth, rubber, plastic and metal that's too complex to recycle.

A UK shoe company has (3) .... up with a design for the world's first 3D printed, made-to-measure shoes which can be composted – turned into soil – at the end of their life. The shoes may (4) .... some people as rather strange. As a result, not everyone will therefore regard them as the (5) .... of fashionable footwear. They are also (6) .... expensive. Their inventors, however, hope this will be the next huge (7) .... in eco-footwear.

The shoes are produced based on in-store foot scans and then take 30 hours to print. Once they are (8) .... out, the shoes can be returned and composted.

1	**A** inside	**B** among	**C** between	**D** including
2	**A** composed	**B** created	**C** combined	**D** constructed
3	**A** thought	**B** made	**C** come	**D** dreamt
4	**A** knock	**B** hit	**C** punch	**D** strike
5	**A** progress	**B** future	**C** prospect	**D** fate
6	**A** totally	**B** absolutely	**C** completely	**D** extremely
7	**A** breakthrough	**B** movement	**C** boost	**D** addition
8	**A** used	**B** worn	**C** tired	**D** spent

Test 4 — Reading and Use of English Part 2

For questions **9–16**, read the text below and think of the word which best fits each gap. Use only one word in each gap. There is an example at the beginning (**0**).

Write your answers **IN CAPITAL LETTERS** on the separate answer sheet.

Example: **0** O N

The city of Tartu, Estonia

The Republic of Estonia is a very beautiful country **(0)** .... the Baltic Sea in Europe. Its capital city, Tallinn, is a popular tourist destination. However, there are also plenty of reasons **(9)** .... explore the country's second largest city, Tartu.

To start **(10)** .... , Tartu is the oldest city in the Baltic states and has one of the oldest universities **(11)** .... the world, founded in the 1600s. Around **(12)** .... quarter of the city's population are students. There's plenty to do **(13)** .... year round and visitors love the film festival **(14)** .... is held every summer, during which movies are shown on the Baltics' largest outdoor movie screen.

There are over 20 museums, including the popular Tartu Toy Museum. Visitors should also **(15)** .... the opportunity to see the Tartu Leaning House. It **(16)** .... built in the 1700s next to Tartu's ancient city walls and leans over even more than the famous Leaning Tower of Pisa in Italy.

Test 4 — Reading and Use of English Part 3

For questions **17–24**, read the text below. Use the word given in capitals at the end of some of the lines to form a word that fits in the gap **in the same line**. There is an example at the beginning (**0**).

Write your answers **IN CAPITAL LETTERS on the separate answer sheet**.

Example: **0** N O V E L I S T

Edith Wharton

The American writer Edith Wharton (1862–1937) is best known nowadays as a **(0)** ...., although her first novel was not published until she was 40. Born into a **(17)** .... New York family, she travelled in Europe with her parents as a child, **(18)** .... becoming fluent in French, German and Italian. She wrote stories from early **(19)** ...., attempting her first novel aged just 11. It attracted such fierce **(20)** .... from her mother, however, that she started writing poetry instead.

NOVEL
WEALTH

CONSEQUENCE
CHILD
CRITIC

Her first published work was a translation of a German poem. She was 15 years old. Her family insisted that it should appear under another name, because writing was considered **(21)** .... as an occupation for a rich American woman. Nevertheless, she refused to be **(22)** .... and eventually became an extraordinarily **(23)** .... writer. By the time of her **(24)** ...., she had published 15 novels, seven novellas and 85 short stories in addition to her poetry, as well as books on design, travel, literature and culture.

SUIT
COURAGE
PRODUCE
DIE

Test 4 — Reading and Use of English Part 4

For questions **25–30**, complete the second sentence so that it has a similar meaning to the first sentence, using the word given. **Do not change the word given.** You must use between **two** and **five** words, including the word given. Here is an example (**0**).

Example:

0 It's over five days since Sam's last message.

   TOUCH

   Sam hasn't ………………………………………… least five days.

The gap can be filled by the words 'been in touch for at', so you write:

Example: | **0** | BEEN IN TOUCH FOR AT |

Write **only** the missing words **IN CAPITAL LETTERS** on the separate answer sheet.

---

25 I don't know why someone put this plant in a rubbish bin – it's in perfect condition!

   THROWN

   I don't know why this plant ………………………………………… – it's in perfect condition, but it's in a rubbish bin!

26 Barbara thinks she will use all the facilities at the hotel.

   HOPING

   Barbara ………………………………………… advantage of all the facilities at the hotel.

27 I had almost run out of time, so I had to rush round the last part of the exhibition.

   LEFT

   I had very ………………………………………… see the last part of the exhibition, so I had to rush round it.

28 Leah wished she had postponed the barbecue until the summer.

   PUTTING

   Leah regretted ………………………………………… the barbecue until the summer.

29 I don't know who owns this car.

   IDEA

   I have ………………………………………… this is.

30 David lives a long way from college, so he has to take the bus every day.

   CLOSER

   If David ………………………………………… , he wouldn't have to take the bus every day.

Test 4 — Reading and Use of English Part 5

You are going to read an article by a woman who loves archaeology, the study of ancient cultures through examining their remains. For questions **31–36**, choose the answer (**A, B, C** or **D**) which you think fits best according to the text.

Mark your answers **on the separate answer sheet**.

The magic of archaeology

A writer and broadcaster explains why she loves archaeology

Archaeology is the study of the human past through material remains, such as buildings, tools or decorative items. Often, the things archaeologists discover are items that were thrown away, lost or buried. This 'rubbish' tells the story of ancient lives. The real value of all these material remains is in the links between them – where part of a stone tool is located in relation to a fireplace or how a site has been reused and reshaped by generation after generation. From single data points, archaeologists build a web of understanding.

When I was a teenager, I watched a TV documentary about an archaeological discovery at the top of Mount Ampato in Peru. Using a wide range of scientific techniques, as well as historical knowledge of ancient societies, the anthropologist-archaeologist-mountaineers were able to work out exactly what had happened at the site. I was astonished to learn that discovering and explaining such mysteries could be an actual job. Archaeology, and the challenge of making the strange familiar, has felt fascinating to me ever since.

To gain some experience before going to university, I found an archaeological project – or 'dig' – that was willing to let my friend and me camp for a week and help out. There was a tent for us all to eat in with chairs, tables and a limitless supply of hot tea served in brown-stained mugs, and the professional archaeologists were the coolest people I'd ever met. They looked too messy and muddy to be top academics, but it was clear they were intellectual and scientific experts, able to work out the story of a complex site that had seen thousands of years of human activity.

Curiosity about these ancient lives is what inspires the work I do now, making TV and radio programmes and writing books about the past. Television shows about archaeology capture the magic of discovering the distant past, the detail of archaeological techniques and several big, tricky questions. Why do humans – through time and across cultures – do so many weird and amazing things? How did people in the past tackle the challenges many still struggle with today – whether that's how to build a rainproof roof, grow food, carry babies comfortably, choose a leader or keep their loved ones safe?

I'm frequently involved with community archaeology projects, too. They often need volunteers and good digs will welcome people with physical disabilities and additional support requirements. Projects need people to clean and process what has been dug up, keep digital and written records, use tech to gather data – from photographing objects and processing lidar (laser) scans to photogrammetry, which uses large numbers of still photographs to build a 3D model of a site or an individual item. They need people who like talking to visitors, as well as people who don't go on site at all, but can work from home instead, looking at documents and maps, completing research or keeping websites and social media accounts up to date.

A few years ago, I volunteered at Chester Farm, near Wellingborough in Northamptonshire, UK. It's a brilliant site, close to a prehistoric (and later Roman) river crossing. There's evidence of more than 10,000 years of human activity along the riverbank and in the surrounding fields. This single site tells the story of the county. On the day I helped out, I was asked to dig in a particular area. The archaeologists knew it was Roman, but they weren't sure whether there was anything interesting there. I worked away and then there it was – the smooth, curved head of a long, thin, white pin. It was a Roman hairpin made of cow bone, in perfect condition. I was the first person to hold it for 1,800 years – the last person to touch it was probably the one who dropped it. It was a truly incredible feeling.

31 What are we told about archaeologists' work in the first paragraph?

   A   It is based on making connections.
   B   Not everyone regards it as important.
   C   It mainly relies on chance discoveries.
   D   Not all of it turns out to be worthwhile.

32 What does the writer suggest happened to her as a teenager?

   A   She learned about a place which she later became obsessed by.
   B   She decided she would never do an ordinary job if she could help it.
   C   She was inspired to consider a career she had not previously heard of.
   D   She suddenly doubted whether she could achieve her professional ambitions.

33 How did the writer feel while she was at the archaeological dig before university?

   A   shocked at some people's appearance
   B   nervous about carrying out a difficult task
   C   relieved that the conditions were comfortable
   D   impressed by the knowledge of those working there

34 In the fourth paragraph, the writer makes the point that

   A   people's priorities have not changed much over time.
   B   it is surprising how little people understand about one another.
   C   TV shows are the most effective way of explaining archaeology.
   D   her shows have provided some interesting solutions to old problems.

35 What does the writer emphasise about community archaeology projects?

   A   the variety of skills that volunteers must have
   B   the amount of work that volunteers have to do
   C   the range of options that are available to volunteers
   D   the degree of responsibility that is given to volunteers

36 The writer tells the story about Chester Farm to show

   A   how dull archaeological sites often are.
   B   how thrilling archaeology can sometimes be.
   C   how important archaeology has always been.
   D   how demanding many professional archaeologists are.

Reading and Use of English Part 6

You are going to read an article about personalities and whether it is possible for us to change ours. Six sentences have been removed from the article. Choose from the sentences **A–G** the one which best fits each gap (**37–42**). There is one extra sentence which you do not need to use.

Mark your answers **on the separate answer sheet**.

Can we change our personalities?

At some point, most of us have been given a neat description of our personality, as if it were a brand of clothing and never changes. This could have occurred during a conversation with a close friend or in a social-media quiz. But according to psychologist and author Dr Benjamin Hardy, who I interviewed recently, the idea that our personality remains the same throughout our lifetime is essentially nonsense.

In his book *Personality Isn't Permanent*, he argues that personality isn't fixed at all. Some changes occur naturally as people go about their lives. **37** He speaks about personality – 'your consistent attitudes and behaviours, your way of showing up in situations' – as a collection of learnable skills, like riding a bike.

There's something unromantic about seeing personal characteristics as learned skills because we tend to think of our personality as key to what makes us *us*. Hardy thinks that's part of the problem. He says our 'identity' – how we choose to define ourselves as a person – is what's important. Personality is just the behaviour that follows on from that. **38** That person might then have confidence and a good sense of humour as a result.

The most important thing is understanding that it's possible to change – both our identity and our personality. This should give us a sense of freedom, Hardy says, because most people have defined their current self too precisely. If someone says, 'I'm shy', that doesn't have to mean they always will be. But because most people's identity is something they think is fixed, they find it really hard to imagine that they could be different. He says the problem isn't that people are unable to change. **39**

The past few years have seen the wellness movement become more and more popular. **40** But there's also been increasing interest in improving our mental state through practices such as meditation. Although many of these affect personality – if you're well rested and in good health, you're likely to be more optimistic – the goal of improving actual personality has rarely been stated. In future, will we attempt to become funnier or more generous with the same determination that currently goes into developing our muscles?

The idea that personality becomes fixed at a certain age has been around for more than a century. One popular theory is that it doesn't change much after the age of 30. According to Hardy, there's an alternative explanation. **41** Whereas if they were trying out more activities or going to more different places for the first time, their personality would keep changing because they'd be out of their comfort zone.

So what do we do if we want to give our personality a boost? **42** Hardy advises starting with imagining the person we would like to be – and says the characteristics will follow. He says it does involve 'deliberate practice', a psychology term referring to a repetitive, highly self-aware process. 'You must always be pushing slightly above your current skill level, getting feedback and some level of coaching. You watch and analyse yourself, just like a football player.' I say it sounds like learning anything else. He says it is. 'Personality is a learnable skill, just like learning how to walk.'

A	So imagine, for example, someone who considers themself powerful and charming.	**E**	That might mean adding some humour or trying to stop being unkind.
B	It makes them think of all the possibilities available.	**F**	It's that they don't believe they can.
C	It has often tended to focus on physical things such as eating, sleeping and exercise.	**G**	People often have a career and family and stop doing so many new things.
D	However, it's also possible for anyone to deliberately alter their character if they wish to.		

Test 4 Reading and Use of English Part 7

You are going to read an article about testing video games as a job. For questions **43–52**, choose from the sections (**A–D**). The sections may be chosen more than once.

Which section mentions

the occasionally uninteresting nature of game testers' work?	43
being able to find out what the video-game industry is really like?	44
attempts to play a game in a way that the makers did not intend?	45
that people can become game testers without having done similar work before?	46
the value of noticing issues before a game is available to the public?	47
the range of aspects of a game that the tester must think about?	48
various potential future opportunities open to game testers?	49
a possible impact on the tester of playing as a job rather than for pleasure?	50
how important the work of game testers is?	51
the chance of arrangements being altered without much notice?	52

Video-game tester – is it the job for you?

A

Many people who love video games believe that becoming a game tester is a simple and enjoyable duty that's made even better by the fact that you get paid for it. It's certainly true that the job can be fun and rewarding. You'll often have access to the newest titles and you'll get an inside look at the gaming business. Testing video games may also match your skills and interests, especially if you appreciate discovering new worlds, paying attention to detail and thinking strategically. And you'll get to use the most recent platforms, allowing you to enjoy the best-quality video games. Being a game tester can lead to a variety of employment prospects if your long-term goal is to work in the gaming business, including game creation, visual design, quality assurance engineering and project management.

B

You can have a significant impact on the gaming industry and community by working as a game tester. Testers must approach the games and gameplay differently from the way they would if playing for pure amusement. By doing so, they can spot technical and creative issues that might have a negative impact on the user experience. Before games are released, testers assist developers in finding and fixing bugs and other aspects that may cause issues. In addition, costs are greatly reduced when post-release errors are avoided. In the end, effective testing improves the overall quality of the game and user pleasure, making it more likely that the game will make a profit. And the games you test may go on to become classics that excite and inspire gamers for years to come!

C

One of the challenges of testing video games is that the testing includes 4D (adding the desired feelings the player should experience) and demands that the tester should be aware of the entire context, not just specific features of the game. That includes graphics, sound, music, game flow, game design, game balance, storytelling, performance and, of course, the game mechanics as a whole. Focusing on all of these elements at once and determining if the game 'feels correct' is the toughest part of my job. It's a different approach from simply enjoying a game at home and some people find it spoils what was once their favourite hobby. Finding a game's weaknesses is, in my opinion, the second-biggest headache. Many gamers do everything they can to test a game's limits and find shortcuts, and a significant number of them will try to hack the game – put simply, they cheat. And that will harm other gamers' experiences and can directly affect the game-maker's profits.

D

To work as a game tester, you need to be flexible because plans can change every day. Having reasonable motor skills is helpful, though you don't really need to be a skilled gamer, as most of the time, you'll be testing basic functions. Nevertheless, being able to use all the controls is important. You also need good oral and written communication skills and should be able to put up with doing the same kinds of sometimes dull tasks again and again. On the plus side, no previous game testing experience is necessary before you apply. You do need to bear in mind that the gaming industry is expanding at a very rapid pace. I have shared my experiences and what I know from friends and co-workers, but there will always be more to add. My final advice would be that if you love games as much as I do and are thinking about working as a professional game tester, I'd say go for it! Win this game!

Test 4 — Writing Part 1

You **must** answer this question. Write your answer in **140–190** words in an appropriate style on the separate answer sheet.

1. In your English class you have been talking about films and the cinema. Now, your English teacher has asked you to write an essay.

   Write your essay using **all** the notes and giving reasons for your point of view.

   'There is such a large choice of films to watch at home now that it is no longer worth going to the cinema.'
   Do you agree?

   Notes

   Write about:

   1. the atmosphere
   2. the screen size
   3. ……………………………… (your own idea)

Test 4 — Writing Part 2

Write an answer to **one** of the questions **2–4** in this part. Write your answer in **140–190** words in an appropriate style on the separate answer sheet. Put the question number in the box at the top of the answer sheet.

2 You see this announcement on an English-language website.

> **Reviews wanted**
>
> **A really great café**
>
> What is your favourite café? What makes it different from other cafés? How could the café be improved?
>
> The best reviews will be posted on our website.

Write your **review**.

3 You have received this email from your English friend, Carey.

From: Carey
Subject: Where to go?

Hi!

I've offered to arrange a special family day out with my grandparents to celebrate their 40th wedding anniversary, but I'm not sure where we should go. I want it to be a lovely day they'll remember!

We could either go out for a meal at a local restaurant or try something really different, like a boat trip.

What do you think we should do?

Carey

Write your **email**.

4 Your English teacher has asked you to write a report on public transport options in your local area for the college magazine.

In your report, you should include information about:

- what public transport options are available now
- any problems that exist with the current options
- any improvements that could be made.

Write your **report**.

Test 4 Listening Part 1

🎧 44 You will hear people talking in eight different situations. For questions **1–8**, choose the best answer (**A, B** or **C**).

1   You hear part of a talk about working life.
    The speaker is pointing out the value of

    A   teamwork.
    B   time management.
    C   communication skills.

2   You hear a woman talking about shopping for clothes.
    What is she explaining?

    A   the reasons why she selects certain clothes to try on
    B   the factors that help her evaluate the clothes she buys
    C   the characteristics of the clothes that suit her personal image

3   You hear two friends talking about a TV documentary on organic gardening.
    How does the man feel about organic gardening?

    A   curious about the techniques involved
    B   enthusiastic about taking it up
    C   concerned about how hard it is

4   You hear two people talking about a crime novel they both read called *Wide Eyes*.
    They agree that it was enjoyable because

    A   it showed how the human mind works.
    B   it maintained their interest throughout.
    C   it dealt well with the issue of justice.

5   You hear part of a podcast in which a woman is talking about approaches to time.
    What approach does she prefer for herself?

    A   being flexible
    B   being productive
    C   being in tune with nature

6   You hear part of an arts programme in which a man is talking about sculpture.
    What is the main reason he thinks stone is popular with artists?

    A   It is very hard to damage.
    B   It is naturally very beautiful.
    C   It is available in many different forms.

7   You hear a woman talking to a friend about her new electric bike.
    How does she feel about it?

    A   relieved that it is easy to maintain
    B   disappointed with how slow it is
    C   concerned about how safe it is

8   You hear two friends talking about reaching the age of 30.
    The man says that he felt

    A   less need to see his friends so often.
    B   less pressure to achieve his life goals.
    C   less desire to go out in search of fun.

Test 4   Listening Part 2

🎧 45) You will hear a man called Charlie Buckingham talking about working as a volunteer at an animal shelter, where animals that have been injured, or are not wanted, are cared for. For questions **9–18**, complete the sentences with a word or short phrase.

Volunteering at an animal shelter

Hearing that people who cannot pay for **(9)** .... for their animals often give them up made Charlie feel sad.

Charlie says **(10)** .... makes a big difference to how likely a dog is to be chosen by a visitor wanting to adopt one from the shelter.

Charlie was asked to do **(11)** .... as his first task when he started as a volunteer at the shelter.

Charlie was surprised to hear that volunteers are advised not to wear **(12)** .... for their work.

Charlie says that **(13)** .... may be the reason that cats are less popular with volunteers than dogs.

According to Charlie, what he calls **(14)** .... is harder than other things for volunteers to provide for the animals.

Charlie thinks that a dog's **(15)** .... is the best indicator of how happy it is.

Charlie says that **(16)** .... is the most appealing characteristic of the dog he would like to adopt.

Charlie says that, apart from money, **(17)** .... are the most regularly donated gifts that the shelter receives from people.

Charlie is pleased that his skills in **(18)** .... have been useful in his role as a volunteer at the animal shelter.

Test 4 — Listening Part 3

🎧 46 You will hear five short extracts in which people are talking about taking dance classes. For questions **19–23**, choose from the list (**A–H**) what each person says caused some difficulty for them. Use the letters only once. There are three extra letters which you do not need to use.

A making slow progress

B lacking a natural talent

Speaker 1 — **19**

C being at a lower level than others

Speaker 2 — **20**

D not being able to concentrate fully

Speaker 3 — **21**

E following instructions

Speaker 4 — **22**

F performing in front of others

G remembering things

Speaker 5 — **23**

H not being fit enough

Test 4 — Listening Part 4

🎧 47 You will hear an interview with a woman called Samantha Caine, who works as a professional food stylist preparing food and drinks for photography, television and advertising. For questions **24–30**, choose the best answer (**A**, **B** or **C**).

24 What reason does Samantha give for choosing to become a food stylist?

   A It enabled her to combine her greatest interests.
   B It offered her the kind of variety she was looking for.
   C It seemed a natural consequence of her previous training.

25 Samantha says that for one of her first assignments, she should have

   A ensured the food remained fresh-looking.
   B done research into the particular requirements.
   C given consideration to what set decoration to include.

26 What did Samantha appreciate about working on the TV drama series *Brookertown*?

   A being in an exciting environment
   B learning about the programme production process
   C seeing her food being enjoyed by the actors

27 What techniques does Samantha avoid as a food stylist?

   A adding food colouring to dishes
   B making food look tastier than it is
   C using ingredients that cannot be eaten

28 When talking about an advertisement for chocolates she worked on, Samantha says she felt

   A relieved to have created what the director wanted.
   B pleased about the unintended effect of some flowers.
   C delighted that sales of the product increased as a result.

29 Samantha thinks her success as a food stylist is due to her

   A desire to listen to others.
   B ability to produce original work.
   C willingness to work under pressure.

30 What does Samantha see as the most important thing for her future as a food stylist?

   A experimenting with a wide variety of food
   B connecting with creative people
   C staying updated on technology trends

Test 4 — Speaking Parts 1 and 2

Part 1 2 minutes (3 minutes for groups of three)

Interlocutor First, we'd like to know something about you.

Shopping

- Where do you like buying clothes from? (Why?)
- Do you ever buy things which are second hand? (Why? / Why not?)
- Is there anything special which you are hoping to buy soon? (What would you like to buy?)
- In the future, do you think you will buy more things online? (Why? / Why not?)
- Do you prefer saving money or spending money? (Why?)

Part 2 4 minutes (6 minutes for groups of three)

Interlocutor In this part of the test, I'm going to give each of you two photographs. I'd like you to talk about your photographs on your own for about a minute and also to answer a question about your partner's photographs.

(*Candidate A*), it's your turn first. Here are your photographs on page C14 of the Speaking appendix. They show **people in situations where speed is important**. I'd like you to compare the photographs and say **why you think speed is important for the people in these situations**.

All right?

Candidate A
1 minute ....

Interlocutor Thank you.

(*Candidate B*), **would you like to work in a professional kitchen? (Why? / Why not?)**

Candidate B
Approximately 30 seconds ....

Interlocutor Thank you.

Now (*Candidate B*), here are your photographs on page C15 of the Speaking appendix. They show **people starting to do things in different situations**.

I'd like you to compare the photographs and say **why the people have decided to start to do these things**.

All right?

Candidate B
1 minute ....

Interlocutor Thank you.

(*Candidate A*), **Do you enjoy running? (Why? / Why not?)**

Candidate A
Approximately 30 seconds ....

Interlocutor Thank you.

Test 4 — Speaking Parts 3 and 4

Part 3 4 minutes (5 minutes for groups of three)

Interlocutor Now, I'd like you to talk about something together for about two minutes.

Some people believe that the best way to learn a new skill is by teaching yourself, but other people disagree. Here are some of the things they think about and a question for you to discuss. First, you have some time to look at the task on page C16 of the Speaking appendix.

Now, talk to each other about **whether you think teaching yourself is the best way to learn a new skill.**

Candidates 2 minutes (3 minutes for groups of three)

Interlocutor Thank you. Now you have about a minute to decide **what the best reason is for <u>not</u> trying to teach yourself when you're learning a new skill.**

Candidates 1 minute (for pairs and groups of three)

Interlocutor Thank you.

Part 4 4 minutes (6 minutes for groups of three)

Interlocutor

- Do you think it is better to learn something new by listening or by doing? (Why?)
- Some people say a good teacher needs to be patient. Do you agree? (Why? / Why not?)
- Some people believe that students should be allowed to leave school at the age of 15 if they want to. Do you think this is a good idea? (Why? / Why not?)
- Some people like to always be learning something new. Why do you think this is?
- Is it better to learn a new language when you are very young or when you are older? (Why?)
- Some companies offer employees the chance to do training courses. How important do you think this is? (Why?)

Thank you. That is the end of the test.

> **What do you think?**
> **Do you agree?**
> **And you?**

Test 5 — Reading and Use of English Part 1

For questions **1–8**, read the text below and decide which answer (**A, B, C** or **D**) best fits each gap. There is an example at the beginning (**0**).

Mark your answers **on the separate answer sheet**.

Example:

| 0 | **A** calls | **B** attracts | **C** invites | **D** appeals |

```
0  A  B  C  D
   ☐  ■  ☐  ☐
```

Stonehenge and Seahenge

Thought to be between 3,500 and 5,000 years old, Stonehenge **(0)** .... around 1.5 million visitors a year. Yet the purpose of this circle of giant stones in southwest England **(1)** .... a mystery. How it was made is also a matter for **(2)** .... – theories about how the 25-ton stones were transported to the area over great distances are many and **(3)** ....

Stonehenge was not the only circular 'henge' monument built in ancient Britain, **(4)** .... Another was Seahenge, a circle of oak columns made 4,000 years ago and rediscovered on an English beach in 1998. It is believed that like Stonehenge, Seahenge was **(5)** .... to be in a specific position in **(6)** .... to the sun on certain days every year. This is thought to have been extremely **(7)** .... in the lives and beliefs of ancient societies. In particular, sunrise on the longest day of the year and sunset on the shortest day were **(8)** .... dates for ancient farmers.

1	**A** continues	**B** stays	**C** remains	**D** keeps
2	**A** debate	**B** question	**C** doubt	**D** wonder
3	**A** varied	**B** wide	**C** mixed	**D** broad
4	**A** besides	**B** meanwhile	**C** indeed	**D** though
5	**A** measured	**B** designed	**C** prepared	**D** controlled
6	**A** reference	**B** connection	**C** comparison	**D** relation
7	**A** major	**B** significant	**C** principal	**D** essential
8	**A** key	**B** main	**C** great	**D** chief

Reading and Use of English Part 2

For questions **9–16**, read the text below and think of the word which best fits each gap. Use only one word in each gap. There is an example at the beginning (**0**).

Write your answers **IN CAPITAL LETTERS** on the separate answer sheet.

Example: **0** O F

Apps for creativity

Nowadays, there are apps for nearly anything you can think **(0)** .... So it should come as **(9)** .... surprise that if you're interested in giving your creativity **(10)** .... boost, there are apps for that, too.

Some of these apps use sound to stimulate your imagination. **(11)** .... instance, you may hear a sequence of sounds that inspires you to make up a story to go with it. Others send you a short text or image every morning which aims to wake up your brain and give you new things **(12)** .... think about.

Many puzzle apps can help your brain to think **(13)** .... different ways, potentially unlocking creative solutions to problems you **(14)** .... been struggling with for a while. And there are apps that help you organise your ideas, with tools **(15)** .... as mind maps.

And last **(16)** .... not least, there are all the apps that encourage you to doodle or draw something – another way of unlocking your brain power!

Test 5 — Reading and Use of English Part 3

For questions **17–24**, read the text below. Use the word given in capitals at the end of some of the lines to form a word that fits in the gap **in the same line**. There is an example at the beginning (**0**).

Write your answers **IN CAPITAL LETTERS on the separate answer sheet**.

Example: 0 V A R I O U S

Mary Anderson

Mary Anderson (1866–1953) was a US businesswoman who worked in (0) .... different fields throughout her life. She made a major (17) .... to transport history by inventing the (18) .... version of a windscreen wiper.

VARY
CONTRIBUTE
ORIGIN

Anderson was in a streetcar – or tram – in 1902 when she observed that the driver kept the windscreen open, even though the weather was (19) .... That was because it was too hard to keep the windscreen clear of snow and thus keep the road ahead (20) .... while the streetcar was moving. Anderson thought of a solution to this problem and employed a (21) .... to prepare a drawing of a hand-operated system that could be used from inside the vehicle.

FREEZE
VISION
DESIGN

Similar devices had previously been created by others, but Anderson's version proved to be the first one that actually worked. Her (22) .... design has, of course, now been (23) .... by more modern ones, but the basic idea remains the same and her concept made driving (24) .... safer.

EFFECT
PLACE
CONSIDER

Test 5 — Reading and Use of English Part 4

For questions **25–30**, complete the second sentence so that it has a similar meaning to the first sentence, using the word given. **Do not change the word given**. You must use between **two** and **five** words, including the word given. Here is an example (**0**).

Example:

0   It's over five days since Sam's last message.

   TOUCH

   Sam hasn't .... least five days.

The gap can be filled by the words 'been in touch for at', so you write:

Example: | **0** | BEEN IN TOUCH FOR AT |

Write **only** the missing words **IN CAPITAL LETTERS on the separate answer sheet**.

---

25   I'll lend you some money, but you must give it back to me soon!

   PAY

   I'll lend you some money as .... me back soon!

26   People all over the world have listened to this song.

   HEARD

   This song .... people all over the world.

27   'Tidy your room, it's a mess!' Steve said to his son.

   CLEAR

   Steve told his .... mess in his room.

28   Sal didn't bring the right kind of clothes for yesterday's wet weather.

   UNSUITABLE

   The clothes that Sal .... for yesterday's wet weather.

29   My cousin thinks it is wrong to play loud music in public places.

   APPROVE

   My cousin doesn't .... played in public places.

30   The very first thing I noticed about the restaurant was how quiet it was.

   STRUCK

   What .... all about the restaurant was how quiet it was.

Making decisions

Our reporter talks to two experts on decision-making

Psychology professor Laurence Alison has specialised in how to make decisions, but in the early days of his career, he focused on the theory, rather than the practical aspects. Now he and his colleague, Neil Shortland, have written a book based on the findings of academic and theoretical decision-making research, making it understandable to the general public. He hopes this will help them make decisions in their everyday lives. Alison says that in normal life, perhaps 1% of the decisions we make are actually life-changing, such as whether to change career or start a family. 'The problem,' he says, 'is that many people are terrified of these decisions. They believe they're bad at making critical choices. You hear them saying things like, "I just wish someone would tell me what I ought to do.".'

In fact, the good news at the heart of the book is that there's almost always a decision that's uniquely right for you – so it's usually best to make your own decisions. It's a question of keeping in mind your personal values and concentrating not on the process, but on the end goal, according to Alison. He says that people worry about making the decision, when what they ought to be doing is thinking ahead and asking themselves what they really want to achieve. Shortland agrees: 'People fail to focus clearly on what matters to them. They see that an option is appealing in one sense, but they don't think about what they need to give up to get it.'

For Alison and Shortland, accepting that there will be regrets is essential for effective decision-making. Fear of regretting a decision later prevents some people from being able to make any decision at all. That's part of why they both believe the biggest danger around decisions isn't doing the wrong thing, it's doing nothing. Alison says that because these big decisions are unusual events in people's lives, they don't have much to compare them to and they lack the skills required. So, people try to keep risk to a minimum and leave things as they are.

Alison and Shortland agree that some personality types find it easier than others to make decisions: they talk a lot about so-called 'maximisers' (who aim for perfection) versus 'satisficers', who will accept something that's 'good enough' and are therefore more effective decision-makers. The problem for the former is that waiting for everything to be perfect might mean missing an opportunity, and also real life is rarely, if ever, perfect. At the heart of good decision-making is the knowledge that in going for one option, you have to give up on other possibilities. The cooler you can be about letting them go, the more efficient your decision-making will become.

So how good are Alison and Shortland at making their own decisions? Shortland says he was recently offered a new job and had to decide whether to go for it or not. He says he had to think very deeply about what he really wanted and that he spent five days making his choice. He does not regard this as a weakness: he says that honesty and knowing what one is really like as a person are what matters and that takes time. Alison says he still has to think about decisions for some time, and some decisions are certainly more difficult than others. 'My stumbling block is sometimes reacting too quickly – not taking notice of my own advice to work out whether or not I need to act at this precise moment or if I can wait a while.' At the moment, they're considering the use of artificial intelligence. AI can play chess, it can spot patterns and warn us about things. But can it tell us which decisions to take right now? Alison and Shortland are looking at the pros and cons. 'This is the hot topic right now and we're in the thick of it,' says Shortland.

line 60

31 What is suggested about Professor Alison in the first paragraph?

  A He is keen to pass on what he has learned.
  B He has changed his attitude towards his subject.
  C He thinks most people are unable to make good decisions.
  D He knows more about abstract ideas than other psychologists.

32 What do Alison and Shortland both say about decision-making in the second paragraph?

  A People often avoid doing it if at all possible.
  B People do not always approach it in the right way.
  C People often end up replacing one problem with another.
  D People are not always willing to take responsibility for themselves.

33 What is said about the link between regrets and decision-making?

  A Regretting poor decisions is essential to learning to make better ones.
  B Doing nothing is better than making decisions and regretting them later.
  C Concern about future regrets can lead to not managing to take decisions.
  D Regrets about past mistakes can limit the ability to take correct decisions.

34 What do Alison and Shortland think about personality types?

  A One type is more successful at decision-making than the other.
  B People prepared to accept bad decisions are making a mistake.
  C Both types can become more effective at making good decisions.
  D People who want things to be perfect make decisions more rapidly.

35 How does Shortland feel about his own decision-making abilities?

  A relieved that they are rarely required
  B determined to show off his knowledge
  C confident that he knows what he is doing
  D embarrassed that they were once quite poor

36 What does Alison mean by the phrase 'my stumbling block' in line 60?

  A an issue he ignores
  B the thing he often forgets
  C what he is afraid of doing
  D something he does badly

Test 5 — Reading and Use of English Part 6

You are going to read an article about buildings in places where it can be very hot. Six sentences have been removed from the article. Choose from the sentences **A–G** the one which best fits each gap (**37–42**). There is one extra sentence which you do not need to use.

Mark your answers **on the separate answer sheet**.

Cool buildings in 40°C heat

If architects are people who like challenges, building schools in Burkina Faso must be a dream job. How can they be kept cool under a baking sun without air conditioning? Temperatures in this part of the world are usually about 40 °C during the hottest season.

Architect Diébédo Francis Kéré grew up in the small village of Gando and knows the challenges well. He and other architects such as Albert Faus are finding brilliant ways to design schools and orphanages – places where children can live if they have no parents or their parents can't care for them – in Burkina Faso, using local materials. **37**   Kéré has spoken movingly in the past about the support he was given as a child by the whole community, with everyone giving money towards his education. 'The reason I do what I do is my community,' he said.

Gando Primary School, built in 2001, was Kéré's first construction after completing his studies. He said that at first, his community didn't understand why he wanted to build with clay – thick, heavy soil that can be made into bricks – when modern buildings were made of glass in other parts of the world. **38**   Men and women then came together to build the school, combining traditional techniques, such as beating clay floors by hand until they are smooth, with more modern technology – in order to seek better comfort.

The Noomdo orphanage was another of his projects. 'The Kéré building provides us with good thermal comfort because when it's hot, we're cool and when it's cold, we're warm inside,' says Pierre Sanou, a social educator at the orphanage. 'We don't need air conditioning, which is an incredible energy saving.' Kéré's buildings use very little concrete. That isn't just because it needs to be transported to the site. **39**   The buildings have very strong walls and very light roofs, so the cool air that enters from below pushes the hot air out from above. The roof at Noomdo is high and curved, with openings at the sides.

Nearby, the Bangre Veenem school complex designed by Faus uses similarly clever ways to cool the building. The complex includes everything from nursery to high school, as well as a professional school. Staff say students are comfortable and can concentrate on their classes. **40**

Faus also kept the transport of materials to a minimum and used the region's own materials and resources. The school is built using laterite, a material native to the area. **41**   'It's a very beautiful material. When families see the buildings, they want their children to go to school,' says Ousmane Soura, an education adviser at the school. Some teenagers even meet inside the classrooms to talk after class or during vacation periods.

'Students can come at night to study and charge their phones,' Soura says. **42**   'Students are more focused because we have a good temperature in class. If the students, the administration and teachers work well, and the environment is favourable in class, the results will be better.'

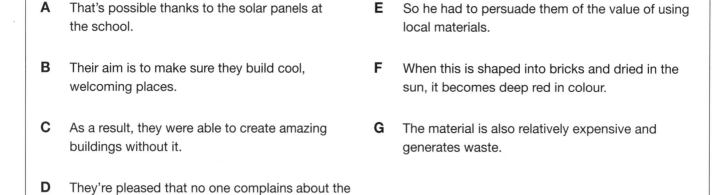

A That's possible thanks to the solar panels at the school.

B Their aim is to make sure they build cool, welcoming places.

C As a result, they were able to create amazing buildings without it.

D They're pleased that no one complains about the heat and wants to go home.

E So he had to persuade them of the value of using local materials.

F When this is shaped into bricks and dried in the sun, it becomes deep red in colour.

G The material is also relatively expensive and generates waste.

Test 5 — Reading and Use of English Part 7

You are going to read an article about four people who went on a train trip together. For questions **43–52**, choose from the people (**A–D**). The people may be chosen more than once.

Which person

refused to accompany their friends sometimes?	43
was tempted to do something selfish?	44
respected someone's need for privacy?	45
accepted some criticism they received?	46
disapproved of someone's attitude?	47
followed some advice they were given?	48
admired someone's courage?	49
denied borrowing something important?	50
tolerated some irritating behaviour?	51
doubted that someone was being honest?	52

Our train trip!

Four young people talk about a two-week holiday they went on together.

A Chen

Four of us went on a two-week train trip together, mainly staying in hostels, but sometimes sleeping on the train. The others were always borrowing my phone charger, which was a bit of a pain – I don't know why they did this because we'd each brought one. I just put up with it, though, and there were times when I needed something of theirs myself, so it kind of worked out, I suppose. We shared all our food and that worked OK – though once I bought a really nice chocolate bar that was quite expensive, and it did cross my mind to go off on my own for a bit and eat it all myself, but I didn't in the end. We saw some amazing places and although I've got loads of photos, I'm glad I kept a diary as well – that was my sister's idea – I'm sure I'll enjoy looking back through it!

B Sefa

The others are crazy about street art and wanted to photograph as much of it as possible wherever we went. It was a way of seeing places we might not have otherwise, but every once in a while, I insisted on doing something alone instead, despite their protests. Overall, it was a great experience, though it goes without saying there were moments when things were a little awkward. Like the time someone couldn't find their phone charger and said I must have used it and that I'd left it behind at the hostel that morning. I said I hadn't and the charger eventually turned up in its owner's backpack, so it all ended well. In general, though, I thought that person should have been more willing to let other people use their stuff – it seemed a little mean. But none of us ever fell out badly, so that was OK.

C Robin

The trip was fantastic and you do learn loads about people by doing something like that together – not all of it positive! We all had the same type of phone charger – I'd actually put my initials on mine to avoid any confusion. But there was one person who kept on using mine anyway and even left it in a hostel once – at least, they said they hadn't, but then insisted on disappearing for a while and I'm sure they'd gone back to get it. It appeared in my backpack later, anyway. And I can't say I'd never do the same kind of thing myself. Only one of us kept a diary. I'd have loved to have been able to take a quick look at it, but everyone has the right to keep some thoughts to themselves! Anyway, we were all still good friends by the end of the trip.

D Bo

We're all very different characters, but we got on really well – at least most of the time. We went most places together, but there was one person who liked going off for walks alone from time to time. I thought that was cool because I'd hesitate to do that in a place I'd never been to before, even with my phone to guide me – I'd be too concerned I might get lost. I love taking photos and sometimes the others had to hang around while I tried to get exactly the right shot. Not everyone was happy about that and in the end, they let me know about it. I had to admit they had a point and tried to speed up a bit after that. There were a few issues with stuff like disappearing phone chargers, but nothing serious. I hope we can go away together again next year!

Test 5 — Writing Part 1

You **must** answer this question. Write your answer in **140–190** words in an appropriate style on the separate answer sheet.

1. In your English class you have been talking about health and using screens. Now, your English teacher has asked you to write an essay.

   Write your essay using **all** the notes and giving reasons for your point of view.

   Should everyone have one day a week when they do not look at screens?

   Notes

   Write about:

   1. interruptions to work or study
   2. sleep
   3. ………………………… (your own idea)

Test 5 Writing Part 2

Write an answer to **one** of the questions **2–4** in this part. Write your answer in **140–190** words in an appropriate style on the separate answer sheet. Put the question number in the box at the top of the answer sheet.

2 You have received this email from your English-speaking friend, Li.

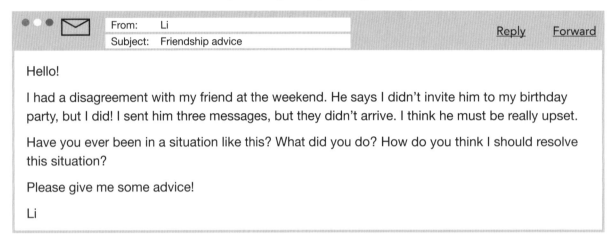

From: Li
Subject: Friendship advice

Hello!

I had a disagreement with my friend at the weekend. He says I didn't invite him to my birthday party, but I did! I sent him three messages, but they didn't arrive. I think he must be really upset.

Have you ever been in a situation like this? What did you do? How do you think I should resolve this situation?

Please give me some advice!

Li

Write your **email**.

3 You see this announcement on an English-language website.

Reviews wanted

Product review

Have you used a new product such as a sports drink or shampoo recently?
What do you like or dislike about the product? What would make it better?
Write us a review of the product and tell us whether you would recommend it to other people.

We will publish the best reviews next month.

Write your **review**.

4 You see this announcement in an English-language magazine.

Articles wanted

An activity that makes me happy

Tell us about an activity you do in your free time that you enjoy. Why does it make you happy? Why is it important for people to have interests outside college or work?

The best articles will be published in our magazine.

Write your **article**.

Test 5 — Listening Part 1

🎧 52 You will hear people talking in eight different situations. For questions **1–8**, choose the best answer (**A, B** or **C**).

1. You hear two friends talking about following the news.
   What does the man say about positive news stories?

   A They tend to be about subjects that are unimportant.
   B They reduce the stress of hearing about depressing events.
   C They help provide a more realistic picture of the world.

2. You hear a podcaster talking about people whose work involves getting paid to sleep.
   What is the podcaster doing?

   A explaining why she was surprised to find out they exist
   B outlining the responsibilities that they have
   C arguing that they have special skills

3. You hear two friends talking about 'binge-watching', watching many episodes of a TV series in one session.
   They agree that

   A there are very few TV programmes they find exciting.
   B watching TV has negative effects on how they sleep.
   C TV programmes are designed to make people keep watching.

4. You hear part of an interview with a footballer.
   How does she feel after hearing there will be very cold weather?

   A unsure how it will affect how she plays
   B worried that matches might be cancelled
   C determined to avoid getting injured

5. You hear two friends talking about a historical novel they both read.
   What do they disagree about?

   A how accurately historical events were described
   B how useful it was for learning about historical events
   C how entertaining the author's writing about historical events was

6. You hear a woman talking about some research she did on being bilingual, growing up speaking two different languages.
   Her aim was to understand how being bilingual

   A affects opinions and attitudes.
   B improves problem-solving abilities.
   C varies depending on surroundings.

7. You hear two friends talking about how they make decisions.
   What do they both find helpful?

   A making time for quiet thinking
   B writing down their options
   C talking to someone they trust

8. You hear an expert talking about education for adults.
   What is he doing?

   A explaining why some lack motivation
   B identifying factors that need to be dealt with
   C considering whether it benefits wider society

Test 5 — Listening Part 2

🎧 53 You will hear a young woman called Polly Smart giving a talk about her experiences as a coach at a summer sports camp for children. For questions **9–18**, complete the sentences with a word or short phrase.

Being a coach at a summer sports camp for children

Polly says that her desire to develop her **(9)** .... was her main motivation for applying to be a coach.

Polly was very impressed by the **(10)** .... on her arrival at the camp.

Polly says that the term '**(11)** ....' was used for what new coaches did on their first day.

Polly enjoyed working with other coaches to think of so-called **(12)** .... games for newly arrived children.

Polly says that **(13)** .... was the sport she felt most nervous about teaching.

Polly appreciated the fact that her sleeping accommodation was close to the **(14)** ....

Polly says that on many occasions she was grateful for the thorough training in **(15)** .... that she'd received.

In the evenings, Polly discovered that the **(16)** .... were more enjoyable than she'd expected.

Polly was surprised at how emotional she felt during the **(17)** .... at the closing ceremony on the last day.

Polly says that she'll remember being at the camp as a time of real **(18)** .... for her personally.

Test 5 — Listening Part 3

🎧 54 You will hear five short extracts in which people are talking about a temporary job they did working as a waiter in a restaurant. For questions **19–23**, choose from the list (**A–H**) how each person says they felt while working as a waiter. Use the letters only once. There are three extra letters which you do not need to use.

A I was pleased to have a nice manager.

B I found it enjoyable to meet lots of people.   Speaker 1 | 19 |

C I was glad that I had to wear a uniform.   Speaker 2 | 20 |

D I was relieved not to find it boring.   Speaker 3 | 21 |

E I appreciated saving money on food.   Speaker 4 | 22 |

F I was proud of making very few mistakes.

G I didn't mind being told what to do.   Speaker 5 | 23 |

H I was surprised how fit it made me.

Test 5   Listening Part 4

🎧 55 You will hear an interview with a man called Darren Mason, who runs a creative writing site called Lineweavers on the internet. For questions **24–30**, choose the best answer (**A**, **B** or **C**).

24 Darren says that he and the other writers who contribute to his site all share

    A a high level of creative energy.
    B an interest in good literature.
    C a desire to make writing a career.

25 Darren's initial purpose for posting his own writing on the site was

    A to find out what people think of it.
    B to challenge himself to take risks.
    C to make himself finish things.

26 What aspect of the site gives Darren most pleasure?

    A the variety of writers who contribute to it
    B the quality of the writing published on it
    C the assistance it gives to newer writers

27 When talking about the poem *Nights like this* that he posted on the site, Darren says he was unsure

    A what inspired him to write it.
    B what some of it really meant.
    C what reaction people would have to it.

28 How does Darren feel about getting critical feedback on his own creative writing?

    A dissatisfied when it is very brief
    B irritated by negative comments
    C determined to learn something from it

29 What does Darren say is the biggest difficulty running the Lineweavers site?

    A having to reject some contributions
    B keeping up to date with technology
    C balancing his other commitments

30 What is the main thing Darren has learned about people from running the site?

    A Their personal experiences can influence what they prefer.
    B There is no limit to what they can find interesting.
    C They can argue about almost anything.

Test 5 — Speaking Parts 1 and 2

Part 1 — 🎧 56 2 minutes (3 minutes for groups of three)

Interlocutor First, we'd like to know something about you.

Home and away
- Would you like to live in another country? (Why? / Why not?)
- Have you ever been on a really long journey? (Where did you go?)
- Tell us something about the area where you grew up.
- What do you think about the place where you live now? (Why?)
- In the future, would you like to live somewhere new or stay where you are now? (Why?)

Part 2 — 🎧 57 4 minutes (6 minutes for groups of three)

Interlocutor In this part of the test, I'm going to give each of you two photographs. I'd like you to talk about your photographs on your own for about a minute and also to answer a question about your partner's photographs.

(*Candidate A*), it's your turn first. Here are your photographs on page C17 of the Speaking appendix. They show **people who are teaching in different situations**. I'd like you to compare the photographs and say **what you think might be difficult about teaching in these situations**.

All right?

Candidate A
⏱ *1 minute* ....

Interlocutor Thank you.

(*Candidate B*), **do you enjoy learning practical skills like sewing? (Why? / Why not?)**

Candidate B
⏱ *Approximately 30 seconds* ....

Interlocutor Thank you.

Now, (*Candidate B*), here are your photographs on page C18 of the Speaking appendix. They show **people on boats in different situations**. I'd like you to compare the photographs and say **why you think the people have decided to spend time on a boat in these situations**.

All right?

Candidate B
⏱ *1 minute* ....

Interlocutor Thank you.

(*Candidate A*), **would you like to go on a trip on a sailing boat? (Why? / Why not?)**

Candidate A
⏱ *Approximately 30 seconds* ....

Interlocutor Thank you.

Test 5 — Speaking Parts 3 and 4

Part 3 4 minutes (5 minutes for groups of three)

Interlocutor Now, I'd like you to talk about something together for about two minutes.

Some people believe that it is better to work alone and other people think it is better to work as part of a group. Here are some of the things they think about and a question for you to discuss. First, you have some time to look at the task on page C19 of the Speaking appendix.

Now, talk to each other about **whether it is better to work alone or as part of a group**.

Candidates 2 minutes (3 minutes for groups of three)

Interlocutor Thank you. Now, you have about a minute to decide **what the best reason is for working as part of a group**.

Candidates 1 minute (for pairs and groups of three)

Interlocutor Thank you.

Part 4 4 minutes (6 minutes for groups of three)

Interlocutor

- Is it easier to work with people you know well or with strangers? (Why?)
- Do you think that it is important to choose a leader for all group work? (Why? / Why not?)
- Do you think it is important for work to be enjoyable or are results all that matter? (Why?)
- Some companies reward workers for getting good results at work. Do you think this is a good idea? (Why? / Why not?)
- Some people prefer to concentrate on work for a long time and other people like taking regular breaks. Which do you think is better? (Why?)
- Is it important to specialise in one area of work or to get experience in a variety of different fields? (Why?)

Thank you. That is the end of the test.

> What do you think?
> Do you agree?
> And you?

Test 6 — Reading and Use of English Part 1

For questions **1–8**, read the text below and decide which answer (**A**, **B**, **C** or **D**) best fits each gap. There is an example at the beginning (**0**).

Mark your answers **on the separate answer sheet**.

Example:

| 0 | **A** point | **B** factor | **C** piece | **D** feature |

0 A ▫ B ▫ C ▫ D ▬

Why some people dislike vegetables

It's an unfortunate (0) .... of evolution that vegetables are so good for us, but aren't immediately tasty to all of us. Humans adapted over thousands of years to enjoy the taste of higher-energy foods because the most immediate risk was not eating enough, rather than (1) .... to long-term health. Vegetables aren't particularly high-energy, but they're (2) .... with healthy substances, including some called 'bioactives'.

Bioactives are part of the (3) .... vegetables taste bitter. Humans developed a dislike of bitter tastes to protect themselves from poisons and possibly as protection from over-eating one (4) .... plant food. So in a (5) .... , plant foods can taste like poison.

For some people, this bitter taste is particularly strong, while others (6) .... notice it. However, if you're in the former category, the good (7) .... is that we can all train ourselves to enjoy vegetables. If we (8) .... including them in our diet, our brain gradually learns that they aren't poisonous and they actually start to taste less bitter.

1	**A** trouble	**B** harm	**C** suffering	**D** ruin
2	**A** packed	**B** complete	**C** full	**D** crowded
3	**A** explanation	**B** motive	**C** reason	**D** cause
4	**A** single	**B** alone	**C** absolute	**D** only
5	**A** manner	**B** truth	**C** fact	**D** way
6	**A** barely	**B** fairly	**C** slightly	**D** virtually
7	**A** idea	**B** news	**C** side	**D** thought
8	**A** ensure	**B** stay	**C** recall	**D** keep

Test 6 — Reading and Use of English Part 2

For questions **9–16**, read the text below and think of the word which best fits each gap. Use only one word in each gap. There is an example at the beginning (**0**).

Write your answers **IN CAPITAL LETTERS on the separate answer sheet**.

Example: **0** A S

Impressionism

The term 'Impressionist' was first used (0) .... an insult in response to an exhibition of new paintings in Paris in 1874 by a diverse group of painters which included Monet, Renoir, Pissarro and Degas.

Modern life and ordinary people having (9) .... good time were popular subjects with many Impressionists. They painted theatres, cafés and popular countryside resorts. Traditionally in French painting, poorer people (10) .... rarely been shown as individuals or people (11) .... should be taken seriously.

Even (12) .... significant to the Impressionists was an interest (13) .... how the human mind processes what it sees. When we look at a landscape or a crowd of people, we do (14) .... instantly see every face or leaf in detail, but as a mass of colour and light. Impressionists tried to express this experience in their paintings.

Today, Impressionist paintings are (15) .... of the best known and best loved in the world. It can be hard to imagine (16) .... revolutionary the movement was once considered.

Test 6 — Reading and Use of English Part 3

For questions **17–24**, read the text below. Use the word given in capitals at the end of some of the lines to form a word that fits in the gap **in the same line**. There is an example at the beginning (**0**).

Write your answers **IN CAPITAL LETTERS on the separate answer sheet**.

Example: `0` `INEXPENSIVE`

Stand-up paddleboarding

Paddleboarding is a relatively (**0**) .... watersport in which a person stands or kneels on a board and uses a paddle – like a canoe paddle, but longer – to move themselves forwards. Modern stand-up paddleboarding is (**17**) .... from Hawaii and was adopted by west-coast American (**18**) .... in the early 2000s. It has been growing in (**19**) .... ever since.

EXPENSE

ORIGIN
SURF
POPULAR

Unlike surfing, which requires waves, it is suitable for people who want to explore coastlines or rivers. Many of the more (**20**) .... priced paddleboards can be filled with air at the water's edge, making them easy to transport.

REASONABLE

Some paddleboards are longer than others, (**21**) .... on how fast people want to go, their (**22**) .... and where they want to paddleboard. The boards also vary in (**23**) ....

DEPEND
HIGH
WIDE

There are places where you're allowed to go along certain waterways, but it's (**24**) .... to go along others. So, if you decide to go paddleboarding and don't want to get into trouble, always check before you set off!

LEGAL

Test 6 — Reading and Use of English Part 4

For questions **25–30**, complete the second sentence so that it has a similar meaning to the first sentence, using the word given. **Do not change the word given.** You must use between **two** and **five** words, including the word given. Here is an example (**0**).

Example:

0 It's over five days since Sam's last message.

TOUCH

Sam hasn't .... least five days.

The gap can be filled by the words 'been in touch for at', so you write:

Example: | **0** | BEEN IN TOUCH FOR AT |

Write **only** the missing words **IN CAPITAL LETTERS on the separate answer sheet**.

---

25 Yalen said that if we didn't leave immediately, we'd miss the train.

UNLESS

Yalen said that we wouldn't catch .... off immediately.

26 Before we went on the camping trip, the organisers made sure we had all the necessary information about the area.

EVERYTHING

The organisers told .... know about the area before we went on the camping trip.

27 I always try not to get angry with my sister, but I don't always manage it!

HELP

Sometimes I just .... my temper with my sister!

28 I made a suggestion for improving the college website and almost everyone agreed.

DISAGREED

Hardly .... my suggestion for improving the college website.

29 The scientists thought that some of the results of the experiment might not be accurate.

ACCURACY

The scientists .... some of the results of the experiment.

30 'Can I save enough money to buy a motorbike?' I wondered.

ABLE

I wondered whether I would .... aside enough money to buy a motorbike.

Test 6 — Reading and Use of English Part 5

You are going to read an article about a woman who decided to move home frequently instead of living permanently in one place. For questions **31–36**, choose the answer (**A, B, C** or **D**) which you think fits best according to the text.

Mark your answers **on the separate answer sheet**.

My life as an urban nomad

I'm typing this at a very lovely handmade desk in a small one-bedroom flat in London. The cosy apartment's dark wooden floorboards are covered with thick Bhutanese rugs. Bedroom bookshelves are full of fascinating travel guides and books on the benefits of cold-water swimming. This feel-good flat has been the ideal place for me to spend the winter, somewhere I felt immediately at home when I moved in three months ago. But by the spring, I'll be living somewhere entirely different, perhaps in a new city, maybe even a new country. These are the exciting unknowns in my nomadic – or wandering – life.

Three years ago, I quit having a fixed place to live in, leaving my home for various locations across the UK and other countries. The notes in my phone reveal that, to date, I've slept in 117 beds, in locations ranging from the Scottish Highlands and coastal Dorset to Armenia's capital, Yerevan, and the Georgian capital, Tbilisi, all while
line 18 successfully holding down a full-time job as a travel writer.

But for most of that time, I've stayed in London, the city I've called home since moving here 19 years ago as a shy yet eager student. Fast-forward to today and my nomadic lifestyle has allowed me to live in several inner-London boroughs over the last 36 months, granting my curious nature permission to run wild. I've seen more of London in the past three years than in the previous ten combined, simply because I've been able to get to know local people's most popular spots, discover streets I've never seen before, as well as some of the best restaurants that non-residents might usually miss. Knowing I'll only be in a certain area for a limited time forces me to really make the most of it.

Mostly, I find my short-term accommodation through friends of friends. Sometimes I've checked in to a hotel and I've also experimented with pet-sitting – staying in people's homes while they're away to look after their pets. And amazingly, I've not once found myself without a place to live. My last permanent home was a wonderfully light-filled flat I rented, with great neighbours, mere footsteps from East London's leafy Victoria Park. It made taking the initial step into nomadism the hardest.

I began by selling off items I knew I wouldn't need and, as a lifelong furnished renter, I didn't have many of the possessions most people collect over the years. I've never owned a bed, for instance, and the same goes for sofas and other large items of furniture. Books rapidly got reduced to just the few I knew I'd read again. Clothing was donated to the local charity shop. I've never been the kind of person who wants to keep things forever, so it was fairly simple to squeeze everything I owned into just a few boxes. Filled with personal souvenirs, photographs, letters, kitchen essentials and a few pairs of particularly special shoes, I put the packages that made up my life into a friend's garage, where they've remained ever since.

Living nomadically, mostly out of a 65-litre backpack, I've become deeply aware of just how much 'stuff' we collect, but don't need. Everywhere – on TV, online, on posters, on the sides of buses – we're exposed to messages encouraging us to buy the latest devices, kitchen appliances, home furnishings, newest fashion trends and miracle beauty products. I'm convinced it's a trap. The endless cycle of wanting to buy things, but having to be cash-rich and time-poor in order to buy them, doesn't feel like living well. I've realised I don't want to spend weekends painting bedroom walls or buying coffee machines and pizza ovens. And so I borrow those items instead. Perhaps it won't work forever. Maybe I'll start to dream of a place of my own. But for now, this is the perfect lifestyle for me.

31 In the first paragraph, the writer highlights

   A how determined she is to have fun.
   B how confusing her life can often be.
   C how delightful her current home is.
   D how keen she is to move elsewhere.

32 What does 'holding down' in line 18 mean?

   A searching for
   B keeping on doing
   C having a break from
   D avoiding focusing on

33 What does the writer say about the places where she has lived in London recently?

   A She chooses them by talking to people who already know them well.
   B She would not explore them so thoroughly if she were there for longer.
   C She was not brave enough to visit them when she first arrived in London.
   D She has discovered new aspects of her personality through spending time in them.

34 What does the writer suggest in the fourth paragraph?

   A It is a pity she was unable to keep on renting one particular flat.
   B Taking care of animals is not something she would ever try again.
   C She has frequently felt concerned she might have nowhere to stay.
   D There was a time when she was almost tempted to change her plans.

35 How did the writer feel about getting rid of her things?

   A It was no problem for her at all.
   B It was not as hard as she expected.
   C It showed her what she valued most.
   D It became easier for her after a while.

36 What opinion does the writer express in the final paragraph?

   A People who lack interest in owning things are very unusual.
   B We should avoid buying new things if we can possibly help it.
   C Wanting to acquire more and more things is a sign of weakness.
   D Being able to afford anything we want may not be a worthwhile goal.

Reading and Use of English Part 6

You are going to read an article in which a psychologist explains why we laugh at certain situations. Six sentences have been removed from the article. Choose from the sentences **A–G** the one which best fits each gap (**37–42**). There is one extra sentence which you do not need to use.

Mark your answers **on the separate answer sheet**.

Why do we laugh when someone trips?

Who among us has never laughed out loud when a friend trips on the pavement or misses a step on the stairs? People being clumsy, losing balance, falling — it's there in comedy films, in online video clips. We laugh and laugh, often unable to stop ourselves.

37 They are, after all, in a difficult situation. Don't worry; our laughter is not the result of a lack of kindness. As a clinical psychologist who specialises in the field of emotion regulation, I'd like to explain some of the different aspects of these situations which have the potential to generate our usually well-meaning laughter.

The first of these ingredients is surprise; more specifically, seeing a person surprised by a situation in everyday life, when it seemed like they had everything under control only a few seconds earlier. This odd situation highlights our errors of prediction: we predicted that what followed X would be Y, but then the events developed in an unexpected way, via B. We made a mistake in our prediction of what would happen. It's no longer logical. **38** In other words, we create a new, more logical, comic explanation for what we witnessed.

Faced with a surprising and odd situation, our brain searches for information that allows us to explain what's happening and to react accordingly. What does the face of the person who trips communicate to us? **39** A research study explored this by asking participants to look at 210 images, each of which showed one of three types: faces looking puzzled; faces showing pain or anger; and people whose bodies were placed in awkward positions and whose face wasn't visible (e.g. the face was hidden by skis or the person's arm).

Twenty landscape images were added to the set of photos in the study. **40** Participants were asked to indicate how funny they thought each image was and their brain activity was recorded. The images with puzzled faces were regarded as funnier than those with faces showing pain or anger, and funnier than the images with bodies in ridiculous positions. The brain data also supported the idea of facial expression as a factor in how funny people found these bizarre situations.

So, when we see a look of confusion, surprise or astonishment on the face of a victim of their own clumsiness, this information creates a context that generates laughter. On the other hand, if we see pain or anger in the expression, we're touched by the suffering of the victim. **41** It seems that our brains can instantly analyse the context of unfortunate situations and recognise whether funny elements are present or not.

Finally, witnessing another person's unfortunate situation causes us to imagine ourselves in the same position and identify with what they're going through and what they must be feeling. This can make us feel uncomfortable, powerless and ashamed. **42** We're basically expressing our relief at not being the victim ourselves. So, let's forgive ourselves for laughing at comical situations involving other people's clumsiness! We aren't laughing at the other person's suffering; we're reacting to their surprise, to the strangeness of the situation and to their confused expression, having worked out that they're not actually really upset and haven't really hurt themselves.

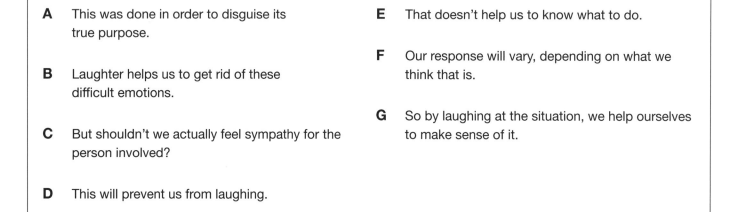

Test 6 — Reading and Use of English Part 7

You are going to read an article about a type of art called *kintsugi*. For questions **43–52**, choose from the sections (**A–D**). The sections may be chosen more than once.

In which section does the writer

tell the story behind a particular *kintsugi* piece?	43
show how highly people once valued certain objects?	44
describe the process and impact of looking at a *kintsugi* piece?	45
link the concept of *kintsugi* with a cultural view of things that are damaged?	46
give an example of the emotional impact of something precious being broken?	47
list various factors which make *kintsugi* pieces different from one another?	48
mention the personal impact that learning about *kintsugi* had on them?	49
say that *kintsugi* is relevant to groups of people as well as individuals?	50
suggest that the artists who now make *kintsugi* pieces are less specialised than the ones who made them in the past?	51
explain why a material was chosen?	52

Kintsugi
The Japanese artform based on the belief that a repaired pot can be stronger

A 'The world breaks everyone and afterward many are strong at the broken places,' wrote the American writer Ernest Hemingway. I found a way to understand this through the idea of *kintsugi* (*kin* = gold + *tsugi* = joining), the repair technique that puts a broken pot back together, but reveals the breaks and scars by highlighting them with gold. The broken object becomes something new, something that almost seems to say out loud, 'I was broken, but now, even though I am not perfect, I am more beautiful and stronger than ever'. *Kintsugi* restores function, adds beauty and tells a story. As our eyes follow the lines of destruction now filled with gold, every crack reveals its tale. This is *kintsugi's* greatest power: its story of loss and recovery, breaking and repair, tragedy and the ability to overcome it. A *kintsugi* repair speaks of strength, uniqueness and the beauty in survival, leading us to a respectful acceptance of loss and suffering.

B Where did the idea of *kintsugi* come from? Accepting breaks and repairs is part of a long-accepted Japanese artistic tradition that appreciates what is not perfect. Japan has the materials for *kintsugi*: ceramics, *urushi* (Japanese lacquer) and gold. However, it was the tea ceremony that was responsible for its development in the early 1600s. The tea ceremony was a high art form, and precious tea bowls were given as rewards for loyalty, often instead of land or money. If such precious objects were broken, they would have been repaired with great care, using the most expensive materials available. Until recently, *kintsugi* was only ever done by artists skilled in *maki-e*, or 'sprinkled pictures'. In this highly sophisticated craft, very beautiful and delicate images are created in powdered gold and silver on a black background.

C Every *kintsugi* piece is unique, based on the original object itself, the way it has broken, the skill and judgment of the artist and the materials used. The quality of the gold varies, so the repair can be delicate or bold, shiny or matt. Other powdered metals are used, such as silver, or none at all. One well-known example of silver *kintsugi* is the tea bowl by Raku Kichizaemon XV called *Nekowaride* (broken by a cat). This precious bowl was a critical piece for the famous potter. One day, when he left his workplace, he left his little dog behind. A cat came in from the street and Raku returned to find the panicked cat running around the walls. Trying to escape, it hit the bowl, which fell and broke into many pieces. Raku's wife collected them and had it repaired using silver, rather than gold, so the repair would age along with the pot.

D *Kintsugi* can be seen as part of the move towards more environmentally friendly living: repair, don't replace. Repairing our own ceramics in this way can encourage us to appreciate the objects we live with. And what if an object has a particular meaning? Perhaps you thought you would never forgive your friend for breaking your grandmother's teapot, the one she used whenever you visited. But repair it and it could become even more special. *Kintsugi* can be a healing act and applies to more than objects. If we recognise that we are all imperfect, the idea of repair could include acts of forgiveness, affection, acceptance or simply a warm hug. This is beneficial at a personal level, but *kintsugi* can also be applied at the community level. In fact, various organisations, such as those drawing attention to global climate change, have been using the idea to challenge our thinking.

Test 6 — Writing Part 1

You **must** answer this question. Write your answer in **140–190** words in an appropriate style on the separate answer sheet.

1. In your English class you have been talking about space exploration. Now, your English teacher has asked you to write an essay.

    Write your essay using **all** the notes and giving reasons for your point of view.

    > 'We should not spend money on space exploration. We need to focus on Earth first.'
    > Do you agree?

    Notes

    Write about:

    1. cost
    2. the future
    3. .... (your own idea)

Test 6   Writing Part 2

Write an answer to **one** of the questions **2–4** in this part. Write your answer in **140–190** words in an appropriate style on the separate answer sheet. Put the question number in the box at the top of the answer sheet.

2   You see this announcement in an English-language magazine.

> Articles wanted
>
> **A book that has changed the way you think**
>
> Tell us about a book you have read that changed the way you think.
> What was it about? How did it give you a new way of thinking?
> Is it important to read books that make us think in a different way?
>
> We will publish the best articles next month.

Write your **article**.

3   You have seen this advertisement online.

> **Holiday Camp Workers needed**
>
> Would you like to work at a holiday camp for children?
>
> We're looking for people who
>
> • have experience of working with young children
> • will enjoy running fun activities to do at the camp
> • can communicate well in English.
>
> Please write to Oliver Harkins, Camp Manager, explaining why you are suitable for the job.

Write your **letter of application**.

4   Your English teacher has asked you to write a report on problems with the college library.

In your report, you should:

- describe the main problems
- explain how these problems affect students
- make recommendations on how to improve the situation.

Write your **report**.

Test 6 Listening Part 1

🎧 60 You will hear people talking in eight different situations. For questions **1–8**, choose the best answer (**A**, **B** or **C**).

1   You hear two friends talking about using a computer keyboard.
    How does the man feel about his typing skills?

    A   satisfied with his level of accuracy
    B   surprised at the speed he can reach
    C   pleased with the improvement he has made

2   You hear two friends talking about supporting a football team.
    What do they agree is the advantage of supporting one?

    A   It makes watching matches more exciting.
    B   It gives a feeling of being part of a community.
    C   It provides a form of relief from the stress of life.

3   You hear part of a psychology podcast in which a woman is talking about making apologies.
    What is she doing?

    A   explaining the need for honesty
    B   outlining the effect of body language
    C   suggesting how to find suitable words to use

4   You hear a woman talking to a friend about choosing a gift for her nephew.
    She would like the gift

    A   to encourage creativity.
    B   to help to develop general knowledge.
    C   to be similar to things she had as a child.

5   You hear a man talking to a friend about using his local buses.
    How does he feel?

    A   reluctant to stop taking them
    B   confused about their schedules
    C   disappointed by their reliability

6   You hear a man talking about teaching children good manners.
    He thinks that too little importance is given to

    A   using the voice to express politeness.
    B   setting an appropriate example.
    C   praise for behaving appropriately.

7   You hear two students talking about a lecture on the history of fashion that they attended.
    The woman suggests the lecture would have been better if

    A   less time had been spent looking at gender differences.
    B   a wider geographical context had been covered.
    C   the focus had extended beyond a specific social class.

8   You hear a news report about a very unusual frog.
    What do scientists say they are unsure about?

    A   what species the frog belongs to
    B   how something grew on the frog's skin
    C   whether the frog will ever be seen again

Test 6 — Listening Part 2

🎧 61 You will hear a man called Ryan Lee talking about working as a set designer for a theatre, designing the scenery and stage for theatrical productions. For questions **9–18**, complete the sentences with a word or short phrase.

Working as a theatre set designer

Ryan says that the **(9)** .... is the starting point for him when he takes on a new production.

Of the subjects Ryan studied at school, **(10)** .... has been more helpful than he expected.

For Ryan, research is key to achieving what he calls **(11)** .... in theatre productions with a historical setting.

Ryan makes sketches, which he usually displays on a **(12)** .... for the director in discussions about set design.

Ryan works closely with the costume designer, who may ask him to avoid certain **(13)** .... in his designs.

Actors often contribute ideas for what to include in what's known as the **(14)** .... of a character they're playing.

Ryan says that the number of **(15)** .... can make creating sets for musicals challenging.

Ryan is particularly keen on plays that deal with **(16)** .... when accepting invitations to work on plays.

Ryan says that designing a theatre set is similar to **(17)** .... in many ways.

Ryan's next project will involve the challenge of representing varying **(18)** .... in the set of the play.

Test 6 — Listening Part 3

🎧 62 You will hear five short extracts in which people are talking about a job they did working with animals. For questions **19–23**, choose from the list (**A–H**) how each person says they benefited from working with animals. Use the letters only once. There are three extra letters which you do not need to use.

A It had a calming effect on me.

B It gave me a strong sense of purpose.　　　　　Speaker 1　[ ] 19

C I enjoyed the way animals responded to me.
　　　　　　　　　　　　　　　　　　　　　　Speaker 2　[ ] 20

D I developed useful skills for other jobs.
　　　　　　　　　　　　　　　　　　　　　　Speaker 3　[ ] 21

E I appreciated how varied each day was.

　　　　　　　　　　　　　　　　　　　　　　Speaker 4　[ ] 22

F I met people with similar interests.

G I felt part of the local community.　　　　　　Speaker 5　[ ] 23

H It increased my energy levels.

Test 6 — Listening Part 4

🎧 63 You will hear an interview with a woman called Amy Rossi, who is the manager of a band called the Velvet Echo. For questions **24–30**, choose the best answer (**A**, **B** or **C**).

24 How did Amy feel when members of the Velvet Echo asked her to manage the band?

  A nervous about what they might require from her
  B uncertain whether she was the right person for them
  C embarrassed that they had such a high opinion of her

25 When asked about wanting to work in the music industry, Amy says that she had always

  A felt passionate about music of many kinds.
  B enjoyed being around people with musical talents.
  C wanted to help less well-known musicians make money.

26 Amy thinks that the Velvet Echo started to attract more fans after changing their approach to

  A their image.
  B their live performances.
  C their way of writing songs.

27 What does Amy say has been the most difficult aspect of managing the Velvet Echo?

  A negotiating a satisfactory recording contract
  B reducing expenses on their last series of concerts
  C dealing with a disagreement between band members

28 The main reason Amy wanted the Velvet Echo to play at the Electric Bandstand concert hall was because

  A it was built to offer very high sound quality.
  B it had been a venue for many successful bands.
  C its design provided a good atmosphere for concerts.

29 What does Amy say about promoting the Velvet Echo on social media?

  A She is surprised by how many new fans used it to discover the band.
  B She is glad that it has strengthened relationships with existing fans.
  C She is pleased that it encourages feedback on how fans see the band.

30 How does Amy feel about the Velvet Echo's new album 'Toucan Fly'?

  A optimistic about how it will be reviewed by critics
  B confident that it will attract a wider audience than previous ones
  C curious to see what reactions there will be to the use of some new instruments

Test 6 — Speaking Parts 1 and 2

Part 1 🎧 64 2 minutes (3 minutes for groups of three)

Interlocutor First, we'd like to know something about you.

Daily routines
- How do you prefer to travel to college or work? (Why?)
- How important is it for you to spend time outside every day? (Why?)
- Are your weekends very different from your weekdays? (Why?)
- Do you often stay up really late at night? (Why? / Why not?)
- How do you find out about the daily news? (Why?)

Part 2 🎧 65 4 minutes (6 minutes for groups of three)

Interlocutor In this part of the test, I'm going to give each of you two photographs. I'd like you to talk about your photographs on your own for about a minute and also to answer a question about your partner's photographs.

(*Candidate A*), it's your turn first. Here are your photographs on page C20 of the Speaking appendix. They show **people saying goodbye in different situations**. I'd like you to compare the photographs and say **what you think the people might find difficult about saying goodbye in these situations**.

All right?

Candidate A
⏱ *1 minute* ....

Interlocutor Thank you.

(*Candidate B*), **did you enjoy going to school when you were a young child? (Why? / Why not?)**

Candidate B
⏱ *Approximately 30 seconds* ....

Interlocutor Thank you.

Now (*Candidate B*), here are your photographs on page C21 of the Speaking appendix. They show **different places where people live**. I'd like you to compare the photographs and say **why you think the people have chosen to live in these places**.

All right?

Candidate B
⏱ *1 minute* ....

Interlocutor Thank you.

(*Candidate A*), **would you enjoy living in a city centre? (Why? / Why not?)**

Candidate A
⏱ *Approximately 30 seconds* ....

Interlocutor Thank you.

Test 6   Speaking Parts 3 and 4

Part 3 66 4 minutes (5 minutes for groups of three)

Interlocutor Now, I'd like you to talk about something together for about two minutes.

Here are some things that some people think are essential for having a close friendship with someone and a question for you to discuss. First, you have some time to look at the task on page C22 of the Speaking appendix.

Now, talk to each other about **whether these things are essential for having a close friendship with someone.**

Candidates 2 minutes (3 minutes for groups of three)

Interlocutor Thank you. Now you have about a minute to decide **which two things are most important for having a close friendship with someone**.

Candidates 1 minute (for pairs and groups of three)

Interlocutor Thank you.

Part 4 67 4 minutes (6 minutes for groups of three)

Interlocutor
- Is it important for friends to always agree with each other? (Why? / Why not?)
- Do you think that where you work is the best place to meet new friends? (Why? / Why not?)
- Is it better to spend time with just one friend or with a large group of friends? (Why?)
- Do you think it is easy to continue a friendship when one person moves away? (Why? / Why not?)
- Some people say that modern technology is having a negative effect on friendships. What do you think?
- Is it better to ask friends or family for advice when you have to make an important decision?

Thank you. That is the end of the test.

**What do you think?
Do you agree?
And you?**

Test 1 Audioscript

LISTENING PART 1

 Training Exercise 3

You hear a woman talking about the creation of new supersonic airliners.

Woman: It seems that experts in the aviation industry are wasting time and resources with their investigations into supersonic flight. My suspicion is it's just about showing off their engineering capabilities. Flights on aircraft like this will surely only be possible for the super-rich, rather than the rest of us. When the supersonic airliner Concorde was conceived back in the mid-1900s, there really was a genuine need to speed up the flow of information and ideas across continents, as in those days, we still relied on printed material or personal interaction a fair bit. Those kinds of reasons for developing aircraft no longer apply in the era of digital online communication.

 Exam practice

You will hear people talking in eight different situations.

One.

You hear two friends talking about bungee jumping.

Man: I'd never do a bungee jump myself.

Woman: Why not?

Man: Well, while I admit it takes a certain amount of guts to go free-falling from a height with just an elastic-style cord attached to you, there are better ways to prove your courage or indulge a need for thrills. You know, more worthwhile ones.

Woman: How dangerous is it?

Man: Everything's safety tested ... I heard the most common issue is feeling dizzy afterwards! How often does anyone come to any real harm? It just makes me wonder what drives anyone to do it. It'd be fascinating to talk to someone who's done one. What do you think?

Woman: I'd love to try it!

Two.

You hear two friends talking about trainers.

Man: What do you think of my new trainers? They weren't that expensive – I got them online, second-hand.

Woman: Wow, you'd never believe it! They look like new. A nice pair usually costs a small fortune. People pay up because they want to be on trend, I guess. Like, trainers are part of having a cool personal style.

Man: Totally. These ones are really perfect! I find new ones tend to take a while to wear in, too. Your feet get really sore if you haven't got the size exactly right. Have you noticed that?

Woman: I can't say I have. I think they're popular for the very reason they're not like that.

Three.

You hear a woman talking about when she studied at a music school.

Woman: I'd always wanted to be a pianist and never questioned my ambition to go to music school. I was thrilled to get in. Suddenly, I was surrounded by others who were passionate about music, extremely talented and completely dedicated to music as a profession. You're expected to put in the hours, day in day out, training, doing exercises, trying to develop greater control and become a better player. Of course, I already knew that was essential, but it soon dawned on me that I'd given up other aspects of my life. You just have to accept you wouldn't get to do many non-music related activities ... and you felt guilty if you did.

Four.

You hear two friends talking about an animated movie they saw.

Man: I watched that animated movie *Close Call* last night.

Woman: Oh yeah, I saw that. The storyline was hard to follow, all those animals – and trying to work out who was meant to be a goodie and who was a baddie. Like that cat, KJ.

Man: That was the whole point ...

Woman: But a movie should let you know where things stand, like whose side you're supposed to be on, otherwise you don't care. I mean, it was obviously written by highly talented scriptwriters and the artwork was incredible, so it was a shame. It's crucial to understand all the different animals or whatever in the story to enjoy a movie like that.

Five.

You hear part of a talk about photography.

Woman: The number of photos taken every day has multiplied enormously since the invention of the smartphone. There's no one thing making it impossible to resist trying to photograph the colours of the sunset, an amazing meal or the cute smile of a child on their first birthday. But I think the primary factor ... it's that human desire to feel connected. Who doesn't post their shots on social media, even if they're only looked at for a split second? It's so easy to capture moments on camera with a click. And, unlike in the past, the photos are instant! I just wonder if we'll ever look at them again.

Six.

You hear a man talking about a documentary.

Man: Last night's documentary, *Nature Watch*, was certainly worth watching. There's so much talk in the media today about endangered species – polar bears, pandas, tigers – and yes, these creatures need attention. I don't deny it's urgent that humans wake up to the reality of our behaviour as we steadily destroy their habitats, polluting the water, air and land they live in. It was just refreshing to see something rather less depressing. The camerawork was stunning, with amazing close-ups revealing how insects, animals and plants interact to create the wonder that we call nature. Observing such things is sure to provoke greater interest in and care about the world we live in.

Seven.

You hear a man telling a friend about a long bike ride he did alone.

Woman: Hey, how was your solo bike ride to the west coast?

Man: It was so cool doing it on my own!

Woman: How was it different?

Man: Your mind can wander much more. You don't have to talk. Or negotiate what kind of pace you want to go at. What I did appreciate was being able to pick which way to go when various options were possible. It can be a bore having to come to some sort of agreement. I could have pushed myself more in terms of speed ... the result of less pressure from seeing how much someone else is doing, I guess. It was darker than I'd planned when I got back.

Eight.

You hear two friends talking about a podcast on food and nutrition.

Woman: Do you listen to the podcast *Foodfile*, all about food and nutrition?

Man: Yeah, I've listened. The presenters get on my nerves, though.

Woman: Don't you think it's an important subject?

Man: It's obvious we should all have more vegetables in our diet ... less processed food, sugar, salt and so on and so on. They make a clear case for all that in every episode. They need to get more in touch with the reality of most people's lives, though. Few people have the time or money to buy fresh products like they recommend. Admittedly, giving up meat saves money and it's good for the environment. They do make that point.

LISTENING PART 2

 Training Exercise 3

You will hear a man called Kevin Pendit giving a talk about organising a festival of short films made by film students around the world.

Man: Hi. I'm Kevin Pendit, here to tell you all about the film festival I organised last year. I'm still a film student and it was my first time doing something like this. I wanted to show short films made by other film students in different parts of the world.

When undertaking a project like this, planning is essential. I had lots of ideas about how to go about generating publicity and I knew that I wanted the film festival to be an example of the creativity and diversity there is out there among young filmmakers. But research is key. I did a lot of this beforehand, so I'd know exactly what I was doing.

The next thing was funding, of course, and I was incredibly lucky. I'd actually negotiated a sponsorship deal with a travel company, but they pulled out early on. Thankfully, a technology company then came forward and agreed to provide financial backing, a lot more generously, in return for having their name in all publicity material.

Of course, there are loads of important factors to consider besides funding. I listened to advice from others and learned that a theme is vital. After considering various ideas, I decided to go with 'community', as I think it's something we're losing in the modern world. I wanted to raise awareness in my target audience, which was primarily younger people.

There were prizes for the best films in different categories, which meant I needed a panel of judges. I knew an arts journalist on a local paper who was happy to join, plus a friend of mine who's a big film expert. I asked one well-known film director to be in charge of the team, but he was too busy, so I turned to my college tutor, who happily took on that role.

 Exam practice

You will hear a woman called Natalya Erikson giving a talk about her work as a curator who organises exhibitions at a museum of contemporary art.

Natalya: Hi. My name's Natalya Erikson and I work as one of the curators at the Richmond Contemporary Art Museum. We're responsible for organising most of what happens at the museum.

Art's my passion and I knew I wanted to have a career related to it. That's mainly due to my mother's influence. She's always been involved in the art world and I followed in her footsteps. She advised me that being an artist requires more than just a love of art. Being an art dealer, she came into contact with many people and an art-teacher friend of hers suggested I go into curating.

I wasn't sure and tried other things before committing myself to curating. I did history at university, rather than an art-related subject. I also volunteered on the student magazine. The writing I did on that served me well, as I do a lot of it in my job now, for example providing information about exhibits. Creating art is something I do in my free time, but it's just a hobby.

People ask what kind of work a museum curator does. I personally prefer the term 'desk days' to cover the most common things I get up to. It could be anything from emailing, communicating with artists by phone, planning exhibitions or organising deliveries of works. Before a new exhibition, it's hectic and I'll be super-busy organising the gallery space, but not every day is action-packed!

The museum where I work has a main collection and we also have visiting collections. These come from all over. There's plenty from artists in Europe and we're growing our collection from Asia and Australia. We have close connections with Africa and it's from there that our most celebrated stuff comes, attracting many visitors.

We sometimes work with art colleges, displaying interesting things from students. For example, we had one exhibition of pencil drawings, with some very unusual choices of subject, or another was of street photography. I adore pottery and I got so much satisfaction curating an exhibition of it not long ago. The student artists received so much praise. The show was incredibly colourful.

The job has many inspiring aspects, which is why I love it, although not everything brings joy! It can be dull recording details. I do that all the time, because we have to know where every piece of work is, where it's going, dates, places and so on. Creating layouts for exhibitions is another matter. I get totally involved. And unlike some art curators, I don't mind applying for loans from potential investors either.

You need certain talents as an art curator. Research is essential, though I often leave that to colleagues who enjoy it more, whereas my speciality is problem solving. I have a gift for it and it comes in handy when you're dealing with people from different areas, all with their own specific agendas, like the media, the general public, buyers and artists themselves! A lot can go wrong.

I often give talks for visitors. At the moment, I'm busy doing the background work for one on photography. I'll discuss its influence on contemporary painting. The subjects I talk about can range from a spotlight on a particular artist to exhibition design.

I'm always interested in buying paintings for our collection. Artists paint on a variety of surfaces, with canvas being the most common, though of course, paper is also used or even wood. I've seen a series of works done on plastic and it's my intention to acquire at least one to show the variety of possible surfaces.

So, for those of you with ambitions for a career as a curator in an art museum, I would recommend a certain amount of caution. Avoid setting your sights too high by aiming for a position in one of the top museums. There's more opportunity to gain experience in small galleries. That's a more realistic ambition to begin with. Occasionally, artists' studios welcome curators, too, to help them organise exhibitions. And step by step, you make contacts and find your place in the art world.

LISTENING PART 3
 Training Exercise 3

Woman: All my previous cooking experience failed to prepare me for the intensity of chef training, producing dishes on a large scale, with so much information to take in: safety instructions, food hygiene, preventing cross-contamination between things like nuts and other foods. To be honest, I'd thought I'd be a more skilled cook than other students and then I put bicarbonate of soda instead of the flavour enhancer MSG into an Asian stir fry. If only I'd bothered to check the label! On top of that, I did it on more than one occasion. I was totally gutted – I mean, so irritated with myself! It made me feel a bit less self-important, anyway!

 Training Exercise 5

Man: I'd heard that my chef training course would be a lot of hard work. And it was. I think I'd have enjoyed it more if there'd been less theoretical stuff – you know, nutrition, kitchen hygiene, menu planning, cost control and so on. But the thing I really appreciated was how positive everyone was about each other's work. The kitchen culture was very much stepping in to lend each other a hand. That meant that you didn't even mind doing less exciting chores like peeling potatoes or scrubbing kitchen surfaces. I really got into the cooking side of the course and I was so proud of my pastry skills by the end.

 Training Exercise 8

1 Woman: I wish there had been fewer boring tasks to do. It always seemed to be me who was asked to do them.

2 Man: I felt very anxious and if I'd been given a choice, I'd have turned down the opportunity to play the role of head chef.

3 Woman: Everything seemed quite easy. I would have liked it if the course had demanded a bit more from students.

4 Man: It was a shame that I had a couple of arguments with other students. I wish I'd kept my temper and, afterwards, I made sure it never happened again.

5 Woman: The recipe was very complex and I got the stages in the wrong order. If someone else hadn't stopped me, I would have done it all wrong.

 Exam practice

You will hear five short extracts in which people are talking about a long-distance train journey they went on.

Speaker 1

A friend and I took the night train across France and into Italy. She wanted us to get a sleeping car – you know with bunk beds, which would have cost far more – but I didn't agree. So we just paid for normal seats and it turned out fine. Actually, I slept through most of the journey, which meant it didn't seem to take that long. If I'd stayed awake though, I'd have caught sight of the mountains at dawn. My friend went on and on about how incredible they were. Such a shame. My dad bought me a guidebook to read on the journey and I never got past page one!

Speaker 2

I travelled from south-west England to Aberdeen in Scotland. It should have taken about ten hours. I changed trains in London and wished I'd gone via Manchester instead. Another passenger warned me that train operations would be held up due to bad weather, but I was already on the way. I hoped he was wrong, but no. At least I'd downloaded some movies on my phone to while away the hours waiting for my connection. I was on my own with nobody to chat to, though I didn't really mind, and later I got to see the stunning valleys and dramatic rock formations passing through the area of the Peak District.

Speaker 3

I'll never forget taking the overnight train from Mombasa on the East African coast to Nairobi, the Kenyan capital. The cost of a sleeping compartment with dinner seemed very reasonable at the time and the journey involved going through a wildlife park, where I even spotted giraffes and zebras. It would have been good to see elephants, but never mind. It was just a pity I'd chosen to travel round Kenya on my own, as I realised it'd have been more fun to share the experience. I did chat a bit to other travellers, though, in Swahili, Italian and Chinese, all of which I speak a little ... and, of course, English.

Speaker 4

I chose to travel to Germany and Switzerland by train recently – far less chance of delays than flying. It all went smoothly and the only issue was something I could have handled differently. I was on a call on my phone and a man asked me to lower my voice. In my very basic German, I responded that it was important and carried on. He pointed out a sign for passengers to avoid using phones. I should have just done as he asked, now I look back on it. I suppose because I'd paid for a first-class ticket, I felt entitled to conduct my business. Still, it's best to be considerate.

Speaker 5

Travelling by train in India, I'd been advised to inform myself of procedures for booking tickets, but it wasn't really necessary, as everyone was so helpful. It was quite an experience and nothing beats passing near the foothills of the Himalayas. Stunning! I'd been unsure about the wisdom of going alone, but in fact, other people on the train were very chatty and I managed to pick up quite a few words of Hindi and other local languages! The journey seemed very long, though, and I remember thinking: if only I'd brought a novel or something like that, as I got fed up with my phone as company when my conversations dried up.

LISTENING PART 4

 Training Exercise 2

Woman: What first made you study sports psychology, Jim?

Man: It's common for people to become sports psychologists to figure themselves out. I've been learning about techniques on my own for ages, but I'll never forget the turnaround in myself when I won a major ski-racing event. The difference was clear. I'd been aware how much your head gets in the way of winning at things long before making a career of it and getting an academic qualification. I've since seen many transformations, assisting sportspeople who lacked sufficient confidence to come out on top. It's very rewarding.

Woman: What's been useful in your work as a sports psychologist?

Man: Well, some athletes have doubts about the mental side, instead focusing on the physical aspects of what they do. Having been in the same position previously, I get that, and they get that I do. It means they're more willing to take on board what I'm putting across. I try to teach them to come back from losing, to look on the bright side and go forward. Developing psychological skills can take a frustrating amount of time. It's hard to play the waiting game, but worth it in the long run.

 Exam practice

You will hear an interview with a man called Abe who is talking about his work as a music producer, directing musicians, both creatively and technically, in the recording studio.

Woman: I'm talking to Abe Halliday, a music producer who uses his technical and creative skills to help musicians make their recordings in the studio. Abe, how did you get into it?

Man: Though sadly lacking in any real talent for playing music, I dreamt of some music-related career. From helping friends in bands improve their sound to managing a really gifted musician, the guitarist and songwriter Alec Wilkins, there have been various stages to pursuing that dream. None of it's been straightforward – there was so much competition, so many barriers to overcome. I hadn't predicted that, but I'm grateful that eventually people realised I had a gift for producing music.

Woman: It must be an enjoyable job!

Man: Absolutely! I'm constantly around people with creative talents and skills, and there are endless possibilities when you're producing music. Obviously, clients have specific requirements I have to go along with, so it's a balancing act getting that right. Messing around with all the tubes and knobs and lights and boxes is totally absorbing. That's got to be the number-one pleasure for me. And musicians are cool people, though, of course, some have less ability than others.

Woman: Are there any negative sides?

Man: When you're using things like microphones, mixing consoles, speakers and so on, maintenance can be an issue. Finding spare parts and people to repair things gets harder all the time. It's not my skill set or what I care about, but there's a lot of accounting and invoices stuff when you run a studio. I'm OK with that side of things. It's part of the job that doesn't bother me. Neither does what some people complain about – having to be in the studio at night or at weekends.

Woman: What are relationships like with musicians you work with?

Man: Mostly, they're great. I always look on the bright side. I had someone recently who was challenging! A very short temper! She wanted everything done her way and kept arriving late or stopping recording to have breaks. I took things in my stride and managed to get round her with flattery – lots of admiring comments about her voice, her insights. She softened and began to take on board what I asked her to do.

Woman: You recently produced the music for a popular advertisement ...

Man: Yes, a well-known sugary snack. I don't eat such things myself, but I don't mind earning money for helping to sell them! And thankfully, the whole process was relatively short and I could get back to what I really do! The music we produced went well with the product and that may be what helped make it so successful with customers, I believe. Ads often use songs that are already famous, so it was good to create something original.

Woman: And you're recording with the band Furious Sleepers, I hear ...

Man: Yes, very soon. We've had a lot of communication about what we want to do together and I'm really looking forward to it. We'll be re-recording some versions of their songs, which they were unhappy with previously. Should be interesting, though less creative than some work. I'm sure the studio will be able to deliver exceptional results for them. We're going to be on a very tight deadline, with a lot to record, but I get a buzz out of living up to high expectations.

Woman: What advice do you have for anyone wanting to do your job?

Man: It goes without saying that you need to actively listen to music so you notice everything. You can't do it without naturally good ears. That's something hard to change. What's really essential is to network, to get to know as many artists, engineers and other professionals as you can. By reaching out to them, you'll widen your options. And don't get stressed about the technical stuff. Everything is constantly evolving and you learn it hands-on in the same way, with practical experience.

SPEAKING PART 1

 Training Exercise 1b

Interlocutor: Where do you live, Kemi?
Kemi: I'm from Nigeria, the north part.
Interlocutor: And you, Yuki?
Yuki: From Kyoto, in Japan. It's a very beautiful city.
Interlocutor: Kemi, do you have any hobbies which you do regularly?
Kemi: Not really. I do like taking photos, but I don't do it that often, usually just when I'm on holiday. I'm too busy with my college work to do hobbies every week.
Interlocutor: Yuki, how often do you go out somewhere with your friends?
Yuki: Most weekends, I think. We just go to the city centre or we meet at one of our houses and just hang out. I like seeing my friends.
Interlocutor: Kemi, tell us about a place you visited which you really enjoyed.
Kemi: Well, I love travelling and I like most places I go to, but my favourite was Portugal. I went there with my family and we visited three or four different cities and ate lots of delicious food. I would like to go back there again.
Interlocutor: Yuki, are you going to any special events or celebrations soon?
Yuki: Actually, yes, it's my uncle's birthday next week and the whole family is going to meet to have lunch together. I'm really looking forward to it.

 Training Exercise 2d

1 Is looking at art in museums something you like doing?
2 How do you feel about doing puzzles with numbers or words?
3 Do you enjoy playing computer games?
4 Tell us about a photo you like.
5 What is your favourite time of year?

 Training Exercise 2e

Interlocutor: Is looking at art in museums something you like doing?
Candidate A: Well, I'm not really into art, but I am keen on going to museums to learn about ancient history. It's fascinating to learn about the lives of people so many years ago.
Interlocutor: How do you feel about doing puzzles with numbers or words?
Candidate B: I know puzzles are really popular at the moment, but I'm not particularly interested in them. Maybe if I'm on a long journey, I'll do some to pass the time, but that's all.
Interlocutor: Do you enjoy playing computer games?
Candidate A: To be honest, I'm not a huge fan of them. I don't mind the ones which you can play with a friend, but most of them are too complicated for me.
Interlocutor: Tell us about a photo you like.
Candidate B: Do you mean a photo I've taken? I took one from the top of a mountain I climbed last year. In the photo, you can really see how high we climbed and how beautiful the scenery was. I absolutely love that photo and I've saved it onto my phone so I can look at it every day.
Interlocutor: What is your favourite time of year?
Candidate A: That's a difficult question to answer. I think I'd rather spend time outside when it's warm, so I suppose I like spring or summer best. I can't stand the cold weather, so winter is my least favourite time of year.

 Exam practice

1 Is it important to you to do some exercise every day?
2 Do you prefer doing team sports or exercising on your own?
3 How interested are you in watching sport on TV?
4 Have you ever been to a live sports event?
5 Would you rather go for a long walk outside or go running in a gym?

SPEAKING PART 2

 Training Exercise 2

Mika: In the first picture, I can see a woman who is standing at the front of a room. It looks like an office. She has a screen behind her, which has charts and information on it. She's smiling at two people sitting in front of her. I imagine these people are her colleagues and she's presenting a business report to them. Everyone seems quite relaxed, so I think they probably all work together on a project and she's sharing some information which they need. She needs to be confident that the information she has is correct. In contrast, the second picture was taken outside, at a ski resort. The people seem happy, like the woman in the first picture. The man on the left is probably a ski instructor and the other people may be learning to ski. Perhaps it's their first time, so they need to be confident that they can learn this new skill.

 Training Exercise 3b

Interlocutor: Asif, would you like to learn to ski?
Asif: Actually, I have skied once before and I quite liked it. Mika mentioned that the people in the photo look happy, but I didn't feel as confident as they seem to be, because I was really worried about falling over. I did actually fall over and it was fine, so I'd like to have another go and I'd be less nervous next time, I think.

 Training Exercise 5

Interlocutor: In this part of the test, I'm going to give each of you two photographs. I'd like you to talk about your photographs on your own for about a minute, and also to answer a question about your partner's photographs. Here are the photographs. They show people in situations where they need to be confident. I'd like you to compare the photographs and say why you think the people need to be confident in these situations.
All right? Thank you.
Would you like to learn to ski?
Thank you.

SPEAKING PART 3

 Training Exercise 3

Interlocutor: Now, I'd like you to talk about something together for about two minutes. Some people think that it's important to plan holidays carefully, but other people disagree. Here are some of the things they think about and a question for you to discuss. First, you have some time to look at the task. Now, talk to each other about whether it's important to plan a holiday carefully.
Candidate A: OK, being flexible. I think if you plan a holiday too much, you don't have flexibility. Do you agree?
Candidate B: Yes, that's a good point. I think you're right. Next, avoiding crowds. If you check the busy times in the place you want to go, you can avoid too many crowds. What do you think?
Candidate A: Yes, so maybe it's good to plan. OK, getting the best price. If you buy your tickets in advance, they're often cheaper, aren't they?
Candidate B: That's true, so it's good to plan. Now, booking activities. In a popular place, you need to book early so it's not sold out.
Candidate A: I agree. Finally, having time to relax. Some people plan too many activities for their holiday, so they're always busy. There's no time to relax. Do you agree?
Candidate B: Yes, absolutely. I hate holidays when there's too much to do.

SPEAKING PART 4

Training Exercise 3

Interlocutor: Some people say that it's better to explore your own country rather than travel abroad. What do you think?
Candidate A: I agree. I, umm, I think it's … it can be … good, er, to visit your own country. Um, in your own country, there are … lots of places you don't know and these are interesting to see, so it's

a good idea. And, er, if you travel abroad, it ... it ... costs more, I think, so it's not such a good idea. That's what I think.

Interlocutor: What do you think?

Candidate B: The discussion about whether travelling locally is better than travelling to other countries is a common one. I'm in two minds about it, actually. Travelling abroad gives you the opportunity to experience things you cannot experience at home, but staying in your own country reduces travel, which is better for the environment, and it's a good way of learning more about where you come from.

LISTENING PART 1

 Training Exercise 2

Woman: My last entry on my blog was about a 10 km run up in hills around 800 metres high. It was tough, I won't lie, and I could have pushed myself harder. Anyway, my posts are getting plenty of hits, which is awesome. I must be doing something right. But I may have taken on more than I can handle, as I'm falling behind on my assignments. The blog about today's run might not be finished until tomorrow because I'm catching up on one. What with college deadlines, I guess I shouldn't have taken on all the training and blogging, but if I hadn't, I might have found excuses for not studying.

 Training Exercise 7

1 I suppose it's inevitable that artificial intelligence will eventually take over most work done by humans ... whether we like it or not.

2 I'm genuinely excited about the prospect of working there. The dynamic environment and interaction with customers sound like a perfect fit for me.

3 Finding the information you're after on this website is virtually impossible. I mean, its design is seriously lacking.

4 I know AI presents some serious challenges, but lots of people say that humans will be able to manage its impact on society, which is good to know.

5 Although I've been offered the post of manager, I don't really want to accept it. Working in retail isn't part of my long-term career goals.

6 This website's pretty impressive. I found navigating through it for the information I needed totally straightforward.

 Exam practice

You will hear people talking in eight different situations.

One.

You hear a psychologist talking about attitudes to time.

Man: There are many expressions like 'seize the day' or 'you only live once'. They basically suggest that we should be concentrating on enjoying ourselves right now, rather than stressing about the future or getting stuck in the past. Yet considering what is to come may be wise when we make choices in the here and now. Various research evidence suggests that writing letters to your future self can steer people away from self-defeating behaviour and encourage them to weigh up the consequences of their actions more thoughtfully. Doing this actually motivates you to be a better version of yourself today. And might well end up giving you better memories, too.

Two.

You hear two friends talking about artificial intelligence.

Man: It's hard to tell the difference between paintings and songs created entirely by AI ...

Woman: Between them and something created by humans? I know AI uses human ideas, but it still seems quite unique ... what it comes up with.

Man: Would you like AI-powered robots doing chores, like cleaning and cooking?

Woman: It'd be brilliant, though I can't imagine a world where things we find uninspiring but are actually complex, like, say, hanging out laundry or even tidying up properly, could be done by anyone other than a human. My big fear is the more science-fiction side of AI. You know, if somehow AI gains authority and starts running human affairs.

Man: Hmm, maybe ...

Three.

You hear a man talking about working in a shop.

Man: A career in retail sales could mean working in a variety of outlets, from small, maybe a boutique or convenience store, to large, say, a department store or supermarket. Most people start out as sales assistants of some sort. The work usually involves dealing with a diverse range of customers, each with unique needs, preferences and behaviours. It's vital to be able to communicate politely and effectively, and to be able to deal with pressure. Most shops experience peak periods, at certain times of day when demand is high. This can create a fast-paced environment and shelves need to be rapidly restocked, transactions processed, all the while responding to customer enquiries.

Four.

You hear two friends talking about cooking without using ready-made ingredients.

Man: I've been trying to cook all my meals just using basic natural ingredients, nothing ready-made ...

Woman: Good idea, but you have to be organised, shopping in advance and stuff. It's hard to eat like that on a daily basis.

Man: You can always just throw some fish in a pan with oil and cook some frozen or canned vegetables. It doesn't always mean following complicated recipes.

Woman: So frozen and canned food don't count as ready-made? That's more manageable, though not everyone's up for more than putting something in the microwave after a long day's work.

Man: True. It takes all sorts and some of us enjoy being in the kitchen more than others.

Five.

You hear a woman telling a friend about an app she likes for booking train tickets.

Woman: You must try this great app, TrainBook.

Man: Why are you so enthusiastic about it?

Woman: Well, I've used several and it comes out on top. I've found if an issue arises, like a train gets cancelled or you need to change tickets, it's no problem to message them, or use the live-chat feature, and get assistance. Most ticket apps aren't like that, though they all help you find the most economical way of getting your ticket from A to B. Some do make it easier than others to work out whether you're getting the best deal. I'm all about doing things quickly, which is why I check them out.

Six.

You hear a man telling a friend about his efforts to develop greater self-discipline.

Woman: How's your self-discipline going since you read that book on the subject?

Man: It's been a game-changer for me, which is great. I've realised how important it is to set clear goals and stick to them, even when things get tough.

Woman: So, are you at the gym before work every morning, like you wanted?

Man: Sure there are days when I've ignored my alarm and put off going, but I'm getting into eating more healthily, less junk and stuff. There's still a way to go, though. I just remind myself of the bigger picture and the satisfaction I'll feel if I accomplish all my goals. I'm confident I can do it.

Seven.

You hear two friends talking about an exhibition they saw.

Man: Well, that was interesting!

Woman: You could say that. Most of the paintings looked as if the paint could have just been thrown at the canvas, but I can tell there must have been more skill than that involved. And in some of them, the effect's quite dramatic.

Man: The artist's got another exhibition coming up soon with a different theme.

Woman: It's amazing there's a demand for it. I suppose people must appreciate his work. Surprising really, as it's quite weird. I'd be interested to find out if he can do anything different, I guess.

Man: I might go to another, I think. Not sure.

Eight.

You hear part of an interview with a novelist.

Man: How much influence has your own childhood had on your writing?

Woman: Well, I deal with the subject of being a child in several of my novels and I'm sure some of that has its origins in – or is loosely based on – memories of things that might have happened to me or emotions I must have been through. I just wish I'd held on to more, as it's all rather vague to me now. As a child, I knew so little of the world, of course. I was sensitive to slight personal upsets and yet I also took so much else in my stride, living in difficult economic circumstances.

LISTENING PART 2

 Training Exercise 2

Man: I think when I first had the idea of running a coffee shop, before opening I was somewhat naïve. I had little idea what would be involved. After opening, it took a couple of years before I really felt confident in the whole project. Before that, it was rough. And that's expressing it mildly. I dealt with virtually everything myself: cleaning, making the coffee, serving customers, doing the accounts.

It was no surprise that good-quality coffee was the number-one priority for the majority of my customers. No one minds slightly higher prices if that's what they get. In the early days, I couldn't always afford to have the heating on, but that didn't seem to bother people in winter. I hadn't realised noise would be such an issue, though. After several people expressed unhappiness about it, I made sure anything I played was at a low volume.

 Training Exercise 3

1 Nobody's ever complained about the quality of coffee here before!
2 Dealing with customers takes up most of my energy when the shop's open.
3 The number of customers depends a lot on what time of day it is.
4 I strongly believe in the importance of serving coffee at the right temperature.
5 Customers sometimes ask how a latte differs from a cappuccino.
6 I was worried about how customers might react to a big price increase.

 Training Exercise 4

1 I never thought I'd be capable of running a business single-handed for so long.
2 All our food's homemade and Sara is responsible for preparing it.
3 She's incredibly good at making delicious homemade pastries.
4 I'm very pleased with the new décor since the coffee shop was redecorated.
5 The relaxed atmosphere in a small coffee shop is preferable to that of a busy takeaway.
6 I remain very confident in the future loyalty of my regular customers.

 Exam practice

You will hear a young woman called Marlene Niall talking about a course in fashion design she has just completed.

Marlene: Hi, I'm Marlene Niall, still buzzing after my three-year course in fashion design. It had been my dream to get into designing clothes since I first developed a passion for fashion around the age of 14. I adored creating my own designs. I used to see them as what I called 'wearable art'. I've since learned that, despite what you see on fashion runways, mostly clothes design is about mixing form – the shape of clothes – and function – what they're for – to create appealing and practical clothing.

The course I wanted to do is popular, so I wasn't sure I'd get in. At my interview, I knew the tutors would be looking for something special. As I showed off a collection of my best designs – my portfolio – I was super-aware of trying to come across as having energy and demonstrating commitment. Actually, it was my open mind that got me selected, apparently … so they said afterwards.

I won't go into much detail, but the course wasn't easy … a lot to take on board, and there were students who'd joined without a previous background in sewing. Having done loads myself, it seriously improved my ability to get assignments done when we created things to deadlines. Drawing skills are something else that make things go more smoothly if you have a background in that.

During the first year, we did some design projects, where you create a design concept and then design and produce the clothes themselves. One was on clothing for children. Most projects are theme-based, so you take the concept, say, the rainbow, and use that as your inspiration. I played around with ideas, including the jungle. That really appealed to me, but it's been done before for kids, so instead I opted for the circus. I just love clowns and stuff. My designs worked out brilliantly, I'm glad to say.

I appreciated learning to use special software that allows you to digitally create clothing designs. You can sketch and draft patterns, and create a virtual prototype – you know, an initial version on screen of an idea. It offers more flexibility and precision than on paper. What made me enthusiastic was its efficiency. You can decide so quickly if a design's going to work.

Another subject area was textiles – the materials we make clothes from. Learning how to work with them is crucial. I love linen for its fresh look and I adore silk for how it hangs. Cotton is fun. It allows for endless possibilities in terms of texture and appearance, which may be why it's usually my first choice for designs. Bamboo made from plant fibres is a new favourite with designers.

In the final year, we got to put on a fashion show with a particular range of designs, like, for example, swimwear or sportswear. It took time and effort both to come up with designs, having gone for airline uniforms, and then make them. I half-wished I'd gone for something simpler, like sleepwear, but my show was a success.

There was an academic element to the course. We had to produce one long written assignment on a fashion-related subject. I played around with ideas, thinking business would be a useful area to deal with in depth. Another option was consumer psychology. I went for that, and it was fascinating, although textile science sounded interesting.

We studied digital branding – basically using digital platforms to establish and promote a fashion brand's identity and image to consumers. Doing it successfully involves effective use of social media, something I'm less confident in, but also storytelling, which I turned out to be good at in an online context, like on a website.

Another thing was work placements, where you get to work somewhere for a few weeks and pick up some industry insights. I got so much out of doing one at a marketing agency. I learned a lot about fashion PR. I observed their interactions with clients and saw how important teamwork is, too. But it was the networking I found especially valuable. It should help me get on in my career.

LISTENING PART 3

 Training Exercise 1

1 I felt like I had to live up to some huge expectations, as so many people had worked really hard to help me get to the final.
2 I put in so much practice before the final. That effort really paid off in the end and I got the gold medal.
3 We all had to perform the same song. I couldn't believe the amount of praise I got. Apparently, I stood out from the rest.
4 My new coach showed me some different ways of doing things and he was impressed by the speed I picked them up at.
5 During my big skating performance, I attempted something I'd practised a thousand times, but I messed up the moves.

Training Exercise 2

Woman: It was amazing how huge the audience was. Luckily, it didn't bother me, as I was so focused on my performance and getting everything perfect and not making any silly errors. Apparently, someone's phone went off in the middle of my song, but I didn't even notice! There were ten singers in total and we all had to perform the same song. I couldn't believe the amount of praise I got. Apparently, I stood out from the rest. It was like a dream come true and I knew I'd got through to the next stage of the competition. My family were in the front row cheering. It was an overwhelming feeling.

 Exam practice

You will hear five short extracts in which people are talking about surfing.

Speaker 1

Living in Western Australia, I've always been into surfing. That feeling of catching the perfect wave and riding it to shore, it's part of getting away from the nine to five and I need it after sweating my way into work and commuting back to the suburbs. It's like a release from all that. I've tried yoga and stuff, but nothing beats surfing. And you meet good people through the sport. There have been a few I didn't hit it off with, I'll admit, but most are chilled and laid-back, but also love adventure. They're willing to take a few risks. I mean, there are some scary sharks out there!

Speaker 2

I went to Bali in Indonesia for a holiday. It's a great place to escape to for people who live and work in cold, dark places in winter! Someone there suggested I try surfing and what an experience it was! I now do it a lot. When I started surfing, it seemed to take ages to pick up the basics. I was pretty useless, but pushing myself to my limits paid off. The feeling of overcoming new challenges – I get so much out of that. You don't have to be in perfect shape physically, but strength and stamina are helpful and it's massively rewarding psychologically, riding the waves on a surfboard.

Speaker 3

Surfing didn't come totally naturally, but I stuck at it and with practice, acquired the necessary skills. It's taken me to some stunning places – remote beaches, tropical islands with jungle – but even in England, there are good beaches for surfing, though you need a different kind of courage to take your board out in the waves there – and a wetsuit to keep you warm. There's an incredible friendliness among surfers, no matter where you are. We look after one another and share similar values. It's unlike anything else I've come across in that respect. When you're surfing, you also realise how powerful the ocean is, so it's wise to take good care.

Speaker 4

Surfers have a reputation for being in good physical condition and I guess it's a cool crowd to be seen with. In fact, there's a wide range of body types among us and no single one is ideal. Surfing's something I do on a daily basis if possible, either before or after work. I prefer going alone, so I seek out the least popular beaches. It's a precious feeling when there hasn't been a good wave for ages and ages, and then one arrives. I've really learned how to wait calmly – something that helps me in other aspects of life. I used to have more difficulty with that sort of thing.

Speaker 5

There's growing awareness among surfers of ocean pollution and I do my bit to spread the word. That's because I've always been a keen environmentalist, wanting to protect nature from harm. It's hard to avoid noticing the problem of trash these days, whether it's on your way to work or at the beach at weekends. What makes surfing a joy for me is that I get to stay in shape doing something I love and, like with any sport, it becomes a way of life. You have to be well-informed to surf, too – safety-conscious about strong currents, rocks, the risks involved, though the dangers of sharks are over-estimated in my view.

LISTENING PART 4

 Training Exercise 1

Woman: I've always been fascinated by buildings. They can cause emotions, such as a sense of wonder or excitement, or even fear. But what really developed my passion for them, and ultimately made me choose my career, was family trips, when my parents would point out significant or beautiful buildings, from old cottages and castles to the earliest skyscrapers. There's such a diversity of styles and each had a story. It made me curious about the past and the culture of times gone by and I think that inspired my desire to train as an architect.

Exam practice

You will hear an interview with a man called Dean Belinsky, who is talking about his interest in science and his career as a science journalist.

Woman: Today, I'm interviewing a science journalist – Dean Belinsky may already be familiar to you from his appearances on TV and his articles in many newspapers and magazines. Dean, when did you first get interested in science?

Man: I remember being fascinated by the sky at night. A neighbour had a telescope and offered to bring it round for me to use. But he said I'd have to wait until the best time to observe, which was in the first quarter of the moon's cycle. I was so impatient, but then when I eventually got to look through the lens, it blew my mind. Suddenly all these different-shaped markings on the moon's surface were visible. That extraordinary moment set me off and it wasn't long before I was learning everything I could about the planets, the names of stars and so on …

Woman: Were you into other science subjects, like chemistry for example?

Man: Yeah, especially chemistry. I'd do experiments at home, mixing up chemicals and stuff. A chemistry professor friend of my parents came round and I showed her the next experiment I had lined up. I was thinking she's going to say it's silly, but in fact she went, 'That could explode, you know'. I had to drop the whole idea, but I thought it was so cool – what she'd said! I hadn't realised I was capable of creating something like that.

Woman: Jumping forward in time, how did you get into your role as a communicator about science?

Man: I'd always known I'd study science and did various degrees and postgraduate studies, and then I started to wonder if this was really what I wanted to do. For some bizarre reason, which is quite mysterious to me, I just had this burning hunger to pass on all the amazing stuff I knew about. I used to chat to friends about science things and I discovered that the more I knew, the more interesting my stories seemed to them.

Woman: And you left a good job as a research scientist …

Man: That's right. I was on great pay, with a long-term contract, but I gave it all up. It doesn't sound modest, but I had a great deal of confidence that somehow I could write and talk about scientific ideas and information in a way that would appeal to people who didn't know so much. I was staying in the same subject area, just doing something else with my knowledge.

Woman: How did you get the job of presenter on the TV series *Sci World*?

Man: I'd written an article about genetic engineering that attracted a lot of attention and I was interviewed on another TV show about it. The producer of *Sci World* saw me and called me up to offer me the job. He said I knew how to research topics thoroughly and could put them across very clearly, but it was my passion he claimed he'd spotted … and a keenness to investigate things that matter to people.

Woman: How do you choose what to write about for magazines and newspapers?

Man: Although it's impossible to be 100% certain what'll go down well, you have a pretty fair idea and one thing that makes me go for, say, the subject of how oil, which I wrote about recently, how it's formed and what it consists of, was there'd been a big oil spill from a ship that was in the headlines. So, there's a reason for knowing about it. There's no single topic there's always a demand for.

Woman: What's the secret to communicating with the public about science, Dean?

Man: There's no magic key. When I'm initially exploring an area I'm going to write about, I try and hold onto what I didn't fully get at first. That makes it easier to figure out what'll be most difficult for people. It's not how you'd talk to colleagues, other scientists. But then again, it's not like you want to remove all the science from it and make it sound like some sort of story designed to be understood by a little kid.

SPEAKING PART 1

 Training Exercise 4

Examiner: Kasper, how did you spend your evening yesterday?

Kasper: As soon as I finished work yesterday, I went to a concert in the park with some friends from my class. We saw a great band and then we went to a café.

Examiner: Maria, do you enjoy taking photos with a phone?

Maria: Actually, I chose a phone with a good camera for exactly that reason and I take pictures all the time. My favourite ones are pictures I take of my friends.

Examiner: When was the last time you did some sport?

Kasper: I try to exercise every day and I went to the sports centre near my college before my lessons yesterday. I used the gym and the pool.

Examiner: Would you rather watch a film in the cinema, on TV or on a computer?

Kasper: I'm not that keen on movies, actually, but when I do watch them, it's usually at home on the TV, because I feel more comfortable there and it's cheaper than the cinema. I don't watch movies on my computer because they don't look very good on a small screen.

Examiner: Tell us what you usually do when the weather is bad.

Kasper: I hate the rain, so on rainy days, I just stay at home and watch TV or I might do something creative, like baking or art. It depends on my mood.

 Exam practice

1 How did you learn to ride a bike?
2 Tell us about your first English lessons.
3 Would you be interested in becoming a teacher?
4 How do you feel about learning online?
5 Do you work best in the mornings or in the evenings?

SPEAKING PART 2

 Training Exercise 3b

Interlocutor: In this part of the test, I'm going to give each of you two photographs. I'd like you to talk about your photographs on your own for about a minute and also to answer a question about your partner's photographs.

It's your turn first. Here are your photographs. They show people protecting the environment in different ways. I'd like you to compare the photographs and say why you think the people decided to protect the environment in these ways.

Candidate: Both of the pictures show people doing positive things for the environment. In the first picture, there's a group of people who seem to have just finished cleaning the beach, because they have lots of bags full of rubbish. They look happy and pleased with the result. I think they have chosen to do this because they can see the benefits immediately. Doing something like this in a group is a good idea because it's more fun and they can encourage each other. I think the action the people in the second picture are taking is more about a change of lifestyle. The results aren't as easy to see, at least not immediately. I think these people are going to work and they decided to go by bike or scooter rather than by car to reduce pollution. Like I say, the results aren't instant, like in the first picture, but it's a good long-term action and I imagine they feel pleased that they're doing something positive for the environment.

SPEAKING PART 4

 Training Exercise 2a

1 Well, today everyone says, 'Just look it up online!' But the problem is, there's a lot of incorrect information online, isn't there?
2 That's a difficult question, I'm not really sure … I suppose, I think it might be because they're afraid of getting it wrong. I mean, if they suggest something, and, er, then there's a problem, they might feel, um, guilty. Do you see what I mean?
3 I don't think we can compare them. I mean, maybe it depends on what the situation is and who is likely to be able to advise you better, so we can't compare them. Maybe your parents have more experience, but compared with your parents, maybe your friends know your likes and dislikes better.
4 That's a very interesting question. A review is just an opinion, isn't it? For instance, if I ask my friends what their favourite book is, I might not like it as much, but that doesn't mean I can't trust them. What's more, it's interesting to find out what other people think.

Test 3 Audioscript

LISTENING PART 1

One.

You hear a podcaster talking about the issue of success in life.

Man: Living up to other people's expectations can be difficult, especially if you've been successful in the past. It can make you set ambitious goals that take you down a path where nothing less than being the best is tolerable. This can lead to a need to compete and to see others' success as some sort of personal failure. As we become more mature and succeed due to our experience and expertise, we often begin to understand and accept that there are always going to be people who are more successful. It's worth noting, too, that competitive types who regularly achieve success may become arrogant, which most would agree is an undesirable characteristic.

Two.

You hear a man telling a woman about the yoga classes he attends.

Woman: How's your yoga course going?

Man: It's great. I admit some of the bending and stretching can be tough. I'm looking for something beyond the physical, though – you know, mental clarity, relief from stress, greater inner peace ... that sort of thing.

Woman: A lot to ask for!

Man: Yeah, well, yoga's popular for very good reasons! What's really remarkable is that it has such ancient roots. They go back thousands of years. Why do you think it's been kept going? Because of what it offers in terms of being good for the mind, body and spirit. And it's possible for anyone, regardless of age, shape or ability, to get something out of it.

Three.

You hear two friends talking about football.

Woman: I really can't stand it when players play defensively in football – you know, focusing on preventing the other team from scoring.

Man: Totally. I'd rather see lots of missed opportunities to score than players not getting anywhere because they're being blocked. In the greatest matches, it's the opposite of defensive.

Woman: That's right. And unpredictability adds excitement. That happens when you've got high levels of energy and both teams play an attacking game.

Man: Good point. You never know what's going to happen next, which makes for more thrills. But if one team scores a lot more than the other, it tends to mean it's one-sided.

Woman: I know what you mean.

Four.
You hear a young man talking to a friend about learning to drive.

Man: Learning to drive's challenging. You know the town hall?

Woman: Yeah?

Man: The road sign there means you're supposed to give way to traffic coming from the right. I've spent hours learning the driving regulations – that's my strong area – but I thought the car approaching was going slow enough to let me go and I drove out.

Woman: There's so much to think about.

Man: True. But the reason I mention it is because it tells me it's about experience. Any beginner could do what I did. Luckily, the other car slowed down in time. It's really not difficult to mess up. Only years of driving help you make good judgements.

Woman: I guess so.

Five.
You hear a woman talking to a friend about a book she has just read.

Woman: Have you read that novel by Harvey Dole?

Man: No. Everyone's talking about it.

Woman: That's why I read it. In fact, the publicity just shows the separation that can exist between excellent marketing and actual literary skill. The novel deals with topics like human relationships, age and culture, as well as politics and various other stuff.

Man: Sounds OK.

Woman: Yeah, it might work better on TV … I mean, the basic plot's exciting. It's just the author's style – he repeats ideas and it's often hard to follow what he means. The hero, the guy the whole story kind of focuses on, isn't that appealing, either. A good actor could do something with the role, though.

Six.
You hear two people talking about space exploration.

Man: I'm not sure how urgent sending humans to the moon or Mars is.

Woman: It's hardly a priority. Despite the media's interest in space tourism, there's limited interest from the public in personal space travel. Most is from super-rich billionaires.

Man: Huge amounts of money are being spent on space-related technology.

Woman: And in the past, some of these innovations have been adapted to benefit humanity, like fire-resistant materials or GPS for navigating and mapping. So, there's value in carrying on with that sort of investment. I'm less convinced about the need to find planets with similar conditions to those here on Earth, however useful it might be in the future.

Man: Really?

Seven.
You hear a man talking about some psychology research.

Man: A recent psychology study investigated social networks, by which I mean the various types of social relationships people have. Most people can maintain connections with around 150 people at most: largely family, friends, neighbours, colleagues, but also people they know through things like sports or social media and online connections. This had already been established previously, so wasn't particularly remarkable. However, more interestingly, the research also showed the quality of personal connection matters. It makes a difference how meaningful and supportive relationships are. And it's amazing how we differ in terms of how much effort we all put into keeping in touch and going out of our way to connect with others.

Eight.
You hear two colleagues talking about their boss.

Man: We're lucky to have Martin as our boss. He's so approachable.

Woman: That's essential for a boss.

Man: And he's open to feedback. You can say if something isn't a good idea and he welcomes it. That's unusual.

Woman: Too right. It's also necessary to be direct with staff. He sometimes lets people get away with things, because he doesn't want to say anything that'd cause negative feelings.

Man: It's good to be like that. Sometimes it's better not to be too straightforward or critical, for the sake of human relations. Anyway, he's very forward looking. He gives us opportunities to try doing things in new ways.

Woman: Which all bosses should do.

LISTENING PART 2

You will hear part of a travel podcast in which a man called Danny Blake is talking about a climb he did with friends and a guide up Mount Batur, a volcano in Bali, an island in Indonesia.

Man: Now on the podcast, I'm Danny Blake. I'll tell you about an unmissable experience for visitors to the island of Bali – climbing the still-active volcano Mount Batur. Going to see sunrise from the top is a popular excursion there and some friends and I booked a tour with a guide.

It all began with meeting our guide Wayan at four in the morning. He supplied us with some necessary items. I knew from information in advance that we'd get a pair of hiking poles for maintaining balance on rough ground and torches to light the track in the dark and also snacks to keep our energy levels up. I couldn't believe I'd forgotten drinking water, so it was a huge weight off my shoulders when Wayan handed me some, luckily included in the price.

Wayan informed us that because Mount Batur's still an active volcano, it's closely monitored, so there were no worries about any danger. At one time, it was believed to have been around 3,800 metres tall, before the top of it collapsed, forming what's called a caldera. Its current peak is at about 1,700 metres, somewhat lower than that of Bali's tallest volcano, which is 3,140 metres high. Fortunately for us, we only had to hike 500 metres up Mount Batur, as we were driven part of the way up.

Dressing appropriately is essential. Take a jacket, definitely. And hiking boots are best, though my hiking sandals were comfortable and meant my feet could breathe. Flip-flops aren't advisable, but plenty of hikers wore trainers, which seemed good enough. I also saw people wearing headlamps – excellent for seeing the way and having hands free.

After a short while hiking, the temperature change was noticeable. Obviously, you get colder temperatures as you get higher. Despite having felt full of energy to start with, I soon felt exhausted – no surprise, given the steepness of the climb, but what was bizarre was the warm air pockets that seemed to come from nowhere, but actually came from the ground, proving we were on a live volcano.

In the group, complaints were heard about how steep it was, although there were brief spells of flatness every half hour or so. Despite being asked for breaks by some, Wayan encouraged us to keep going and make do with snacks like energy bars. It wasn't that bad, but it was a shame the lack of light prevented any photo opportunities.

There were many other hikers on the volcano and someone mistook the tiny white sparkles from their torches in the distance for fireflies. Wayan said they were just flashlights. Personally, I thought they looked like little diamonds. Rather beautiful in the black of night.

The climb time was two and a half hours and by the end, the physical effects were noticeable. Anyone can do the trek, but don't take that to mean it's a complete joke. It was a leg workout! And you notice there's less oxygen available. The way down's easier, but a real ankle twister, as it's also easy to fall over!

Along the way, there were loads of monkeys around, eager to grab climbers' snacks. I witnessed one making off with a chocolate bar someone had put down and if I hadn't spotted it in time, I might have had my sunglasses seized. They were lying on my backpack, which a daring monkey had approached, probably smelling the bag of nuts inside!

Everyone began taking photos as first light arrived. The sunrise was stunning, with the sky shaded in gorgeous reds and pinks. It was actually quite hard to get a picture without tourists in view, so it was great that one of mine really showed the clouds off well. They looked like a blanket below the tops of other nearby volcanoes.

On top of Mount Batur, the scenery's dramatic, with black lava rocks from different eruptions clearly visible. What was really striking was that they were so varied. The colours ranged from deep black to dark grey, some sharp and jagged, others more rounded. And the rocks were quite slippery on the way down.

LISTENING PART 3

You will hear five short extracts in which people are talking about learning to play a musical instrument.

Speaker 1

I've never been musically gifted, but in my 40s, I got this idea in my head of learning to play the piano. I'm not sure why – maybe something to do with my mum having been a talented pianist. I know I could never be as good as her, so it's not as if I've got any major expectations of myself. I do practise fairly regularly, but I can't say I've improved that much. I certainly avoid letting anyone else hear me ... for fear they'll laugh! Even so, I'm quite proud of myself for taking on a challenge and it's something to do when I get bored at the very least.

Speaker 2

Taking up the saxophone's been a real source of joy, even if it's a bit painful for other people listening when I'm practising! I just have to stick at it and maybe one day I'll sound like a true professional! I actually thought it'd feel far more of a chore getting round to practising every day, but I actually look forward to it. A couple of friends of mine took up the sax and when they realised how much commitment it would take, they gave up. I can't imagine getting like that. I know I've got a long way to go before I'm any good, but I've never been a quitter.

Speaker 3

Learning to play guitar hasn't been 100% smooth sailing, but I'm noticing some major improvements and I'm feeling ready to do a performance for my mum and dad and their friends. They keep begging me to. They're both musicians and were always telling me I should learn to play. Even though I was a bit of a late starter, I've totally got into it. Yet it seems like only yesterday that I was a complete beginner. Anyway, I've set myself an ambitious target – to master both acoustic and electric guitar within a year or at least play them in a way that'll make people sit up and listen!

Speaker 4

Playing a musical instrument's supposed to be good for your intellect, which would be handy, as I'm doing a degree in maths. I'm still waiting for an increase in brainpower! Anyway, I wanted a challenging instrument, so I went for the violin. I'm finding I feel like playing far more on some days than others. It depends so much on being in the right mood. Having said that, I'm doing OK, though I may have been over-ambitious thinking I'd be able to reach a decent level by practising seven hours a week. I've been told by other violinists you need to do about three hours daily, so I'm going to have a go!

Speaker 5

Playing drums looked like fun to me and it's lived up to that. I've been learning for a year and it's funny how it breaks the ice in social situations. Everyone loves chatting about music, which is a bonus, as I didn't know many people in my area and I find making conversation awkward. I've now made friends with a guy who plays guitar and meeting up to play together's become a regular thing. I thought I wasn't good enough to play with anyone else, but he's about the same level as me, so it works out well. Who knows? We could start a band if anyone else wanted to join us.

LISTENING PART 4

You will hear an interview with a woman called Claire Kaledos, who is a personal trainer and helps people with personal health and fitness goals.

Man: With me is Claire Kaledos to tell us about her career as a personal trainer, helping people achieve their health and fitness goals. Claire, what qualifications do personal trainers need?

Woman: Most start with a basic diploma. Obviously, that's essential if you want a job somewhere like a gym or other professional institution. I hadn't realised how crucial these certificates are in the case of someone getting injured in a session and wanting to take you to court. It means you'll get proper insurance for that. And of course, as I well knew, the diploma was just the beginning of my journey towards being a true expert.

Man: How soon did you start working after qualifying?

Woman: There are so many people qualifying, so it took time to get established. I was taking on clients in a couple of gyms, not a huge income, but doing what I loved, and in my early 20s, it really set me up well for keeping myself in good shape. I must admit the job's a lot for a young person to handle, advising others about such serious matters as health. I hadn't really taken on board what a big thing that was.

Man: You use social media a lot for publicity, don't you?

Woman: Yes, it's a must. And you have to create an image for yourself. All personal trainers try to come across as dynamic, someone who can inspire people in their workouts. That's such a common approach for social media, so to stand out more, I focused on how fresh and original I was, trying out the latest techniques and keen to experiment with cutting-edge tech. I felt it was too early to be impressing others with my expert teaching and huge knowledge of my subject!

Man: You're now self-employed. Is that difficult?

Woman: I thought it'd take ages before enough people were seeking out my services that I'd be able to support myself and I was really anxious about that. But it didn't take long before I'd built up a list of fitness fans willing to sign up with me, and I could let go of my worries and calm down! To be honest, the accounting and submitting tax forms I have to do come far less naturally than advising people on fitness!

Man: I heard you recently worked with the actor Jake Greenford!

Woman: Jake's one of several celebrities I've been privileged to train, I'm proud to say. He had to increase his muscle power in a short space of time for a particular action movie and, you know, he was truly shocked when I went through what it'd involve. It meant some major lifestyle alterations! The physical work was tough for him, as I pushed him really hard. In the end, he and his director were both absolutely thrilled with his new look after our sessions, though.

Man: So what issues do clients have doing personal training?

Woman: Well, if someone has an injury, or pain from one, that can make them feel like quitting, but it's fairly rare, as we really try to avoid injuries! If people had more time, my job'd be considerably easier. Everyone seems to struggle to fit their sessions into their daily or weekly routine. Oh, and you occasionally get people saying they haven't got what it takes to achieve the outcomes they're aiming for, but, hey, that's what I'm there for – to encourage them and make them feel that, yes, they can do it!

Man: Have you changed during your years as a personal trainer, Claire?

Woman: Oh, I think my awareness has grown of how important it is to look after your body and mind. It's about being able to recognise your own needs and take the necessary steps to improve your well-being. If I can do that personally, I can help others do the same – I've always wanted to help people in some way. It's fascinating how different we all are and yet we all share similar emotions. And it's increasingly clear to me that we need to get the fitness message across, now so much work involves sitting at a desk all day.

SPEAKING PART 1

Interlocutor: First, we'd like to know something about you. Where do you live, Mayumi?
Mayumi: I'm from Tokyo, Japan.
Interlocutor: And you, Stefan?
Stefan: I'm from Switzerland. I live in Zurich.
Interlocutor: Mayumi, how do you usually celebrate important events in your family?
Mayumi: Oh, we like to organise a special meal. We cook traditional Japanese food at home or sometimes we go out to a restaurant. I prefer staying at home.
Interlocutor: How would you like to celebrate your next birthday, Stefan?
Stefan: With my friends.
Interlocutor: Why?
Stefan: Because my friends and I like having parties together and that's a good way to celebrate a birthday.
Interlocutor: Mayumi, do you like taking lots of photos of important events?
Mayumi: Well, it depends on the event. If it's a celebration with family or friends, it's nice to take some photos, but not too many. I prefer to spend time chatting. But a big event like a festival is a nice time to take photos.
Interlocutor: Stefan, have you ever entered any competitions?
Stefan: Sports competitions, yes. I like swimming and I've entered a lot of swimming competitions. I've even won some of them. I'm entering one next week, actually, so I'm doing a lot of training at the moment.
Interlocutor: Thank you.

SPEAKING PART 2

Interlocutor: Stefan, it's your turn first. Here are your photographs. They show people who need to prepare well in different situations. I'd like you to compare the photographs and say what you think the people might find difficult about preparing for these situations.
Stefan: The first photo is of a music performance. I imagine it's some kind of classical music. There's a group of people singing and a woman is playing a piano. There's also a woman at the front, I think she's the conductor. Everyone has to prepare for their own role in this performance so that they can perform well. That takes a lot of training. I think it'll be difficult for them all to prepare together, because it's hard to find a time when everyone can meet. If they don't prepare well, the concert might not be good. I think all the people in the second picture also need to prepare well, but in slightly different ways. The children are doing some kind of science experiment, so they need to be prepared with the right kind of safety equipment. They need to know what they're doing. The teacher needs to prepare by making sure the children all know what they have to do and that they understand how to keep themselves safe. They're all wearing white coats to protect their clothes, gloves to protect their hands and special glasses to protect their eyes, for example. I don't think it's particularly difficult for them to prepare for this experiment, but it is important to prepare carefully.
Interlocutor: Thank you. Mayumi, do you enjoy classical music?
Mayumi: To be honest, no, I don't. I find it really boring, because it's usually quite slow and I prefer loud rock music. When I hear music, I want to dance, I don't want to just sit and listen, so a concert like the one in the first photo isn't for me.
Interlocutor: Now, Mayumi, here are your photographs. They show people showing things in different situations. I'd like you to compare the photographs and say why you think the people have decided to show these things.
Mayumi: So, in the first picture, a man's showing something, whereas in the second picture, a friend is showing something. In the first picture, I suppose they're in a garden and the man's showing the other two men what he's grown or what he needs to do on his garden. Maybe he's proud of what he's grown or he's hoping to get their help with something, like mending a fence or planting some new things. The woman in the second picture is showing her friend some clothing. It looks like a T-shirt. The women are in a shop, so I suppose she's showing her friend because she wants her advice on whether she should buy it or not. Or maybe the woman holding the T-shirt thinks her friend would like it. She seems happy, so she's enjoying the shopping experience. It looks like a nice shop because it's very bright and the clothes look good.
Interlocutor: Thank you. Stefan, do you enjoy shopping with friends?
Stefan: Oh yes, I really do. I try to go shopping with friends once or twice a month. We don't only look for clothes, though. Sometimes we shop for books or posters. Shopping with friends is much more fun than shopping on your own, because you have someone to get advice from.

SPEAKING PART 3

Interlocutor: Now, I'd like you to talk about something together for about two minutes. Here are some things many people think are helpful when someone moves to live somewhere new and a question for you to discuss. First, you have some time to look at the task. Now, talk to each other about whether you think these things are helpful when someone moves to live somewhere new.
Stefan: OK, I've never moved to live anywhere new, but I imagine it's difficult at first, mainly because you don't know people. So, I think this point about joining clubs or societies is a good one. That way, you can meet people.
Mayumi: I agree. If it's a club, like a sports club, you'll find it easy to speak to people and make friends. Do you think it's a good idea for someone to invite people to their home?
Stefan: Oh, I don't know. Maybe after a while, but I wouldn't say it's the first thing people should do.
Mayumi: I completely agree. It takes some time for people to feel confident and relaxed with people so that they want to invite them to their home, doesn't it? Which brings me to the point about decorating their home. If people do that, they'll feel happy about how it looks and then maybe they'll want to have visitors.
Stefan: Yes, but if they spend all their time at home doing work on their house, they won't have time to meet people and, like we said, that's one of the most important things. So, how about giving gifts to neighbours?
Mayumi: Like flowers or a cake? That could be nice and it's important for people to have a good relationship with their neighbours.
Stefan: Exactly, so doing something nice, like giving a present, is a good start!
Mayumi: OK, so the last point is about walking around the local area. How do you think this would help?
Stefan: Well, they'd get to know the area, like where the shops are, where to get the bus, that kind of thing.
Mayumi: Yes, and maybe they'd meet people at the same time.
Interlocutor: Thank you. Now you have about a minute to decide which two things are most helpful when someone moves to live somewhere new.
Mayumi: Well, I think we've already agreed that meeting people is the most helpful thing, because that way, the person wouldn't feel lonely.
Stefan: Yes, and if they get to know local people, these people can show them around the area. So, should we choose the point about joining clubs or societies? I think we said that's the easiest way to meet people.
Mayumi: Definitely. We need one other point, don't we? I know you felt it's not a good idea to stay in the house all the time, but I still think decorating the house or apartment is a good idea. It'd make the person feel comfortable. What do you think? Is that OK for the second point?

Stefan: Yes, I see what you mean. If people balance decorating their home with meeting people by joining clubs, then they've done the two most important things. Let's choose those.

SPEAKING PART 4

Interlocutor: What do you think someone new to the area where you live would enjoy about living there? Mayumi?

Mayumi: Personally, I really appreciate how easy it is to get around and reach the places you want to be, so I can get to the city centre easily for shopping or I can get out into the countryside easily. But I think it's the city which is the biggest attraction for people – it's not like all the cities you see where the shops are all the same, it's got lots of independent businesses and it's a nice place to walk around.

Interlocutor: What do you think?

Stefan: Where I come from is a bit more rural. Of course, there are cities quite close by, but we don't go to them often, only when we need something we can't get in our local towns. I think someone moving here would really like how friendly it is and how peaceful it is. If they come from a busy city, though, they might get a bit bored.

Interlocutor: Stefan, do you think that it's a good idea to live in the same place your whole life?

Stefan: I think these days, very few people live in the same area where they were born their whole lives, because it's so easy to travel to different places. I don't think I'd like to live in another country, but in another part of my country would be a great experience, I think.

Interlocutor: Do you agree?

Mayumi: I see what Stefan means. I think it can be good to stay in the same area, because that usually means you have family nearby and you don't lose touch with them. I wouldn't mind staying in my area, as long as I can travel to other places on holiday!

Interlocutor: Why do you think people choose to live in a capital city?

Stefan: Well, capital cities often have the best facilities, all the things we've already mentioned. Talking about entertainment again, if you want to see a famous singer or actor, they're more likely to go to a capital city than to a smaller town.

Mayumi: Well, yes, but do you really think that's why people choose to live in capital cities? I think it's probably true that they don't actually choose this, it's just where the best jobs are and that's why they end up living there.

Stefan: That's an interesting point – maybe it isn't a choice, just the only option. I hadn't thought of that.

Interlocutor: Some young people like to stay at home when they study at college or university. Other young people think it's better to move away from home to study. What do you think?

Stefan: In my country, students usually live at home. It's cheaper and more convenient, so that's probably why. What about in your country?

Mayumi: It's the same. It's very unusual to move to another city or another country. I do think there are some advantages to moving away, such as learning to be more independent.

Stefan: That's what I was thinking. If you have to live away from home, you have to learn how to look after yourself …

Mayumi: So university becomes more useful. You're learning about life as well as learning a subject.

Stefan: But it is so expensive to live independently. I think I'd still choose to live at home if I could.

Interlocutor: Do you think that living in another country is easier now than it was in the past?

Stefan: I suppose one thing that makes it easier is technology, because it's easier to translate from one language to another and it's easier to keep in touch with people at home.

Mayumi: That's true. With the internet, it's also so much easier to find out about the rules and laws of a new country. But you still have to live there and get to know the lifestyle – I think that's something people can only learn by being there, so technology doesn't help.

Stefan: I agree. But I do think that travelling and moving to a new country is more common than it used to be, so that probably makes it easier.

Mayumi: That's a good point. I imagine that a hundred years ago it was quite unusual to move to live in a different country, but now it's not.

Interlocutor: Thank you, that is the end of the test.

Test 4 Audioscript

LISTENING PART 1

One.

You hear part of a talk about working life.

Woman: The workplace can be a stressful environment if you're under pressure to get things done as quickly and efficiently as possible, especially if the project in question isn't straightforward. It's sensible to bear in mind that you aren't the only person who can solve problems and to have the self-awareness to get others involved when needed. Talking to colleagues about how you can cooperate together to get things done may well be the best solution. If you can come up with ways of sharing out the load, it can be more effective as a strategy than going it alone, especially when you're unlikely to meet a deadline otherwise.

Two.

You hear a woman talking about shopping for clothes.

Woman: I often find myself heading towards the changing room in a shop with something I've picked up without thinking through properly whether it's something I'm likely to wear more than once. Once it's on in front of the mirror, I assess it more coolly. So I'll consider as truthfully as possible how good I look in it – is it my style? And also, whether I'd be happy to wear it for longer than the few minutes it's on me in the changing room and on multiple occasions. Then there's the issue of whether it's good value for money. If something passes these checks, it might just be worth investing in.

Three.

You hear two friends talking about a TV documentary on organic gardening.

Man: I'm going to watch that documentary you recommended tonight – the one on organic gardening.

Woman: I'll be interested to hear your views on the programme, as you love gardening.

Man: I'm sure it'll be fascinating. The biggest issue is preventing insects and other pests that can damage plants. And that's a major challenge, even when you use chemicals and things. I suppose something that's common to all gardening is the need for good soil for growing anything – getting your soil healthy is key. You have to do things like add organic substances to the soil and also cover the soil surface to conserve moisture.

Woman: Yes, and keep weeds down.

Four.

You hear two people talking about a crime novel they both read called Wide Eyes.

Man: *Wide Eyes* was a brilliant read in the end, don't you think? It certainly gave me some insights into what makes people tick, you know – why they behave as they do.

Woman: Well, personally, I think its outstanding point was how each chapter ended on a cliff-hanger, so you wanted to go on to the next one to find out what happened.

Man: There's no doubt it did that and I liked the way it all ended with Ronnie – you know, the bad guy – getting caught like that.

Woman: I actually felt sympathy for him, so it was slightly disturbing when the police took him away … despite him obviously being guilty, of course.

Five.

You hear part of a podcast in which a woman is talking about approaches to time.

Woman: Time can be viewed in many different ways. For example, certain cultures value punctuality and efficiency more than others. That's what I tend to identify with, as someone who finds schedules necessary and who has a need to be constantly getting things done. However, it's interesting how some cultures place greater value on meaningful relationships and experiences than on completing tasks within set timeframes, where it's less about achievement and more about connection, either with other people or with the rhythms of life, such as night and day or the coming and going of the seasons. Relating to time like this differs notably from my own chosen way of doing things.

Six.

You hear part of an arts programme in which a man is talking about sculpture.

Man: Stone has been used to create sculptures throughout the ages. It has countless benefits. For example, the range of textures available, from soft limestone to rocky granite, offers great freedom to an artist, with each kind presenting unique challenges and opportunities. Chief among the qualities it is chosen for is its capacity to survive tough conditions, such as harsh weather or being roughly handled. This cannot be said of metals or wood, although all these various materials have visual appeal of one sort or another. Each has patterns within it that add to the qualities that can make a sculpture attractive to the eye.

Seven.

You hear a woman talking to a friend about her new electric bike.

Man: Wow, I love your new e-bike!
Woman: Yeah, it's cool for riding around town.
Man: Very wise to wear a helmet, though!
Woman: Yeah, well, it's common sense to protect yourself, although I don't feel at risk on the roads, you know, from cars and other vehicles.
Man: Does it have a guarantee?
Woman: Yeah, for two years. I worried that'd be enough before I bought it, but now I realise it's such a simple design that keeping it in good condition's not a problem. There isn't much that could go wrong. And it's so convenient for getting round, so it doesn't matter that it doesn't get up to very high speeds.

Eight.

You hear two friends talking about reaching the age of 30.

Woman: Can you remember what it was like to turn 30?
Man: It wasn't that long ago! Things changed, but often in good ways, like I had more self-confidence. I remember being aware that there was still a lot I wanted to do, although I'd made a fair amount of progress in my career.
Woman: Did your friendship circle get smaller?
Man: Yeah. I still had the same energy for adventure, exploring new places and having a good time, but I was more independent, so it didn't bother me that I wouldn't spend so much time with people I knew, who were entering different life stages, like moving home, getting promoted at work or bringing up kids.

LISTENING PART 2

You will hear a man called Charlie Buckingham talking about working as a volunteer at an animal shelter, where animals that have been injured or are not wanted are cared for.

Man: Hi, I'm Charlie Buckingham, here to talk about going to an animal shelter in my town, where I help by volunteering at weekends. The shelter takes care of animals that have been injured, lost, abandoned or mistreated – mostly dogs and cats. I discovered that not everyone can look after their animals properly. Sometimes it's due to lack of knowledge or education and sometimes lack of funds. While food for most animals is generally affordable, it's upsetting that it's medical treatment that can be costly. That's the major cause of owners deciding not to keep an animal and eventually the poor things end up at the shelter.

Fortunately, animal shelters exist to take care of unwanted animals and some of these are adopted by new owners, who visit the shelter and choose from the animals there. With dogs, for example, certain things affect their chances of being adopted, training being the primary one. If they've been taught to behave appropriately, their appearance doesn't matter much, although occasionally size is relevant, as some people want a big dog or a small one.

Staff at the shelter instruct new volunteers in the daily tasks. These range from preparing and distributing food and water to more fun jobs like playing with the animals or walking them. Cleaning is what we're busiest with and that's what I remember taking up the whole day when I began volunteering.

Wearing suitable clothes is important and jeans and T-shirts are best. I didn't know open-toed shoes like sandals aren't recommended, but it makes sense. What was unexpected was the tip to avoid perfume. Apparently, it can overwhelm the sensitive noses of animals and cause them discomfort or stress. And obviously, dangly earrings and things like that aren't appropriate.

Some volunteers are fans of dogs, while others prefer cats. I think dog people are the majority. Allergies to cats are common, which is probably why fewer volunteers go for them. Cuteness is a quality in animals, which makes puppies and kittens so appealing, but older animals have qualities like loyalty or affectionate behaviour. Most of us at the shelter are drawn to animals of all kinds.

All animals need love, but those who've had a hard time in the past have special requirements. The dedication of volunteers is impressive, doing their utmost to make sure the animals get what they need. It's what I'd describe as quality time that's sometimes in short supply. We'd all like to have more of it with individual animals, but there's so much to do, making sure the shelter runs smoothly.

I love seeing dogs in my care looking healthy and happy. There are certain things that indicate well-being, such as a good appetite. You can also tell a lot from happy-looking eyes or a healthy coat and skin. Plus, a happy dog makes the right sounds, not growls of fear. For me, it's the tail I look at. If it's wagging from side to side, it's the surest sign of happiness!

I'm planning to adopt a dog from the shelter myself. His name's Archie and he's full of playfulness. What's really remarkable about him is his intelligence. That's what made me set my heart on adopting him. He's had a tough life full of difficulty, but his gentleness is obvious.

The shelter's always trying to raise money and the public are generous with financial donations. We also get other gifts, anything from food bowls to towels. Even office supplies are helpful. Most things are welcome, especially toys for animals, which fortunately, we get more than anything else. It doesn't matter if they're old and used. Our animals love them.

It's not just skills with animals that volunteers need. We raise funds by selling second-hand things we've had donated and we have a weekly open day showing visitors round. I help with website posts advertising things for sale that we've had donated. I'm less good at writing descriptions of the items, but my photography abilities come in handy, so potential customers can see an image of something they might buy.

LISTENING PART 3

You will hear five short extracts in which people are talking about taking dance classes.

Speaker 1

Woman: Taking hip-hop dance classes was great. It's a very dynamic type of music and dancing to it, you need stamina and strength. I struggled with that – you know, the demands on energy of the moves – but the whole experience opened my eyes to the value of regular exercise. And I enjoyed getting caught up in watching other people – some of their dancing was very impressive – and also thinking about the words of the music along with the dance steps. Our instructor sometimes got us to do individual performances and I often fell over. It's easy to lose your balance, but I wasn't the only one, luckily.

Speaker 2

Man: I did salsa classes, which it's super-important to be fit for – it's such a physically demanding dance style. I loved that sensation of feeling my whole body working. Fantastic! For me, keeping my focus was the real test. My mind wandered a bit when we had to repeat steps again and again. The teacher was so patient, trying to communicate the different dance concepts to students of varying skill levels. I'm not naturally a fast learner, but I still achieved more than I expected in a short time. We even put on a show at the end of the course, which friends and family came along to.

Speaker 3

Woman: I took flamenco dance classes in Spain. Understanding and interpreting music ... it's an essential aspect of dance and something that doesn't come naturally to everyone. Learning the footwork, positioning your body, your arms and also timing – all that requires a good memory, along with practice, but it's rewarding once you've mastered a set of steps. Although I memorised things and could do them perfectly without an audience, I was clumsier with my feet when I knew I was being observed. Frustrating, as it wasn't like I'd forgotten what to do! Anyway, I really got into the emotional intensity of flamenco, but I also appreciated the effects it had on my physical well-being.

Speaker 4

Man: I took ballroom dance classes, inspired by seeing it on TV. I've always had a gift for dancing when it's quite free and natural, but I wasn't sure what I'd be like keeping in step with a partner. Choreography is the whole art of combining movements and when you're not used to learning sequences, it can be quite challenging to recall the steps, especially in more complex routines. That's something I had to work hard on, anyway. Fortunately, our tutor was very effective at getting across what to do and demonstrated everything to us clearly. I also had a nice dance partner and together, we made pretty satisfying progress.

Speaker 5

Woman: I started tap dance classes last year. There are always things that could distract you from what you should be giving your attention to, but I loved how the classes took my mind off my worries and I could get lost in what I was doing. Some students already knew the steps and were just there to perfect them or show off. I think it made me feel rather insecure about my own ability and knowledge compared to them. But I tried not to let that put me off, as I'm a perfectly good dancer in other dance styles and it was just a matter of time and practice for me.

LISTENING PART 4

You will hear an interview with a woman called Samantha Caine, who works as a professional food stylist, preparing food and drinks for photography, television and advertising.

Man: Food stylists work with food to make it visually appealing for purposes such as photography, television and advertisements. With me is food stylist Samantha Caine. What made you choose this career, Samantha?

Woman: Hi. Well, I'd always known I'd do something food-related. I studied at cookery school, worked in restaurants and set up my own recipe blog. Taking photos for that caught my imagination and the more I saw what food styling involves, the more I realised how suited I was to it, because there are so many avenues to explore – every commission presents a new challenge. It's allowed me to learn about some fascinating subjects, too ... like art and history and technology.

Man: Tell us about one of your first assignments.

Woman: I remember one for a magazine recipe section. It was simple enough – to cook the dishes and arrange them for the photographer. I knew exactly what was wanted and I'd thoroughly checked the details of it all, I thought ... but it was a lesson for me, as the dishes weren't at their best after several hours under studio lights. I ended up wishing I'd paid more attention to that than all those little extra touches, such as the right tablecloth, plates and bowls that match nicely and so on.

Man: What was it like working on the TV drama *Brookertown*?

Woman: I was really thrilled to be asked to coordinate the food in the scenes involving eating and drinking. And I couldn't help noticing the eagerness of the cast tucking into what I'd prepared both during and after filming. That was super-rewarding. Being on the set of a TV production is a nerve-wracking experience – there's so much going on and the atmosphere can be extremely tense, so I did my best to make sure I didn't get in the way of camera operators and other important people on the set.

Man: Food stylists use certain techniques. Are there any you avoid?

Woman: Well, the whole aim of them is to ensure things are arranged to have as appealing an appearance as possible in the final image. For example, edible glue might be used to hold things together to look better or oil gets sprayed on to make something shine attractively. I'd rather not do that if it means things are unlikely to get consumed afterwards. Ideally, any tricks of the trade add flavour and there are ways to enhance the pink of a strawberry milkshake or the blueish purple of a fruit jam with a food dye and for them to taste delicious.

Man: I loved your work on the ad for a famous brand of chocolates.

Woman: Thank you. Of course, the true measure of an ad for something like chocolates is if more customers buy them! The director in charge had a specific mood in mind for the setting and we filmed outdoors in a garden on a sunny day. I was so concerned about the chocolates melting. Some roses I'd put nearby saved them due to the lovely shadow they cast. I'd like to say it was what I'd anticipated, but it was more of a fortunate coincidence.

Man: So, what's the secret of your success, Samantha?

Woman: A food stylist has to manage lots of conflicting demands. The key talent is coming up with a visual arrangement that is unique and stands out. That's my real gift, I think. I admit I find it highly stressful preparing food in a short space of time, while making sure I'm following the various instructions I'm getting from the client, the photographer or any other people involved.

Man: I see. So, Samantha, what about the future?

Woman: A significant challenge that affects how food is advertised is keeping pace with rapidly evolving communication methods, such as social media and digital platforms. While I'm also keen to work with evermore diverse dishes from around the world, I'd have to say that's my priority. There's no shortage of individuals with style and imagination competing for this type of work as demand grows.

Man: Thanks so much.

SPEAKING PART 1

Interlocutor: First, we'd like to know something about you. Where do you live, Paola?

Paola: I'm from Buenos Aires, the capital of Argentina.

Interlocutor: And you, Saleh?

Saleh: I'm from Syria.

Interlocutor: Paola, where do you like buying clothes from?

Paola: To be honest, I don't buy many clothes. When I do, I prefer to buy them from the market, because they're cheaper there. Sometimes I buy from a big department store if I need something special.

Interlocutor: Do you ever buy things which are second hand, Saleh?

Saleh: Not really.

Interlocutor: Why not?

Saleh: Well, because I prefer things which are new, so I know they're in good condition. Sometimes, second-hand things have damage or problems.

Interlocutor: Paola, is there anything special which you're hoping to buy soon?

Paola: That's a difficult question, let me think. Oh yes, it's my dad's birthday next month, so I need to buy him a present. I haven't decided what to buy yet. Maybe a book, because he loves reading.

Interlocutor: Saleh, in the future, do you think you'll buy more things online?

Saleh: Well, I already buy a lot of things online because it's so convenient and usually I can get better prices. But I don't buy clothes online at the moment and maybe in the future I'll do this more, I'm not sure.

Interlocutor: Thank you.

SPEAKING PART 2

Interlocutor: Saleh, it's your turn first. Here are your photographs. They show people in in situations where speed is important. I'd like you to compare the photographs and say why you think speed is important for the people in these situations.

Saleh: OK, speed is obviously very important in the second picture, because it's a car race. I don't know much about car racing, but it looks like the car has stopped for repairs. There's a person on the left with a tyre, so maybe they need to change the tyre. I can see a huge crowd in the background and it's also getting dark, so I imagine it's important to do these things quickly because people are watching the race and maybe it's nearly the end. If they are too slow, the car will not win the race. The other picture is quite different. The people are working quickly, but calmly. Speed is important because the food needs to be hot when it's served to customers. But they need to stay calm. If they make a mistake, the food won't look good or maybe they'll forget something and it won't taste good. In both pictures, there's a team of people and this helps them to work quickly, because they all have different jobs to do.

Interlocutor: Thank you. Paola, would you like to work in a professional kitchen?

Paola: I don't think so. I do love cooking, but there's a lot of pressure in a kitchen like that. They might look calm, but I'm sure they aren't! I imagine it's also pretty hot and noisy in a kitchen like that, too, so I'd rather just cook at home in my own kitchen.

Interlocutor: Now, Paola, here are your photographs. They show people starting to do things in different situations. I'd like you to compare the photographs and say why you think the people have decided to start doing these things.

Paola: OK. Looking at the first picture, it looks like they are starting a race, but not a very serious one. Everyone looks very happy and they are all different ages, so I think this is some kind of organised race for fun or for charity. It looks like it's quite cold, because a lot of the people are wearing hats and warm exercise clothing and the sky looks rather cloudy, but the people don't seem bothered by that. I imagine they are starting this race because it's a fun thing to do. In the second picture, on the other hand, I suppose the people are starting a journey by train or by plane, so that's something they are about to do, unlike the race, which is already starting. There's a businessman with just one case and a group of people, possibly a family, getting lots of luggage out of the car. I imagine the businessman is feeling OK about his journey. It's just for work, but the other people are feeling excited about starting their trip to go on holiday.

Interlocutor: Thank you. Saleh, do you enjoy running?

Saleh: I'd probably enjoy something like in the first picture, but I wouldn't enjoy serious running. Doing it with a group of people like in the picture does look fun, but I think it'd be boring just to run by yourself or for a serious competition.

SPEAKING PART 3

Interlocutor: Now, I'd like you to talk about something together for about two minutes. Some people believe that the best way to learn a new skill is by teaching yourself, but other people disagree. Here are some things they think about and a question for you to discuss. First, you have some time to look at the task. Now, talk to each other about whether you think teaching yourself is the best way to learn a new skill.

Saleh: So, a new skill, that could be something like a sport or learning to drive or art …

Paola: Yes, anything really, and I think what the skill is affects whether teaching yourself is a good idea or not, don't you?

Saleh: Definitely! I mean, you can't teach yourself to drive, can you? And that's linked to this point about learning correctly.

Paola: That's right. For some skills, you need an expert – someone who really knows the skill and can give you the correct information. Maybe that's not so important for other things, like learning to paint or to dance. What do you think?

Saleh: I don't know. It can still be helpful to have a teacher. It's like this point here about getting advice. If you do everything by yourself, how will you get the advice you need to make progress in the skill?

Paola: Well, the internet is great for that. You can find videos explaining how to do anything, so you have advice and information about how to do it correctly, but you're still teaching yourself.

Saleh: That's a really good point. And I suppose a reason why people think teaching yourself is the best way is because you can do it for free! I mean, you don't have to pay for lessons, you can just get the information you need online.

Paola: I hadn't thought of that, it's an interesting point. This point here is also a positive one – feeling satisfied. If you manage to teach yourself something, it must feel great.

Saleh: Exactly, and I think that's the main reason why people prefer to teach themselves. It feels more like a personal achievement. If you teach yourself, you're thinking more, you're more involved in your learning.

Paola: Yes, but what about having enough time to learn? Is it quicker to learn by yourself or with a teacher? I suppose that depends on what you are learning.

Saleh: Exactly, and on how often you can learn.

Interlocutor: Thank you. Now you have about a minute to decide what the best reason is for <u>not</u> trying to teach yourself when you're learning a new skill.

Paola: Do you think it's that first point we mentioned, about learning correctly? I mean, even with online videos, it's possible that you will make a mistake. In contrast, a teacher can explain things to you.

Saleh: I suppose so, but we didn't talk much about having enough time to learn. Do you think teaching yourself takes a lot longer? That could be a reason not to do it, because you have to do lots of research and maybe you need to practise more.

Paola: Well, with a teacher, you probably only have lessons once or twice a week, particularly if they're expensive, like we said. But if you're teaching yourself, you can maybe do some practice every day, so it could actually be quicker to teach yourself. So I don't think that is the main reason not to do it.

Saleh: I take your point, so maybe we'll stick to that first idea: the main reason not to teach yourself is because you may not learn correctly.

Paola: Yes, I completely agree with you.

SPEAKING PART 4

Interlocutor: Do you think it's better to learn something new by listening or by doing, Paola?

Paola: That's a good question. Like we said before, it's good to have someone explaining things to you, like a teacher or someone in an online video. But I don't think you really know how to do something until you have practised it yourself.

Interlocutor: What do you think?

Saleh: I completely agree. If you listen, you know something in theory. If you do something, you really know it.

Interlocutor: Saleh, some people say a good teacher needs to be patient. Do you agree?

Saleh: I agree 100%, that's why I know I couldn't be a teacher! A teacher needs to listen to the students and explain things many times. For that, you need to be patient.

Interlocutor: Do you agree?

Paola: I do agree that patience is important, but I don't think it's the most important thing. What's important is that a teacher knows the subject very well and can explain it clearly.

Interlocutor: Some people believe that students should be allowed to leave school at the age of 15 if they want to. Do you think this is a good idea?

Paola: Well, I don't know what all the rules are in different countries. In some countries, it's possible to leave school at 14 years old, but many students stay until they're 17 or 18 and I think that's a good idea, because they can get their qualifications, which will help them get a good job.

Saleh: I see what you mean, but some students don't want to keep learning school subjects. They want to do something practical, so I think they should be allowed to leave school in that case.

Paola: You mean if they want to be a mechanic or a cook, for example? Yes, that's an important point. They're good jobs, too, and people can learn to do them while working, better than learning at school.

Interlocutor: Some people like to always be learning something new. Why do you think this is?

Saleh: Maybe it's because they're interested in a lot of things. I don't know really.

Paola: That could be the reason. Or it could be because they like to have a goal, something to aim for. They don't want to just sit and watch TV in their free time.

Saleh: Yes, I suppose that could be the reason.

Interlocutor: Is it better to learn a new language when you are very young or when you are older?

Saleh: Oh, I'm sure it's better when you're very young. Children can generally learn things more quickly than adults, so the same is true for languages.

Paola: I agree. In particular, they can learn the pronunciation more easily, don't you think?

Saleh: Yes, they just copy the sounds they hear without thinking about it.

Paola: And think about children who grow up learning two languages, because their parents speak different languages. They seem to learn easily.

Saleh: But it's different if the children have to go to classes, that might make it more difficult – I mean if they can't practise the language often enough.

Interlocutor: Some companies offer employees the chance to do training courses. How important do you think this is?

Saleh: I think it's really important for the company and for the employee. The company gets more skilled workers and the employees can develop their own skills for the future.

Paola: Yes, that's true if it's training for work. I've heard some companies let their employees do training for other things which are not directly related to their job. I think this is also a good thing, because it makes workers feel more satisfied. It's like a kind of bonus. A happy worker will be a worker who wants to stay with the company, so it's definitely important.

Interlocutor: Thank you. That is the end of the test.

Test 5 Audioscript

LISTENING PART 1

One.

You hear two friends talking about following the news.

Woman: So, often the news ends with an upbeat positive story, doesn't it?

Man: Yeah, and that helps to balance up the false impression you get from endless accounts of disasters or negative stuff like economics, where things always seem to be going wrong. The news focuses on things that are bad in the world because they're the exception, not the rule.

Woman: True.

Man: I mean, more cheerful stories can't really make up for some of the awful things you hear about, but it's great to have them. And things like new medical research or an individual's achievements are motivating, even if they're probably very different in terms of significance to most people.

Two.

You hear a podcaster talking about people whose work involves getting paid to sleep.

Woman: When I wanted to buy a new mattress recently, it was a source of comfort to discover there are people that test products like this to provide feedback to the companies that produce them. It meant I could buy my mattress safe in the knowledge it'd been fully checked out. You might think, 'Wow! What a relaxing job!' But, believe it or not, these so-called professional sleepers are expected to be attentive while they're hard at work, apparently, in order to supply detailed reports on their experiences. It still sounds like a pretty ideal job, and I'm convinced the majority of us could apply for the position! What do you think?

Three.

You hear two friends talking about 'binge-watching', watching many episodes of a TV series in one session.

Man: I watched the whole series of *Nightwalk* in one evening!

Woman: Nine episodes in one session! It's so rare to want to binge-watch like that! I must admit I did it recently with that detective series *Inspector Smith* – one I couldn't stop watching! I've heard it's bad for your sleep patterns if you do it at night, so not a recommended behaviour. Everything in moderation, I say. If it's only occasional – which is me – there's no harm done, I reckon.

Man: I wish there were enough series out there that made me want to! Not every TV programme's like *Nightwalk*.

Woman: The majority are more likely to send me to sleep!

Four.

You hear part of an interview with a footballer.

Man: How do you feel about the very low temperatures forecast for the next few weeks?

Woman: Well, winter's a big change – you adapt your training and playing style to suit the colder conditions. It's unclear how long this coming icy spell'll last. There's a greater risk of injury, as muscles tighten up, so more chance of pulling or straining something. The worst outcome would be that bitter disappointment, when you've prepared for a game, you're in the right zone and then it gets called off. I'm just hoping that won't be the case. The cold does sharpen my focus, so I'm looking forward to more opportunities to score some goals.

Five.

You hear two friends talking about a historical novel they both read.

Woman: That novel *The Owl in the Castle* was fascinating. I couldn't put it down.

Man: It's an incredible dramatic story and based on accounts of what really happened from different sources. Although, I think the novelist altered certain facts here and there. There were some chapters it'd be unwise to base an understanding of history on.

Woman: It's common for writers to invent things in order to explore certain themes in their novels. This one was no different. And it still gives you plenty of insight into what went on in those times.

Man: With fiction like that, it's the story that counts, but writers have a duty to be informative, too.

Six.

You hear a woman talking about some research she did on being bilingual, growing up speaking two different languages.

Woman: I wanted to explore certain questions in my investigations into the subject of growing up speaking two languages – in other words, being bilingual. I was already aware of many beneficial effects for bilingual people. One of these is how well they find solutions when presented with puzzles and other tricky challenges. It's been demonstrated in several studies that they have advantages. My interest was in the factors that influence their psychological development – to know more about the way the environment someone is in can produce different results. And what influences the choice of language when a bilingual person wants to express particular feelings or views about things.

Seven.

You hear two friends talking about how they make decisions.

Man: Decisions can be so hard.

Woman: Yeah, some are harder than others! It's sensible to discuss choices with a close friend or relative.

Man: Chatting with another person could influence you into doing something you wouldn't have done otherwise. I'd rather find a break in my schedule to reflect on possibilities ... somewhere peaceful. It's more worthwhile than putting down all the pros and cons on paper, which I've also heard recommended.

Woman: By setting aside a few moments to give things some calm attention, it's amazing how that clarifies what to do. But yeah, listing alternatives in a notebook ... it's supposed to make it easier to process them. Personally, I'd be happy to try that.

Eight.

You hear an expert talking about education for adults.

Man: By providing education programmes for those who have left school and are working or unemployed, many social problems will be addressed. This kind of education provides an obvious means of overcoming numerous issues, such as shortages of particular skills. Many adults, however, face obstacles when it comes to accessing education. These may include financial problems, lack of time due to work or family responsibilities. This can mean that, though eager to participate, they are unable to attend regularly or to complete courses they sign up for. It is, therefore, vital that those in authority show understanding of such matters and find ways to enable them to achieve their learning goals.

LISTENING PART 2

You will hear a young woman called Polly Smart giving a talk about her experiences as a coach at a summer sports camp for children.

Polly: Hi, I'm Polly Smart, here to talk about the summer job I did after graduating – as a coach at a sports camp for children during school summer holidays. There are so many reasons to apply to be a coach. For one, it's great for your CV when you have very little work experience. Being a coach boosts self-confidence when you're new to the world of work. And it's the perfect environment for improving leadership skills – they're crucial for many careers and that was what made me decide to put in my application.

I was nervous arriving at the camp, looking around the place I'd spend the coming months. It was near a lake with rocky hills in the distance. I was struck by how huge the swimming pool was and there were various buildings I felt curious about – I suspected some were sports facilities, which turned out to be correct.

There was a meeting for new coaches that morning, where we received lots of instructions and heard we'd get guidance as necessary along the way. The assignment of duties was according to our knowledge of different sports and we spent the morning and afternoon shadowing. That's what they called working with someone who'd been there before and could guide us.

A hundred children were due to arrive the following day and the plan was to start with games. One of the coaches introduced us to some that promote teamwork among kids and then we had to come up with what are known as 'ice-breaker' games. It's a way for everyone to get to know each other and it was fun thinking of entertaining ideas. Games were part of most activities – anything from role-playing to quizzes.

When the kids got there, it wasn't long before sports sessions got going. Imagine leading one for 30 children aged 11 to 13. I was nervous! I taught rules and techniques for volleyball, tennis and basketball. Tennis gave me more anxiety than basketball, as I've played it less, but volleyball wasn't a problem at all. The kids were fantastic and mostly did what I asked them to do!

I was exhausted that night! Us coaches slept in small cabins four to a room, while the kids were in larger cabins nearby. The one I was in was located right by the dining hall, which meant waking every morning knowing breakfast was on its way. Nice! I'd have liked to be nearer the internet router, though, as the WiFi was rather slow. There were plenty of showers and bathrooms, but they got busy before breakfast.

Coaches had full training in everything safety related and also in basic medical treatment. Fortunately, I hardly used that. Record keeping was something else we got careful guidance in. It's a nuisance, as we had to fill things in for almost everything we did, but it's necessary in case anything goes wrong and actually, I'm glad I was trained to do it properly, as it was a very useful skill.

Each evening, we kept the kids busy after a day of sports. It was campfire cooking a lot of the time, along with music and songs. I'm no good at cooking or singing, but it was still fun. It was talent shows I was concerned about. Performing's not my thing, but they ended up being a real laugh – I don't regret taking part!

After four weeks, the kids were due to leave and another group would arrive. There was a closing ceremony each time with prize-giving and feedback activities. I knew the goodbyes would be sad – I cry easily! But it was the speeches that really moved me. It was so unexpected to be in tears, hearing such lovely things said about me.

Summer camp was an experience to remember. I found it particularly memorable as a period that involved genuine self-discovery. It opened up new parts of my character. I heard others talk about being full of optimistic feelings – seeing such enthusiastic and loving kids gives great hope for the future.

LISTENING PART 3

You will hear five short extracts in which people are talking about a temporary job they did working as a waiter in a restaurant.

Speaker 1

I spent several months as a waiter in a hotel restaurant. I learned loads about customer service, food hygiene and just food in general. The chefs there were very good and waiters got to sample the dishes, which was a real bonus! We had to wear special black trousers and white shirts, and to tell the truth, it made it easier not having to worry about what to put on for work, something I appreciated. The shifts varied – some were full-on busy, with no time to get bored, while others were slow and dull and the manager would be trying to find something for us to do.

Speaker 2

I spent some time working at a seaside restaurant, where people would come off the beach for lunch or snacks. There was a constant stream of customers and it was amazing how many variations on an order people can request – small this, large that, no salad and so on. Even so, I hardly got any wrong, unlike some of my colleagues. That gave me satisfaction. The boss kept a close eye on how hard we worked. We were constantly taking customers' orders, coming and going from the kitchen and even though I'm using to running and exercising at the gym, I'd be exhausted by the end of the day.

Speaker 3

The restaurant I worked in part-time was in a small town, with just a few regular customers. They loved to strike up conversation, especially when things were quiet – there was rarely much to do. The days could have felt very long and I'd been warned it might be like that, but each one of those customers had a story to tell and they kept me interested in working there. It's just a shame there weren't more of them! They were very quick to remind me if I forgot some detail of their favourite order or something like that or if I had a stain on my jacket or trousers!

Speaker 4

I'll never forget my uniform working in a burger bar, with a red cap and red apron. I felt funny, but customers could spot me easily! Most of them were really nice – oh, unless their food wasn't exactly what they ordered! The boss was friendly enough, too, but very strict, constantly issuing instructions to staff. Anyway, I never thought it'd be so good for me working in a burger bar – not because of the discount burgers we were allowed, something I avoided – but, because it was on three floors, it really kept me in shape. I was up and down, rushing here and there all day, with barely a moment's rest.

Speaker 5

I worked briefly in a quite expensive restaurant, waiting on really wealthy customers. I learned a lot about providing a quality customer-service experience – we were instructed to take it as if everyone that walked in the door was literally the boss, since they were paying us indirectly. Actually, they were mostly pretty polite and pleasant. Every day was different and the menu changed regularly. It was great trying all the dishes – one big advantage of the job – as it meant not having to pay for stuff to prepare meals at home. I was less keen on the smart uniform, though, as I was responsible for washing and ironing it.

LISTENING PART 4

You will hear an interview with a man called Darren Mason, who runs a creative writing site called Lineweavers on the internet.

Woman: Today, our topic is creative writing. Darren Mason set up and manages Lineweavers, an internet site dedicated to the craft of creative writing.

Man: Hi there.

Woman: Darren, many other writers contribute to your site. Is there anything special that brings you all together?

Man: It's hard to say. We're a whole bunch of poets, storytellers and literary critics and some put in more to the site than others. Naturally, we have varying amounts of motivation and drive, but I'd say we possess a desire in common to pursue our passion for great writing of all kinds, both reading it and creating it. And some of us, though by no means everyone, have ambitions to do it professionally.

Woman: Did you start the site to post your own writing?

Man: Yes, that's how it all started. Previously, I'd had a tendency to leave things uncompleted ... just continually going back to them and revising and rewriting. Putting work out there on the site was a way of drawing it to a close and saying 'This is complete'. It was fascinating to observe how the number of reactions from readers steadily built and I discovered this made me want to experiment and be more daring creatively and encourage others to do the same.

Woman: What aspect of the site are you most pleased with?

Man: Another difficult question. I'm happy that people of all ages participate, sending in their writing, but reaching a broader, more diverse range is still a major goal. I guess I take the greatest pride in offering a platform to support the less experienced, suggesting how to go forward with ideas. There's a real sense of community around shared creativity – it's great if the writing's brilliant, which some certainly is, but it's more about working towards excellence.

Woman: Tell me something about one of your own poems on the site.

Man: One I posted recently, called *Nights like this*, is a good example. Readers have responded positively to my work, which is very reassuring, and this was no exception. The poem itself is slightly mysterious, based on some dreams I'd had and I had doubts myself about certain lines, to be honest, what my own understanding of them was. That's OK, I think. Poetry is all about interpreting things for yourself.

Woman: I see. So, how do you feel personally about getting critical feedback?

Man: When I write a poem or a story myself, I want criticism I can use in a helpful way. It doesn't knock my confidence, though it isn't always useful. I've found it necessary to ignore things I totally disagree with. I have the most respect for other views when someone's gone into great detail and closely analysed the writing at length. Some criticism is the opposite, which isn't what I'm looking for at all. I don't mind fault-finding remarks if they're well thought out.

Woman: What do you find difficult about running the Lineweavers site?

Man: Well, I also do a full-time job, so I schedule evenings and weekends for working on the site. In truth, it's such a labour of love that I couldn't say that's an issue. What's tougher for me is reading a poem or story sent in and realising it's not suitable for the site. You can't accept everything and it feels cruel breaking that news. As for the technical demands of managing a site, web design, accessibility on different devices and so on ... that could be a significant challenge. Luckily, it's one of my areas of knowledge, thanks to my day job.

Woman: Running the site means you learn a lot about people, doesn't it?

Man: Yes, it does. Although everyone involved loves creative writing, there's very little that humans aren't capable of disagreeing about, on every subject under the sun. I don't think I was so aware of that until I took this on. Of course, I knew very well that we're all the products of our backgrounds and the events that have shaped us in our lives, which in turn affects what we choose to read and write about.

SPEAKING PART 1

Interlocutor: First, we'd like to know something about you. Where do you live, Pilar?

Pilar: I'm from near Seville, a beautiful city in the south of Spain.

Interlocutor: And you, Matteo?

Matteo: I'm from Florence, in Italy.

Interlocutor: Pilar, would you like to live in another country?

Pilar: I've never thought about that. I like travelling, but living somewhere different can be hard. Maybe if it was a country where I could speak the language, that would be better.

Interlocutor: Have you ever been on a really long journey, Matteo?

Matteo: Lots of times.

Interlocutor: Where did you go?

Matteo: Oh, I took a long train journey from the north to the south of Italy. It was OK at first, but a bit boring after a while. I think the journey was eight hours and that's a long time to be on a train.

Interlocutor: Pilar, tell us something about the area where you grew up.

Pilar: My home was in a small village near Seville, not in the city centre, but it was easy to go into the city when we wanted to go shopping. I enjoyed growing up in a village, because it was quieter and the views were amazing. We had orange trees surrounding our house.

Interlocutor: Matteo, what do you think about the place where you live now?

Matteo: It's a very famous place for tourists, because of all the art, so it can get very busy, especially in the summer. I don't like it so much then, but in the winter, when it's quieter, I love living there, because it's so historical and beautiful.

Interlocutor: Thank you.

SPEAKING PART 2

Interlocutor: Matteo, it's your turn first. Here are your photographs. They show people teaching in different situations. I'd like you to compare the photographs and say what you think might be difficult about teaching in these situations.

Matteo: In the first photo, there's a man teaching in a room with a large group of young adults, whereas in the second photo, the woman is teaching a smaller group of children and they're working closely together. In the first photo, the students all have a laptop in front of them and I imagine teaching like this is difficult because the students may be distracted by the screens and not pay attention to the teacher. There may also be problems if the technology doesn't work properly and I suppose the room could get quite hot or noisy with all those devices working. It doesn't look like there's much space either, so it's difficult for the teacher to get to individual students to help them, like he's doing in this picture. The interaction is more personal in the second photo. It looks like a teacher teaching a small group of students to sew on a machine. The two girls on the right are concentrating hard, but it might be difficult to teach this skill if not all the children can see properly. Other children are doing something else, so maybe they have to take it in turns to get close to the machine. A positive thing about this kind of teaching is that the children will see the results of what they are learning immediately.

Interlocutor: Thank you. Pilar, do you enjoy learning practical skills like sewing?

Pilar: Yes, I do. Like Matteo said, it's good when you can see the results of what you are learning, so if you are sewing or cooking, you can see the thing you made immediately. With more academic subjects, it's more difficult to get those instant results, I think.

Interlocutor: Now, Pilar, here are your photographs. They show people on boats in different situations. I'd like you to compare the photographs and say why you think the people have decided to spend time on a boat in these situations.

Pilar: I think the experience for these people on the boats is very different. In the first picture, it looks a bit like a sailing race. The weather doesn't look great and the sea seems to be quite rough. I suppose the two men are part of a sailing team and they're working hard to win a race. I imagine this is their hobby or they could be professional sailors, so that's why they've decided to go on the boat. They seem quite relaxed, despite the difficult situation, so I suppose they're quite experienced. In contrast, the people in the second photo have decided to go on a boat to relax. The weather's nice and the water's calm and going on a boat is a great way to go sightseeing. They can get a nice view of the colourful buildings from the water. I suppose going on the boat was part of their holiday experience and they don't have to worry about sailing the boat, they're just tourists. There are quite a lot of boats on the water, so it might not be as relaxing as they expect it to be and it might be quite noisy.

Interlocutor: Thank you. Matteo, would you like to go on a trip on a sailing boat?

Matteo: I'm not sure. I wouldn't enjoy it if the weather was bad like in that photo, but if it was a sunny day and the water was calm, then it could be a fun thing to do. I would want to do it with someone experienced, though, just in case there were any problems.

SPEAKING PART 3

Interlocutor: Now, I'd like you to talk about something together for about two minutes. Some people believe that it's better to work alone and other people think it's better to work as part of a group. Here are some things they think about and a question for you to discuss. First, you have some time to look at the task. Now, talk to each other about whether it is better to work alone or as part of a group.

Matteo: OK, so these are different things to consider when deciding on the best way to work.

Pilar: Yes, and we need to decide whether they're a good thing for working alone or working as a group. If we look at this first one – the time available – I guess that could be an advantage for either way of working. If you work with other people, you can share the different jobs, so you may complete the task more quickly …

Matteo: But if you work on your own, you don't need to waste time discussing who's going to do what, you can just get on with the work. It's definitely an important thing to consider. But I do think 'a range of skills' is a reason why people may work better as a group.

Pilar: I agree. In your group, there might be someone who's really good at something you find more difficult, so that's a strong reason to work as a group.

Matteo: Oh, and look at this point about the type of work – that's really important, isn't it?

Pilar: Definitely. Some jobs just need a lot of people, you know – something like a building project – whereas other jobs, like writing reports or researching information, can more easily be done by one person.

Matteo: That's true. It might be the case that having many people can make a job harder to complete, yet sometimes it's impossible to finish something without more people being involved.

Pilar: The problem is, in a group, there'll be different people with different personalities and that can cause problems. Maybe people won't agree on something or they'll want to do something in a different way.

Matteo: And that's linked to the earlier point about the time available. You might actually waste time arguing about things rather than getting the work done.

Pilar: I agree. So, the final point is about feeling satisfied. I take this to mean that if you're working alone, you can feel proud that you've achieved the work yourself, but if you're part of a group, maybe you don't feel the same level of satisfaction. Do you agree?

Matteo: I do. It's difficult to say you did a job well if you weren't completely responsible for it.

Interlocutor: Thank you. Now you have about a minute to decide what the best reason is for working as part of a group.

Pilar: Well, we did say that having a range of skills is important, because it helps to get the job done well. You can use each other's skills to make sure the job gets done to the best of your ability.

Matteo: Yeah, that's a definite advantage of working as a group. There's also that point about the type of work – you know, maybe some jobs just need more people to do them. What do you think?

Pilar: Yes, that's an important thing to consider, but I'd argue that it's the range of skills rather than the number of people that's the strongest reason why people might choose to work together on something.

Matteo: Fair enough, you've convinced me! I'm happy to go with that choice.

SPEAKING PART 4

Interlocutor: Is it easier to work with people you know well or with strangers? Pilar?

Pilar: That's an interesting question. I guess if you work with people you know, you can be more relaxed with them, but if you work with strangers, you can focus more on the work and you won't be so distracted by chatting about other things.

Interlocutor: Do you agree?

Matteo: I'm not sure. It's true that people who know each other might waste time chatting, but even if you work with strangers, you need to create a good atmosphere, so you might waste time getting to know them ... I mean, breaking the ice.

Interlocutor: Do you think it's important to choose a leader for all group work? Matteo?

Matteo: Actually, I do. Even though people are sharing the responsibility, they need someone to make sure everyone's doing what they're supposed to do and that there aren't any problems.

Interlocutor: Do you agree?

Pilar: Yes, completely. We mentioned possible arguments in group work earlier and that's a reason to have a leader. Also, if there's no one in control, a lot of time can be wasted discussing what needs to be done, rather than actually doing it.

Interlocutor: Do you think it's important for work to be enjoyable or are results all that matter?

Matteo: That's a really tricky question. I suppose it depends on who's answering. For the worker, making work enjoyable is important, but the manager may be more concerned about the results.

Pilar: To a certain extent, but I think a good manager would also want their workers to be motivated, otherwise they would just move to a different company.

Matteo: Yes, I agree, I think a balance is important.

Interlocutor: Some companies reward workers for getting good results at work. Do you think this is a good idea?

Pilar: You mean by giving them a bonus? That'd definitely encourage people to work well, wouldn't it?

Matteo: Yeah, but sometimes a project might not be successful for reasons the workers can't control. Like increasing sales, for example, if the economy is weak, so this system is only fair if the workers get a good basic salary.

Pilar: Yes, they need to know that their income's good enough for their lifestyle and the bonus is extra, not essential.

Interlocutor: Some people prefer to concentrate on work for a long time and other people like taking regular breaks. Which do you think is better?

Matteo: I'm definitely the first kind of person. When I have a job to do, I like to start working early in the morning and keep going until it's done.

Pilar: Not me! I have to stop for breaks – you know, to get a drink or something to eat or to go outside and get some fresh air. Otherwise, I find I can't make progress.

Matteo: So that could mean we wouldn't work well in a team!

Pilar: Exactly! Our working styles are too different!

Interlocutor: Is it important to specialise in one area of work or to get experience in a variety of different fields?

Pilar: I think that really depends on what the work is. If you work for a large company, moving to different teams to learn a bit about different parts of the job can be very useful experience.

Matteo: Yes, but if you're a specialist, like maybe a special kind of scientist or creator, then I think it's better to stay with one kind of work, so that you can get more and more experience.

Pilar: I agree, there's no point in changing teams or jobs just for the sake of it, is there?

Interlocutor: Thank you, that is the end of the test.

 **Audioscript**

LISTENING PART 1

One.

You hear two friends talking about using a computer keyboard.

Woman: You're a pretty good typist!

Man: I wouldn't expect anyone to notice. But yeah, the result of taking several online courses and putting in plenty of practice! As I use a keyboard so much for the writing I do in my job, it's been a really worthwhile investment of time. I used to be painfully slow. I was encouraged to try after hearing that typing fast and without many errors is relatively achievable if you put in the effort.

Woman: I'd have thought you make more mistakes when you're typing fast.

Man: Well, the software self-corrects a lot of mine, but it'd still be worth trying to reduce the number.

Two.

You hear two friends talking about supporting a football team.

Woman: When you support one particular team, the game has more meaning for you. You get far more involved in the emotions of winning or losing.

Man: You certainly identify with one side more than the other. But it's also a form of escapism from everyday challenges and issues – you transfer your hopes and fears onto this team. But when everyone's singing together in the crowd, I think the sense of belonging is what's really important.

Woman: You get something special out of it, hugging one another in the joy of a goal or the despair of missing one – a form of connection to others. That's the main thing, I guess.

Three.

You hear part of a psychology podcast in which a woman is talking about making apologies.

Woman: Apologising is necessary at times to repair relationships. However, not many of us know how to do it effectively. It's vital to choose what you say carefully, so you sound sincere, as if you mean what you're saying. People can tell when what's been said doesn't match the true feelings of the speaker – our physical movements communicate messages unconsciously. Take eye contact – avoiding it could lead to what you say coming across as not sincerely meant. Even if you say 'I'm so sorry', this may not help unless you look as if you mean it. And remember, saying 'I'm sorry if I upset you' doesn't work at all!

Four.

You hear a woman talking to a friend about choosing a gift for her nephew.

Woman: I'm trying to find something for my nephew Sam's seventh birthday.

Man: What have you got in mind?

Woman: Well, I've been looking at different books. You know, parents always approve if you give kids things related to reading – learning useful things for school is seen as super-important! My sister, Sam's mum, is very much like that! She and I got given lots of educational books when we were little. Though, I remember cuddly toys were what we were always asking for. We wanted dolls and animals and played games with them in original and imaginative ways. Ideally, my present should be something that inspires that sort of thing.

Man: I'm sure you'll have no trouble finding something suitable.

Five.

You hear a man talking to a friend about using his local buses.

Man: I'm fed up with the buses round here.

Woman: Why's that? I thought you used them all the time.

Man: That's only down to necessity. Unfortunately, there's zero alternative.

Woman: There are several bus routes from where you live into the town centre, aren't there?

Man: Yes, and in theory there should be loads of options, especially since they updated the timetables and supposedly added more buses on some routes, which I was optimistic about. But they still seem very irregular and rarely turn up at the time stated. I'd find another way of getting into town if I had any choice in the matter.

Woman: Sounds like you need to make a complaint.

Six.

You hear a man talking about teaching children good manners.

Man: Adults, particularly parents and teachers, are responsible for educating children about the need for good manners. It's well understood that we need to be models of politeness for our children, so they see and hear good manners in action. An area that's often neglected is that of tone. It's all very well teaching children things like 'please' and 'thank you'. Yet, even if the words are polite, if they don't sound it due to the way they're delivered, then it's meaningless. In my view, many parents pay insufficient attention to this, though I think there is awareness of the value of positive encouragement, offering comments to show approval when children get it right.

Seven.

You hear two students talking about a lecture on the history of fashion that they attended.

Man: What did you think of the lecture?

Woman: Well, it dealt primarily with what Europeans wore in the last few centuries – which was fair enough, as the next few are supposed to be going into fashion in other areas of the world. It's a massive subject. There are so many different styles of dressing just in Asia. It's a pity there wasn't more in this one, though, on clothing worn by other sectors of the population besides the rulers and the very wealthy. But it was interesting how both men and women used to give similar attention to their outfits, compared to the emphasis on female fashion in more recent times.

Man: True.

Eight.

You hear a news report about a very unusual frog.

Woman: Scientists researching different species of frog, lizard and snake in the foothills of an Indian mountain range during the rainy season came across an intriguing sight. It was a tiny gold-backed frog with a mushroom attached to its back. The frog changed positions several times, but the mushroom remained in place. The team claim to be considering possible theories. It could be that the humid atmosphere, combined with the slight wetness of the frog, allowed the mushroom to survive or that bits of wood got stuck to the frog, providing suitable conditions for growth. However, they don't hold out any hope of a repeat sighting to confirm it either way.

LISTENING PART 2

You will hear a man called Ryan Lee talking about working as a set designer for a theatre, designing the scenery and stage for theatrical productions.

Man: Hi. I'm Ryan Lee, here to tell you what it's like to work as a theatrical set designer for plays and musicals. Basically, I create the set, which includes the scenery and overall look of the stage.

With any new production, the director's vision will dictate what you do in terms of set design, but I'll always read the script multiple times before anything, so I can begin to visualise the story, as well as its central concept and general atmosphere. Often the writer includes instructions related to set design, which the director may want to use.

Some set designers study the subject at university, while others learn on the job, which is what I did. Some subjects from school have been useful. For example, I did art – I was always creative – also drama, which is how my interest in theatre developed. Literature's the subject I wouldn't have predicted as being so valuable, but having read the classics adds to my understanding of what a writer's trying to do in a play.

Plays with historical settings are a favourite. It requires lots of research to get the sets right and to attain the realistic magic – that's the term I use – that comes from in-depth learning about a period, its architecture, its furnishings and so on. It's amazing how things just seem to work out.

Sketching ideas is the next step after research, in preparation for discussion with the director, to see if we're thinking along the same lines about set design. These sketches could be done with a pencil or pen or digitally, but I'll print them out and show them on a board rather than exhibit them on a screen. After all, we're not producing something for TV.

The costume designer and I are ultimately responsible for the visual appearance of a production. We'll share ideas about the styles of décor I've chosen, the outfits and the materials that the characters will be wearing. Colours are significant, so it's common for costume designers to request that I stay away from one, as it won't go with the costumes.

Actors spend a lot of time thinking about the psychological world the characters they play inhabit, as well as the physical one. It's common for them to make suggestions to me about their character, especially about things to go into what we call their living space. Sometimes they mention prop ideas, like books their character would read.

Musicals are more light-hearted than serious drama, but tend to have impressive sets, so I'll need extra assistants. What causes issues when planning sets is that numerous dance scenes might take place and the set must accommodate them all. But it's fun seeing lots of actors jumping on and off the furniture and thinking about where to place the musicians on the stage.

Plays might deal with darker or more complex themes. I've designed for many where the setting was domestic and the focus was on personal relationships, which is relatively easy set wise. Anything to do with social issues appeals to me. That's the kind of theme I always go for when I'm contacted with offers. It's interesting but very demanding when plays have a fantasy theme, with plenty of scope for imagination.

People often ask me what set design's similar to. I've heard it said it's like playing chess, thinking ahead before every move. Personally, I'd compare it to composing music. You select notes, balance them with others and collaborate with people to bring it to life. That seems truer to what I do than, say, painting a picture, which seems relatively straightforward in comparison!

I'm looking forward to my next project – a play centred around one man in a cabin in the mountains. The temperature of the cabin changes throughout the play and I have to find original ways to suggest that, when obviously in the theatre it isn't actually changing at all. The stage will also be a revolving circle, so the audience witness events from different perspectives. Should be interesting!

LISTENING PART 3

You will hear five short extracts in which people are talking about a job they did working with animals.

Speaker 1
I worked at a sanctuary for old or sick donkeys in my local area for a couple of years. An interesting experience, as the other workers came from a real variety of backgrounds and the job required plenty of teamwork. What was amazing was how positive I felt being around donkeys all day. It was their reactions to human contact. Once they trusted me, they were so affectionate, but they're definitely influenced by your level of experience and confidence. Most tasks we had to do were very physical – with a strict daily schedule of feeding and cleaning. There were occasional relaxed moments, but it was mostly very energetic, tiring work.

Speaker 2
I used to be a professional dog walker, before training as a vet's nurse. In the area our family lived, lots of people couldn't walk their dogs every day due to work commitments, so there was plenty of demand. I remember what a relief it was from the stress of daily life as the parent of three kids. It made me feel more at ease with life, spending the whole day walking around, bumping into people I knew. Despite seeing the same dogs regularly, you have to be someone who understands dogs and their different moods. Plus you need plenty of physical stamina and enjoy spending long hours just walking.

Speaker 3
My years working at a race-horse stable were very memorable. I was only a stable hand – responsible for taking care of the horses, feeding and watering them, grooming them to keep their coats shiny and healthy and mucking out the stables to keep them clean and well organised. It was back-breaking work, but it really taught me that horses all have individual personalities and mixing with them gave me unique experiences on a daily basis. That factor was a big plus, as things never got monotonous or boring. I tried to create a calm environment for the horses, as they react dramatically to something like a sudden loud noise or movement.

Speaker 4
After leaving school, I saw an ad at a local photographer's for a part-time assistant to help when photographing people's pets. In fact, several of my animal-loving friends brought their pets in to be photographed while I was working there. The photographer himself wasn't really an animal person, so it was fulfilling for me to be given so much responsibility at a young age and I felt extremely motivated. Sometimes the animals were a bit nervous and I had to calm them down, which wasn't always easy at all and occasionally we had to give up. But it was rewarding to see the final outcome if the photographs turned out well.

Speaker 5
My work now as a zoology professor is all about studying animals, but I got some practical experience during university holidays working on a dairy farm. Cows are peaceful creatures and don't seem complex, but they have varying personalities and form strong connections with one another, so that when separated, they become stressed and need to be settled down. Some of the other workers were also students who shared my fascination with them. In fact, I made some useful contacts. I remember one important task was checking on the newborn calves to see how well they were feeding. It was wonderful and extraordinary observing them becoming more lively and active!

LISTENING PART 4

You will hear an interview with a woman called Amy Rossi, who is the manager of a band called the Velvet Echo.

Man: Today, I have Amy Rossi with me in the studio. Amy manages the band the Velvet Echo.

Woman: Hello. Good to be here.

Man: Amy, when did you become the manager for the band?

Woman: Around six years back. We were all friends and I followed what they were doing pretty closely. One day, they just said, 'Will you be our manager?'. 'Why me?' I asked and they gave this whole list of reasons, saying I had all the right qualities. It made me uncomfortable hearing such praise, but I did feel I knew them well enough and what they needed to be able to help them. It was the business and promotion side of things they lacked awareness of.

Man: I see. And have you always wanted to work in the music industry?

Woman: Well, I've hung out with people who were into creating music – rock, punk, hip hop, indie, you name it – since I don't know when. I was envious of their abilities and just got a buzz out of being in their company. Being a practical kind of person, I thought about what it took for musicians to become successful, especially financially, but the people I knew, with all that commitment and love of music, had little idea about all that. I can't say I ever had any ambitions to be a music-industry person, though.

Man: So, what helped the Velvet Echo attract more fans?

Woman: They thought about how to adapt their approach. On stage playing for an audience, they had a strong look – very diverse, with two striking female guitarists, an extrovert male lead singer and a keyboardist and drummer, both with eye-catching hairstyles. Dan, the singer, created most of the tunes and he'd also come up with the words. When they decided to do all that as a more cooperative effort, working together, things seemed to take off musically. And their fanbase just grew and grew.

Man: Great stuff. So, how difficult is it managing the band?

Woman: Well, I organise tours, book venues and so on. I try to cut costs where I can and sort out the best deals for them. For example, it was a major struggle to get decent terms for them with the music company who are producing, distributing and promoting their next couple of albums – probably the trickiest thing I've had to do. The group have sometimes had a difference of opinion and I provided support and guidance, but they rarely argue, unlike some groups!

Man: You were very keen for them to do a series of concerts at the Electric Bandstand Hall.

Woman: Yeah, it's been renovated to improve the acoustics, so it now offers a great sound experience. The whole vibe and mood of the place, the layout of the stage, plus the dance area – all that had long made it seem like the ideal venue to play live. I knew I was right. And some top bands expressed interest in playing once they heard how well the Velvet Echo went down there.

Man: Cool! So, you use social media a lot for promoting the band?

Woman: Yes, it's an amazingly effective method and a very well-proven one, of increasing exposure and visibility. More fans get to hear about the band and those who are already fans can engage and interact with the band if they want to. The opportunity it offered to get insights into what fans thought was also valuable. It's good to see how they feel their views are welcomed, like by taking part in surveys we hold on the platforms or just posting comments.

Man: So, the band's latest album, 'Toucan Fly', is out next week.

Woman: Yes, it's very adventurous. With certain tracks, the inclusion of some saxophone, trumpet and violin sounds are a variation from previous albums. But that's sure to expand the number of followers and admirers of the band and, in concerts, experimenting with that bigger sound's been a huge hit. Whether music journalists will be so enthusiastic is another matter, of course, despite mostly writing positively about the band's live performances.

Man: Well, good luck!

SPEAKING PART 1

Interlocutor: First, we'd like to know something about you. Where do you live, Carla?

Carla: I'm from Luxembourg, a small country in Europe.

Interlocutor: And you, Li?

Li: I'm from China.

Interlocutor: Carla, how do you prefer to travel to college or work?

Carla: I'm working at the moment and I prefer to go there by bike. It takes about half an hour, but I find that's a great way to get some exercise and clear my mind for the day. I can't drive and the public transport is so unreliable, so cycling to work is the best option for me.

Interlocutor: How important is it for you to spend time outside every day, Li?

Li: I'd say it's absolutely essential. I love being outside, even if it's just for a short walk. I don't even mind if the weather's bad.

Interlocutor: Carla, are your weekends very different from your weekdays?

Carla: Quite different, yes. I get up early during the week, but I don't need to do that at the weekend. I like to stay in bed with a cup of coffee and a good book. I just take my time to relax at the weekend, because my working week is so busy.

Interlocutor: Li, do you often stay up really late at night?

Li: Not really.

Interlocutor: Why not?

Li: Well, I have quite a long journey to work and I like to start early to avoid the traffic jams, so for that reason, I prefer to go to bed early during the week. It's different at weekends, of course.

Interlocutor: Thank you.

SPEAKING PART 2

Interlocutor: Li, it's your turn first. Here are your photographs. They show people saying goodbye in different situations. I'd like you to compare the photographs and say what you think the people might find difficult about saying goodbye in these situations.

Li: In both of the pictures, the people saying goodbye seem happy and positive, so it doesn't look like the situations are very difficult, but maybe they're hiding some emotions. The first photo shows a woman saying goodbye to people in an office. I suppose they're her colleagues and she's leaving her job. She's holding a box with a plant, some notebooks and maybe a coffee cup, which I think were on her desk, so I imagine she's moving to a new job or maybe just to a new office. She might be a bit worried about the change and a bit sad that she's leaving her colleagues, who all seem very friendly. In the photo below, a mother and a father are saying goodbye to their children, who look like they're going off to school. The children are wearing a school uniform and they have school bags. Everyone seems very happy and excited, but maybe they're a bit nervous, too. Maybe it's the first day of the school year and the parents or the children are a bit worried about how things will go. The children are probably excited about being with their friends again, though, and the parents look very proud.

Interlocutor: Thank you. Carla, did you enjoy going to school when you were a young child?

Carla: Yes, because of my friends, like Li said! It was fun to see them and play with them every day, so I was always excited about going to school.

Interlocutor: Now, Carla, here are your photographs. They show different places where people live. I'd like you to compare the photographs and say why you think the people have chosen to live in these places.

Carla: The first photo shows a very impressive apartment. It looks like it's high up and there are views of a city. The windows are huge, so there's a lot of light in the room, and it looks very modern, with a lot of space. I think the man has chosen to live there because he likes modern buildings and the convenience of living in a city centre. I imagine it would be easy to get to places from the apartment and there are probably lots of shops and restaurants in the surrounding area. The decoration in the apartment does look a bit simple, so maybe it's not a family home, just a home for one person. In contrast, the second photo is of a wooden house in the countryside. It's also got big windows, so I imagine it's bright inside, like in the apartment, especially on sunny days like in this picture. The house is in a field and I can't see any other buildings nearby, so it's completely different from the other photo. I'd say the woman has chosen to live there because she likes to enjoy nature.

There's a cow in the picture, so maybe she's a farmer. The scenery is beautiful and it must be a very peaceful place to live, but the problem is, she has to drive everywhere if she wants to go shopping or for entertainment, so it's not as convenient as the apartment in the first photo.

Interlocutor: Thank you. Li, would you enjoy living in a city centre?

Li: I live in a small town at the moment and I enjoy that, but I don't think I could live in a really big city like New York or London. I do like the convenience of town living, but I think I'd find a city too noisy and busy.

SPEAKING PART 3

Interlocutor: Now, I'd like you to talk about something together for about two minutes. Here are some things that some people think are essential for having a close friendship with someone and a question for you to discuss. First, you have some time to look at the task. Now, talk to each other about whether these things are essential for having a close friendship with someone.

Carla: Where shall we start?

Li: What about this point, about liking the same things? Do you think this is essential for a close friendship?

Carla: Important, yes, but not essential. It's possible to have different interests and still be friends with someone, don't you think?

Li: I completely agree. My best friend loves sport and I hate it, but we're still friends!

Carla: OK, so let's move on to this point about being honest. I do think this is really important.

Li: Definitely. If you can't trust someone, it's difficult to imagine how they can be your friend.

Carla: Yes, that's what I think. Honesty is so important in a friendship.

Li: OK, moving on, let's talk about whether it's important to see each other regularly. I suppose it depends on what you mean by 'regularly'. I mean, I like to see my friends every week, if I can, but not every day. I like to have time on my own as well.

Carla: That's a good point. Like we discussed earlier, you might have different interests from your friends and if you see them too often, there's no time to do the things that you enjoy. So, what do you think about being the same age? Is that important?

Li: I do think it helps. If you're the same age, then you have similar lives, like you'll both be studying or both be starting a family, so it's an easier way to have something in common.

Carla: Yes, but maybe that matters less the older you get. When I was at school, all my friends were in the same year as me, but now that I'm working, I have some friends who are five years younger or older and we still get on fine.

Li: I think that's a good point – our needs change and so our friendships can change.

Interlocutor: Thank you. Now you have about a minute to decide which two things are most important for having a close friendship with someone.

Li: We didn't have time to talk about the last point – coming from similar backgrounds. Do you think this means money?

Carla: Maybe, or just family background, experiences, education. I think it can mean a lot of things and I do think it's one element of a friendship, but not the most important one.

Li: I couldn't agree more. You can be friends with all kinds of people, so I think we can reject that one. I'd say one of the most important factors is being honest, like we said. I mean, this is essential for a close relationship.

Carla: Absolutely. And can I suggest 'liking the same things' as the other one? That may be influenced a bit by age or background, but not totally. And there may be some differences in your likes, but you have to like some of the same things to have things to talk about and do together.

Li: I agree. Let's go with those two choices.

SPEAKING PART 4

Interlocutor: Carla, is it important for friends to always agree with each other?

Carla: I think it's nice if they do, but, in reality, friends may have arguments or just different opinions about things. If they're good friends, this should be OK.

Interlocutor: Do you agree?

Li: Yeah. I think it's impossible to always agree with someone. The important thing is that the disagreement does not become a big argument. Friends should respect each other's opinions.

Interlocutor: Do you think that where you work is the best place to meet new friends? Li?

Li: I think it's the easiest place to meet people, because that's where you spend most time, so there's more chance of meeting people. However, I think it's good to have friends who you don't work with as well.

Interlocutor: What do you think?

Carla: I agree with Li. It's easy to become friends with someone you see almost every day, but there are other places to meet friends, like when you're doing your hobby or at a party. You can meet friends anywhere, really.

Interlocutor: Is it better to spend time with just one friend or with a large group of friends?

Li: I don't think one thing is better than another. It depends on what you're doing. What do you think?

Carla: I completely agree. Sometimes it's nice to be with just one friend, just chatting together, but sometimes you want to be with lots of friends, for example if there's a celebration. I suppose the only problem is if the group is so large that you can't get to talk to everyone or maybe someone feels left out.

Li: That's a good point. Some people are quite quiet and they may prefer to meet up in smaller groups or just one to one.

Interlocutor: Do you think it's easy to continue a friendship when one person moves away?

Carla: Well, it's pretty easy nowadays because we have social media and emails, so you can keep in touch easily.

Li: Yeah, it's not like in the past, when maybe you had to wait days or weeks for a letter. But I do think it can be difficult to keep the friendship the same. The person who moves away will have new experiences and will meet new people, so their personality or interests may change.

Carla: I see what you mean.

Interlocutor: Some people say that modern technology is having a negative effect on friendships. What do you think, Carla?

Carla: Well, like I said, social media and emails can be a good way of keeping in touch with friends who don't live near you. I suppose the problem is when friends who live close to each other prefer to send messages rather than actually meeting up.

Interlocutor: What do you think, Li?

Li: That's a very good point. I know some people who make a plan to meet and then just send a message to cancel at the last minute. It's too easy to do things like that and it makes me think that the friendship isn't important to them.

Carla: Yes, that's what I meant. It depends how the technology is used.

Interlocutor: Is it better to ask friends or family for advice when you have to make an important decision?

Carla: That really depends on the decision. Friends can be good people to discuss decisions with, but parents may have more experience, so they may be able to give better advice.

Li: Absolutely. A friend will know what's important to you, what you like, but someone from your family may know what's a good decision and also what's a bad decision. I think it's better to ask friends <u>and</u> family.

Interlocutor: Thank you. That is the end of the test.

Teacher's notes & keys

Test 1
Reading and Use of English
Part 1

Task type:
Multiple-choice cloze with one example plus eight gaps. There are four multiple-choice options for each gap.

Training
Lead-in

Explain to students that collocations are a combination of two or more words that are usually used together. Ask students to think of some collocations in their own language.

1 Ask students to complete the exercise individually, then to check their answers in pairs. After that, check the answers as a class.

| 1 charge 2 adjustments 3 chances 4 pressure 5 appearance
| 6 account 7 use 8 emphasis 9 connection 10 advantage
| 11 action 12 breakthrough 13 revenge 14 questions

2 Ask students to do the exercise individually, then to check their answers using the answers for Exercise 1 to help them. Check the answers as a class.

| 1 take 2 make 3 put 4 make 5 take 6 make 7 put 8 make
| 9 take 10 put 11 take 12 make 13 take 14 take

Extension

a Ask students to think of other verb–noun collocations which use *make*, *take* and *put* (e.g. *make a decision, take charge/control, put aside*). Students can use a dictionary or look online if appropriate. Ask pairs of students to choose three or four collocations and write sentences using them.

b Put students into groups and draw a table on the board with *make*, *take* and *put* at the top of each column. You can also add more columns (e.g. with *have*, *hold*, *set*). Groups try to think of as many collocations as possible using each verb. Invite one member of each group in turn to fill in a column in the table. The completed table could be added to their vocabulary records.

3 Ask students to match the words and then to check their answers in pairs. Check the answers as a class.

| 1 e 2 c 3 f 4 a 5 b 6 d

4 Students can do the exercise individually before checking their answers in pairs. Check the answers as a class.

| 1 conveniently located 2 densely populated 3 brightly coloured
| 4 bitterly disappointed 5 closely connected 6 strictly forbidden

5 Students can do the exercise in pairs. Check the answers as a class.

| 1 C 2 A 3 D 4 C 5 B 6 D 7 C 8 A

Lead-in

Candidates are often tested on prepositions in the Use of English tasks, especially in Parts 1, 2 and 4. In Part 1, an option that would make sense in a gap may be incorrect because it can't be followed by the preposition that comes after the gap.

Exercise 6 focuses on which prepositions are used with particular verbs, and Exercise 7 focuses on which prepositions are used with particular adjectives.

6 Ask students to do the exercise individually, then to check their answers in pairs. When you check the answers as a class, ask students to tell you how the **incorrect** verb could be used in the same sentence.

1 We will *answer* your queries as soon as possible.
2 She has *focused on* the history of science throughout her career.
3 Everyone here is *allowed* some time off in the evenings.
4 They eventually *managed to contact* me.
5 My best friend doesn't *agree with* eating meat.
6 The teacher *advised* us *not to spend* more than two hours on our homework.
7 I will *give* you as much information as I can.
8 They were wrongly *blamed for* breaking the window.

| 1 respond 2 specialised 3 entitled 4 succeeded 5 approve
| 6 discouraged 7 provide 8 accused

7 Ask students to look at the photo and the title before reading the text. Then tell them to read the text quickly and answer these questions: *Did the writer do other sports before joining the team?* (Yes: *I've always been quite good at sport …*) *Does the team seem to be successful?* (Yes: *… for our winning so many matches*.)

Ask students to do the task individually before checking their answers in pairs. Then check the answers as a class.

| 1 D 2 B 3 A 4 C 5 C 6 B 7 D 8 B

Lead-in

In Use of English Part 1, candidates are often tested on words that are similar in meaning. Exercise 8 focuses on verbs with similar meanings.

8 Ask students to do the task individually, then to check their answers in pairs. Then check the answers as a class.

| 1 D 2 D 3 A 4 D 5 A 6 C 7 B 8 C

Lead-in

Fixed phrases are often tested in Use of English Parts 1, 2 and 4. In Part 1, the 'lexical' or 'vocabulary' words in the phrase are frequently tested.

9 Ask students to do the exercise individually, then check the answers as a class.

| 1 heart 2 sign 3 mind 4 far 5 pain 6 sudden 7 fact

10 Again, students can do the exercise individually, then check answers in pairs. Check the answers as a class.

> 1 heart 2 do 3 impression 4 track 5 took 6 due 7 make

Extension
Ask pairs of students to write a dialogue using some of the fixed phrases and idioms in Exercises 9 and 10. Pairs could then perform the dialogue in front of the class. While students listen to each dialogue, they could tick each idiom or phrase they hear from Exercises 9 and 10.

Exam practice
Tell students that the whole Reading and Use of English test takes 1 hour and 15 minutes, including the time it takes to fill in the answer sheet. There are four Use of English tasks and three Reading tasks. If they spend 15 minutes each on the Reading tasks, that leaves candidates 30 minutes to do the four Use of English tasks.

Remind students that they should always read the text for Part 1 quickly before they start looking at the options so that they know what the topic is.

> 1 B 2 B 3 A 4 C 5 C 6 D 7 A 8 D

Part 2

> **Task type:**
> Open cloze with one example plus eight gaps.

Training
Lead-in
Candidates need to be able to use articles, quantifiers and determiners accurately, and they will be tested in the exam, either in Use of English Part 2 or Part 4 (or both). They are also important in the Writing test and students need to be aware of them in Use of English Part 3. For example, they may need to decide whether to use a singular or a plural noun.

1 Ask students to read the text quickly and decide why the baby penguins are described as 'brave' in the title. (They jump into the sea from high up, even though they have never swum before and can't fly.)

Ask students to do the exercise individually, then to check their answers in pairs. Check the answers as a class.

> 1 Some 2 a 3 The 4 these 5 the 6 enough 7 a

2 Students should do the exercise quickly in pairs. Check the answers as a class and make a note of any items that students are still getting wrong.

> 1 no 2 Every / Each 3 much 4 None 5 Little 6 lots / plenty
> 7 many / any 8 one 9 little 10 both

Extension
Ask pairs to write two or three sentences like the ones in Exercise 2, each with two options. Students can then write an exercise for the whole class to do in another lesson.

Lead-in
As mentioned in the notes for Part 1, candidates need to know how to use prepositions correctly. The prepositions in Exercises 3 and 4 are some of the ones listed at B2 level on the English Vocabulary Profile. However, in Part 2, candidates are also likely to be tested on prepositions listed at lower levels, especially in longer, more complex sentences.

3 Students can do this exercise individually, then check their answers in pairs. Check the answers as a class.

> 1 with 2 of 3 in 4 at 5 in 6 on 7 with 8 in

4 Students can do the exercise in pairs. Check the answers as a class.

> 1 with 2 to 3 from 4 with 5 to 6 on 7 to 8 from

Extension
When correcting the students' work, make a note of any mistakes they make using prepositions and correct these as a class.

Lead-in
Quickly revise relative pronouns and relative clauses with the students. Remind them that non-defining relative clauses give extra information and must be between commas. We can't use *that* as a relative pronoun in these clauses (e.g. *Sam*, **who works in the same office as me**, *is very clever*). Defining relative clauses contain essential information, without which the sentence doesn't make much sense on its own. We don't use commas before or after these clauses (e.g. *Do you know the name of the person* **who/that wrote the screenplay for this film**?).

5 As a class, look at each sentence in turn and ask students whether the relative clause is defining or non-defining. (All the ones between commas are non-defining.) Students can do this exercise in pairs. Then check the answers as a class.

> 1 that / which 2 which 3 whose 4 who 5 which 6 whom
> 7 where 8 what

6 Students could do this for homework or individually in class. Check the answers as a class.

> 1 This is the house where I used to live. / This is the house (that/which) I used to live in.
> 2 Is that the person who/that helped you when you fell off your bike?
> 3 I wonder whose backpack this is.
> 4 The only part of the film that/which confused me was the ending.
> 5 Paolo's friend Linda, who studies maths, managed to fix his laptop.
> 6 I'm having dinner with Tao, whose parents are fantastic cooks.

Exam practice
Lead-in
Ask students for three good things about playing computer games and three bad things. Write them on the board. Then tell students to read the text quickly, ignoring the gaps. Ask them to check if any of their ideas are in the text. Then give students up to 15 minutes to do the task. They will have less time to do this task in the exam, but they shouldn't worry about that at this stage.

> 9 what 10 As / Like 11 with 12 their 13 everyone / everybody
> 14 in 15 without 16 little

Part 3

> **Task type:**
> Word formation in a text with one example plus eight gaps. Each gap corresponds to a word. The stem of each missing word is given at the end of the line with the gap in it.

Training

In Part 3, candidates must form words by, for example, changing a noun into an adjective or an adjective into an adverb. They will need to add suffixes and/or prefixes to words. They will also need to know about spelling changes and irregular ways of changing words from one part of speech to another. The activities here cover some of the words that candidates may come across, but there are many more. If students are keeping vocabulary records, these will not only be useful for recording what they learn here, but also for recording words they learn in future. They could record 'word families' (e.g. *fair / fairness / fairly / unfairly / unfairness*).

Lead-in

Candidates need to decide what type of word is needed – known as the *part of speech* – in each gap. This will usually be a noun, an adjective, an adverb or a verb.

1 Ask students to work in pairs and write the parts of speech on the lines next to the words. Check the answers as a class.

> 1 verb 2 adverb 3 noun 4 adjective 5 adverb 6 adjective
> 7 noun

2 Ask students to give examples of suffixes. Write them on the board. Then ask students to do the exercise in pairs. Check the answers as a class.

> 1 socialise / socialize 2 naturally 3 partnership 4 effective
> 5 wrongly / wrongfully 6 peaceful 7 payment

Extension

Students can write a list of the suffixes they used to form the words they wrote in Exercise 2. They can then add to the list as they find more words with different suffixes.

3 Ask students to decide in pairs what kind of word is needed in each gap (1 noun, 2 noun, 3 adverb, 4 adjective, 5 adverb, 6 adjective, 7 noun, 8 verb). Then, students should try to complete the gaps individually. After they have checked their answers in pairs, check them as a class.

> 1 guidance 2 patience 3 necessarily 4 encouraging 5 steadily
> 6 mysterious/mystifying 7 approval 8 specify

4 Tell students that they must spell their answers correctly. The words in this exercise are ones that often cause spelling problems for students. Students can complete the exercise individually and check their answers in pairs. Then check the answers as a class.

> 1 happily 2 independent 3 suspicious 4 successful 5 beautifully
> 6 fascinating 7 negatively 8 appearance

Extension

Divide the class into groups and ask them to look up different spelling rules online. If it isn't appropriate to do this in class, they could do it for homework. One group could look up the rules for extending words ending in -*y*, another group could check the rules for adding -*ly*, and another group for adding -*ful*. Then each group can explain the rule they checked to the rest of the class.

Lead-in

If the word needed to fill a gap in Part 3 is a noun, candidates must decide whether the noun is singular or plural. They should look for clues in the text before and after the gap to decide whether a plural is needed.

5 Do the exercise together as a class and discuss the reasons for the answers. Tell students that there may be gaps in the exam task that have more than one possible answer and that in those cases, any correct answer will be accepted. However, students should only write one answer on their answer sheet.

> 1 player / players 2 players 3 players 4 player / players
> 5 player 6 players

Lead-in

If the word that candidates have to form in Part 3 is a verb, they will need to think of what tense or form the verb should be in.

6 Ask students to look at the first sentence. Ask them what the missing verb is (*widened*) and write it on the board. Then ask students to do the rest of the exercise in pairs. After that, check the answers as a class.

> 1 widened 2 widening 3 widen 4 widen 5 widens

7 Ask students to work in pairs and decide what kind of word should go in each gap. Check the answers as a class. Then ask students (again, in pairs) to complete the gaps and check their answers using a dictionary or by looking online. Check the answers as a class.

> 1 originally 2 generosity 3 observations 4 ambitious
> 5 decisive 6 unfriendly

Exam practice

Ask students to read the text quickly to find out whether it is about one new species or several (several – 100 were found in less than a month).

Look at the example as a class. This is an opportunity to check that students remember the difference between adjectives ending in -*ed* and adjectives ending in -*ing*.

Remind them that nouns may need to be plural and that some items may need a prefix as well as a suffix.

> 17 discoveries 18 scientists 19 knowledge 20 unbelievable
> 21 including 22 Additionally 23 roughly 24 expectations

Part 4

Task type:
Key word transformation of six separate sentences (with one example). Each pair of sentences consists of one full sentence followed by a second sentence with a gap that can be filled with up to five words.

Training

In Part 4 of the Reading and Use of English paper, candidates can be tested on a wide range of grammatical structures, fixed phrases, phrasal verbs, etc. The following activities practise some of the language that is commonly tested. Further revision may be needed to deal with any weaknesses that students have. This will also be useful preparation for the Writing paper.

Lead-in

Candidates may be tested on reporting verbs in Part 4, as well as in Part 1. The verbs may also be useful when they are writing stories. Parts 5 and 7 can also test the meaning of these verbs. Exercise 1 focuses on both their meaning and their grammar.

Exercise 2 focuses on grammar and word order, which are also important, and are often tested in Part 4.

1 Ask students to complete the exercise individually, then to check their answers in pairs. After that, check the answers as a class.

> 1 invited Toni to their
> 2 advised Louis to take up
> 3 refused to play football
> 4 accused Tomas of breaking
> 5 offered to bring
> 6 demanded to know what was

Extension

Ask students to note down the verbs they are less confident in using in their vocabulary records. Ask them to write sentences containing each of these verbs and check with you to make sure they are correct.

2 Remind students about word order in reported questions and about the 'backshift' of tenses (present continuous → past continuous, past simple → past perfect simple, etc.) in reported speech.

Students can do the exercise individually, before checking their answers in pairs.

> 1 where the supermarket was
> 2 who had / who'd left the flowers
> 3 if / whether my cousins were coming
> 4 what the teacher thought

Extension

Students each write a direct question on a slip of paper. Collect all the slips, mix them up and give each student someone else's question. Students have to write the correct reported question. They can check their answers in pairs, then with you as a class.

Lead-in

Candidates may be tested on comparative and superlative forms in Part 4. These forms may also be tested in Part 2 and a comparative adjective may be tested in Part 3. Students should be familiar with these forms. Use Exercise 3 to check what they know and what they need to practise more.

3 Students can complete the exercise individually, then check their answers in pairs. After that, check the answers as a class.

> 1 more, more 2 least 3 as, as 4 little 5 much more 6 fewer
> 7 most 8 more

Extension

Ask students to think about which structures they found most difficult in Exercise 3. Ask them to write sentences using these structures. Students check their answers in pairs. Go round the class as they are working and help them if necessary. Encourage them to try using some of these structures in their own writing.

Lead-in

Candidates are often tested on three-part phrasal verbs in Part 4. These are also often tested in Parts 1 and 2.

4 Ask students to work in pairs to complete the phrasal verbs and match them with the meanings. After that, check the answers as a class.

> 1 forward, b 2 for, d 3 with, f 4 out, c 5 on, a 6 up, e

5 Ask students to do the exercise in pairs. Then check the answers as a class.

> 1 put up with 2 run out of 3 looking forward to 4 come up with
> 5 cut down on 6 stood up for

Exam practice

Remind students that they get two marks for each sentence in this part, so even if they make a mistake, they can still get one mark. Also remind students that they can only write a maximum of five words in the gap and cannot change the given word. In the answer key, the part to the left of the vertical line is given one mark, and the part to the right is given one mark. There is sometimes more than one possible correct answer.

> 25 thanked Jain | for coming up
> 26 the better | it will
> 27 if / whether he was | keen on
> 28 of / about cutting down | on
> 29 refused to | put up
> 30 as demanding as | I had / I'd

Part 5

Task type:
A text followed by six four-option multiple-choice questions.

Training

Lead-in

In Part 5, candidates are asked different types of questions about the text. The questions can be about attitudes and opinions, or about feelings (of the writer or someone in the text). Candidates could also be asked what the writer is 'doing' in one of the paragraphs – these questions are about function, e.g. justifying an opinion or criticising someone / something. The questions always follow the order of the text, but there may occasionally be one question at the end asking about the whole of the text, or about what the title of the text could be. As with all parts that involve a text or texts, students should always read the text quickly before looking at the questions so they know what they are reading about. There may be words in the text that students don't know. Tell them not to worry about this. If they need to understand a word or phrase to answer a question, they should try to work out the meaning from context (the text around the word and the topic of the paragraph or the text as a whole).

1 Explain that sentences 1–5 might appear in a text about learning to play chess and each one expresses one of the opinions a–e. Students can do the matching in pairs, discussing their answers as they go along. Check the answers as a class.

> 1 b 2 e 3 c 4 d 5 a

Extension

Pick a topic (e.g. football or going to the cinema) and ask pairs of students to write three short opinions (a, b, c) about it on a piece of paper. Then ask them to pass the piece of paper to another pair of students. Each pair of students should now write a sentence expressing one of the opinions (a–c) on the same piece of paper before passing it on to a third pair of students. Students should now try to work out which of the three opinions is expressed in the sentence.

2 Ask students to read the extract quickly. Check the answer as a class.

> Some new neighbours are moving into the house next to Dan and Lucy or into the flat below.

3 Students can look at this in pairs. Then check the answers as a class.

> **1** looks down on ('Far too old-fashioned')
> **2** welcomes ('She imagined herself knocking on their door with the cake she'd just baked. Or maybe they could come round for dinner …')
> **3** Dan ('They must be pretty fit – and care about the environment.')

4 Ask the students to read the paragraph quickly, then check the answer to the question as a class.

> (to) draw (objects)

5 & 6 Ask students to do these individually, then discuss their answers in pairs. Check the answers as a class.

> D is correct. ('I'm not brilliant at drawing and had been a bit worried that signing up for the intermediate class might have been too ambitious. However, I soon realised that no one else was that great either, which cheered me up.')
> A is wrong because the writer thought the intermediate class might be too advanced for him.
> B is wrong because the writer had been worried that other people might find him irritating. He doesn't mention feeling irritated himself.
> C is wrong because at first, he couldn't see the objects that the teacher brought in, but he was never puzzled by them.

7 Ask students to work through the two examples in pairs, discussing their answers as they go along. Then check the answers as a class.

> **1** C (The only things mentioned in the extract that make sense after *preserving* are *town centres* and *one or two buildings*. But the town centres are being modernised, so they are not being preserved. The old buildings are what the writer says should be a priority.)
> **2** B (After two things are mentioned, *the former* refers back to the first thing. Here, the two things are *tree frogs* and *lizards*. The first thing mentioned is *tree frogs*.)

Exam practice

Ask students to read the text quickly to find out what it is about. Then, ask where the writer travelled to during the cruise. (Possible answers could be all or some of the following: Norway / the most northerly part of Europe / Trondheim / Bodø / the top Arctic edge of Europe / Honningsvåg / the island of Magerøya / Nordkapp / Europe's most northerly point / the Barents Sea / Skarsvåg.) If students are not familiar with this part of the world, you could show them these places on a map (either now or after the students have done the task). Also, after students have done the task, you could look for colour images of the Northern Lights.

Tell students to answer questions 31–36 individually, underlining the parts of the text which give them the answers. In the exam, they will have about 15 minutes to do this part.

Then ask them to compare their answers in pairs and explain why they chose each answer. Check the answers as a class, making sure all the students know why each answer is correct.

> **31** C **32** B **33** A **34** C **35** D **36** D

Part 6

> **Task type:**
> A text with six sentences missing. Underneath the text, there are seven sentences. Six of these sentences fit in the gaps in the text.

Lead-in

In Part 6, candidates have to look for ways in which ideas in the sentences below the text may be linked to ideas in the text. To do this, students need to understand referencing and also know how linking words and phrases are used to connect ideas. These linking words and phrases, as well as referencing, will also be useful in their own writing.

1 This exercise should help students to focus on the kinds of words they should look for in the text and options to help them to do Part 6 tasks.

Ask students to do the exercise individually. Then ask them to discuss their answers in pairs. Afterwards, check the answers as a class.

> **1** there **2** them / these **3** so / that / this **4** then
> **5** Others **6** afterwards / there / elsewhere

2 Students can do the exercise in pairs. Then, check the answers as a class.

> **1** c **2** a **3** d **4** b

3 Students do the exercise individually. They then check their answers in pairs.

> **1** In contrast **2** Furthermore **3** Nor **4** for instance
> **5** In spite of this

Extension

Ask students to use at least three of the linking words and phrases from Exercises 2 and 3 in their next writing homework.

Exam practice

Ask the students if they consider themselves competitive people.

Ask them to read the text quickly to find out what kind of sport the writer does (cycling).

Ask students to underline linking words and phrases and words used for referencing in options A–G. They should use these to help them choose the correct sentence for each gap. In the exam, candidates have about 15 minutes to do this task.

> **37** G **38** E **39** C **40** F **41** A **42** D

Part 7

> **Task type:**
> Ten multiple-matching questions about several short texts or one long text divided into sections.

Training
Lead-in

In Part 7, functional verbs such as *accept* or *stress* often appear in the questions. Candidates need to know what these verbs mean and recognise their functions in the text(s).

1 Explain to students that the sentences are all examples of people saying things, and that the verbs in the box

are all function verbs. Each function matches one of the statements. Students can do the exercise in pairs. Then, check the answers as a class.

> 1 disapprove 2 confess 3 recommend 4 question 5 stress
> 6 accept 7 deny

2   Explain that the statements 1–8 are all examples of sentences that could appear in Part 7 texts. The options below them are all function verbs, and only one verb matches the statement in each case. You could do this exercise as a whole class.

> 1 emphasising 2 defending 3 challenging 4 respects
> 5 criticising 6 approves of 7 claiming 8 proposing

Extension

Students could look up the meanings of the other function verbs and write examples of statements illustrating these (in their vocabulary records, if they are keeping them). This could be done in class or for homework.

Exam practice

Ask students if they know what an escape room is and if they have ever been to one. If they have, what was it like? Did they solve the puzzle(s)? Did they enjoy it?

If students don't know what an escape room is, ask them to read the beginning of text A to find out.

Ask students to read the text quickly to see if the four people went to the same escape room or to different ones. (Each person went to a different escape room.)

Ask students to answer questions 43–52, underlining the parts of the text that give them the answers. In the exam, they will have about 15 minutes to do this task.

> 43 B   44 D   45 A   46 B   47 C   48 D   49 A   50 C   51 D   52 B

Test 1
Writing
Part 1 (essay)

> **Task type:**
> An essay of 140–190 words giving an opinion and providing reasons for the opinion. Three points must be covered: two are given and the candidate must think of a third point to include.

Training

Lead-in

Ask students what online classroom learning is. Ask whether they have done any, and what they enjoyed or did not enjoy about the experience. Divide the class into two groups. Ask one group to discuss the advantages of online classroom learning and ask the second group to discuss the disadvantages. Write their ideas on the board.

Now tell students that they are going to look at the Part 1 essay task. The Part 1 essay is compulsory and the format is always the same. The general topic is given before the task, and usually takes the form of 'In your English class you have been talking about …'. There is a question, or a statement followed by a question, which candidates must answer. Under the question are two notes. Candidates must cover these in their essay. They must also think of a third point to include.

1a Ask students to read the essay task.

1b Ask students what *online classroom learning* means.

> Attending a class online

1c Ask students what they have to write about in the essay.

> The advantages and disadvantages of online classroom learning

1d Ask students to look at the first note. Ask them to look at the board and find any advantages or disadvantages relating to location. Then elicit further ideas from the class.

1e Ask students to look at the second note and ask them to think of any advantages or disadvantages relating to connecting with other students. Elicit other ideas from the class.

2 Go through the first question as a class. Ask them to work in pairs to decide which note each of the remaining sentences refers to.

> a 2   b 1   c 1   d 2   e 1   f 2

3a Students work in pairs or small groups to discuss the ideas. Draw their attention to the Tip to help them decide. Then discuss each of the ideas as a class.

> variety of tasks, qualifications (The other points either reflect the general topic or overlap with notes 1 and 2.)

3b Ask students to look at the points they choose for note 3 and to discuss the advantages and disadvantages of each. They should do this individually, then compare their ideas with a partner. They then discuss the ideas as a class.

3c Ask students to work in small groups to think of ideas for the third point. Explain that when they are thinking of a third note during the test, they should make sure that there is enough to write about.

Lead-in

Ask students what they already know about writing essays. Write their ideas on the board and ask the class to evaluate them.

4a Ask students to read the three essay structures and discuss in pairs which structure they think is the best and why.

> All the structures are suitable, but B will make the writing more concise and keeps similar ideas together. This makes it easier to follow the line of argument.

4b Ask students to read the sentences and decide which paragraph they would put them into, using structure B from Exercise 4a. Look at the first sentence as a class and discuss where it belongs in the essay.

> 1 Paragraph 1, note 2 (advantage)
> 2 Paragraph 2, note 1 (disadvantage)
> 3 Introduction
> 4 Paragraph 2, note 3 (disadvantage)
> 5 Paragraph 1, note 3 (advantage)
> 6 Conclusion
> 7 Paragraph 1, note 1 (advantage)

4c Ask students to discuss in pairs or small groups what the most important disadvantage of note 2 could be. Each student writes a suitable sentence for this note, following the style of the sentences in Exercise 4b.

> For example, it can be harder to create lasting friendships when you have little opportunity to talk to other people in person.

Lead-in

Elicit words that are used during online meetings. Remind students that they should use words and phrases relating to the topic in their essay and to vary them as much as possible.

5a Ask students to read the sentences and look at the words and phrases in bold. Ask whether they are formal or informal (informal). Then ask students to work with a partner to match the phrases with their more formal equivalents in a–g. Go through the answers as a class.

> 1 b   2 f   3 c   4 a   5 e   6 g   7 d

5b Focus students' attention on the Remember box. They then look at sentences 1–6 and decide whether they are formal or informal. Go through the answers as a class and ask students to provide reasons for their choices.

> 1 I   2 F   3 F   4 I   5 F   6 I

Lead-in

Elicit linking words of any kind that might be used in an essay and make a list on the board.

6a Ask students to look at the sentences in Exercise 4b and underline any linking words and phrases.

> **to add information**: Additionally, Similarly, What is more
> **to compare and contrast ideas**: despite, On the other hand, However

6b Students complete the exercise individually, then check answers in pairs. Then check the answers as a class.

Adding information	Comparing and contrasting
besides	even so
equally	even though
furthermore	in contrast
in addition	nevertheless
likewise	nonetheless
moreover	on the contrary
not only … but also	whereas

Extension

When students do any writing, they should include a range of linking words and phrases. Ask them to check that they have done this when they do any writing in class or for homework.

Exam practice

Ask students to read the task. Ask what they think of when they hear the words *artificial intelligence*. Explain that this is often shortened to *AI*. Ask them how AI can be used for language practice.

Ask students to look at the question and notes 1 and 2. Explain any language if necessary or provide examples. Ask them to think of a third note.

In the test, students should spend about 40 minutes planning, writing and checking their essay.

Students can write the essay in class or for homework. After planning the essay, they should spend about 30 minutes writing it. Focus their attention on the checklist in the Advice box and ask them to use this to check their work at the end. Remind students that they should always check their answer carefully in the actual exam, including spelling and punctuation.

> **Sample answer**
> Language practice can be done in person and online with artificial intelligence (AI). There are advantages and disadvantages to both methods.
>
> Practising with a real-life partner provides authentic conversation, whereas the advantage of using AI is that work can be personalised: learners choose the topic in addition to the vocabulary or grammar focus. What is more, there is a wide choice of engaging interactive materials. Another thing to consider is feedback: whether you are working online or face-to-face, you can gain useful feedback, though it may be quicker online.
>
> Language practice may be less personalised in person: there is always someone else to consider. However, online, it can take a long time to find what you'd like to practise. There may be limited access to resources in a one-to-one situation. In contrast, the drawback of online study is that technology may fail. It is also difficult to verify that feedback is accurate online; even in face-to-face situations, students are reliant on others to provide accurate information.
>
> Whichever way students practise language, there are excellent opportunities to progress and although it may be in different ways, both methods can be helpful.
>
> **Commentary**
> - This is a good answer.
> - All content points are addressed (notes 1 and 2, and own idea).
> - Reasons are given for the ideas expressed.
> - The candidate has used an appropriately semi-formal style.
> - Ideas are organised into logical paragraphs, with an introduction and conclusion.
> - There is a range of suitable vocabulary and grammatical structures.

Part 2 (article)

> **Task type:**
> An article of 140–190 words giving opinions and/or providing information, in response to an advertisement in a magazine or on a website.

Training

Lead-in

In the article task, students should think about who the reader of the article is and remember to write their article for this reader. Explain that the article should be interesting to read and make the reader feel involved.

1a Elicit some examples of hobbies and interests from the students. Then ask them to look at the titles and explain any new vocabulary (e.g. *thrill-seekers*). Ask students to look at the topics and decide which title might belong to an article about each topic.

> 1 a   2 b   3 d   4 e   5 c

1b Ask students whether they think the titles are interesting and to explain their reasons (e.g. because they refer to the topic of the article and draw the readers' attention).

2a Students complete the task in pairs and check answers as a class.

> 1 and 3 grab the attention of the reader more because they are rhetorical questions.

2b Ask students to change the sentences to rhetorical questions. Go through the first one as an example with the class.

> **Suggested Answers**
> 1 Are you wondering whether you're too old to take up competitive sport?
> 2 Have you ever fancied learning to play an instrument?
> 3 Would you like to get some tips about strengthening your relationships?
> 4 Do you have some / any free time to do an interesting new project?

Lead-in

Explain to students that using a variety of adjectives can make an article more interesting to read and that they should do this in the exam task. Elicit some adjectives and write them on the board. Encourage students to come up with some interesting or dramatic adjectives.

3a Ask students to read the example. They then complete the task in pairs or small groups. Students share answers with the class. Write the most interesting adjectives on the board.

> **Suggested answers**
> 1 frustrating / irritating   2 terrible / awful / horrendous   3 freezing
> 4 impossible   5 hilarious   6 fantastic / brilliant / wonderful / superb
> 7 ancient   8 terrifying   9 delicious   10 exhausted

3b Ask students to choose the more dramatic adjective in sentences 1–5.

> **Answers**
> 1 thrilling   2 fascinated by   3 overwhelmed by   4 unbelievable
> 5 priceless

3c Ask students to look again at sentences 1–5 in Exercise 3b and underline the adverbs that go before the adjectives.

Explain that with dramatic, or absolute, adjectives, it is also possible to use absolute adverbs, such as *totally*, *completely* and *absolutely*.

Note: *really* can often be used in place of the absolute adverbs for a similar (but less dramatic) meaning.

> absolutely, totally, completely

Extension

Ask students to write sentences using the dramatic adjectives they came up with in Exercise 3a and to include an absolute adverb before each adjective.

Lead-in

Explain that in the article task, it is good to include opinions about the topic. Elicit phrases for expressing opinions (e.g. *I think / believe, In my opinion*). Write students' examples on the board.

4a Students complete the task in pairs. Go through the answers as a class. Then ask students to compare the phrases on the board from the Lead-in task with the ones in Exercise 4a.

> 1 see   2 conclusion   3 concerned   4 tend   5 convinced
> 6 seem   7 Personally   8 agree

4b Students look at the phrases and decide which can introduce an opinion. They discuss their ideas in pairs or small groups. Then check the answers as a class.

> The most likely ones are: *To my mind, ...*; *If you ask me, ...*; *I don't know about you, but I ...* . However, they could all be used if the writer continues with their own opinion.

4c Ask students to read the sentence endings and match them with the sentence beginnings from Exercise 4b. Explain that there may be more than one correct answer. Then check the answers as a class.

> **Suggested answers**
> 1 Imagine what you could
> 2 To my mind / If you ask me / Whether you believe it or not
> 3 To my mind / If you ask me / Whether you believe it or not
> 4 Listen to this!
> 5 I don't know about you, but I
> 6 To my mind / If you ask me / Whether you believe it or not

Exam practice

Ask students to discuss the questions in pairs and encourage them to give reasons for their ideas. Remind them that they need to answer all the questions in their article.

Candidates should spend about 40 minutes planning, writing and checking their Part 2 task in the exam.

Students can write their article in class or for homework. When they have finished, they should check their work carefully.

> *Sample answer*
> **A fantastic way to spend the day in Marshton**
> Fancy going somewhere exciting for the day? Then come to the village of Marshton! It's small, but as far as I'm concerned, what it lacks in size, it makes up for in fun!
>
> Not everyone would agree, but you can have a great time as a young person in a rural village. My online friends often ask whether I get bored. Definitely not! That's because there's lots to do: we've got an amazing outdoor pool, some cool cafés and a village hall where they hold all kinds of activities, like games nights and parties.
>
> What could someone do if they came to visit for a day? In addition to the incredibly beautiful views of the nearby White Mountains to photograph, Marshton has an ancient castle with a truly thrilling history. There's also a brilliant woodland nature trail, with fascinating sculptures made from fallen trees. Once visitors have done all that, they'll be starving! So they should head along to Bistro Burgers to build their own burger from the huge range of delicious ingredients on offer.
> Who said the countryside was boring?
>
> *Commentary*
> • This is a very good answer.
> • All the questions are addressed.
> • Reasons are given for the opinions expressed.
> • A title is used.
> • The article is organised clearly into paragraphs.
> • It uses some rhetorical questions.

Part 2 (letter)

> **Task type:**
> The letter task in Part 2 tests your ability to write a letter, such as a letter of application for a job. You should write 140–190 words.

Training

Lead-in

Ask students what they know about writing letters (for example, who they might go to and so on).

1a Ask students to read the notice. Ask who has written the notice, why they have written it and what interested readers should do.

> Apply for the role of Events Manager of the community festival in the town

1b Students complete the task in pairs and check answers as a class.

> 1 B 2 C 3 B 4 B 5 O 6 O 7 C

Lead-in

Ask students whether they should use formal or informal language in a letter to the town council member (formal).

2a Students decide which phrases are suitable ways to start a formal letter. Elicit when the remaining phrases might be used, for example, when writing to a friend.

> Dear Mr Jackson,
> To whom it may concern
> Dear Sir or Madam,

2b Elicit possible ways to finish a letter which starts with one of the phrases in Exercise 2a. Then ask students to look at the phrases and decide which are suitable to use at the end of a formal letter. Go through the answers as a class.

> Yours faithfully,
> Yours sincerely,

Lead-in

Elicit the meanings of *work experience* (unpaid work in an organisation to get experience) and *volunteering* (unpaid work helping others in society). Invite students to give some examples or provide some of your own (e.g. answering calls in an office or helping people to pack their bags in a supermarket). Ask students about their own experiences of work experience or volunteering, or how they help other people in their daily lives.

3a Focus students' attention on the Tip. Explain that when they plan their answer in the test, they should think about the vocabulary related to the topic that they can use.

Then ask them to look at the phrases in Exercise 3a. Explain any unfamiliar vocabulary (e.g. *prospects*).

Students match the phrases with the definitions. Check the answers as a class and elicit some ideas for each one (for example, if you have a sense of community, you might help elderly people in your neighbourhood or pick up litter).

> 1 c 2 i 3 d 4 j 5 g 6 a 7 h 8 f 9 e 10 b

3b Ask students to decide which phrases are connected to volunteering, work and work experience.

> **volunteering**: contribute to society, a sense of community, charity, give something back
> **work and work experience**: relevant qualifications, improve your career prospects, develop your CV, skills and experience, internship, discover your strengths and weaknesses (The three latter phrases could also be used in connection with volunteering.)

Extension

Ask students to think of other skills and abilities that volunteering and work experience might give people.

Exam practice

Ask students to read the task and, in pairs, discuss ideas on why wildlife protection is important.

Remind students that they need to answer all the questions in their letter. In the exam, candidates should spend about 40 minutes planning, writing and checking their letter.

Students can write their letter in class or for homework. When they have finished writing, they should check their work carefully.

> *Sample answer*
> Dear Ms Tome,
>
> I would like to apply to volunteer on one of your farms. Looking after the countryside is very important to me and I believe that I have suitable skills for this role.
>
> I enjoy spending time in the countryside and I have always been interested in nature. I have recently taken a course in wildlife conservation, so this volunteering position would allow me to put some of that knowledge into practice and further extend my skills. In my opinion, it is vital to protect wildlife so we can maintain the planet's biodiversity for future generations.
>
> I do not have any direct experience of working as a volunteer on a farm, but I regularly help my neighbours with their gardens. I always give them advice on planting flowers that attract bees, using rainwater to water the garden and other strategies to help the environment.
>
> I would very much like to be considered for this role and look forward to hearing from you.
>
> Yours faithfully,
> Edward Brown
>
> *Commentary*
> - This is a very good answer.
> - All the points are addressed.
> - Reasons are given for the points raised.
> - The candidate has written the letter in an appropriately formal style.
> - The letter is organised well and is divided into clear paragraphs.
> - The letter has a suitable greeting and ending.

Part 2 (report)

> **Task type:**
> A report of 140–190 words written for a specific English-speaking audience.

Training

Lead-in

Ask students what a report is and why someone might write one. (It can be a review of an event or evaluation of a specific topic, with recommendations and/or a conclusion based on the writer's opinions. Reports are often written by students or by people at work.) Elicit what they already know about reports.

1a Ask students to read the report. Tell them not to worry about the words in bold at this point. Ask them to work in pairs to discuss what went well at the event and what did not. Discuss the answers as a class.

> **what went well:** spacious and clean changing facilities, some snacks, well-organised races with time for competitors to prepare
> **what did not go well:** limited parking leading to queues and some competitors being late for their races, snacks ran out, no quiet area, one race overlooked so some swimmers were unable to compete

1b Refer students to the Tip box and explain that in the exam task, it is useful to include headings in their report because it helps to organise the information. Elicit what the first and last section might include and what the headings might be (*Introduction, Recommendations / Conclusions*).

Ask students to look at the statements. Explain that they should refer back to the report in Exercise 1a to check. Check the answers as a class.

> Statements 1, 2, 4 and 6 are true.

Extension

Tell the students that you attended a conference that had some problems. Write these complaints on the board:

The queues were so long that some people missed the start.

There were problems with the microphones, so the sound quality of the presentations was bad.

The seats were very uncomfortable.

Ask students to write some recommendations so that future events will go more smoothly. They should aim to write a short paragraph as in the report in Exercise 1a.

Lead-in

Focus students' attention on the Remember box. Provide an example of an active sentence transformed to the passive voice, e.g. *Nobody emptied the bins and there was rubbish everywhere.*
→ *The bins had not been / were not emptied and there was rubbish everywhere.*

2a Ask students to look at the words in bold in the report in Exercise 1a and ask whether they are active or passive verb forms.

> They are in the passive voice. This makes the writing more formal. Also, the result of the action itself is more important than who or what performed the action.

2b Ask students to look at the first sentence and write it on the board. Ask a volunteer to come to the board and rewrite the sentence in the passive voice. Ask the rest of the class to check that it is correct and make any amendments. Students then complete the rest of the task in pairs. Check the answers as a class.

> **1** No seat numbers were put on the tickets, / Seat numbers were not put on the tickets, so no one knew where to sit.
> **2** Too many people were let into the festival and not enough facilities were provided for them all.
> **3** The participants weren't sent the address for the event.
> **4** The kitchens hadn't been cleaned or tidied, so the cooking event couldn't go ahead.
> **5** The game was cancelled at the last minute, but no one / nobody was informed.

Exam practice

As a class, discuss some ideas of what a college might do to encourage students to help the environment.

Remind students that they need to include all the points in their report. They should spend about 40 minutes planning, writing and checking their report.

Students can write their report in class or for homework. They should write their report in about 30 minutes and use the checklist to make sure they have done what they should.

Sample answer
Introduction
This report aims to provide information about how college students are encouraged to care for the environment.

How students help the environment
Students help to look after the environment in several ways. Firstly, there are recycling bins where we can place different kinds of waste, such as cans, bottles or banana skins. Secondly, we are encouraged to switch off lights and turn off taps to save energy and water. What's more, we have planted a roof garden to provide a habitat for insects.

The importance of helping the environment
It is crucial to educate people about the environment. Climate change is a huge problem that is affecting how we, animals and plants live. If we do not work to protect the future of our planet now, there may not be one!

Recommendations
I would strongly recommend encouraging staff to travel by public transport to college, as most students do. We could also reduce the amount of meat that is offered in the canteen. Finally, we should collect rainwater to water plants around the school when the weather is hot and dry.

Commentary
- This is a very good answer.
- All the points are addressed with examples.
- The candidate has written the report in a suitably formal style.
- The report is clearly organised into sections with appropriate headings.
- A range of vocabulary and grammatical structures is used.
- The candidate has written the correct number of words.

Test 1
Listening
Part 1

> **Task type:**
> Multiple choice. Eight questions. One multiple-choice question per text (short monologue or dialogue), each with three options.

Training

1 The aim of this activity is to make students aware of the different possible focuses that questions in Part 1 might have. Tell students that in the exam, they will hear and read a sentence giving the context of each recording. This will help to prepare them for what they will hear. This sentence will also tell them how many speakers they will hear on each recording (one or two). Tell students that there will be a variety of types of question. For example, the question might focus on the overall topic or general meaning, or a specific detail, or the speaker's purpose, attitude, opinion or feelings. If there are two speakers, the question may focus on whether they agree or disagree about something. Ask students to look at questions 1–6 and match the different question focuses with a–f. Sometimes the context sentence is followed by a question (1, 2, 4, 6) and sometimes by a sentence stem (the first part of a sentence) (3, 5) that will be correctly completed by one of the three answer options. In these examples, the multiple-choice options have been omitted.

> **1** c **2** a **3** b **4** f **5** e **6** d

2 The aim of this activity is to give students a full example of a Part 1 task while thinking about question focus.

Ask them to look at options a–f and to read the context sentence and question given. They should choose which option best matches the question.

> d

3 Play the recording and ask students to choose the correct option for the question.

> c

4 Ask students to check their answers by reading the audioscript. Ask them to underline things that are said that support the correct option. Below are examples of what they might choose to underline. Afterwards, give students the chance to listen for a second time. It can be useful to listen and read at the same time as it helps students to match the written and spoken sounds of English.

> It seems that experts in the aviation industry are <u>wasting time and resources with their investigations into supersonic flight</u>. My suspicion is <u>it's just about showing off their engineering capabilities</u>. Flights on aircraft like this will surely <u>only be possible for the super-rich, rather than the rest of us</u>. When the supersonic airliner Concorde was conceived back in the mid-1900s, there really was a genuine need to speed up the flow of information and ideas across continents as in those days, we still relied on printed material or personal interaction a fair bit. <u>Those kinds of reasons for developing aircraft no longer apply</u> in the era of digital online communication.

5 The aim of this activity is to help students widen their vocabulary so that it is easier to match the meaning of what they hear on recordings with the meaning of what they read in tasks. Ask students to match the adjectives with the synonyms. Encourage them to use dictionaries if necessary and to keep a written record of vocabulary that is new to them.

> 1 c 2 f 3 g 4 d 5 e 6 h 7 a 8 b

6 The aim of this activity is to further widen students' vocabulary. Ask students to match the adjectives with the antonyms. Encourage the use of dictionaries and the keeping of written records of vocabulary that is new. Tell students that many of the words in Exercises 5 and 6 will appear in the recordings for Test 1.

> 1 c 2 h 3 b 4 f 5 g 6 e 7 a 8 d

Exam practice

Tell students that they will hear eight different recordings. Remind them to pay attention to the context-setting sentence as this will give them useful information about what they will hear. Remind them, also, to read the questions and options carefully before each recording. Suggest that they underline key words to prepare themselves. For the first one or two recordings, it might be useful to stop and let students compare their answers with a partner to give them confidence before listening to the rest of the recordings and answering the questions. You could also refer them to the Advice section to help them with questions 1 and 2.

Remind students not to leave a multiple-choice question unanswered. If they are not sure what the correct answer is, they should choose the one that best fits what they understood. Tell students that if there's a word in the options they do not know, they should look for clues in the context around the word to help them work out the meaning.

After listening

Check the correct answers with students. Ask them to say which words in the recording give the correct answer. It may be useful to focus on any vocabulary which caused them problems. After clarifying and checking the meaning, perhaps using dictionaries, encourage students to make a note of new words and phrases in their vocabulary records. You could also ask them to try to identify the question focus of each of the eight questions in Part 1.

> 1 B 2 A 3 A 4 B 5 A 6 C 7 B 8 C

Extension

Give students as many opportunities as possible to listen to short extracts from dialogues or monologues spoken by native speakers of English at this level. As they practise hearing texts like this, they will become more familiar and comfortable with what is expected from them in Listening Part 1.

Part 2

Task type:
Sentence completion. Ten sentences to complete with between one and three words. One speaker (monologue).

Training

1 Ask students to read the context-setting sentence and ask them some questions: *Who will be speaking? What will he talk about?*

> He will talk about organising a festival of short films made by film students around the world.

2 The aim of this exercise is to encourage students to try to guess what words might fit in the gaps in the sentences, both in terms of meaning and grammar. Look at the first sentence together and ask questions: *What words could go in this gap? What kind of things might be important stages in planning a film festival?* Possible answers include 'sponsorship' and 'getting funding'. Then tell students to look at the other gaps and think of possible words that could go in each one. Remind them to look carefully at the words both before and after the gap. This will help them decide on likely meaning and also whether, if the missing word is a noun, it should be singular or plural. Get them to compare their ideas with a partner. Possible answers for the second gap are a type of company, e.g. a film or construction company.

3 Remind students that each sentence will have some sort of 'cue'. In other words, the speaker will use words that help students to identify which sentence they should be focused on. This is so that they do not get lost and are guided through the recording. Also remind students that they will hear 'distractors'. In other words, the speaker will talk about other things that sound possible for the gap, but do not fit it correctly. Play the recording for students to complete the gaps.

Play the recording a second time, then give students a chance to compare their answers.

> 1 research 2 technology 3 theme 4 college tutor

4 Ask students to look at the audioscript and check their answers.

5 Tell students to underline the cue words in the audioscript that help them identify which sentence to focus on.

> Hi. I'm Kevin Pendit, here to tell you all about the film festival I organised last year. I'm still a film student and it was my first time doing something like this. I wanted to showcase short films made by other film students in different parts of the world.
>
> When undertaking a project like this, planning is essential. I had lots of ideas about how to go about generating publicity and I knew that I wanted the film festival to be an example of the creativity and diversity there is out there among young filmmakers. But research is key. I did a lot of this beforehand, so I'd know exactly what I was doing.
>
> The next thing was funding, of course, and I was incredibly lucky. I'd actually negotiated a sponsorship deal with a travel company, but they pulled out early on. Thankfully, a technology company then came forward and agreed to provide financial backing, a lot more generously, in return for having their name in all publicity material.
>
> Of course, there are loads of important factors to consider besides funding. I listened to advice from others and learned that a theme is vital. After considering various ideas, I decided to go with 'community', as I think it's something we're losing in the modern world. I wanted to raise awareness in my target audience, which was primarily, younger people.
>
> There were prizes for the best films in different categories, which meant I needed a panel of judges. I knew an arts journalist on a local paper who was happy to join, plus a friend of mine who's a big film expert. I asked one well-known film director to be in charge of the team, but he was too busy, so I turned to my college tutor, who happily took on that role.

Exam practice

Before starting, give students time to read the instructions, where the context is given, and also to pay attention to the task title. Remind them that all this will help prepare them for what they are about to hear.

You could ask some questions to focus them on the context: *Who are you going to hear speaking? What is she going to talk about?* You could also ask them if they know anything about art museums and get them to predict some possible vocabulary they might hear (e.g. *exhibits, exhibition, collection, photography, conservation, creativity*).

Remind students how important it is to use the time before the recording starts to read the sentences and to guess what words might be used to complete them. Remind them also that they should only write the words they hear (no more than three, and usually one or two) and that they shouldn't change the words at all.

After playing the recording for the first time, you could let students compare with a partner before listening for the second time. When you check the correct answers, tell them to look carefully at their spelling and make a note of any words that they had problems with. Write the correct answers on the board so that students can check their spelling.

> 9 dealer 10 writing 11 desk days 12 Africa 13 pottery
> 14 recording details 15 problem solving 16 photography
> 17 plastic 18 small galleries

Extension

Encourage students to view listening exercises as a chance to expand their vocabulary. Recommend that they note down new words whenever they listen to or watch TV or films in English. Encourage them, also, to use their dictionaries to check both meaning and spelling. Point out that in English, words frequently sound slightly different from the way they are written.

Part 3

> **Task type:**
> Multiple matching. Five short monologues. Five correct answers; eight options to choose from.

Training

1 Tell students to look at the example of a Part 3 task. Explain that all five speakers will talk about the same basic topic. You could prepare students for the topic of chef training by asking some questions: *What might someone learn about on a chef training course? Would you like to do a chef training course? What might be easy or difficult about it?*

2 Now ask students to read the eight options carefully to prepare for listening. They could underline key words (e.g. *pleased, recognised, better than others, annoyed, less pleasant tasks*). Remind them that three of the options do not match any of the speakers and that they may hear things that sound a little similar, but are an incorrect match. They will have some examples of this when they listen to the first speaker.

3 Tell students that they are going to listen to the first speaker. They should choose the option that best matches what she says. You could also remind students that in the full version of the test, the five speakers will be a mix of male and female and may have slightly different accents from each other.

Play the recording of the first speaker. Before playing the recording for a second time, remind students that they should use this opportunity to check and confirm the correct answer.

> C

4 Now let students read the audioscript, and check their answers. Ask them to underline information that confirms the answer. You could ask the following check questions: *Did she read the label on the bicarbonate of soda?* (no) *Does she regret not reading it?* (yes)

> All my previous cooking experience failed to prepare me for the intensity of chef training, producing dishes on a large scale, with so much information to take in: safety instructions, food hygiene, preventing cross-contamination between things like nuts and other foods. To be honest, I'd thought I'd be a more skilled cook than other students and then I put bicarbonate of soda instead of the flavour enhancer MSG into an Asian stir fry. If only I'd bothered to check the label! On top of that, I did it on more than one occasion. I was totally gutted – I mean, so irritated with myself! It made me feel a bit less self-important, anyway!

5 Ask students to listen to the second speaker and to choose the correct option.

> G

6 Tell students to underline words that give them the correct answer. After this, you could ask them to mark in different ways words that might lead them towards the wrong option (see text in italics below). The aim of this is to reinforce their awareness of distraction in the text and options.

> I'd heard that my chef training *course would be a lot of hard work. And it was.* I think I'd have enjoyed it more if there'd been less *theoretical stuff – you know, nutrition, kitchen hygiene, menu planning, cost control,* and so on. But the thing I really appreciated was how positive everyone was about each other's work. The kitchen

> culture was very much stepping in to lend each other a hand. That meant that you didn't even mind *doing less exciting chores like peeling vegetables or scrubbing kitchen surfaces*. I really got into the cooking side of the course and I was so proud of my pastry skills by the end.

7   The speakers from Exercises 4 and 7 use grammatical forms to express a wish for things to have happened differently (the language of regrets). Focus students' attention on the following two sentences.

  1 If only I'd bothered to check the label!
  2 I'd have enjoyed it more if there'd been less theoretical stuff.

  Explain the importance of understanding language like this for listening tasks, in order to identify feelings of regret or wishing the past to have been different. You could focus students on the use of the past perfect tense after *if* and *if only*.

  Ask students to complete sentences 1–5 with the correct forms of the verbs. The aim of this activity is to give students practice of conditional forms and the language of regret.

  > 1 had been
  > 2 'd / had been given, 'd / would have turned down
  > 3 'd / would have liked, had demanded
  > 4 'd / had kept
  > 5 hadn't stopped, 'd / would have done

8   Play the recording for students to check the correct forms. Then ask students to match each sentence to one of the options in Exercise 2. The answers do not necessarily relate only to the 'regret' structures.

  > 1 B   2 D   3 H   4 F   5 E

Exam practice
Lead-in

You could ask students to talk about long train journeys they've been on before they listen. Ask them what the best and worst things about their journeys were. Tell them to read the instructions for Part 3 and ask them some questions: *How many people will you hear speaking? Will they be speaking alone or with someone else? What will they talk about?* Tell them to read the options carefully and check they understand. Encourage them to underline key words and ideas.

Play the recording and, at the end of the task, give students time to compare their answers before feedback.

> 19 F   20 E   21 G   22 A   23 B

Extension

Ask students to find a podcast or video of someone talking in English about travelling to different countries. Advise them not to worry if they can't understand it all, but to use it as an opportunity to practise listening and learn some new vocabulary.

Part 4

> **Task type:**
> Multiple choice. An interview or exchange between two speakers. Seven three-option multiple-choice questions.

Training

1   Start by introducing the topic of sports and sports psychology, and by asking students to discuss the questions. This will prepare them for the topic of the listening material to come.

2   Tell students to read the instructions in Exercise 2. Ask some questions: *Who will you hear being interviewed? What will he be talking about?* Give students time to read the two multiple-choice questions. Encourage them to underline the words they think are important. Before they listen to the recording, remind them that the interviewer's questions will help them know which question to answer. Remind them also that the words Jim, the sports psychologist, uses will be different from the options, although he will talk about similar things. Play the recording twice, then let students compare their answers.

> 1 C   2 C

3   Tell students to underline the words in the audioscript that confirm the correct options. Then ask them to think about why the other options are incorrect. Remind them that the speaker will usually mention things related to all three options, but only one option will be the correct answer.

> **Woman:** What first made you study sports psychology, Jim?
> **Man:** It's common for people to become sports psychologists to figure themselves out. I've been learning about techniques on my own for ages, but I'll never forget the turnaround in myself when I won a major ski-racing event. The difference was clear. I'd been aware how much your head gets in the way of winning at things long before making a career of it and getting an academic qualification. I've since seen many transformations, assisting sportspeople who lacked sufficient confidence to come out on top. It's very rewarding.
> **Woman:** What's been useful in your work as a sports psychologist?
> **Man:** Well, some athletes have doubts about the mental side, instead focusing on the physical aspects of what they do. Having been in the same position previously, I get that and they get that I do. It means they're more willing to take on board what I'm putting across. I try to teach them to come back from losing, to look on the bright side and go forward. Developing psychological skills can take a frustrating amount of time. It's hard to play the waiting game, but worth it in the long run.

4   The aim of this activity is to develop students' vocabulary and learn some common verb–noun phrases to talk about ambition and achievement. Tell students that this is a common theme in Part 4 interview tasks, but of course there are a huge range of other possible topics for the interview. Encourage students to use dictionaries and remind them to record any new phrases in their vocabulary notebooks.

> 1 a career   2 barriers   3 inspiration   4 a path   5 fulfilment

5   This activity also aims to develop vocabulary: idiomatic language that might be used when talking about achievements. Encourage students to use dictionaries and remind them to record any new phrases in their vocabulary notebooks.

> 1 d   2 c   3 f   4 a   5 b   6 e

Extension

Recommend that students listen to and watch videos online of interviews with people talking in English. This will help them to become familiar with the typical progress of an interview from questions about how someone got started in their interesting activity to questions about details of the high and low points, the difficulties and successes, through to questions about the interviewee's advice for others and future goals.

Exam practice

You could prepare students for the topic of music and the work of a music producer by asking the following questions: *What kind of music do you enjoy listening to? What other jobs are there besides musician that are related to music? Do you know anything about what a music producer does?* You may need to explain that a music producer is a professional in the music industry who manages and directs musicians, both creatively and technically, when they are making a recording.

Remind students to use the context sentence to help them think about and predict the sort of topics that will be covered in the interview. You could ask some check questions: *Who is being interviewed? What is he being interviewed about?* Remind students also that the interviewer's questions will help them know what question they should focus on as they listen and that the questions will follow the order of the recording. Tell students that they should use the second listening as a chance to check and confirm their answers from the first listening.

After listening, allow students compare their answers with each other before checking the correct answers as a class.

> 24 B   25 B   26 B   27 A   28 B   29 C   30 C

Speaking
Part 1

> **Task type:**
> A conversation between one examiner, known as the interlocutor, and each candidate. In Part 1, candidates answer questions on a variety of topics related to their everyday life. The interlocutor has three sets of topics to choose from and each topic has four questions. The questions asked may be on the same topic, or they may be about different topics.

Training
Lead-in

Before students open their books, ask: *Who do you talk to in this part of the test? What do you talk about?* Then ask students to look at the Task information section in their books to check the answers.

1a In pairs, students look at the choice of topics and decide which ones are suitable for Part 1 questions. Check answers as a class.

> future plans, friends, hobbies, travel experiences, your birthday

1b Students will hear two candidates answering questions in Part 1 of the test. While they listen, students tick the topics from Exercise 1a they answer questions on.

> Kemi: hobbies, travel experiences; Yuki: friends, future plans

1c Students listen to the recording again and write down the questions they hear. In feedback, draw students' attention to the Tip about responding to the question using the appropriate tense. Discuss how they can also demonstrate their range of grammar by using different tenses in their responses.

> (Kemi) Do you have any hobbies which you do regularly?
> Tell us about a place you visited which you really enjoyed.
> (Yuki) How often do you go out somewhere with your friends?
> Are you going to any special events or celebrations soon?

1d Refer students to the topics in Exercise 1a which were not suitable for Part 1 of the Speaking test. Focus on *environmental problems* and talk about why it is less suitable, then elicit suggestions about how it could be adapted for Part 1. (It is a general topic which does not focus on personal experience. A typical Part 1 question could be *Do you do anything to improve the environment?*)

Ask students to work in pairs to think of ways to make the more general topics from Exercise 1a suitable for Part 1 of the Speaking test. Go through answers as a class.

> **Possible answers**
> facilities in the local area – Where is your favourite place to go near where you live?
> important news stories – Do you prefer to read about the news or to listen to it on the radio or watch it on TV?
> new inventions – Is it important for you to always have the latest devices?
> public transport in your country – How often do you travel by bus?
> the lives of famous people – Is there a famous person you would like to meet?

2a Expressing likes and dislikes is a common feature of Part 1 responses. Write a general topic, e.g. *sport*, on the board and draw two faces: ☺ and ☹. Then elicit responses from students. Write the language for expressing likes and dislikes they use on the board. They may only use simple verbs *like, don't like, hate*. Tell them there are different ways to express likes and dislikes and they should try to vary the expressions they use to demonstrate a range of language.

Ask students to look at the comments from candidates in the exercise. They need to complete the sentences by writing one word in each gap. Students check their answers in pairs, then check as a class.

> 1 keen   2 in, rather   3 mind / care   4 bear / stand   5 watching
> 6 into   7 fan

2b Students now match the comments with the Part 1 topics from Exercise 1a. Tell them that it may be possible to match some comments with more than one of the topics.

> 1 hobbies   2 travel experiences, future plans   3 future plans
> 4 your birthday   5 friends   6 hobbies, your birthday
> 7 hobbies, travel experiences, future plans

2c Ask students to close their books. Elicit some different ways of asking questions about likes and dislikes. Students then look at the questions in the exercise and underline the different question structures used. Remind them they need to listen carefully to what they are asked so that they can respond appropriately.

To practise the language from Exercise 2b, students work on their own to write an answer to each question. In feedback, focus on any common issues with accuracy.

2d Students can now practise answering the questions. Play the recording and pause after each question for them to answer.

2e After students have answered the questions, play the recording of two candidates answering the same questions. Students listen to find out if the candidates have the same opinions as them. Review the language from this section by asking students which expressions from Exercise 2b the candidates used.

A: Well, I'm not really into art, but I am keen on going to museums to learn about ancient history. It's fascinating to learn about the lives of people so many years ago.
B: I know those are really popular at the moment, but I'm not particularly interested in them. Maybe if I'm on a long journey, I'll do some to pass the time, but that's all.
A: To be honest, I'm not a huge fan of them. I don't mind the ones which you can play with a friend, but most of them are too complicated for me.
B: Do you mean a photo I've taken? I took one from the top of a mountain I climbed last year. In the photo, you can really see how high we climbed and how beautiful the scenery was. I absolutely love that photo and I've saved it onto my phone so I can look at it every day.
A: That's a difficult question to answer. I think I'd rather spend time outside when it's warm, so I suppose I like spring or summer best. I can't stand the cold weather, so winter is my least favourite time of year.

Exam practice

1 For exam practice, students work in pairs to ask and answer the questions. Draw attention to the Advice box and remind students to give an extended answer: they should aim to say two or three sentences or spend around 20 seconds on each answer. When they are practising the questions, encourage them to time each other's answers so that they get an understanding of what an extended answer feels like.

2 Play the recording and pause it for students to answer. Ask students to whisper their answers so they don't distract each other, or nominate one or two students to say their answer out loud.
Monitor while students are talking. In feedback, discuss how successful they were at giving extended answers.

Part 2

Task type:
An individual 'long turn' for each candidate, based on two photographs and a related question. The 'long turn' candidate speaks for around one minute. After each long-turn response, the second candidate answers a question connected to one of the photographs. The second candidate can speak for up to 30 seconds. If necessary, the interlocutor will ask a follow-up question (*Why? / Why not?*) to encourage the second candidate to extend their response.

Training
Lead-in

Ask students to read the task information at the top of the page. Check understanding by calling out key numbers (1, 2, 4, 30) and asking students what these numbers refer to in a Part 2 task.

1 Ask students to close their books. Elicit some suggestions for tips for this part of the test. Prompt ideas by writing *You should …* and *You shouldn't* on the board.
Ask students to complete Exercise 1.

You should …
- make guesses about what the photographs show. (The question from the examiner always begins with *say why / what you think*, so candidates are expected to speculate. Speculating about the photographs is a good way of demonstrating a range of language.)
- talk about the similarities and differences between the photographs. (Candidates should compare the photographs, using a variety of comparative expressions.)
- use linking words. (Linking words and cohesive devices are important for comparing the photographs.)
- listen to what your partner says. (Candidates have to answer a short question about their partner's photographs. They should listen to what their partner says to help them start thinking of vocabulary they can use. They don't need to mention what their partner said, but this can be a good way of showing that they were listening.)
- answer the question above the photographs. (Candidates may choose to spend half the time comparing the two photographs and the other half on answering the question. It doesn't matter which order they do this in, but it is important not to forget to answer the question.)

You shouldn't …
- ask your partner what they think about the photographs. (In this part of the test, candidates do not interact with each other.)
- choose your favourite photograph and talk about it. (The task is to compare the two photographs.)
- describe everything you can see in the photographs. (Candidates need to compare the photographs and also answer the question.)
- stop talking as soon as you have answered the question. (One assessment focus of this part of the test is candidates' ability to organise an extended response. The examiner will stop the candidate speaking after one minute.)
- make suggestions to your partner. (Candidates should not interrupt their partner while they are speaking.)
- speak for a minute about your partner's photographs. (Candidates are asked a simple question after their partner's long turn. They have up to 30 seconds for their answer. The examiner will interrupt them if they speak for too long.)

2 Ask students to turn to page C1. Ask them to tell you the topic (feeling confident) and the question (*Why do the people need to feel confident in these situations?*). Tell students they will now listen to a candidate doing this task. While they listen, they should think about the advice in Exercise 1 and consider the candidate's performance.

Positive points: The candidate uses appropriate linking words to compare and contrast the pictures. She speculates about the pictures, using appropriate language.
Negative points: The candidate gives a detailed description of the two pictures, but only makes a brief reference to the question for the second picture.

3a Ask students to think about the follow-up question for Mika's partner. Students brainstorm some ideas in small groups, then share with the whole class.

3b Play the recording of Asif's follow-up question and response. Students listen to find out what the question is and to comment on Asif's performance.

The question is: *Would you like to ski?* Asif follows the examiners' advice: he uses linking words and he does not talk for too long. He briefly mentions his partner's response, which shows that he was actively listening.

4a Refer to the advice in Exercise 1 about giving an extended answer for one minute. Discuss with students how giving reasons for a comment is one way of extending their response, and appropriate use of linking words and expressions demonstrates their ability to organise what they say.
Students work with a partner to match the sentence beginnings and endings. Monitor while they are working to note down any difficulties they have with the expressions. In feedback, focus on what kind of word or structure comes after each expression (e.g. noun, -*ing* form, clause).

1 d **2** a **3** e **4** b **5** f **6** c

4b To practise the expressions for giving reasons, ask students to cover up Exercise 4a. They need to use one word to complete the sentences which refer to photo B on page C1.

Students do the exercise in pairs, then check the answers as a class. In feedback, allow variations in response, as indicated in the key below.

1 Given / Seeing
2 as / since / because
3 as / since / because
4 Due / Owing
5 due / thanks / owing
6 because

5 Ask students to reflect on what Mika and Asif did well and what they could do better. Tell students that they will now talk about the same photographs using the tips they have been talking about.

Students work in pairs. Tell them you will play the recording twice. The first time, one student does the long-turn response and the other answers the follow-up question, then they swap roles. If space allows, move students so that the pairs are not sitting too close to each other. Ask them to use low voices when they speak so that they do not disturb each other.

Play the recording and pause after the examiner reads the instruction for the long turn. After one minute, start the recording again. Allow 30 seconds for students to respond to the follow-up question.

Exam practice

Students look at the photos on pages C2 and C3. Ask them what the two topics are (taking a break, making changes) and ask them to read the task instructions in the book.

Students work with a partner to complete the task. Check the timing and make sure they move on after one minute for the long turn and 30 seconds for the follow-up question. Monitor and make notes for feedback on examples of good performance and any key language issues.

Sample answers
Candidate A (long turn)
The first thing I notice about these pictures is that the first one is outside, whereas the second one is inside, and there's a difference in why they're taking a break. In the first picture, the four people look like builders. Two of them are holding helmets and one of them is wearing a bright jacket for safety. It looks like they're outside a building site because I can see different materials in the background. They have snacks – sandwiches, I think – and bottles of water, so I imagine they've been working for several hours and they're hungry and thirsty. On the other hand, the woman in the picture below is taking a break from painting. She's having a drink and looking at the work she's done. It looks like she's in an art studio, maybe in her own home. I imagine she needs to take a break because she had to concentrate hard to do her work and needs to rest her eyes. She probably also needs to see if she's happy with her work or whether she needs to make any changes. So, the main difference is the first picture shows people who need physical rest and the second picture shows someone who needs a rest from concentrating hard.
Candidate B (follow-up question)
Well, I'm certainly not an artist and I don't have all the equipment the woman in that picture has, but I do like painting pictures just for fun and just for myself. I prefer drawing or painting pictures outside, like pictures of scenery or nature.

Candidate B (long turn)
OK, the first picture shows a family and they're changing a room in their house. In the second picture, the woman is changing the girl's hair by cutting it. I suppose when you think about it, the people in the second picture might be having different feelings about the change. The woman, who looks like she might be the girl's mother, might be feeling nervous because it's possible she's not a professional hairdresser and she might make a mistake. The girl could be excited that she's going to look different, so I don't think she's finding anything difficult about the experience. The changes in the first picture are going to take longer to make. The man is showing the baby the new colours for the walls and the woman seems to be repairing a door. She's looking on her phone, so I wonder whether she's unsure about what she's doing and so needs to check instructions, and that's what she's finding difficult. They also probably have to choose between the two colours on the wall and that might be difficult because if they don't like the choice they make, it'll take quite a long time to change it again.
Candidate A (follow-up question)
I'd love to decorate my bedroom at home. It's been the same colour for ages and I'd like to paint it a brighter colour, like red or orange. The trouble is, I have so much stuff in my room and so it's a big job to decorate it. Maybe I'll just get some bright cushions and curtains instead.

Part 3

Task type:
A two-way conversation between the candidates. The interlocutor does not get involved in the discussion. The interlocutor introduces a scenario and tells candidates what they need to discuss. They have a sheet with the question and five prompts to guide the discussion. After around two minutes, the interlocutor asks the candidates to try to reach a decision about one aspect of the discussion topic. They have around one minute for this stage, and it doesn't matter if the candidates don't manage to make a decision in that time.

Lead-in

Ask students to read the task information at the top of the page. Ask them if they have any time to read the task before they start speaking and elicit the timing for the different stages of this part of the test.

1a Students complete the task in pairs. In feedback, focus on the importance of listening: listening to the examiner's introduction to start thinking about the topic and listening to your partner during the discussion so you can respond appropriately.

What the examiner does	What you need to do
The examiner introduces the topic.	Listen carefully. Think about your opinion on the topic. Think of useful vocabulary.
The examiner gives you the task.	Read the question and the options. Think about which option to start your discussion with. Think of useful vocabulary.
The examiner reads out the discussion question.	Talk to your partner. Talk about each of the prompts. Take turns. Listen carefully.
The examiner reads out the decision question.	Talk to your partner. Try to reach an agreement. Listen carefully.

1b Students complete the advice in pairs. In feedback, you can ask students if they can think of any other advice to share.

What the examiner does	Advice
The examiner introduces the topic.	You can ask the examiner to **repeat** what they say if you need to.
The examiner gives you the task.	Don't **rush** through all the prompts. Don't **start** speaking until the examiner tells you to.
The examiner reads out the discussion question.	Don't try to **reach** an agreement yet. Don't worry if you **run** out of time to discuss all the prompts. You can ask the examiner to **repeat** what they say if you need to. Ask your partner to **give** their opinion. Try to **link** the prompts to the main question on the page.
The examiner reads out the decision question.	It's OK if you don't **agree** with each other. You can ask the examiner to **repeat** what they say if you need to. You can agree to **disagree** with your partner. Ask your partner to **give** their opinion.

2 Students look at the sample task. Ask questions to check understanding of the task, e.g. *What is the topic of the discussion? How many ideas should you try to discuss? Do you need to decide straightaway the main reason why it's important to plan holidays carefully?*

3 Students listen to two candidates doing the first part of the task. They discuss their thoughts with a partner before discussing as a whole group.

Positive: They discuss all the points. They ask each other's opinions. They both have an equal chance to speak.
Negative: They don't spend long on each point. They don't connect the points to each other.

4 Explain that the candidates' main weakness was how they organised their discussion (Discourse Management) and how they developed the interaction (Interactive Communication). To address these issues, they need to connect the prompts and move the discussion forward. Students should use a variety of cohesive devices to make these connections.

Elicit some suggestions of ways to link the prompts in the sample task. For example, points which express related ideas or points which express opposite ideas can be linked.

Students work together to complete the table by filling in the gaps in the expressions. Check the answers as a class and elicit any more ideas students have for connecting ideas. In feedback, discuss how 'extent' is another element of Discourse Management, i.e. the candidates could have said more about each prompt. Discuss how it is better to address two or three prompts in some depth than to refer to all the prompts quickly and superficially.

Suggested answers
1 Let's 2 Shall 3 about 4 Moving 5 On 6 However 7 In
8 whereas / while 9 as 10 more 11 addition 12 equally

5 Ask students to cover Exercise 4 and work with a partner to complete the expressions. They can then look at Exercise 4 to check.

1 whereas / while 2 equally / both 3 let's 4 how / what
5 contrast 6 What 7 shall 8 In 9 However

6 Students now practise the task in Exercise 2. Monitor while they are talking and make a note of good use of cohesive devices and any errors which you need to focus on during feedback.

Extension

Extend the practice by also giving students the decision question to discuss. For this task, the decision question is *Now you have about a minute to decide what the two most important reasons are for making detailed holiday plans.*

Make students aware that the question asks for two reasons and remind them that they need to listen to the examiner's question carefully so that they don't miss details like this.

Exam practice

Students complete the task in pairs. Tell them when the initial two minutes are over so that they know it's time to move on to the decision question.

Monitor and give feedback on what went well and what they need to work on. Focus on their Discourse Management in particular.

Sample answer
A: There are lots of good reasons to buy food from a supermarket, aren't there? It's certainly the most convenient way because you have everything in one place.
B: That's true, as long as it's a big supermarket. Although the biggest ones are often outside a town so, unless you have your own transport, they're difficult to get to. That means they're not always convenient. What do you think about the choice?
A: Well, you can find almost everything you want in a supermarket. I suppose if you are looking for something special, you may have to go to an independent shop, but that's not usually the case.
B: Yes, and lots of supermarkets now sell food from different countries, so the choice is good.
A: Do you think the cost of things in supermarkets is better? Or is it cheaper to buy from a market, for example?
B: I hadn't thought of that; that's a good point. Supermarkets often have special offers which are interesting. So, what else do we need to discuss? Ah, yes, the environment. Well, there's the issue of driving to supermarkets I already mentioned …
A: … and the point about international food. That has to be imported and that's not good for the environment.
B: Also, there's lots of packaging at a supermarket. Lots of plastic.
Interlocutor: Thank you. Now you have about a minute to decide what the best reason is for <u>not</u> buying food from a supermarket.
A: Well, we didn't talk about service and I think that's an important thing.
B: You mean if you buy food from an independent shop, the service is better?
A: Yes, exactly, but I'm not sure that's the main reason to avoid supermarkets. What about the environment?
B: That's what I was going to say – it's something that people are thinking about more and more, and supermarkets do cause a lot of environmental problems.
A: Agreed. Let's choose that.

Part 4

Task type:
Questions on topics related to the Part 3 collaborative task
Candidates may be asked to answer questions individually, or the interlocutor may prompt them to discuss a question together. When one candidate is answering a question, the other candidate(s) should listen carefully, because the interlocutor may ask a follow-up question, such as *What do you think?*, *Do you agree?* or *And you?*

Lead-in

Ask students to look at the task information for Part 4. Then ask them to close their books. Elicit what they have to do in Part 4 (answer questions) and what the questions are about (the topic in Part 3).

1 Students complete the table in pairs. Then, check the answers as a class.

Part 1
You talk about personal topics.
You talk on your own.
The part lasts two minutes.
The examiner may ask you *Why?* or *Why not?*
The questions are all about you.
The questions are shorter.

Part 4
You talk about general topics.
You talk on your own.
You talk with your partner.
The part lasts four minutes.
The examiner may ask you *Why?* or *Why not?*
The examiner may ask you if you agree with your partner.
The questions may focus on how your opinion compares to other opinions.
The questions are longer.

2 Focus on the topic of the Part 4 questions. Students look back in their books at the Training section for Part 3. What will the Part 4 questions be about? (travelling / holidays)

Elicit some suggestions of suitable Part 4 questions. Then, students work individually to match the two halves of the example Part 4 questions before checking answers with a partner.

Draw students' attention to the Tip about common question structures and work with them to underline these in the examples. These structures can be used for all topics, and being familiar with them will help students with the longer questions in this part of the test.

Discuss that the examiner may ask *Why?* or *Why not?* after any of these questions to encourage candidates to extend their answer. Talk about using examples and reasons to give a longer response to all questions.

1 d **2** e **3** a **4** b **5** c

<u>Some people say that it's better to</u> explore your own country <u>rather than</u> travel abroad. <u>What do you think?</u>
<u>Should</u> travelling by air for leisure <u>be</u> banned?
<u>Is it always important to</u> read reviews of places before deciding where to go?
<u>Do you think it's true that</u> taking photos of places spoils the experience?
<u>Some people believe that</u> travelling helps them understand more about the world. <u>Do you agree?</u>

3 Students listen to two candidates answering the same question. Ask them to think about how the responses are different. Discuss the second candidate's strategy (rephrasing the question gives him thinking time so he can structure his response more effectively).

The first candidate gives an opinion quickly, but then hesitates and repeats words. The second candidate takes some time before answering and organises the response effectively.

4 Tell students that rephrasing the question as the second candidate does is one useful strategy. 'Filler' expressions can be used in the same way. These are expressions which don't answer the question, but they give the speaker time to think without leaving a silence.

Students complete the task in pairs. Then check the answers as a class.

1 Let me think.
2 That's a difficult question to answer.
3 That's not something I've thought about before.
4 I've never thought about that before.
5 To be honest, …
6 What an interesting question!
7 Would you mind saying that again?

5 Students look at the expressions from Exercise 4 and decide which of the words from the list they can substitute. In feedback, elicit more suggestions from students.

That's not **an issue** I've **considered** before. (Sentences 3 and 4)
I've never **considered** that before. (Sentences 3 and 4)
What **a fascinating** question! (Sentence 6)
Would you mind **repeating** that? (Sentence 7)
Let me **see**. (Sentence 1)
That's a **tricky** question to answer. (Sentence 2)

6 Students now work in groups of three practising the questions from Exercise 2. One student takes the role of examiner, and the other two are candidates. Remind students to swap roles.

Exam practice

Ask students to open their books to the section for Part 3 on page C5. Ask them what the Part 4 questions will be about (shopping / food).

Students work in pairs, taking it in turns to ask and answer the questions. Monitor and make notes to give feedback on language and techniques. Aim to give positive feedback, as well as suggestions of areas to work on.

Sample answer

Interlocutor: Some people say that being able to buy all types of food all year round is a positive thing. Do you agree?

A: Not entirely. Of course, I do like it if I can get my favourite food whenever I want, but I know that's not good for the environment.

Interlocutor: Why do you think some people choose to grow their own fruit and vegetables?

B: That's an interesting question and I think there are several reasons. Firstly, so that they know where the food comes from, you know, there are no chemicals on it. And secondly, because it's cheaper, maybe? I'm not sure.

Interlocutor: Do you think that cooking for yourself is always better than buying convenience foods?

A: Not always, no. Sometimes you need something quick and that's what convenience foods are. I know they may not be healthy, but they are a useful option on busy days.

Interlocutor: What do you think?

B: I agree up to a point. I mean, they are useful, but cooking for yourself is so much healthier and cheaper. Maybe it's not always better, but I try to cook as much as I can.

Interlocutor: Is it better to go shopping regularly and only buy a few things each time or to buy larger quantities less often?

B: Well, shopping for food is boring, so I'd say going less often is better, but I suppose it depends on your situation. You need a car to go and buy large quantities.

Interlocutor: Do you agree?

A: I hadn't thought about that, you know, how you transport large amounts of shopping. It's a good point. But if you can, I agree it's the best option. Not because shopping is boring, but because you save time and probably money buying in this way. The only thing I would say you have to buy more frequently is fresh food, like fruit, vegetables and milk.

B: Oh yes, that's a good point. So it's impossible to avoid going to the shops more often!

Interlocutor: Thank you. That's the end of the test.

Extension

Students look at the Part 4 Exam practice questions in their books and plan extended answers. Ask them to think about arguments for and against the statements in each question; this helps with giving a balanced response.

Test 2
Reading and Use of English
Part 1

Task type:
Multiple-choice cloze with one example plus eight gaps. There are four multiple-choice options for each gap.

Training
Go through the questions with the class.

There are eight questions in Part 1.
There are four options in each question.

Lead-in
Candidates may be tested on phrasal verbs in Part 1. Phrasal verbs may also be tested in Parts 2 and 4, and candidates may need to know what various phrasal verbs mean in all parts of the Reading and Use of English test. Candidates should also try to use some phrasal verbs when they do the Writing test.

1   Tell students that the verbs in the first box can sometimes be followed by more than one of the words in the second, but that in this exercise, they should try to match words to form phrasal verbs that match the specific definitions. In addition, tell students that some of these phrasal verbs can also have other meanings. For example, *put off* has two meanings, but only one meaning appears in definitions 1–5.

Students can do this exercise in pairs. Check the answers as a class.

1 go through **2** run into **3** count on **4** go for **5** date from

2   Ask students to do this exercise in their pairs, then check the answers as a class.

1 dates from **2** go for **3** went through **4** ran into **5** count on

3   Ask students to do the task individually, then check their answers in pairs. Check the answers as a class.

1 out **2** off **3** out **4** up **5** off

4   Remind students to change the form of the phrasal verbs, as necessary.

1 turn up **2** falling out **3** shows off **4** died out **5** took off

5   You could do the exercise as a class. To check students understand the meaning of each phrasal verb, ask them to suggest a sentence that includes each one.

1 e **2** b **3** d **4** a **5** c

6   Ask students to do this exercise in their pairs, then check answers as a class.

1 summed (everything) up **2** put (you) off **3** get (your point) across **4** sort (it) out **5** worn (me) out

7   Create a table on the board with rules a–c at the top of each of three columns. Ask students for examples of phrasal verbs from Exercises 1, 3 and 5 that fit into each column.

Ask students to find two new phrasal verbs to add to each column. They could use dictionaries or look online (if appropriate) to help them.

Examples of phrasal verbs that could be added:

a: *make up, turn on*

b: *sit down, grow up*

c: *look after, deal with*

1 c **2** b **3** a

Lead-in
In Reading and Use of English Part 1, candidates are often tested on words that are similar in meaning. Exercises 8 and 9 focus on nouns with similar meanings.

8   Ask students to do the task individually, then check answers in pairs. Check the answers as a class.

1 opinions / views **2** view **3** attitude **4** attitudes / ideas **5** means **6** way / means **7** risks / dangers **8** danger **9** process / method

9   Explain to students that you are going to look at four sentences from Exercise 8: sentences 2, 3, 5 and 8. Look at the example in Exercise 9 together, which is based on sentence 2 in Exercise 8. Then tell students that in pairs, they should rewrite sentences 3, 5 and 8 using the incorrect option in each case. Check the answers as a class.

Suggested answers
3 I wish I knew what her opinion of this proposal is.
5 What's your favourite way of travelling?
8 If you go along that path, you're at risk of falling!

Exam practice
Remind students that they should spend a maximum of ten minutes on Part 1 in the exam.

1 D **2** C **3** D **4** A **5** B **6** B **7** C **8** A

Part 2

Task type:
Open cloze with one example plus eight gaps.

Training
Go through the questions with the class.

Students should always read the whole text quickly before starting to think about which words go in the gaps so they have an idea of what the text is about before they start.

Only one word can be written in each gap. Contractions (e.g. *don't*, *she'll*, *I'm*) count as two words (*do not*, *she will*, *I am*), so these will never be the answer to any of the questions.

Lead-in
Candidates will be very familiar with auxiliary verbs, but it is useful to revise them and remind them that auxiliary verbs are often tested in Reading and Use of English Part 2. Ask students to think of active verb tenses that require the auxiliary verbs *be* and *have* in various forms (e.g. the present and past perfect, present and past continuous). Students don't need to know the grammatical terms for these tenses; they can just give you examples. Remind them that passive forms involve using the auxiliary verb *be*.

1 Ask students to complete the exercise individually, then to check their answers in pairs. After that, check the answers as a class.

1 would   2 had   3 ought / need / have   4 were   5 have / need
6 could   7 have   8 is

Lead-in
When candidates are doing a Part 2 task in the exam, they need to understand how ideas in the text are connected. For example, two ideas or things might contrast with each other (*... but ...*) or they might be part of a list of points (*... and ...*). Students need to think about how ideas are connected so that the text makes sense when they have completed the gaps.

2 Ask students to work in pairs and discuss how the ideas in each sentence are connected before they complete the gap. Check the answers as a class and make sure students understand how the ideas are connected.

1 apart   2 as   3 view   4 Not   5 whereas   6 Owing
7 long   8 order

Lead-in
Candidates are often tested on these words in Part 2. They may also need to use them in Part 4. It is also good to use them correctly in the Writing and Speaking tests.

3 Tell students that the sentences are all part of the same story about some hikers. Ask them to do the exercise in pairs. Check the answers as a class.

1 so   2 too   3 enough   4 very   5 such

4 Tell students that this is the rest of the story. Ask them to work in pairs to correct the mistakes in the sentences. These are the kinds of mistakes that candidates often make in the Writing test. Check the answers as a class.

1 They saw ~~too~~ many mountain goats on the rocks.
2 Eventually, it wasn't ~~so~~ light **enough** for them to see the path clearly.
3 Luckily, they reached the village before it was ~~very~~ **too** dark for them to walk safely.
4 They were ~~too~~ **very** relieved to have finally reached their destination.
5 It was ~~so~~ **such a** lovely place that they stayed there for a week!

Extension
Keep revising these structures in future classes if students are still having trouble with them.

Exam practice
Check that students know what solar panels are (devices that convert sunlight into electricity using special solar batteries or cells). Ask them to read the text quickly to see what the solar batteries (or cells) are going to be used for.

Remind students that they should take a maximum of ten minutes to do this exercise in the exam.

9 long   10 too   11 a   12 been   13 not   14 able   15 it   16 up

Part 3

Task type:
Word formation in a text with one example plus eight gaps. Each gap corresponds to a word. The stem of each missing word is given at the end of the line with the gap in it.

Training
Go through the questions as a class.

The word at the end of each line with a gap is the stem of the word needed for that particular line. It can't be used to form a word gapped on a different line.
The word in capitals must always be changed.

Lead-in
In Part 3, candidates sometimes have to add a prefix to the beginning of the word in capitals at the end of the line. A suffix may also need to be added at the end of the word.

Ask students to think of as many prefixes as they can. Write them on the board. Ask students (in pairs) to think of one or two words which have each prefix. Write the words on the board and check whether the words are nouns, verbs, adjectives, etc.

1 Ask students to complete the exercise in pairs. Then check the answers as a class.

1 im   2 un   3 in   4 dis   5 il   6 un   7 mis   8 ir

2 Students can do the exercise individually, then check their answers in pairs. Check as a class.

1 inexperienced   2 unlock   3 unaware   4 irregular
5 misunderstand   6 immoral   7 illegal   8 disorganised

3 This exercise could be done for homework and checked at the beginning of the next class.

1 rebuilding   2 dissatisfied   3 interactive   4 irresponsibly
5 informally   6 misleading   7 impatiently   8 illegally   9 repaid
10 unreliable

4 Divide the class into three groups and ask group A to do 1–3, group B to do 4–6 and group C to do 5–9. They can use a dictionary or look online to check their answers.

> 1 heat 2 anxiety 3 height 4 thought 5 proof 6 depth
> 7 length 8 vision 9 maintenance

5 Ask each group to find the three sentences which can be completed with their words.

> 1 height 2 proof 3 thought 4 length 5 vision 6 anxiety
> 7 maintenance 8 heat 9 depth

6 This can be done as a whole class. Compound nouns are only occasionally tested in Part 3. Remind students that the answer will never be a word with a hyphen, e.g. *well-known*.

> 1 underground 2 waterproof 3 worthwhile 4 Furthermore
> 5 breathtaking

Extension

Students can note down any new words, along with sentences showing how they can be used, in their vocabulary records.

Exam practice

In the exam, students should spend a maximum of ten minutes on Part 3.

> 17 beneficial 18 energetic 19 length 20 lifestyle 21 unlike
> 22 behaviour / behaviours 23 daily 24 automatically

Part 4

Task type:
Key word transformation of six separate sentences (with one example). Each pair of sentences consists of one full sentence followed by a second sentence with a gap that can be filled with up to five words.

Training

Go through the questions with the class.

> The word in capital letters must not be changed in any way. The word in capital letters counts as one of the words in the answer. Contractions count as two words.

Lead-in

This is a short review of some passive forms. In the actual exam tasks, candidates can gain two marks per sentence transformation, so they usually have to do more than simply change a passive form to an active one, or a passive form to an active one.

Remind students that when they do Exercise 1, they should pay attention to the verb tense in the first sentence and they should use the same tense for the verb *be* when they complete the second sentence.

Passive forms are often tested in Part 2, as well.

1 Ask students to complete the exercise individually, then to check their answers in pairs. After that, check the answers as a class.

> 1 will be found 2 was given 3 tree is said to be
> 4 teach all the classes 5 Have you been offered 6 are going to sell
> 7 was believed to be 8 are being chosen

Lead-in

Candidates are often tested on these forms in Part 4.

2 Ask students to complete the exercise individually, then to check their answers in pairs. Then check answers as a class.

> 1 to see 2 living 3 drive 4 talking 5 to go 6 to sit
> 7 throwing 8 trying

3 Ask students to work in pairs to match the sentence halves. Then check the answers as a class, discussing the differences in meaning together.

> 1 c 2 e 3 f 4 a 5 d 6 b

Extension

If students are keeping vocabulary records, they could note down verbs which are followed by *to* + infinitive or an infinitive without *to*. They could also list verbs which can be followed by either form, sometimes with a change of meaning (as in Exercise 3).

Lead-in

Candidates are often tested on conditional forms in Part 4 and in Part 2. Practising these verb forms is also useful for the Writing and Speaking papers.

4 Ask students to complete the exercise in pairs before checking the answers as a class. Highlight the difference between talking about likely situations in the future (sentences 4 and 5) and imaginary or unlikely situations in the present / future (sentences 1, 2 and 3).

> 1 could afford 2 didn't have to, was / were 3 wouldn't be, went
> 4 got, 'd have 5 look, will you help

Lead-in

Ask students how they think Selim feels when it starts to rain. Ask them if they have ever done anything like this themselves. How did they feel? Write *I wish ...*, *If only I ...* and *If I ...* on the board and ask the students for one or two examples using each structure to express regret about the past.

5 Ask students to complete the exercise in pairs, then check the answers as a class.

> 1 had / 'd checked
> 2 had / 'd known, was going to rain, would have / 'd have postponed
> 3 had / 'd brought
> 4 had / 'd planned, would not / wouldn't all have had to go

6 This exercise revises the structure *have* + past participle. It was used in Exercise 5 after *would* in the third conditional structures. It is also used after *should* for regrets about the past and after other modal verbs when speculating about the past.

> 1 must have seen 2 should not / shouldn't have lent
> 3 may have changed 4 can't have read

Exam practice

Go over the rules for this part again with the students:

- Write between two and five words.
- Contractions count as two words.
- Never change the given word.
- Spell everything correctly.

- Make sure that the second sentence means the same thing as the first sentence.
- Remember that there are two marks for this question, so it's possible to make a mistake, but still get one mark.

> 25 each / every child | was given
> 26 to stop | using her
> 27 could afford | to
> 28 didn't / did not | turn up
> 29 is thought | to be
> 30 have | paid attention to

Part 5

> **Task type:**
> A text followed by six four-option multiple-choice questions.

Training

Go through the questions with the class.

> There are six questions to answer.
> There are four options in each question.
> The questions are in the same order as the text. Occasionally, there may be a question about the whole text. If there is a question like this, it will always be question 6.

Lead-in

In Part 5, candidates may be asked a question about 'writer purpose' – why the writer has written this part of the text (e.g. to explain something, highlight something, complain about something).

1 Ask students to read the text quickly. Check the answer as a class.

> In a city

2 Ask students to look at the first word in each of options A–D and think about what each verb means. Check as a class and ask students to give examples of the kinds of things people sometimes say when they are criticising, justifying, explaining and emphasising.

Students can then answer the question individually before discussing their answer in pairs. Check the answer as a class.

> D
> 'I see it as my responsibility to ensure that I never make anyone feel uncomfortable'; 'I do my best to stay away from busy areas'; 'When I do end up running through a crowded neighbourhood, I am always extremely careful to spend as little time as possible there.'

3 Ask students to do this in pairs. Check the answers as a class.

> 1 B 2 C 3 A

Extension

Ask students how they feel about runners in crowded places. Do they run themselves? Ask pairs of students to write a sentence which criticises, justifies, explains or emphasises something about runners / running. You could also use other verbs, e.g. *recommending*, *admitting*, *admiring*. Write the sentences on the board or ask students to read them out. Then ask the class to guess what the writer purpose is in each sentence.

Lead-in

In Part 5, candidates may be asked what a word or phrase in the text means. Candidates are not expected to already know this word or phrase, but they should be able to work out the answer from the text around it.

Ask students to read the paragraph quickly to find out what it is about (someone called Jim who is looking for a job).

4 Ask students to do the exercise individually, then to check their answers in pairs.

> C

Exam practice

Ask students if they watch or play football. Have they heard of Sabitra Bhandari? Ask them to read the text quickly to find out three things about the player. If they have heard of her / know about her, they can look for three things that they did not already know.

Students should spend approximately 10–15 minutes doing Part 5 in the exam. Remind them that it is a good idea to underline the part of the text that gives them the answer.

> 31 D 32 B 33 A 34 C 35 C 36 A

Part 6

> **Task type:**
> A text with six sentences missing. There are seven sentences after the text. Six of these sentences fit in the gaps in the text.

Training

Go through the questions with the class.

> There are six gaps in the Part 6 text.
> There are seven sentences to choose from, so there is one option that doesn't fit anywhere in the text.

Lead-in

The sentences must fit in the gaps grammatically (e.g. if there's any referencing, it must work). However, the sentence must also follow on logically from the sentence or sentences before it. In addition, the sentence(s) after the gap must make sense after the chosen option.

1 Look at sentence 1 with the whole class as an example. Options a and b both follow sentence 1 grammatically, but only option a makes sense: there's a contrast between people growing up in the same city (and both being artists), but never actually meeting until this point. Option b doesn't make sense because the reason why the two people don't speak the same language is not that they grew up in the same city – that isn't logical (even in a multilingual city).

Ask students to do sentences 2–5 in pairs, then check the answers as a class. Ask individual students to explain to the rest of the class why one option is wrong and one correct in each case.

> 1 a 2 b 3 a 4 a 5 b

Lead-in

This is further practice of linking words which may be useful for students to know when they are doing Part 6 tasks. They are also useful for understanding texts in general and for students' writing.

2 Ask students to do the exercise individually, then check their answers in pairs. Check the answers as a class.

> **1** Nevertheless **2** Alternatively **3** Finally **4** Besides **5** Otherwise **6** Meanwhile **7** Consequently

Extension
You could ask students to include some of these linking words in their next writing homework. They could use the words from the box and/or the underlined words or phrases in the sentences. They're all potentially useful.

Exam practice
Ask the class what adjectives they would use to describe mice. Tell them to read the text quickly, ignoring the gaps. Do the adjectives they thought of describe the mouse in this text? Remind students that they should spend about 15 minutes on this task in the exam. Tell them that it would be helpful to underline linking words and phrases in the text near the gaps and in the options, as well as reference words (e.g. *them*, *its*).

> **37** E **38** D **39** C **40** G **41** F **42** A

Part 7

> **Task type:**
> Ten multiple-matching questions above several short texts or one long text divided into sections.

Training
Go through the questions with the class.

> Students have to answer ten questions.
> The questions do not follow the same order as the information in the text(s).

Lead-in
Students need to understand what kinds of feelings, attitudes or opinions are being expressed in different parts of the text in order to answer the Part 7 questions. This is also useful for Part 5 tasks.

1 Explain to students that they are going to read some extracts from Part 7 texts. Each extract is followed by a sentence about what the writer is expressing in that extract. These are the kinds of ideas that might appear in Part 7 questions. Students could do the exercise in pairs. Then check the answers as a class.

> **1** thoughtful **2** sophisticated **3** worrying **4** amused **5** unrealistic **6** unhelpful **7** bitter **8** encouraging

Lead-in
Explain to the students that in Part 7, they often need to look for 'paraphrases' – different ways of saying the same thing. The words in the question will be different from the words in the short text or section of text which matches the question, but the idea will be the same. This is also useful for answering questions in Part 5 and for doing Part 4.

2 Ask students to match the sentences and extracts individually, then check their answers in pairs. After that, check and discuss the answers as a class.

> **1** e **2** c **3** b **4** f **5** a **6** d

Extension
If students are keeping vocabulary records, they could record the adjectives in sentences 1–6. Ask them to write sentences showing what some of the adjectives mean and how they are used.

Exam practice
Ask students if they like travelling / would like to travel to new places. Then ask them who wrote this text and what it is about (Alastair Humphreys, an explorer, a man who decided to explore his local area for a year). Remind students to always read the rubric, the title and the byline (if there is one) before starting a task because it will give them useful information about the text and its content.

Ask students to read the text quickly to find out whether the writer's experiences were enjoyable (yes).

Students should spend about 15 minutes on this task in the exam.

> **43** C **44** A **45** D **46** C **47** B **48** D **49** B **50** A **51** D **52** C

Writing

Part 1

> **Task type:**
> An essay of 140–190 words giving an opinion and providing reasons for the opinion. Three points must be covered. Two are given and the candidate must think of a third point to include.

Training
Ask students to discuss the questions with a partner. Then discuss them as a class.

> Yes, you always have to write an essay.
> You are given two notes to write about.
> You must include one point (or note) of your own.
> You have to write 140–190 words.

Lead-in
Discuss holidays as a class. Ask students what they usually do during their holidays. Ask about places they have been to that they enjoyed and places they would like to go to. Encourage them to give reasons for their answers.

1a Ask students to read the exam task and discuss the questions with a partner. Check the answers as a class.

> The general topic is travel / holidays. The notes are about destination and cost.

1b Draw students' attention to the first Tip. Explain that when they are asked to answer a question in the essay task, they should decide whether they generally agree or disagree before they start writing. Tell them that they can provide a balanced view if they wish. They do not need to choose just one side of the argument to agree with.

Students work in small groups to think of suitable third points. Then discuss their ideas as a class. Ask the class to say which ideas would work best and why.

> *Suggested answers*
> activities, modes of transport, weather, food, places to stay, types of holiday

1c Ask students to look at the second Tip. Explain that it is useful to think of words connected to the topic as they plan their answer. Students complete the definitions in pairs.

> 1 self-catering 2 local speciality 3 budget 4 all-inclusive
> 5 connection 6 vacancy 7 peak season / off-season 8 itinerary

1d Students put the words and phrases from Exercise 1c into the sentences, working individually or in pairs. Then go through the answers as a class.

> 1 peak season 2 vacancies 3 budget 4 itinerary 5 connection
> 6 local speciality / specialities 7 Self-catering 8 all-inclusive

Lead-in

Write the following headings on the board: *Strong* and *Weak*. Explain that when giving opinions in an essay, students may wish to express strong opinions or less strong opinions. Ask them to work in pairs to think of stronger and weaker phrases for offering opinions. You may wish to give an example: *I absolutely agree that …*; *I'm not sure that* (the statement 'Holidays are hard work' is completely true). Then go through the students' ideas and write any suitable phrases on the board.

2a Ask students to read the phrases and ask them what they are all used for.

> They are used to give opinions.

2b Explain to students that they should try to use a range of phrases in their essay to express how strongly they agree or disagree with any points raised in the task.

Ask them to discuss the answers with a partner. Then go through the phrases as a class, eliciting whether each one is strong or not. Discuss how to use the phrases.

> I fully agree; I completely disagree; I firmly believe that …

2c Students read the answer to the question in Exercise 1a and underline the phrases that introduce the writer's opinions. Then ask students to read the second Tip. Ask whether the student's answer gives reasons or examples (yes). Elicit the opinions and reasons given.

> I would tend to agree with; I think; I'm of the opinion that; my view is that

2d Ask the students to think about the idea they had for the third point in Exercise 1b. Ask them to read the answer in Exercise 2c again, then write a short paragraph using their third point, remembering to include their own opinion using some of the language they have just practised.

> **Suggested answer**
> I personally believe that friends are more likely to want to spend time in similar ways than parents and children. People of the same generation often share interests, though this is not necessarily the case, of course.

Extension

Ask students whether they agree or disagree with the student's opinions in Exercise 2c and why. Encourage them to offer alternative opinions, using phrases from Exercise 2a.

Lead-in

Elicit the purpose of an introduction and a conclusion in an essay. Ask what kind of information goes into each section.

3a Students complete the task. Check the answers as a class. Then discuss other ways of starting / concluding an essay (e.g. *It is said that …*; *It is commonly / widely believed that …*; *The idea that …*; *Recently, there has been a lot of debate about …*).

Explain that it is fine to start an essay by repeating the task's statement or question, or by giving a direct opinion about the topic (e.g. *Many people prefer to go on holiday with friends rather than family* or *It is more important than ever to consider climate change when choosing a holiday*).

> 1, 4, 5 and 6.
> We do not usually use the phrases *talk about* and *say* in written tasks. The writer could use verbs like *discuss* or *evaluate* instead. The other phrases are fine to use.

3b Ask students to choose the correct options, then check their answers with a partner. Check the answers as a class.

> 1 sum 2 conclusion 3 considered 4 Overall 5 Last

Lead-in

Write these sentences on the board: *1 People often find it difficult to choose where to go on holiday. 2 People have many different opinions about what makes a good holiday.* Under the first sentence, write the prompt *It*. Under the second sentence, write the prompt *There*. Ask students to rewrite the sentences so that they mean the same, using the word given.

1 *It is often difficult (for people) to choose where to go on holiday*. Explain that we don't have to include *for people* when we start a sentence with *it* because this makes the statement impersonal (but we can include it if we want to).

2 *There are many different opinions about what makes a good holiday*.

4 Explain that we can use *It* and *There* to start sentences and that these can be useful in essays. This also provides another kind of structure to vary students' writing.

Do the first sentence with the class as an example. Students then complete the task in pairs. Check the answers as a class.

> 1 It (is often said) that travel broadens the mind, but I'm not sure I agree.
> 2 There (are many) different opinions about what makes ethical tourism.
> 3 It (can be) challenging to order food from a menu in another language.
> 4 There (are several possible solutions) to the challenges of travelling alone.
> 5 It (can be expensive to go) on holiday when you have to pay for tickets and entry fees.
> 6 It (is especially hard) to choose where to go on holiday with a budget. / It (is especially hard) to go on a budget holiday.

Exam practice

Elicit kinds of places to stay (e.g. a campsite, a hotel, a hostel) and their advantages and disadvantages. Then ask students to read the task. Ask them to look at the question and the two given notes. Ask them to think of a third note that is not connected to comfort or the environment (e.g. cost, weather conditions, noise).

In the exam, candidates should spend about 40 minutes planning, writing and checking their essay.

Students can write the essay in class or for homework. After they have finished writing, they should check their work carefully.

> **Sample answer**
> There are clear advantages to camping over staying in hotels. While camping appears to be the cheaper option of the two on the surface, if it is your first camping trip, it will be necessary to invest in a lot of equipment. An all-inclusive holiday in a resort hotel might work out to be inexpensive in comparison. However, once you've got everything you need, camping will almost certainly cost less.

It is often thought that camping is cold and uncomfortable. However, this needn't be the case. With the right location and equipment, and with options like 'glamping', where everything is set up for you, it can be almost as cosy as staying in a hotel room.

I firmly believe that if you camp locally and ensure you take away all your rubbish when you leave, camping is better for the environment. Hotels use significantly more resources in terms of energy and water despite their best efforts to reduce their usage to a minimum.

Overall, I would say that camping is the better choice for a holiday because it is generally cheaper, can be luxurious and is more environmentally friendly.

Commentary
- This is a very good answer.
- All content points are addressed (notes 1 and 2, and the candidate's own idea).
- Reasons and examples are given for the opinions expressed.
- The candidate has used an appropriately semi-formal style.
- Ideas are clearly organised into paragraphs on the same topic.
- The essay includes some vocabulary related to the topic and a range of structures.

Part 2 (email)

Task type:
An email of 140–190 words written in reply to an email or part of an email from an English-speaking person.

Training
Lead-in

Ask students how often they write emails and who they write to. Ask what kind of information is included in the emails they write and receive.

Explain that it is important to structure their email in a logical way so that it is clear and makes sense. They should also include an appropriate opening and closing phrase.

1a Elicit common phrases for opening and closing an email. Write students' ideas on the board. Then explain that they are going to learn some more phrases for beginning and ending an email. Students complete the task. Check the answers as a class.

1 E   2 S   3 S   4 S   5 E   6 E   7 S   8 E   9 E   10 E

1b Focus students' attention on the second Tip, and explain that they should read the task carefully to understand who has sent the email and reply using an appropriate level of formality. Students complete the task in pairs. Check the answers as a class.

They can all be used in informal emails, depending on the context. Some phrases (*Dear*, *Regards*, *Best wishes*) can also be used in semi-formal emails.

Lead-in

Elicit what makes written language informal (contractions, exclamation marks, use of slang, some phrasal verbs, etc.) and encourage students to give some examples.

2a Ask students to read the emails and say whose email is formal and whose email is informal. Ask them to give reasons for their answers.

Bailey's email is informal and the reply from Ellis is formal. The informal email uses informal vocabulary, like *really* instead of *very*, and uses exclamation marks and question tags. The formal email uses more formal words like *register* instead of *sign up*, fewer contractions and more complex sentence structures.

2b Draw students' attention to the words in bold in the first email in Exercise 2a and elicit what they are examples of. Do not confirm answers at this point. Then ask students to look at the language features and match them with the words in bold in the email. Check the answers as a class.

1 Hi!   2 I've   3 (I know you've done some courses,) haven't you?
4 really

2c Remind students that the language features in Exercise 2b are often used in informal writing. Ask them to look at the phrases from Ellis's answer in Exercise 2a and rewrite them using informal language.

Suggested answers
1 Hi, Bailey!
2 Great to hear from you!
3 You're right – I did a course on bike mechanics.
4 They were really cool.
5 I think you're really patient.
6 What about signing up for a course?
7 Let me know what you decide to go for!
8 Write back soon!

Extension

Students could rewrite the whole of Ellis's answer in an informal style using appropriate language. This could be done in class or for homework.

Lead-in

Elicit phrases for giving advice and write them on the board. Ask what people often need advice for and how often the students ask for or give advice. What kind of advice do they ask for and give?

Focus students' attention on the Tip and explain that they should avoid repeating the same phrases in their writing.

3a Students complete the sentences individually, then check their ideas with a partner. Check the answers, inviting different students to read out their completed sentences. Point out that sentences beginning with *Why don't you …* or *How about …* usually end with a question mark.

Suggested answers
1 taking up a new sport?
2 think about what you're interested in.
3 signing up for something completely different?
4 to consider your strengths.
5 do an online search?
6 doing something outdoors.
7 figure out what you're good at?
8 get ideas from other people.
9 look out for ads around town.
10 asking around amongst friends and family.

3b Students do the task individually. They can discuss their answers in pairs.

Suggested answers
1 What about + -ing verb   2 If I were you, I'd + infinitive
3 How about + -ing verb   4 It might be a good idea + to + infinitive
5 Why not + infinitive   6 You might try + -ing verb
7 Why don't you + infinitive   8 Maybe you should + infinitive
9 You could always + infinitive   10 It's worth + -ing verb

Lead-in

Ask students what courses they would like to do. Encourage them to say why they would like to do these courses.

4a Students look at the task. Explain that there may be more than one combination for some of the words. Students do the task in pairs, then check the answers as a class.

> *Suggested answers*
> content creation, creative writing, music composition, portrait painting, pottery making, script writing, web design

4b Explain that the phrases in this exercise make useful collocations (words that go together, shown in brackets in the key). Tell students that some of these can be easily confused in English and that it is a good idea to learn some useful collocations to use in their writing.

Ask students to look at the sentences and do the task in pairs. Then check answers as a class. Explain that the sentences also provide ideas for talking about why people should do courses.

> **1** build (build confidence) **2** contacts (make contacts)
> **3** pick up (pick up skills) **4** sharp (keep your mind sharp)
> **5** tons (make tons of friends) **6** boost (give something a boost)

Exam practice

Elicit the names of sports that can be done outdoors. Then ask students to say which ones are not too challenging. Explain that they can use their imagination in their answers. Remind them that they are being tested on their English, not their ideas, but that their ideas should be realistic, make sense and answer the questions properly.

In the exam, candidates should spend about 40 minutes planning, writing and checking their email.

Students can write the email in class or for homework. After they have finished writing, they should check their work carefully.

> *Sample answer*
> Hey, great to hear from you, Dan!
> I'm glad you're interested in taking up something new and I can certainly recommend some amazing sports for you to try.
> Yes, I do loads of fantastic outdoor sports like climbing, scuba-diving and sailing. I run extreme marathons, too! I love them because they give me a real buzz – there's a lot of adrenaline rushing round your body when you're halfway up a rockface staring out at an incredible landscape, or when you come face to face with a fascinating sea creature!
> Some sports can be tricky for beginners and you don't want to do one that pushes you too hard, do you? Why don't you try something like hiking or trekking first? These sports don't need a ton of experience or expensive equipment. If you tried one like this, you'd get an idea of whether doing outdoor sports is something you enjoy. Then you can take it from there! I'd be perfectly happy to come along with you and maybe show you some amazing trekking routes, if you'd like.
> Hope to hear back from you soon!
> Channing
>
> *Commentary*
> • This is a very good answer.
> • The candidate has answered all the questions.
> • Reasons are given for the advice offered.
> • The candidate uses a range of informal language features.
> • The email is organised well into paragraphs.
> • The email starts and finishes appropriately.
> • The candidate has written between 140 and 190 words.

Part 2 (review)

> **Task type:**
> A review of 140–190 words giving information and opinions, usually in response to an advertisement in a magazine or on a website.

Training

Lead-in

Elicit what a review is and what kind of things people write reviews about. Ask students whether they ever read or write reviews and what they are about.

1a Ask students to look at the list and decide with a partner which ones people might write reviews about. Check the answers as a class.

> All of them except a celebrity, a job or an animal.

1b Students complete the task in pairs. Then check the answers as a class, encouraging students to give their reasons.

> **1** an app **2** a website **3** a meal **4** a film **5** a campsite **6** a game

1c Ask students to look at the first extract and underline the adjectives that describe the app (*inexpensive* and *user-friendly*). Then ask them to circle the adverbs which go before the adjectives (*relatively* and *not very*). Ask what the adverbs are doing (describing the intensity of the adjective, i.e. explaining how inexpensive and how user-friendly the app is).

Students complete the rest of the exercise with a partner. Then check the answers as a class.

> **1** relatively inexpensive, not very user-friendly
> **2** truly outstanding, really straightforward
> **3** way too tough, a bit too rich
> **4** incredibly true to life, especially impressive
> **5** pretty remote, extremely eco-friendly
> **6** exceptionally low quality, very poor, truly groundbreaking
> The adjectives describe the things that are being talked about. The adverbs tell us about the intensity of the adjective.

Extension

Ask students to use the adjectives and adverbs from Exercise 1b to describe the last film they saw, an app they use regularly and a book they have read. Ask them to write one sentence each for the different topics and share their ideas with a partner or in small groups.

Lead-in

Ask students if they have ever been to an outdoor adventure centre or whether they know what happens at one. Elicit outdoor activities that people might enjoy doing (e.g. rock-climbing, kayaking). Ask which activities students would like to do and why.

2a Ask students to read the review. Tell them not to worry about the numbered gaps for now. Explain that they should write down the topics that are mentioned, as in the example (food). Then check the answers as a class and invite students to read out the relevant part of the review.

> location, staff, choice of activities, accommodation, food, cost, facilities

2b Students work in pairs to complete the text. Remind them to look for connections between ideas and vocabulary before and after each gap to help them. Check the answers as a class.

> 1c 2g 3e 4a 5f 6b 7d

2c Ask students to answer the questions and explain how they arrived at their answers.

> The reviewer enjoyed the trip overall. They liked the setting, the friendly and knowledgeable instructors, the ziplining, the hot showers and comfortable beds and the well-cooked food. They were less keen on the lack of things to do when an activity was cancelled, the small size of the cabin, the lack of food choice and the fact that you had to pay extra for the spa. Yes, they would recommend the centre.

2d Ask the students to find and underline the descriptive language in the review in Exercise 2a.

> The centre's in a beautiful setting; in general, it was an enjoyable trip; They were extremely friendly and knowledgeable; the ziplining … was brilliant; the cabin was tiny; the shower was hot and the beds were particularly comfortable; the meal plan … was relatively inexpensive; The food was cooked to a high standard; there wasn't a huge choice; The spa looked stunning

2e Explain to students that it doesn't matter how they order the information in their review, but that it should always be presented in a logical order. Students then look at the two example structures. Ask which they prefer and why (both are fine). They then read the review in Exercise 2a again and decide which structure it follows. Check the answer and invite students to read out the relevant sections.

> B

2f Ask students to look at the list of places and things. Write *café* on the board and elicit points that might be mentioned in a review of a café (e.g. the food, the service, the location, the cost). Students then work with a partner to make a list of possible points for each item on the list. When they have finished, ask students to share their ideas with the class.

> Students' own answers

Lead-in

Write the following list on the board: *skateboard shop, shopping centre, cinema, hotel room, holiday apartment, book, sports club, concert, restaurant*. Then ask students what features of each item they might review.

3a Ask students to look at the words in the box and decide which ones describe good things or bad things (good: *bonus, positive*; bad: *disappointing, downside, drawback*). Students then complete the sentences. Check the answers as a class.

> 1 disappointing 2 positive 3 found 4 downside / drawback
> 5 downside 6 bonus 7 major 8 minuses

3b Draw some shapes on the board (e.g. stars, circles, squares) of different sizes for students to compare. Point to two shapes in turn and ask students to compare them. Review comparative forms if necessary. Students then complete the exercise individually before checking their answers with a partner. Then check the answers as a class.

> 1 much more 2 least 3 as 4 in 5 more 6 challenging

Exam practice

Elicit types of shops. Then ask what people might include in a review about the different kinds of shop.

Candidates should spend about 40 minutes planning, writing and checking their review in the exam.

Students can write their review in class or for homework. After they have finished writing, they should check their work carefully.

> *Sample answer*
> Last week, I visited the clothing shop Be Bright Fashion in the city centre after seeing an advert for it online. I thought it looked really cool on the advert and the range of clothes for people my age seemed very impressive, so I wanted to check it out.
> When I got there, I saw that the store wasn't quite as big as it looked online, but the way it was decorated with lots of bright colours was really attractive. There was particularly good music playing – far better than in other shops I usually go to – and even a DJ! That made the shop feel really different and new. Another bonus was the 20% discount they were giving to the first hundred shoppers.
> When I looked a bit closer, though, although the clothes were on trend, many of them were quite poor quality and that really let them down. The prices weren't as low as I had expected, either.
> Would I recommend this shop to other people? Probably not. It's a nice shopping experience, but the clothes just aren't good enough – sorry, Be Bright Fashion!
> *Commentary*
> • This is a very good answer.
> • The candidate has addressed all the points in the task.
> • Reasons are given for the writer's opinions.
> • An appropriately informal style is used.
> • There is a good range of vocabulary and grammatical structures.
> • The correct number of words has been written.

Listening

Part 1

> **Task type:**
> Multiple choice. Eight questions. One multiple-choice question per text (short monologue or dialogue), each with three options.

Training

Students choose the words. Then check the answers as a class.

> • In Part 1, you will hear **eight** short recordings – these are usually **both monologues and dialogues**.
> • You will answer **multiple-choice** questions about the recordings.
> • You will hear each text on the recording **twice**.

1 The aim of this activity is to develop students' awareness of how understanding of the speaker's feelings and attitudes may be tested in Part 1. Ask students to look at the context sentence and question to identify the attitude or feeling.

> how satisfied the speaker is with something

2 Tell students to listen and choose the correct answer. Play the recording twice. Students compare answers in pairs.

> C

3 Students can read the audioscript to check their answer.

4 Ask students to identify the modal verbs and the verbs that follow them, and to underline them.

> My last entry on my blog was about a 10 km run up in hills around 800 metres high. It was tough, I won't lie, and I <u>could have pushed</u> myself harder. Anyway, my posts are getting plenty of hits, which is awesome. I <u>must be doing</u> something right. But I <u>may have taken on</u>

more than I can handle, as I'm falling behind on my assignments. The blog about today's run might not be finished until tomorrow because I'm catching up on one. What with college deadlines, I guess I shouldn't have taken on all the training and blogging, but if I hadn't, I might have found excuses for not studying.

5   Ask students to match the modal verb forms they have underlined with the descriptions. After checking the answers, remind students of the importance of understanding the use of modal verbs.

> 1 I could have pushed myself harder
> 2 I might have found
> 3 I shouldn't have taken on
> 4 I must be doing
> 5 I might not be finished
> 6 I may have taken on

6   The aim of this activity is to develop students' awareness of the range of attitudes and feelings that might be tested in Part 1.

> 1 P   2 N   3 P   4 P   5 P   6 N   7 N   8 P   9 N   10 N

7   Ask students to decide which adjective most appropriately describes each of the six speaker's attitudes and feelings. Play the recording twice if necessary and encourage students to compare answers. You may wish to refer them to the audioscript and to have them read and listen again.

> 1 resigned   2 enthusiastic   3 critical   4 reassured   5 reluctant
> 6 appreciative

Exam practice

Tell students that they will hear eight different recordings. Remind them to read the context-setting sentences, as these will give them useful information about what they will hear. Remind them, also, to read the questions and options carefully before each recording. Suggest that they underline key words to prepare themselves. For the first one or two recordings, it might be useful to stop and let students compare their answers with a partner to give them confidence before they listen to the rest of the recordings and answer the questions.

Remind them not to leave a multiple-choice question unanswered. If they are not sure what the correct answer is, they should try and make a good guess. If there's a word in the options they do not know, they should look for clues in the context around the words to help them guess the meaning.

After listening

Check the correct answers as a class. Ask students to say which words in the recordings give the correct answers. It may be useful to focus on any vocabulary which caused problems for them.

> 1 B   2 A   3 C   4 B   5 B   6 A   7 C   8 C

Extension

You could ask students to discuss their own attitudes to the following topics: AI, different websites and apps, working in a shop, and any other topics that they might be interested in that come up in tasks. They could try and decide if any of the adjectives used in this section apply to their own attitudes. Encourage them to think about what their attitude is and apply the adjectives to a variety of topics as they encounter them.

Part 2

Task type:
Sentence completion. Ten sentences to complete with between one and three words. One speaker (monologue).

Training

Students choose the correct words. Then check the answers as a class.

> • In Part 2, you will hear a text that lasts three or four minutes with **one speaker**.
> • You will complete **ten** sentences with information from the recording.
> • You will hear the recording **twice**.

1   The aim of this activity is to reinforce the importance for students of using the context, both in terms of meaning and grammar, to predict the kind of words that they need to listen for in Part 2.

> Possible answers for 1 are adjectives such as *hard, challenging*.
> Possible answers for 2 are nouns such as *coffee, prices, food, service*.

2   Before playing the recording, remind students that the focus is on listening for detail and that they should not change the words they hear. Instead, they should write only the word or words that they hear the speaker use on the recording. After listening, encourage students to compare answers. Play the recording twice.

> 1 rough   2 noise

3   The aim of this activity is to develop students' confidence with common verbs that are followed by prepositions. Any of these verbs could feature in a Part 2 task. Ask students to complete the sentences with the correct preposition. Remind them that the verbs used in the sentences usually require a specific preposition to follow them. Let students check their answers by listening to the recording. Draw their attention to the weak pronunciation form of the prepositions. They should notice how the important words, e.g. verbs, take the main stress and the preposition sound is weak and unstressed.

After checking the answers, encourage students to underline the verbs in the sentences and to note in their vocabulary records any verb–preposition combinations that they were unsure about.

> 1 about   2 with   3 on   4 in   5 from   6 to

4   Ask students to complete the sentences with the correct preposition. Remind them that the adjectives usually require a specific preposition to follow them. Allow students to check their answers by listening to the recording.

> 1 of   2 for   3 at   4 with / about   5 to   6 in / about

Exam practice

Before starting, you could lead into the theme of fashion design by asking students to predict possible topics and words they might hear in relation to a fashion design course, e.g. *style, trend, different types of clothing, sewing, fabric, sewing machine, equipment, cutting, scissors, pattern, outfit, lectures, workshops, tutors, classmates, career, project, assignment, presentation*. More abstract words might include *creativity, imagination, originality*, etc.

Tell students to look at the task instructions. Remind them to use the time before the recording is played to try to predict likely words or types of words that could fit the gaps in the sentences. Play the recording twice, then let students compare answers.

> **9** wearable art **10** open mind **11** sewing (skills) **12** circus
> **13** efficiency **14** cotton **15** airline uniforms
> **16** consumer psychology **17** story(-)telling **18** networking

Extension

Give students a topic, e.g. business, fashion, the environment, and tell them to look up three new nouns at a B2 level that are useful for talking about this topic.

The online *Cambridge English Dictionary* gives the level (B1, B2, C1, etc.) of many words. Alternatively, students could use an online resource such as English Vocabulary Profile. Get them to share their words and explain them to each other. This will encourage them to build their vocabulary and prepare them for possible Part 2 task topics.

Part 3

> **Task type:**
> Multiple matching. Five short monologues. Five correct answers, eight options to choose from.

Training

Students choose the correct options. Check the answers as a class.

> In Part 3, you will hear **five** short recordings of about 30 seconds each – these will be **monologues**.
> You will match the correct option with each recording from a choice of **eight** options.
> You will hear each recording **twice**.

Lead-in

To prepare for the topic of competitions, ask students some questions: *Have you ever entered a competition? What types of competition do you often see on TV? Why do you think people enter competitions? Why do some people do better than others?*

1 Remind students that they need to be able to understand the same meanings expressed in different ways. Ask them to read through the options, perhaps underlining key words, before you play the recording. Remind them that they will only hear very short extracts. They will hear a full version of a Part 3 speaker in Exercise 2.

Play the recording twice if necessary. You could pause between each speaker and let students compare answers.

> **1** B **2** D **3** G **4** A **5** F

2 The aim of this activity is to develop students' awareness of distraction (things that are said which might tempt students to choose the wrong answer). Play the recording and ask students to identify anything the speaker says that might have tempted them to consider one of the other options.

> Option H may distract because she says, 'It was amazing how huge the audience was …', but wrong because she says, 'Luckily, it didn't bother me'. Option F may distract because she mentions 'silly errors', but she was focused on not making them. Option E may distract because 'someone's phone went off in the middle of my song', but this is wrong because she 'didn't even notice'. Option B

> might have distracted some students as the speaker mentions her family cheering, but there is no suggestion of pressure.

3 Ask students to underline the three phrasal verbs used and to explain their meanings.

> The phrasal verb *go off* means 'to ring loudly or make a loud noise'. The phrasal verb *stand out* means 'to be much better than other similar things or people'. The phrasal verb *get through* means 'to go forward or advance'.

4 Ask students to choose the most suitable phrasal verb from the box, changing the form where necessary (e.g. to the past simple).

> **1** stood out **2** came up with **3** put in **4** paid off **5** messed up
> **6** lived up to **7** got along **8** pick up

Exam practice

You could prepare students by giving them the topic of 'surfing' and asking them to predict words or phrases that might come up when people are talking about this subject (e.g. *waves, ocean, sea, water, board, beach, skill, balance, ride, powerful, freedom, safety, danger, thrills*).

Remind students to read the task carefully and underline key ideas before they listen. Play the recording twice and, at the end of the task, give students time to compare their answers.

> **19** G **20** A **21** C **22** B **23** H

Extension

Ask students to find a podcast or video online of people talking in English about an outdoor activity. Remind them that some video channels have subtitles or captions that can help them follow what is being said. Advise them not to worry if they can't understand it all, but to use it as an opportunity to practise listening and to learn some new vocabulary.

Part 4

> **Task type:**
> Multiple choice. An interview or exchange between two speakers. Seven three-option multiple-choice questions.

Training

Students choose the correct options. Check the answers as a class.

> In Part 4, you will hear **an interview** lasting three or four minutes.
> You will answer **seven** multiple-choice question with **three** options.
> You will hear the recording **twice**.

Lead-in

You could lead into the topic of architecture by asking students to discuss some questions about the subject, e.g. *Do you take an interest in the architecture around you? Are there any buildings that you particularly like because of the style in which they are built?*

1 Tell students to read the question carefully and prepare to listen. They could underline key words in the question and options. Play the recording twice and let students compare their answers with a partner.

> B

2 Ask students to look at the audioscript to check their answers.

3 Ask students to look at the underlined words and identify the thing(s) or idea(s) that the words refer to.

They: buildings
what: family trips (and her parents pointing out buildings)
each: significant or beautiful buildings
It: the fact that there is a diversity of styles and a story for each building
that: being curious about the past

4 Ask students to choose the most suitable word to complete each sentence. More than one word may be possible.

1 appealing
2 stunned / astonished
3 modest
4 bizarre / extraordinary / impressive / mysterious / remarkable
5 eager
6 appealing / extraordinary / impressive / remarkable

Extension

Tell students to find interviews with experts, e.g. scientists, architects or any other expert in a field that interests them. The interviews could be from podcasts, radio or online videos, especially ones that offer English transcripts. Encourage students to watch part of these interviews and to notice the different feelings, attitudes and opinions expressed by the speaker. They could set themselves a target of identifying five new words or phrases to learn from the interview.

Exam practice

Prepare students for the topic of science and science journalism. You could ask if anyone enjoys reading about science in the news, or watches TV programmes about science. Ask which areas of science interest them most, e.g. biology, astronomy, chemistry, physics, technology. Ask what kind of skills a science journalist needs to have.

Remind students that, before listening to the recording, they should make sure they understand the context and read the options so that they know what to listen for. Play the recording twice. After listening, let students compare their answers with each other before checking the answers as a class.

24 C   25 A   26 B   27 B   28 A   29 B   30 C

Speaking
Part 1

Task type:
A conversation between one examiner and each candidate. In Part 1, candidates are asked questions on a variety of topics related to their everyday life. Candidates are assessed on their performance throughout the whole test, so candidates' performance in Part 1 is taken into account when examiners decide on the final marks.

Training
Lead-in

Students work on their own to complete the statements about Part 1, then check with a partner. Check the answers as a class, clarifying information about Part 1 if necessary.

For Part 1 of the Speaking test, all the questions are about **personal** topics.
You need to talk to the **examiner**.

Your questions will be **different from** your partner's questions.
The total time is **two** minutes.
The questions will be connected to **more than one** topic.

1 Students close their books. Focus on the personal / everyday topics that are covered in Part 1 of the test. Elicit some ideas from students about what these topics could be.

Students open their books and read the questions. Ask them what the topic is (free time / hobbies). Students complete the questions using only one word in each gap. Draw students' attention to the Tip and discuss how questions may be about the past, the present or the future.

1 How / Where   2 Do   3 When   4 Would   5 Tell

2 Talk to students about how the same questions can be asked in different ways. Being familiar with different question structures will help students prepare for this part of the test.

Students work with a partner to rewrite the questions from Exercise 1. Model the first example and monitor to offer support as required. In feedback, accept any suitable alternative answers.

1 did you do   4 you prefer
2 taking photos with a phone   5 do you spend your
3 you last do

3 Students look at the answers to the questions from Exercise 1 and share their thoughts with the class. Focus on what is good (the candidates answer the question) and what could be better (the answers could be extended by adding information; the candidates could use different words rather than repeating the words from the question).

4 Students listen to two candidates answering the same question and note down the extra information the candidates give and the words they use to avoid repeating the question exactly.

	Information added	Alternative words used
1	Added details about the activity itself, the time of the activity and the people they spent time with.	Replaced *yesterday evening* with *as soon as I finished work*.
2	Added a reason (why she chose her phone) and an example (her favourite photos).	Replaced *photos* with *pictures*.
3	Added details about where and what.	Replaced *do sport* with *exercise*.
4	Added reasons and comparison.	Replaced *film* with *movie*.
5	Gave more than one example. Added a reason.	Replaced *bad weather* with *rainy days*.

5 Ask students to work with a different partner. They take it in turns to ask and answer the questions from Exercise 1.

Extension

To extend this practice, ask students to write some more questions on the topic of free time. Encourage them to use a variety of question words and to focus on the past, the present and the future.

Exam practice

Students work in pairs to ask and answer the questions. Monitor to check for answers which are appropriate and extended. Check for any key language errors which you can use for error correction in feedback.

Part 2

> **Task type:**
> An individual one-minute 'long turn' for each candidate, with a brief response from the second candidate lasting about 30 seconds. This part of the test gives candidates a good opportunity to demonstrate their ability to produce an extended stretch of language which is clearly organised. These elements are assessed under Discourse Management.

Training
Lead-in

Students work with a partner to choose the words that correctly describe Part 2 of the Speaking test. Check the answers as a class, clarifying information about Part 2 if necessary.

> You and your partner have **different** photographs to talk about.
> The examiner **will** tell you what the photographs are about.
> The question **is** written down for you.
> You **answer** a question about your partner's photographs.
> The total time is **four** minutes.

1 Ask students for ideas about how they can prepare for Part 2 of the Speaking test. Tell students that Exercise 1 has some comments from students who practised Part 2 in their class and asked their teacher for feedback. Students work with a partner to match the comments from the students with the teacher's response.

In feedback, discuss the additional points in the key. Also remind students that performance is assessed over the full test, not just one part, so one slip need not have a big impact on the final score.

> **1 c** (The response does not need to devote the same amount of time to both photos, but candidates do need to mention both of them.)
> **2 a** (The focus of this part is on producing an extended stretch of language, so candidates should keep speaking for the full minute.)
> **3 b** (It is not a problem if the examiner has to stop a candidate speaking. Candidates need to organise their response so that they cover the required elements early in their long turn.)
> **4 d** (Comparing the photos is one element of this task. Candidates also need to answer the question. This is written above the photos as a reminder.)
> **5 f** (Control of grammatical forms is just one element of the Grammar and Vocabulary criterion on the assessment scale. There are four other criteria as well.)
> **6 e** (Candidates should learn some expressions for saying what something is when they don't know the exact word (e.g. *Something you use for … / Something like a …*).)

2 Students now focus on the follow-up question stage of Part 2 in the same way as in Exercise 1. This time, students need to think of what feedback to give. Students work in small groups to discuss the comments from students and decide if what they did was OK or give advice on something they should do differently next time.

> **Suggested answers**
> **I didn't agree with what my partner said about the photos.** That's fine. You will be asked a specific question about the photos. You will not be asked to comment on what your partner said.
> **I talked about both of the photos.** That may be OK. It depends on the question you are asked. You may be asked to choose one of the photos or to comment on a detail in one of the photos.
> **I described what I could see in the photos.** You only have about 30 seconds, so don't waste time describing the photos. Make sure you answer the question.
> **I was able to answer the question very quickly.** OK, but use the time you are given to demonstrate your range of language and how you can organise your response.

3a Ask students how they are assessed in the Speaking exam. Accept all valid suggestions (pronunciation, organisation, etc.). Focus on 'language' and discuss that this relates to range and control (accuracy).

Students work on their own to identify and correct the common language errors, then check with a partner. Check the answers as a class. Then do Exercise 3b.

> 1 Both of the pictures **show** people doing positive things for the environment.
> 2 … there is a group of people who seem to have just finished **cleaning** the beach …
> 3 They look ~~like~~ happy and pleased with the result.
> 4 I think they have **chosen** to do this because they can see the benefits immediately.
> 5 **Doing** something like this in a group is a good idea.
> 6 … they can encourage each **other** …
> 7 … the results are not as **easy** to see …
> 8 They decided to go by bike or scooter rather **than by** car.

3b Students look at the pictures on page C6. Elicit the common theme (the environment / being green). Tell students they will hear a candidate talking abouts these two photos. He uses the same language as in Exercise 3a, but without the errors. Students listen to check their answers to Exercise 3a. Play the recording again if needed, then discuss any language points students found difficult. Talk about whether the candidate gave a good answer to the question.

4 Students work with a partner to practise the Part 2 task. The student who is listening reads the question and stops the other student speaking after one minute. They then swap roles. At the end, they give each other feedback. Monitor for whole-group feedback.

Extension

Encourage students to keep a record of their own common errors. Students can make posters with common errors to put on the classroom wall.

Exam practice

Students work in groups of three to complete the task, taking it in turns to be Candidate A, Candidate B or the examiner. The examiner needs to check the timing so that the long turn is no longer than one minute and the follow-up question response is no longer than 30 seconds. Monitor and make notes for feedback on performance and language control.

> **Suggested answers**
> **Candidate A (long turn)**
> In both pictures, there's one person who looks rather uncomfortable. In the first picture, it's the girl in the middle. The girls either side of her actually look very comfortable because they are asleep. All three of them are sitting in a vehicle, probably the back of a car. There's not much space, and so the girl in the middle can't get comfortable.

> If she tried to move, she'd wake the other girls up, so she just has to put up with it. In contrast, the woman in the second picture can find a way to make herself more comfortable if she wants to. For example, she could get up and move around or do some exercises. I reckon she's finding it difficult to get comfortable because she's been sitting at her desk for a long time. Maybe her chair isn't suitable for working at a desk, or she's just uncomfortable because she's been working on her laptop for so long. I can see that she's got a special place for her laptop, but maybe she needs something better to help her work more comfortably.
>
> **Candidate B (follow-up question)**
> I'm not keen on travelling long distances by car, actually. If I have to go a long way, I'd rather take the train or fly, if it's not too expensive. On long car journeys, even if I have enough space, I get bored because it's difficult to read in a car without feeling sick.
>
> **Candidate B (long turn)**
> The first thing I notice about these photos is that one is inside and the other is outside. In the first picture, the man seems to be by a river in quite a remote place. He's kneeling down and he's taking a photo of a bear walking near him. The camera looks like an expensive one, so maybe he's a professional photographer. I can't see anyone else around, and I think he's chosen to be alone so that he can take as long as he wants to get the best pictures. Maybe if other people were there, he wouldn't be able to get so close to the bear. He needs to be as quiet as possible, and having other people with him would make this more difficult. The woman in the second picture also looks like she'd like to be quiet, but I think this is because she's tired from working. I can see a laptop in the background, so maybe she's been working on that for a long time and she needs a break without anyone disturbing her. She's got a cup in her hand and she's lying on the sofa – maybe she wants to have a short sleep before she goes back to work, so if someone came in the room to talk to her, she wouldn't be happy.
>
> **Candidate A (follow-up question)**
> Well, if I have something to do, like taking photographs, maybe, but for a long walk in the countryside, I'd rather be with someone else so I have someone to talk to and I don't have to worry about getting lost.

Part 3

> **Task type:**
> A discussion between the candidates. Candidates receive spoken instructions and written stimuli. There is a two-minute discussion followed by a one-minute decision-making task. For a test taken by three candidates, they have three minutes for the first discussion. The discussion element of the activity makes it particularly suitable for assessing Interactive Communication, but all the other assessment features (Grammar and Vocabulary, Discourse Management, Pronunciation and Global Achievement) are also assessed in this part.

Training

Lead in

With closed books, ask students to say how Part 3 is different from Part 2 of the Speaking test. Students open their books and work independently to complete the statements about Part 3, then check with a partner. Check the answers as a class, clarifying information about Part 3 if necessary.

> For Part 3 of the Speaking test, you talk **with your partner**.
> You have **two questions** to discuss.
> You **do not need** to discuss the prompts in a particular order.
> You need to try to reach a decision in the **second** stage of this part of the test.
> The total time is **four** minutes.

1a Students close their books. Write on the board *getting advice from other people* and brainstorm situations in which people might want to get advice. Accept any answers. Students open their books and compare their ideas with the prompts in the sample task on page C9. Elicit some alternative ways of expressing the points in the prompts, e.g. *finding a new job – getting work / employment; buying a piece of technology – purchasing gadgets*.

Students look at the task. Ask them whether the different prompts are all equally important (to elicit the need to use comparative structures in this part of the test). Also focus on superlative structures, which will be needed in the second stage, when they try to reach an agreement (e.g. to find *the best, the most difficult, the most important*).

1b Students work on their own to complete the comparative and superlative expressions with the words from the box. Explain that they will be able to use more than one word in some expressions, with a possible change of meaning.

Students check their answers with a partner. In feedback, discuss words which give a similar meaning (e.g. *much / far / a lot*) and words which express opposite meanings (e.g. *not quite as / not nearly as*). Note that for sentences 2 and 3, the choice of *quite* or *nearly* changes the meaning.

> **1** much / even (big difference)   **2** quite (small difference) / nearly (big difference)   **3** nearly (big difference) / quite (small difference)   **4** much / even (big difference)   **5** as (no difference)   **6** by (big difference)   **7** less (small difference)   **8** near (big difference)

Extension

Draw students' attention to the Remember box and discuss how sentence stress is one feature of the pronunciation assessment. Model and practise the sentences from Exercise 1b using sentence stress appropriately for emphasis.

2 Remind students that after the two-minute discussion, the examiner will ask a new question so that candidates can try to reach an agreement. For this task, it could be *Now you have about a minute to decide in which situation it is most important to get advice from other people.*

Students look at the sample Part 3 task on their own and choose three situations in which they think it is most important to get advice from other people. They then compare their choices with a partner, giving reasons, and try to reach an agreement. Monitor for feedback.

Exam practice

Students work in pairs or groups of three to complete the Exam practice task. Control the timing to give students an idea of how long they have for their discussions. Monitor carefully for use of language and techniques. In feedback, focus on any use of comparative / superlative structures you heard.

> *Sample answer*
> **A:** I suppose if more tourists visit a town, there's the opportunity to create more local businesses, like shops and cafés, or even museums and entertainment places.
> **B:** Yes, and if there are more businesses, there are more jobs for local people, like it says here. But the problem is that some of these jobs may not be available all year. I mean, in the winter, when there aren't so many tourists, there's less need for workers.
> **A:** That's a good point. Some tourist towns are really quiet when it isn't high season. Also, going back to that idea about local businesses,

I guess there's a risk that prices will be high in towns where more visitors go, and this can be a problem for local people. Anyway, what about the point about public transport? Is this a positive reason for encouraging tourism in a town?
B: I think it is. Because it's important to make it easy for visitors to get around, towns which encourage visitors are likely to provide more public transport and the prices may be lower.
A: That's true. It could be a problem if there are too many visitors, though, for example when local people need to travel to work and there's no space on the buses or trains. What do you think about the environment? I think that might be the biggest issue.
B: What do you mean?
A: Well, more people can cause more problems for the environment. You know, more rubbish, more noise, more traffic.
B: I see what you mean. So, when visitors first start coming to a town, there are lots of benefits, but then there may be problems if the number of people isn't controlled.
A: Exactly. I think I've read about this situation in lots of popular tourist places.
Examiner: Thank you. You now have about a minute to decide what the best reason is for trying to increase the number of tourists who visit a town.
A: Like we said before, jobs and local businesses are two positive things. Some businesses wouldn't exist without visitors, so this has to be one of the most important things.
B: Yes, but we didn't talk about accommodation. Is that also a benefit? I mean, building more hotels and apartments for visitors …
A: To be honest, I think that's a disadvantage. If tourists are renting apartments, for example, it's more difficult for local people to find somewhere to live. I still think local businesses is the best reason.
B: I agree. It's a good long-term benefit of having visitors to a town. Let's go with that one.

Part 4

Task type:
A discussion on topics related to the Part 3 collaborative task. The assessor will continue to evaluate all the assessment criteria (Grammar and Vocabulary, Discourse Management, Pronunciation and Interactive Communication) and the interlocutor will be getting ready to give a Global Achievement mark.

Training
Lead-in

Ask students to work with a partner. They should try to be the first pair to complete all four sentences. When they have finished, they shout *Stop!* and give their answers. The other students say whether they agree or disagree.

Check the correct answers as a class.

For Part 4 of the Speaking test, you **do not discuss** your decision in Part 3.
The examiner asks you **some** of the questions on their list.
You **may** talk to your partner.
The total time is **four** minutes for a pair of candidates.

1 Students close their books. Explain that candidates are assessed throughout the test, and Part 4 is their last opportunity to demonstrate their ability. It is also the examiners' chance to confirm the marks that they will give. Elicit suggestions from students about what they are assessed on.

Students open their books and work with a partner to match the points the examiners consider when deciding on the mark with the assessment categories. In feedback, introduce the points in the key below.

Grammar and Vocabulary
The range of structures used.
The range of vocabulary used.
Using language which is accurate and appropriate.
(Candidates should try to balance range with accuracy. Very accurate responses using only simple language will not get a high score because range is also needed.)

Discourse Management
Using a range of linking words and cohesive devices.
Giving extended responses.
The amount of hesitation and repetition.
The organisation of ideas.
(Candidates should aim to always give an extended response in order to demonstrate a wider range of language.)

Pronunciation
Saying individual sounds clearly.
Using word and sentence stress accurately.
Using intonation appropriately.
(The focus here is on how clear a candidate's speech is for the listener. It's not about losing an accent.)

Interactive Communication
Responding to questions appropriately.
Taking an active role in conversations.
The amount of support needed in conversations.
(At different stages of the test, candidates will need to initiate discussion, respond to comments and answer questions. They should take an active role in discussions, making sure they stay on track.)

Extension

Ask students to consider their own strengths and the areas they need to work on. Students can use this focus to draw up an action plan to prepare for the Speaking test.

2a The questions in this activity are linked to the Part 3 Training task. Ask students what the topic of that was (getting advice). They look at the questions, then listen to the recording. They need to decide which of the questions each of the candidates answers.

Students check their answers with a partner. Then check the answers as a class. In feedback, discuss how the candidates avoided repeating exactly the same words that appear in the question, which is a good way of demonstrating a range of vocabulary.

a 3 **b** 2 **c** 1 **d** 4

2b Students look at the assessment descriptors in Exercise 1. Focus on Interactive Communication and ask: *Did all of the candidates respond to the questions appropriately?* (They did. They all answered the question and gave appropriate details.)

Now ask students to look at the Discourse Management descriptors. Play the recording again and ask them to make notes on the candidates' performance for Discourse Management. Ask: *What did they do well? What could they improve?*

Allow students to discuss their ideas with a partner. Then discuss the answers as a class.

Suggested answers
1 Clear organisation of ideas, but response is short – it could be extended more.

2 Extended response, with an example. But there is hesitation and ideas are not clearly organised.
3 Extended response, with examples and reasons. But there is repetition of vocabulary (*compare, maybe, better, parents, friends*).
4 Uses a range of cohesive devices, and ideas are organised clearly.

3 Students choose one of the questions from Exercise 2a. Make sure all the questions have been picked by at least one student. Students stand up and walk around the class, asking different classmates their question. In feedback, ask students to report back on the responses they heard, e.g. *Were they extended? Were they relevant? Were they clearly organised? Was there much hesitation or repetition?*

4 Students look at questions b and c in Exercise 2a. Discuss how this question wording is often used in Part 4 questions, with different variations, e.g. *Some / Many people say / believe / think … .* The statement is always followed by a question for the candidate, such as *Do you agree? What do you think?* or *Do you think that's true?*

Tell students that it can be useful to acknowledge the point made in the statement. This gives them some time to think and also the opportunity to react to the statement, either agreeing or disagreeing with it. Students work with a partner to match the beginnings and endings of the phrases which can be used to acknowledge the point.

Check answers as a class, and elicit alternative options (e.g. *I see = I understand / I get; a valid point = a fair point*). Also discuss how the phrases can be used in isolation or at the start of a longer comment (e.g. *That's a valid point, but …*).

1 f **2** a **3** e **4** b **5** c **6** d

5 Students practise using the phrases with the responses in the recording. Play each candidate's response. Then pause the recording so that students can acknowledge the point made by the candidate and then say whether or not they agree.

Exam practice

Ask students to look at the Speaking Part 3 task on page 107. Ask them what the Part 4 questions will be about (towns and cities / tourism).

Students work in groups of three to do the Speaking Part 4 Exam practice task on page 108. Encourage them to acknowledge their partners' points. Monitor and encourage them to move on to the next question after one or two minutes. Make a note of strengths and areas to work on related to Discourse Management.

Sample answer
Examiner: Is going shopping in a city centre a good way of using our free time?
A: I think that really depends on the person. Personally, I find shopping really boring, so I buy most things online, but I do like going to walk around the centre of my city. It's really beautiful and there's a good atmosphere.
Examiner: Do you think it's a good idea for all city centres to be closed to traffic?
B: To be honest, I'm not sure how practical that is. Maybe in the middle of the day, it's a nice idea. Then people can walk around without worrying about cars. However, businesses in the city centre, I mean, the shops and cafés and so on, they all need deliveries, so closing the centre to all traffic all day will make it difficult for them.
Examiner: Do you think cities should preserve historical buildings or replace them with buildings which are more suitable for modern living?

A: Like I said, my city is really beautiful and that's because of all the old buildings. I would hate to lose them.
Examiner: What do you think?
B: I take your point, and I do agree. I certainly don't think we should destroy old buildings, but I do think they need to be made suitable for modern life, and that means there need to be some changes, at least inside the building.
Examiner: Some people say that town centres as they are today will eventually disappear. Do you agree?
B: It's true that city centres are changing, certainly where I live. Shops are closing all the time, especially small independent ones. I don't know whether this will continue, though. I can't imagine city centres disappearing completely.
Examiner: Do you agree?
A: It doesn't surprise me that people are concerned about changes to cities, and I agree that lots of shops are closing. But they are often being replaced with other facilities, like cafés or restaurants. Town centres might be different in the future, but I completely agree that they won't disappear.
Examiner: Thank you. That is the end of the test.

Test 3
Reading and Use of English
Part 1
1 C **2** B **3** A **4** A **5** D **6** A **7** C **8** B

Part 2
9 Apart **10** as **11** by **12** of **13** order **14** fact **15** What **16** the

Part 3
17 breathtaking **18** beautifully **19** inspiration **20** impressive
21 educational **22** accessible **23** admission **24** unlimited

Part 4
25 didn't / did not expect | you to
26 make / put in | a (very) great
27 every single player | looks
28 'd / had bought | enough food
29 why Ferda decided | to give
30 growing vegetables | can (sometimes) be

Part 5
31 C **32** C **33** B **34** D **35** B **36** A

Part 6
37 E **38** C **39** G **40** D **41** A **42** F

Part 7
43 B **44** D **45** A **46** C **47** D **48** A **49** B **50** C **51** D **52** B

Writing
Part 1

Sample answer
I partly agree with the statement 'People should be banned from nature reserves'.

The main reason I agree with the statement is that visitors can cause damage to habitats. They may walk on important plants or enter areas where there are birds' nests or animal dens. Even if this is accidental, it still causes damage. Similarly, they often leave behind litter, which creatures living in the nature reserves may eat. Another problem is noise, which can disturb animals as they try to carry out their daily activities.

However, having the option to visit nature reserves means the opportunity to learn about the world around us and the ways in which we can maintain it for future generations. It would be a huge loss to both humans and the natural world if visitors were kept away from such places. Provided that we are respectful and follow rules, the problems caused by damage, litter and noise can be kept to a minimum.

On balance, I think the best solution would be to limit visitor numbers to natures reserves, so that visitors can enjoy the natural world and plants and animals remain protected.

Commentary
- This is a very good answer.
- All content points in the task are addressed (notes 1 and 2, and the candidate's own idea).
- Examples and reasons are given for opinions.
- The article is written in an appropriately formal style.
- The essay is organised clearly into coherent paragraphs.
- There is a range of suitable vocabulary and grammatical structures.

Part 2

Question 2
Sample answer
Dear Mr Harrow,
I would like to apply to work in the marketing department at your company. I believe that I have the right personal qualities, in addition to the relevant skills and experience.

As a frequent user of several social media sites, I understand what makes one successful. People want user-friendly sites that have up-to-date, relevant functions which make it easy to make connections with others. What is more, I understand the importance of online safety for everyone.

Although I have not lived in an English-speaking country before, my English skills are excellent, as I have a university degree in English and I use English in my professional life on a daily basis.

I am a great member of a team, as I have good communication skills and I am always ready to help other team members.

If you gave me the opportunity to have an interview at your company, I would be happy to discuss my skills and experience more.

I look forward to hearing from you.
Yours sincerely,
Jenna Greaves

Commentary
- This is a very good answer.
- All the points in the task are addressed.
- Reasons are given to support why the candidate would be suitable for the role.
- An appropriately formal style is used.
- The letter starts and finishes suitably.
- The letter is organised clearly into paragraphs.
- A good range of vocabulary and structures is used.

Question 3
Sample answer
The most interesting TV series I've ever seen just has to be *Flying Up High*, which I watched with my family last month. It's truly unmissable!

What made it so interesting? Although the plot at first seems very familiar, it has some amazing twists and these keep you on the edge of your seat throughout the series. The sense of mystery and drama built up through each episode and the ending was truly unpredictable. Casting Anna Lisette Linden as Nova was an inspirational move. She's a relatively new actor, but she's already shown herself to be very flexible in terms of the roles she's played and she's totally believable.

What I took away from the series was that there's no point in 'fighting' what happens to you in life. I don't mean that you should just give up the minute a problem comes along, but that you should accept what's happened and find ways to move forward in a positive way.

I would definitely recommend this series to all age groups. It's five stars from me!

Commentary
- This is a very good answer.
- All the questions in the task are answered.
- The candidate explains their opinions clearly.
- The candidate uses an informal, direct and natural style.
- Ideas are organised into paragraphs.
- The candidate uses a range of suitable vocabulary and grammatical structures.
- The correct number of words has been written.

Question 4
Sample answer
The best presents are the thoughtful ones
When people think of great presents, expensive luxury items often come to mind. Not to mine, though!

The best present I've ever received was a 'time token'. When it first arrived in my inbox, I had no idea what it was. But my friend, who knew how busy I was with work, a baby and a house to run, was kindly offering to help! She said she'd give up her free time to babysit, clean or help with other chores I was struggling to get done.

Her kind gift allowed me to go to the cinema one night without having to ring a million babysitters to find one who was free. She also brought some tasty food for an early dinner – *and* cleaned the kitchen afterwards!

Do I prefer giving or receiving presents? I should say giving them. And I do enjoy choosing thoughtful gifts – or making them when I have time – for friends and family. But if I'm absolutely honest, I love trying to guess what's inside a neatly wrapped package meant just for me. Maybe I just like the suspense!

Commentary
- This is a very good answer.
- All the questions in the task are answered.
- Reasons are given for opinions.
- The article is in an appropriately informal style.
- The candidate writes personally.
- Ideas are organised into paragraphs.
- A range of vocabulary and grammatical structures are used.

Listening

Part 1
1 B   2 C   3 A   4 C   5 C   6 B   7 A   8 B

Part 2
9 (drinking) water   10 1,710   11 hiking sandals
12 warm (air) (pockets)   13 breaks   14 diamonds
15 (a) leg workout   16 sunglasses   17 clouds   18 varied

Part 3
19 H   20 A   21 E   22 D   23 G

Part 4
24 A   25 B   26 C   27 B   28 A   29 C   30 B

Test 4
Reading and Use of English

Part 1
1 B 2 A 3 C 4 D 5 B 6 D 7 A 8 B

Part 2
9 to 10 with 11 in 12 a / one 13 all 14 which / that 15 take
16 was

Part 3
17 wealthy 18 consequently 19 childhood 20 criticism
21 unsuitable 22 discouraged 23 productive 24 death

Part 4
25 was / has been | thrown away 26 is / 's hoping to | take
27 little time | left to 28 not | putting off 29 no idea | whose car
30 lived / moved closer | to college

Part 5
31 A 32 C 33 D 34 A 35 C 36 B

Part 6
37 D 38 A 39 F 40 C 41 G 42 E

Part 7
43 D 44 A 45 C 46 D 47 B 48 C 49 A 50 C 51 B 52 D

Writing
Part 1

Sample answer
Nowadays, many people watch films at home, as there are a lot of movies available to choose from. However, is it still worth going to the cinema to watch a film there?

Firstly, the atmosphere at the cinema is very different from the one at home. At the cinema, it can be enjoyable to watch a film along with many other people who are all experiencing the same thing. On the other hand, at home, people can relax and they can stop and start a film if they want to.

Secondly, although the size of screens at home has increased in recent years, a cinema screen remains significantly larger than any screen at home, which makes the film seem more dramatic and exciting.

Thirdly, while at the cinema there are delicious snacks that are only available there, at home it is possible to eat a greater variety of healthier snacks or even a meal while watching a film.

In conclusion, there are advantages and disadvantages to watching a film in the cinema and at home and it is probably best to enjoy doing both at different times, depending on the occasion.

Commentary
- This is a very good answer.
- All points are covered (notes 1 and 2, and the candidate's own idea).
- The candidate has given reasons for their ideas, with examples.
- The essay is written in an appropriately formal style.
- The essay is well organised and coherent.
- A variety of words and phrases are used to link ideas.
- A range of vocabulary and grammatical structures is used.

Part 2

Question 2
Sample answer
What do people want from a really great café? In my opinion, great food, a great atmosphere and great prices! That's exactly what you get at Ajay's Place.

I go to Ajay's about once a month with a friend and our babies. It has a beautiful sea view and the cakes there are delicious. The café is warm and cosy, and the staff are very friendly. It's easy to get there by bus and the prices are fairly low in comparison with other similar cafés in town.

What makes it different from other cafés is that you can select the music they play. That means you don't have to listen to someone else's choice of songs all the time, which is absolutely brilliant.

The only downside to the café is that it hasn't been decorated for a few years and it's starting to show its age. If the café were painted a new bright, fresh colour, it would be even better.

But overall, I would definitely recommend this café.

Commentary
- This is a very good answer.
- The candidate has answered all the questions in the task.
- The candidate has given reasons for their answers.
- The review is written in an appropriately informal style.
- A good range of vocabulary and grammatical structures is included.
- The candidate has written the correct number of words.

Question 3
Sample answer
Hi, Carey
How are things? It's great that you're arranging the special day for your grandparents.

A boat trip sounds very exciting and it would certainly be a different type of day for them to remember. You could go somewhere new and take lots of beautiful photos of what you see on the trip. Perhaps you'd see some rare wildlife? But a delicious meal in a local restaurant sounds relaxing and fun, too! I went to a fantastic Malaysian restaurant last week. I could send you the address, if that would be useful.

If I were you, I'd make a list of everyone who's going to come and see if it's possible for them all to go on the boat trip. If the boat's too small, maybe you could go for a meal at a restaurant for your grandparents' wedding anniversary and then go on a boat trip another day with just a few people. If the celebration isn't a surprise, it might be a good idea to ask your grandparents which option they prefer.

Looking forward to hearing from you!
Asha

Commentary
- This is a very good answer.
- The candidate has given appropriate advice.
- It is written in a suitable informal and friendly style.
- The email starts and finishes in an appropriate way.
- There are clear paragraphs.
- A range of vocabulary and grammatical structures is used.
- The candidate has written the correct number of words.

Question 4
Sample answer
<u>Public transport in our local area</u>
<u>Introduction</u>
The aim of this report is to describe the current public transport options in our local area, highlight some problems with these options and make recommendations for improvements.

<u>Current public transport options</u>
Public transport services inside the town currently include buses and trams. The fares are low and affordable for most people living here.

There are very frequent bus services in and around the centre of town and a direct train line into the nearest city.

<u>Problems with the current public transport options</u>
Unfortunately, there are not enough buses between local villages and the town. This makes it difficult for people without their own car to access the town. The local trains tend to be very crowded, which makes journeys unpleasant.

<u>Suggested improvements</u>
I would strongly recommend that more buses be added on routes between local villages and the town so that people can shop and attend appointments in town more easily. There should also be more local trains at popular times of the day so that journeys can be more comfortable for people.

Commentary
- This is a very good answer.
- The candidate has addressed all the points in the task.
- Examples have been included to support the candidate's viewpoints.
- The report is clearly organised into sections, each with a relevant heading.
- An appropriately formal style has been used.
- The candidate has used a range of vocabulary and grammatical structures.
- The candidate has written the correct number of words.

Listening

Part 1
1 A 2 B 3 C 4 B 5 B 6 A 7 A 8 A

Part 2
9 medical treatment 10 training 11 cleaning 12 perfume
13 allergies 14 quality time 15 tail / tail wagging 16 intelligence
17 toys (for animals) 18 photography

Part 3
19 H 20 D 21 F 22 G 23 C

Part 4
24 B 25 A 26 C 27 C 28 B 29 B 30 C

Test 5
Reading and Use of English

Part 1
1 C 2 A 3 A 4 D 5 B 6 D 7 B 8 A

Part 2
9 no 10 a 11 For 12 to 13 in 14 have 15 such 16 but

Part 3
17 contribution 18 original 19 freezing 20 visible 21 designer
22 effective / efficient 23 replaced 24 considerably

Part 4
25 long as | you pay
26 has been heard | by
27 son to | clear (up / out) the
28 (had) brought | were unsuitable
29 approve of | loud music being
30 struck me | first of

Part 5
31 A 32 B 33 C 34 A 35 C 36 D

Part 6
37 B 38 E 39 G 40 D 41 F 42 A

Part 7
43 B 44 A 45 C 46 D 47 B 48 A 49 D 50 B 51 A 52 C

Writing

Part 1

Sample answer
Should people have a regular break from looking at computers and other devices? This is a good question and one that we ought to be conscious of, given the number of devices we have.

There are many positives to having mobile devices and laptops, such as instant communication and access to information. However, it may be a good idea for us to turn off our phones during moments when concentration is required so that we are not interrupted while we are completing important tasks.

In addition, the blue light emitted by many devices can make it more difficult to fall and stay asleep because it overly stimulates our brains.

There have also been accidents caused by people walking around outside while staring at a screen when they should have been looking where they were going.

Would taking one day off a week away from screens solve these problems? In my opinion, it would make little difference to the problems caused by interruptions, sleep issues or the risk of accidents. However, it might allow us to switch off and take a break from the pressures of life for a while.

Commentary
- This is a very good answer.
- The two given points are addressed.
- A relevant third point is included.
- Reasons are given for the opinions expressed.
- An appropriate style is used.
- Ideas are clearly organised into coherent paragraphs.
- The candidate uses a range of suitable vocabulary and grammatical structures.

Part 2

Question 2
Sample answer
Hello, Li

I'm really sorry to hear about what's happened with your friend. I don't get it – why didn't the texts arrive? You never know – perhaps there was a problem with the signal or something.

Anyway, try not to worry. I'm sure you'll be able to resolve the situation if you're good friends. He knows deep down that you wouldn't *not* invite him to your birthday party.

Actually, something similar *did* happen to me. My friend thought I'd spread a rumour about him, but I really hadn't. We had a good chat and by the end of it, he understood that I thought of him as such a good friend that I'd never spread rumours – and we're absolutely fine now!

If I were you, I'd do something similar. Maybe you could invite your friend to go for a coffee and explain the situation properly, face to face. You must still have the texts on your phone. Show him those and then he'll be reassured that you *did* invite him, but the technology let you both down. I'm positive he'll understand.

Let me know how it goes!

Write soon,

Jasmine

Commentary
- This is a very good answer.
- All the questions are answered fully.
- The candidate gives relevant examples to support their ideas.
- The email is well organised.
- Appropriate opening and closing phrases are used.
- The language is in a suitably informal style.
- A range of vocabulary and grammatical structures is used.
- The candidate has written the correct number of words.

Question 3
Sample answer
<u>Shine make-up</u>

As a make-up artist, I'm always using new products. Some of them are great and some of them not so great.

Recently, I tried a new brand of foundation called Shine after seeing an advert on TV for it. The advert said that it's smooth and easy to apply. Unfortunately, this wasn't the case. It's quite thick and you need to use a lot of the product to cover the face. Although the price seems reasonable, when you take this into account, it makes it much more expensive. This is disappointing.

However, the product isn't all bad: the foundation stays on the face all day and it's suitable for sensitive skin. The packaging is really attractive and the foundation itself comes in a container that you can later reuse, which is great for the environment.

The product should be a bit cheaper, because at the moment, it ends up being quite expensive given the amount you need to use.

Overall, I wouldn't recommend Shine to other people because there are other products on the market that are cheaper and easier to use.

Commentary
- This is a very good answer.
- All the points in the task are addressed.
- The candidate includes full descriptions and clear reasons to support their opinions.
- The review is in an appropriate style.
- A range of suitable vocabulary and grammatical structures is used.
- The candidate has written the correct number of words.

Question 4
Sample answer
<u>More than just a ball game</u>

Do you ever wish an activity could go on forever? That's how I feel about volleyball. Every Saturday afternoon, my friends and I get together to play volleyball and every time I wish the game could continue forever.

We first started meeting to play volleyball together a few years ago. Initially, there were just a few people, but now we're a large group because it's become so popular.

Our volleyball matches make me happy because there's such a fantastic atmosphere. We're always laughing and joking while we're playing. I'm not a very competitive person, so if my team loses, I don't mind at all.

It's really important for people to have interests outside college or work so they can relax and unwind. If they're feeling stressed about something, taking part in a different activity can help them forget about their problems. In addition to this, it's often an effective way to meet new friends.

Volleyball might just be a sport, but, for me, it's more than that – it's what makes me happiest in life.

Commentary
- This is a very good answer.
- All points in the task are addressed.
- Reasons are given for the opinions expressed.
- The candidate uses an appropriately informal style.
- The article is well organised and coherent.
- The candidate writes personally.
- A good range of vocabulary and grammatical structures is used.

Listening
Part 1
1 C **2** B **3** A **4** B **5** B **6** C **7** A **8** B

Part 2
9 leadership skills **10** (huge) swimming pool **11** shadowing **12** ice(-)breaker **13** tennis **14** dining hall **15** record(-)keeping **16** talent shows **17** speeches **18** self(-)discovery

Part 3
19 C **20** F **21** D **22** H **23** E

Part 4
24 B **25** C **26** C **27** B **28** A **29** A **30** C

Test 6
Reading and Use of English
Part 1
1 B **2** A **3** C **4** A **5** D **6** A **7** B **8** D

Part 2
9 a **10** had **11** who / that **12** more **13** in **14** not **15** some **16** how

Part 3
17 originally **18** surfers **19** popularity **20** reasonably **21** depending **22** height **23** width **24** illegal

Part 4
25 the train | unless we set **26** us everything | we needed to **27** can't / cannot help | losing **28** anyone / anybody | disagreed with **29** doubted / questioned | the accuracy of **30** be able to | put

Part 5
31 C **32** B **33** B **34** D **35** A **36** D

Part 6
37 C **38** G **39** F **40** A **41** D **42** B

Part 7
43 C **44** B **45** A **46** B **47** D **48** C **49** A **50** D **51** B **52** C

Writing
Part 1

Sample answer
There are those who say that space exploration should not be allowed because we should focus on Earth first. Others claim that space exploration is useful for us.

Space exploration is exciting, but it comes at great financial cost. For example, sending a rover with a camera into space to land on a planet costs billions of dollars. Sometimes machinery is destroyed on landing and money is wasted. There are so many problems that need fixing on the Earth that it seems trivial to find out what is on Mars when the money could be spent on these issues. We also need to think more about protecting our own environment so that future generations can benefit from our beautiful planet.

This is not to say that there are no positives to space exploration. Exploring the universe can help us improve our knowledge of what is around us and it can lead to some useful technology being invented. All this can help improve life on Earth in the future.

In conclusion, there are both positives and negatives of space exploration and we should take these into consideration when discussing its value.

Commentary
- This is a very good answer.
- All points are addressed (notes 1 and 2, and the candidate's own idea).
- Reasons and examples are included to support opinions given.
- An appropriately formal style is used.
- Ideas are organised into coherent paragraphs with a suitable introduction and conclusion.
- A range of vocabulary and grammatical structures is used.

Part 2

Question 2
Sample answer
It was a book about thinking that changed the way I think myself. In fact, the book is called *Thinking* and it raises lots of philosophical questions, such as 'Do people ever really change?'.

The book challenged me to consider many new ideas and different viewpoints. One of the most interesting questions that changed the way I think was 'Do we have to be happy?'. People often work very hard to never feel sad or disappointed or bitter. But the book made me think that these emotions are part of being human, and by trying to shut them away, we don't deal with problems well. Instead, we should embrace these feelings and allow ourselves to cope properly with the things that life sends our way.

I believe it is very important to challenge our ways of thinking by reading different books. By doing so, we learn not only about ourselves, but about others, too. This makes us kinder and more thoughtful to those around us, even if they are very different in terms of background or personality. *Thinking* will make you think that way, too!

Commentary
- This is a very good answer.
- All points in the task are addressed.
- Reasons are given for the opinions expressed.
- An appropriate style is used.
- The candidate writes personally.
- The article is organised clearly into coherent paragraphs.
- A range of suitable vocabulary and grammatical structures is used.

Question 3
Sample answer
Dear Mr Harkins,

I would like to apply for the role of Holiday Camp Worker. I think the role would be very interesting and I enjoy working with children.

I have experience of working with children of all ages, from toddlers to teenagers, from my recent job as a Play Assistant in hospitals. I spent time with children, organising fun games and activities, and before I started that role, I did training on how to keep children safe.

I am a creative and active person. I love playing games and doing outdoor activities myself and I would very much enjoy helping to run such activities for young people. I enjoy playing many different sports, as well as doing arts and crafts, and I play the guitar. I believe that these would be useful skills for the camp.

I can communicate well in English, as I studied it at school, and I have attended additional weekend English courses since leaving school.

I am happy to provide references and enclose my current CV. I would be available to start work immediately.

I look forward to hearing from you.

Yours sincerely,

Poppy Smith

Commentary
- This is a very good answer.
- All the points are addressed.
- Reasons are given and relevant examples included.
- The letter is well organised in paragraphs.
- Suitable opening and closing formulas are included.
- An appropriately formal style is used.
- A range of suitable vocabulary and grammatical structures is used.

Question 4
Sample answer
<u>The college library</u>
<u>Main problems</u>
The library was designed several decades ago, so it is not always suitable for modern activities. For example, there are not enough electrical sockets for students using laptops. In addition, the number of students has increased over recent years, so there are not enough desks for students to use. Furthermore, some areas of the library do not have enough lights.

<u>How the problems affect students</u>
The fact that students cannot use their laptops easily means that they cannot study efficiently in the library. As the library is too crowded, some students do not go there and do not have a chance to benefit from the resources there. The lack of lights makes it difficult for students to study in all areas of the library.

<u>Recommendations</u>
As many books can be accessed now online, I would recommend that the older reference books be stored somewhere outside the library and more space be made inside the library for desks for students. Also, more electrical sockets should be added near the desks so students can study more efficiently. More lights should be added, too.

Commentary
- This is a very good answer.
- All the points in the task are fully addressed.
- The candidate has given reasons for their answers.
- The report is written in an appropriately formal style.
- A title is included.
- Points are clearly organised into sections with relevant subheadings.
- The candidate uses a range of vocabulary and grammatical structures.

Listening

Part 1

1 C   2 B   3 B   4 A   5 C   6 A   7 C   8 B

Part 2

9 script   10 literature   11 realistic magic   12 board   13 colours
14 living space   15 dance scenes   16 social issues
17 composing music   18 temperature(s)

Part 3

19 C   20 A   21 E   22 B   23 F

Part 4

24 C   25 B   26 C   27 A   28 C   29 C   30 B

Reading and Use of English

OFFICE USE ONLY - DO NOT WRITE OR MAKE ANY MARK ABOVE THIS LINE — Page 1 of 2

CAMBRIDGE English

Candidate Name		Candidate Number	
Centre Name		Centre Number	
Examination Title		Examination Details	
Candidate Signature		Assessment Date	

Supervisor: If the candidate is ABSENT or has WITHDRAWN shade here ○

First Reading and Use of English Candidate Answer Sheet

Instructions
Use a PENCIL (B or HB).
Rub out any answer you want to change using an eraser.

Parts 1, 5, 6 and 7:
Mark ONE letter for each question.

Parts 2, 3 and 4: Write your answer clearly in CAPITAL LETTERS.

For example, if you think A is the right answer to the question, mark your answer sheet like this:

For parts 2 and 3, write one letter in each box.

Part 1	Part 2	Do not write below here
1 A B C D	9	9 1 0
2 A B C D	10	10 1 0
3 A B C D	11	11 1 0
4 A B C D	12	12 1 0
5 A B C D	13	13 1 0
6 A B C D	14	14 1 0
7 A B C D	15	15 1 0
8 A B C D	16	16 1 0

Continues over ➡

OFFICE USE ONLY - DO NOT WRITE OR MAKE ANY MARK BELOW THIS LINE — Page 1 of 2

Reading and Use of English

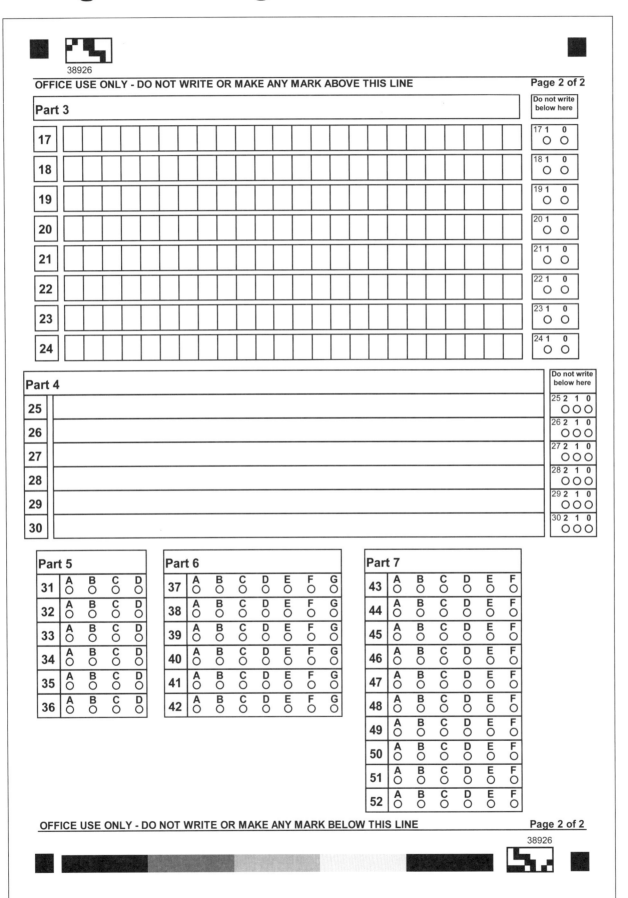

Listening

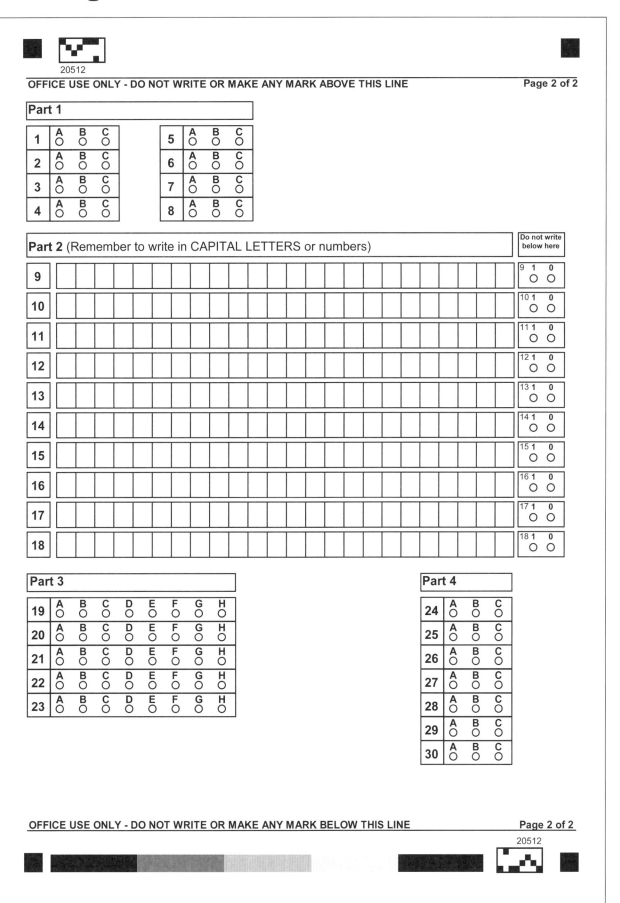

Writing

Part Two Answer
You must write within the grey lines.

Write your question number here:

Acknowledgements

Our highly experienced team of *Trainer* writers and exam reviewers have worked together to bring you *B2 First Trainer 3*. We would like to thank Carole Allsop (writer), Carole Bartlett (writer), Tom Bradbury (reviewer), Helen Chilton (writer), Anthony Cosgrove (reviewer) and Helen Tiliouine (writer) for their work on the material.

The authors and publishers acknowledge the following sources of copyright material and are grateful for the permissions granted. While every effort has been made, it has not always been possible to identify the sources of all the material used, or to trace all copyright holders. If any omissions are brought to our notice, we will be happy to include the appropriate acknowledgments on reprinting and in the next update to the digital edition, as applicable.

Key: RUE= Reading; SPK=Speaking; WRI= Writing; T= Text.

Text
RUE T1: Telegraph Media Group Limited for the adapted text from 'Why have leisure sports become so competitive' by Chris Moss, *Telegraph Media Group Limited*, 15.07.2014. Copyright © 2014 Telegraph Media Group Limited. Reproduced with permission; **RUE T2**: Guardian News & Media Ltd for the adapted text from 'Feeding cattle to breaking barriers: Nepal goal machine Sabitra Bhandari' by Sudesh Baniya, *The Guardian*, 05.03.2024. Copyright © 2024 Guardian News & Media Ltd. Reproduced with permission; Guardian News & Media Ltd for the adapted text from 'House-proud Welsh mouse may be "tidying" for fun, say scientists' by Linda Geddes, *The Guardian*, 08.01.2024. Copyright © 2024 Guardian News & Media Ltd. Reproduced with permission; Guardian News & Media Ltd for the adapted text from 'I've made secret discoveries on my doorstep: a year-long journey across my local OS map' by Alastair Humphreys, *The Guardian*, 17.01.2024. Copyright © 2024 Guardian News & Media Ltd. Reproduced with permission; **RUE T3**: Guardian News & Media Ltd for the adapted text from '"Be bold – that's the fun part": the ultimate expert guide to upcycling furniture' by Nell Card, *The Guardian*, 28.04.2024. Copyright © 2024 Guardian News & Media Ltd. Reproduced with permission; **RUE T4**: Guardian News & Media Ltd for the adapted text from 'Road to ruins: how I discovered the magic of archaeology' by Mary-Ann Ochota, *The Guardian*, 24.02.2024. Copyright © 2024 Guardian News & Media Ltd. Reproduced with permission; Guardian News & Media Ltd for the adapted text from 'Are our personalities set in stone, or can we work on – even improve – them?' by Jamie Waters, *The Guardian*, 10.01.2021. Copyright © 2024 Guardian News & Media Ltd. Reproduced with permission; Endava for the text adapted from 'The Joy and Challenge of Being a Video Game Tester' by Gabriela Elena Miroiu. Copyright © 2024 Endava. Reproduced with kind permission; **RUE T5:** Guardian News & Media Ltd for the adapted text from 'How to make big decisions more easily' by Joanna Moorhead, *The Guardian*, 05.06.2022. Copyright © 2024 Guardian News & Media Ltd. Reproduced with permission; Guardian News & Media Ltd for the adapted text from '"We don't need air con": how Burkina Faso builds schools that stay cool in 40°C heat' by Elia Borras, *The Guardian*, 29.02.2024. Copyright © 2024 Guardian News & Media Ltd. Reproduced with permission; **RUE T6**: The National Gallery for the adapted text from 'Guide to Impressionism'. Copyright © 2024 The National Gallery. Reproduced with kind permission; Guardian News & Media Ltd for the adapted text from 'I gave up renting in London to live nomadically – it's dramatically enriched my life' by Lydia Swinscoe, *The Guardian*, 12.02.2024. Copyright © 2024 Guardian News & Media Ltd. Reproduced with permission; Genevieve Beaulieu-Pelletier for the adapted text from 'Why do we laugh when someone falls down? Here's what science says', by Genevieve Beaulieu-Pelletier, *The Conversation*, 13.03.2023. Copyright © 2023 Genevieve Beaulieu-Pelletier, Psychologist, lecturer and associate professor, Université du Quebec à Montréal (UQAM). Reproduced with kind permission; Guardian News & Media Ltd for the adapted text from '*Kintsugi* helped me to understand my brother's death' by Bonnie Kemske, *The Guardian*, 10.04.2021. Copyright © 2024 Guardian News & Media Ltd. Reproduced with permission.

Photography
All the photos are sourced from Getty Images.
RUE T1: Eva-Katalin/E+; Trevor Williams/Photodisc; FGM/E+; Paul Souders/Stone; James Warwick/The Image Bank; JohnnyGreig/E+; Alistair Berg/DigitalVision; Deborah Faulkner/Moment; Sammyvision/Moment; John Giustina/The Image Bank; Kelly Cheng/Moment; Robert Och/500Px Plus; **RUE T2**: Luis Alvarez/DigitalVision; Mint Images RF; Sue Barr/Image Source; Jackyenjoyphotography/Moment; Betsie Van Der Meer/Stone; David Clapp/Stone; shapecharge/E+; Robert Brook/Corbis; **SPK T1**: Sarah Mason/DigitalVision; Michelangelo Gratton/DigitalVision; ProfessionalStudioImages/E+; Frazao Studio Latino/E+; sturti/E+; vgajic/E+; **SPK T2**: Alistair Berg/DigitalVision; Maskot/DigitalVision; Cohen/Ostrow/Photodisc; Su Arslanoglu/E+; Paul Souders/Stone; Mavocado/Moment; **SPK T3:** Hill Street Studios/DigitalVision; Catherine Costa/E+; Maskot; Thomas Barwick/DigitalVision; **SPK T4:** Klaus Vedfelt/DigitalVision; Jon Feingersh/The Image Bank; Caia Image/Collection Mix: Subjects; AzmanL/E+; **SPK T5:** skynesher/E+; vgajic/E+; Steve Schwarz/Moment; Bo Zaunders/Corbis Documentary; **SPK T6:** Dimensions/E+; Hispanolistic/E+; Drazen_/E+; LOUISE BEAUMONT/Moment; **WRI T1:** Drazen_/E+; shapecharge/E+; somethingway/E+; triloks/E+; SolStock/E+; simonkr/E+; **WRI T2:** DMP/E+; Caia Image/Collection Mix: Subjects.

Cover Photography by Momodine/E+.

Audio
Audio production by Mat Clark/Sonica Studios Ltd.

Typesetting
Typeset by QBS Learning.

Test 1 Training — Speaking Part 2

Why do the people need to be confident in these situations?

A

B

Test 1 Exam practice Speaking Part 2

Candidate A   Why do the people need to take a break?

A

B

Test 1 Exam practice — Speaking Part 2

> Candidate B   What might the people find difficult about making these changes?

A

B

Test 1 Training   Speaking Part 3

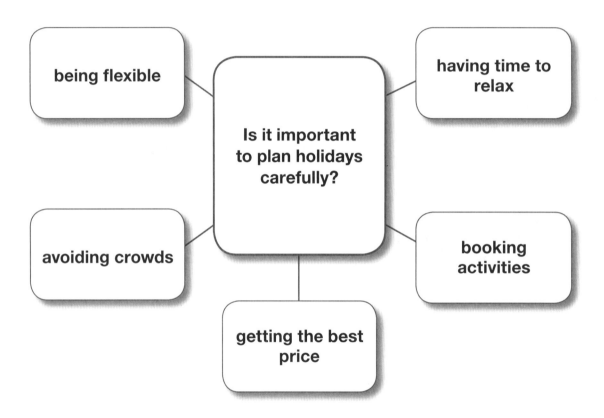

Test 1 Exam practice — Speaking Part 3

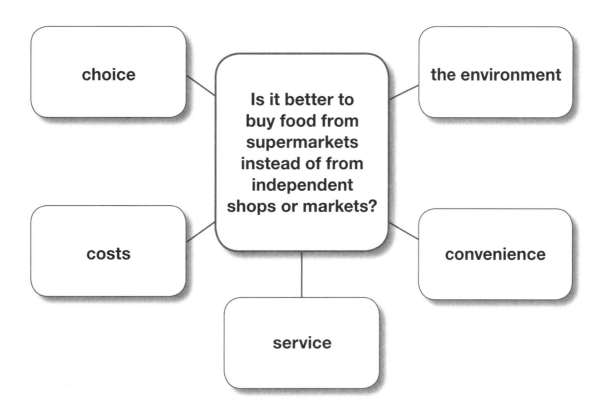

Test 2 Training — Speaking Part 2

> Why have the people decided to protect the environment in these ways?

A

B

Test 2 Exam practice — Speaking Part 2

> Candidate A   Why are the people finding it difficult to get comfortable?

A

B

Test 2 Exam practice — Speaking Part 2

> Candidate B   Why might the people want to spend time alone?

A

B

Test 2 Training — Speaking Part 3

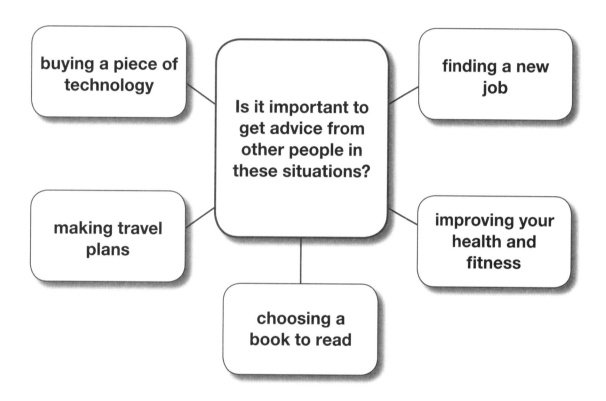

Test 2 Exam practice — Speaking Part 3

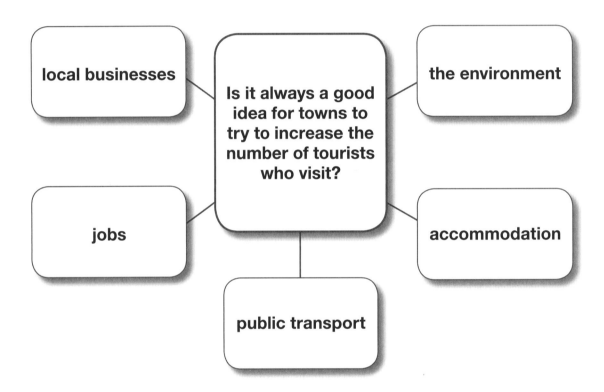

Test 3 — Speaking Part 2

Candidate A   What might the people find difficult about preparing for these situations?

A

B

Test 3　Speaking Part 2

> Candidate B　Why have the people decided to show these things?

A

B

Test 3 — Speaking Part 3

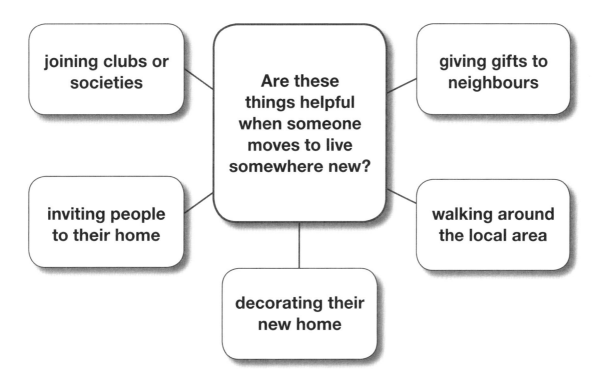

Test 4 — Speaking Part 2

Candidate A   Why is speed important for the people in these situations?

A

B

Test 4 — Speaking Part 2

Candidate B   Why have the people decided to start to do these things?

A

B

Test 4 — Speaking Part 3

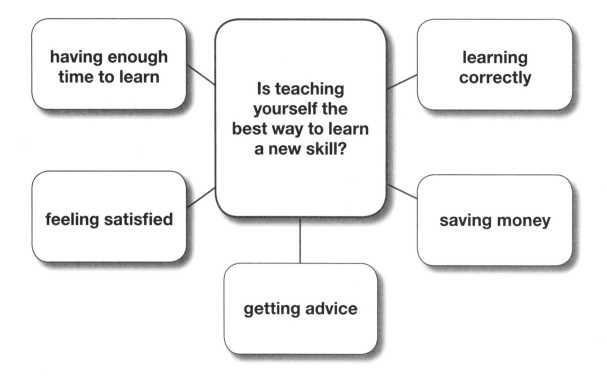

Test 5 — Speaking Part 2

Candidate A   What might be difficult about teaching in these situations?

A

B

Test 5 — Speaking Part 2

Candidate B   Why have the people decided to spend time on a boat in these situations?

A

B

Test 5 — Speaking Part 3

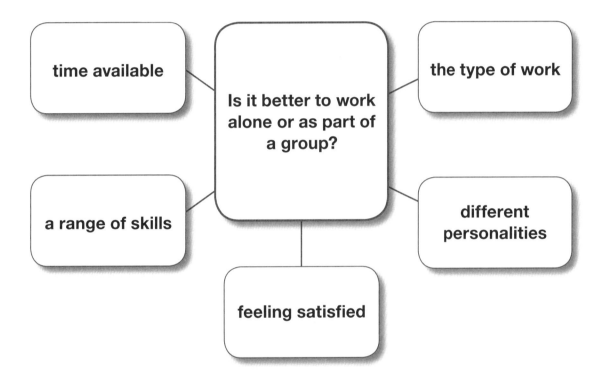

Test 6 — Speaking Part 2

Candidate A What might the people find difficult about saying goodbye in these situations?

A

B

Test 6 — Speaking Part 2

Candidate B   Why have the people chosen to live in these places?

A

B

Test 6 — Speaking Part 3

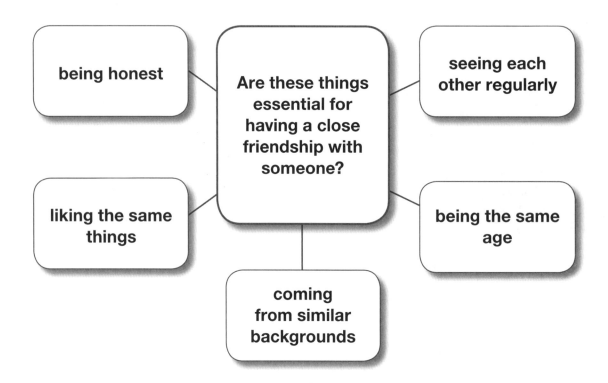